WRITING THE SKY

WRITING THE SKY

OBSERVATIONS AND ESSAYS ON DERMOT HEALY

Edited, with an Introduction,
by Neil Murphy & Keith Hopper

DALKEY ARCHIVE PRESS

Copyright © 2016 by the contributors
Foreword copyright © 2016 by Neil Jordan
Introduction copyright © 2016 by Neil Murphy & Keith Hopper

First edition, 2016
All rights reserved

   Library of Congress Cataloging-in-Publication Data

Names: Murphy, Neil, editor. | Hopper, Keith, editor.
Title: Writing the sky : observations and essays on Dermot Healy / edited,
  with an introduction, by Neil Murphy & Keith Hopper.
Description: First edition. | Victoria, TX : Dalkey Archive Press, 2016. |
  Includes bibliographical references.
Identifiers: LCCN 2016010908 | ISBN 9781564789242 (pbk. : alk. paper)
Subjects: LCSH: Healy, Dermot, 1947-2014--Criticism and interpretation. |
  English literature--Irish authors--History and criticism. | Healy, Dermot,
  1947-2014.
Classification: LCC PR6058.E19 Z95 2016 | DDC 823/.914--dc23
LC record available at https://lccn.loc.gov/2016010908

Partially funded by a grant by the Illinois Arts Council, a state agency

www.dalkeyarchive.com

Victoria, TX / McLean, IL / Dublin / London

Dalkey Archive Press publications are, in part, made possible through the support of the University of Houston-Victoria and its programs in creative writing, publishing, and translation.

Printed on permanent/durable acid-free paper

CONTENTS

Foreword ... ix
   NEIL JORDAN

Editors' Introduction ... xiii
   NEIL MURPHY & KEITH HOPPER

Acknowledgements ... xxi

Section I: Writers and Artists on the Writer

The Plough ... 3
   DERMOT HEALY

Constellations ... 4
   MICHAEL LONGLEY

Alone in a Landscape: The Poetry of Dermot Healy ... 5
   COLM TÓIBÍN

Ballinfull, 3 July 2014 ... 15
   HARRY CLIFTON

"Only myself, said Cúnla" ... 16
   TIMOTHY O'GRADY

Wings 2/6: Memories of Dermot Healy ... 29
   PATRICK McCABE

Song in the Grass ... 40
   KATE FAGAN

Sea-strangeness: Memories of Dermot Healy ... 49
   TESS GALLAGHER

Dermot Healy: A Cavan Antaeus ... 56
   RONAN SHEEHAN

The Bend for Healy ... 64
   RODDY DOYLE

A Song for Ireland ... 66
   DANNY MORRISON

"Anonymous is best . . ." ... 72
   PHILIP Ó CEALLAIGH

After the Event GLENN PATTERSON	76
Dermot Healy: Newcomer, Mentor, Old Hand ALANNAH HOPKIN (& AIDAN HIGGINS)	78
The Rogue Wave MICHAEL HARDING	84
A Short History of *Force 10* (A Journal of the North-West) BRIAN LEYDEN	87
Reading *Force 10* GEORGE O'BRIEN	93
Form CAROLINE BRACKEN	99
Sligo Occult: On Dermot Healy's Radical Style KEVIN BARRY	100
"Testing, said a voice. Testing, one two three . . ." MIKE McCORMACK	104
The Eve of St John EOIN McNAMEE	110
A Goat's Song: A Writer's Appreciation ANNIE PROULX	112
Review Essay: Dermot Healy's *Sudden Times* ANNIE PROULX	124
On *The Bend for Home* MOLLY McCLOSKEY	128
A Lift MARY O'MALLEY	136
Remembering Dermot Healy and *I Could Read the Sky* NICHOLA BRUCE	137
Profile: Interview with Dermot Healy (1999) VINCENT BROWNE	143
At the End of the Day GARRY KEANE	148
Land of Dreams GERALD DAWE	155

Section II: Critical Responses

"The small stone that no one sees gives all the balance":
Unique Perspective and Personal Idiom in the Works
of Dermot Healy   159
    SEÁN GOLDEN

Dermot Healy—Art into Life: Life into Art   182
    BILL SWAINSON

The Importance of Being Dermot: Healy's Idiosyncrasies   197
    THIERRY ROBIN

"The Passionate Transitory":
Dermot Healy and the Sense of Place   210
    KEITH HOPPER

Reveries of the Solitary Self in *Banished Misfortune*   231
    FLORE COULOUMA

Dermot Healy's Heterotopias:
Fanacross and Northern Ireland in *Fighting with Shadows*   246
    JACK FENNELL

"The orchestra of memory":
Music, Sound and Silence in *A Goat's Song*   259
    GERRY SMYTH

Dermot Healy's *A Goat's Song*: "To give some
form to that which cannot be uttered"   277
    NEIL MURPHY

Guilt Trips: Dermot Healy's *Sudden Times*
and the Meaning of Sin   292
    PAUL FAGAN

Psyche's Garden: The Labour of Mourning
and the Growth of the Self in *Long Time, No See*   314
    DERMOT McCARTHY

Mister Psyche's Microcosmos   331
    CATHERINE HOFFMANN

The Bend for Home: Truth, Beauty, Such Things   349
    DEREK HAND

Dermot Healy:
  Local, National and International Drama   365
    MICHELLE C. PAULL

Banished Misfortunes?:
  Dermot Healy and the Rise of the Posthuman   382
    MICHAEL CRONIN

Select Bibliography   399
Contributors   417
About the Editors   429

Foreword

"Banished Misfortune" was the first story I read by Dermot Healy. It seemed as if this stranger had a passport to that imaginary country everyone wanted to inhabit at the time—magic realism. But there was nothing faux Gabriel García Márquez about these pages, no imitation Southern American Gothic either, the story was recognisably, almost impossibly Irish (as was the tune it took its title from, one of the best). It was also rural, involved a family, a road trip. It had more than that again, an engagement with language that was frothy, bubbling, ironic, and almost spookily magical. The magic of puns, misappropriated names, strange and outmoded rural beliefs. I had a publishing interest at the time, called the Irish Writers Co-operative, and had to track down this genius, if not to publish him then at least to meet.

There was always damp around him, rain, mist, damp carpets and bedcovers, pots to hold dripping water from a leaking roof, and towards the end, erosion; enormous waves that threatened to drag his cottage into the ocean. There was rain here, anyway, on the journey up towards Cavan, through a succession of low hills, down a narrow lane eventually that turned into a sea of mud. Across the mud into a rented cottage where Dermot sat among piles of newspapers, books, Guinness bottles, ashtrays, with Anne-Marie, his first wife, and Dallan, his first child.

He had already published poetry, chosen by Seamus Heaney in a Faber anthology. He had a pale beard, whitish hair, and he already looked the age most people would remember him as, somehow young and old at the same time. He had a maddeningly tangential way of talking about things, writers, ideas, politics, country people and realities. It would seem like nonsense and a strange kind of genius at the same time, and one was never quite sure that he meant what he said, or even understood what he said, but one was always embarrassed to admit that one didn't understand, or get it, and would try to share the kind of wheezing laughter that would conclude every comment. He resisted my offer to publish a collection of his stories, and had already decided, probably wisely, to seek out an English publisher. But we got to know each other and became friends.

From his conversation, and his acquaintance, he gave glimpses of a childhood and an adolescence that seemed impossible to me. He had been born in Finea, Co. Westmeath and brought up in Cavan, where his father, who died early, was a guard and his mother ran a legendary cake shop. And when I went to visit him there once I got a glimpse of the kind of childhood that would have led to his strange mixture of anarchy and imaginative indulgence. An extraordinary group of aunts, and a mother, all sharp-tongued, doting of course, with an irreverent, rural attitude towards everything, every rule, certainty, and shibboleth. A community surrounded him that seemed to have slipped through the cracks of everything that made Ireland the intolerable thing it was, at the time. Or maybe there was a world and a reality always there, just barely obscured by the middle-class mores most of the country seemed to abide by. Whatever this strange country was, Dermot Healy had grown up in it, and seemed to have been left quite alone to thrive in it. The best account of this world, of course, is in his memoir, *The Bend for Home*. He drank an old man's drink, Guinness from the bottle, with a gin or whiskey chaser (and many of them). He played pool exceptionally well. And beyond the pool table, seemed to take no exercise at all.

We kept track of one another, over the years. He moved to London. His daughter, Inor, was born. He published a novel, *Fighting with Shadows*, then moved to Belfast while working on another, which would become what most think of as his masterpiece, *A Goat's Song*. He lived in East Belfast, through the worst of the Troubles, and his living there exhibited that extraordinary, gravitationless quality with which he moved through things. Given what was going on at the time, he could have been shot, or worse. But when one searched him out in those Protestant streets, the locals would happily give directions to where the one they called "the Irishman" lived.

His last move was to a cottage by the sea in Ballyconnell, Co. Sligo, further down the coast from Rosses Point, where I was born. I would go to visit him there and again have the extraordinary sense of encountering a hidden landscape beneath or beside the one I thought I had known, with secrets, rituals, relationships that only he seemed to have discovered. Was it real or imagined? Or was it part of some elaborate joke this trickster was enacting on the world at large? He had me drive once, round the roads at the foot of Ben Bulben, which was, as usual, shrouded in wet cloud. Dermot guided me over a gentle slope, and told me to turn off the engine at the bottom of it. I turned it off, dutifully, and asked him why I was doing this. Just wait, he cautioned me. And I waited a minute, and to my amazement, the car drove itself backwards up the slope. The car, like Healy himself, was defying gravity. What's going on, Dermot, I had to ask. He laughed, and like the great magician that he was, revealed nothing and told me to drive on home.

Later that night his wife Helen told me it was an optical illusion, what seemed to be a downward hill was in fact an upward slope. I felt almost cheated when I heard this. Healy couldn't fly, after all. But maybe that was his art. To persuade us that he could.

—Neil Jordan

Introduction

In Aidan Higgins's view, the late Dermot Healy (1947–2014) was the natural heir to the experimental narrative tradition in Irish literature—a counter-realist tradition which includes Joyce, Beckett, Flann O'Brien, and Higgins himself (21). As such, Healy's work continually extended the technical range of fiction and drama, and he repeatedly explored questions of knowing and being in a lyrical, earthy, and deeply contemplative fashion. Many other Irish writers have offered similar testament to the importance of Healy's work. Timothy O'Grady, for example, claims that Healy's *A Goat's Song* (1994) is Ireland's "most ambitious novel since Beckett's *Trilogy*" ("Dermot Healy: An Interview" 26) while Annie Proulx calls it "an exceptional novel, one of those rare books that permanently colour one's ideational map of place and human behaviour" (121). More generally, Patrick McCabe considers Healy's fiction to be "truly revolutionary work, and high literary art" (qtd in O'Grady, "Only Myself" 21) while the late Seamus Heaney hailed him as the poetic heir to Patrick Kavanagh: "Kavanagh was the poet of, as he said, 'the passionate transitory,' bits and pieces of the everyday snatched out of time. He was the poet of praise for those things. It isn't just nature poetry, it's gratitude for the whole gift of existence in Healy"[1] (qtd in Keane, n. pag.).

Despite these writerly accolades and comparisons, Healy's writing was consistently overlooked for the major literary prizes and, partly as a result of this neglect, he has not yet received proper international attention for his varied and ambitious body of work. Outside of Ireland, Healy is probably better known as a novelist, but he was also an accomplished poet, short story writer, playwright, actor, and screenwriter. A generous and gregarious man, Healy was also a great literary enabler: he founded and edited the regional journals *The Drumlin* and *Force 10*, and taught creative writing classes for prisoners as well as for local community groups. Indeed, one of the hallmarks of Healy's own work is its unalloyed celebration of community spirit, allied to a strong social conscience.

However, Healy's prolific fluency across a range of forms and genres perhaps made him difficult to pigeonhole, and this creative eclecticism may have served to complicate his critical reputation. Moreover, Healy was always fascinated by borderlands and liminal states of mind, and he frequently transgressed the conventional boundaries between poetry, drama and fiction, and between fiction and reality. In all of Healy's novels and stories there is a productive tension between the representation of complex lives and events, and the modernist desire to find new ways of expressing the rich subjectivity of these lives. Though usually set in small provincial towns, Healy's fictional worlds perpetually approach the edge of myth, and his vivid sense of place is rendered with an almost shamanistic intensity. These strange landscapes and fractured lives can sometimes appear rather alien to metropolitan critics, which may well account for some of the more tentative and confused responses to his fiction. Consequently, part of the motivation behind publishing this volume is to address the extraordinary neglect of one of Ireland's most gifted and industrious modern writers. The aim is to acknowledge Healy's immense creative achievement while also establishing an initial body of critical work, drawn from a variety of vantage points. The collection includes a broad spectrum of writerly responses—short memoirs, poetry, and commentary-reportage—and an array of literary-critical perspectives covering the entire range of Healy's work: his poetry, short stories, novels, and plays, as well as Healy's own memoir, *The Bend for Home* (1996), and his editorship of *Force 10*.

Many of the writerly contributions in this volume blend memoir with critical commentary. In Neil Jordan's "Foreword," for example, the exciting emergence of Healy's story "Banished Misfortune" is remembered for its "frothy, bubbling, ironic, and almost spookily magical" language, and as a moment which marked the beginning of many years of mutual engagement and friendship between the two writers. A fusion of critique and remembrance drives other contributions, as in Timothy O'Grady's "Only myself, said Cúnla," which spirals outwards from Healy's funeral to offer fulsome testimony to the significance of Healy's *oeuvre*: "one of the greatest achievements in all of Irish literature." O'Grady ultimately settles his gaze on *A Goat's Song*, which he argues belongs in the same company as Flann O'Brien's *At Swim-Two-Birds* (1939), Máirtín Ó Cadhain's *Cré na Cille* (1949), and the work of Joyce and Beckett. Similarly, Patrick McCabe offers us a glimpse into "Catweazle" Healy in Cavan, Dublin, Brixton, Granard, and Longford town, all the while marvelling at the uniqueness of his persona; Tess Gallagher's memories of Healy's unique presence revolve around a sense of what she calls "sea-strangeness" (a term borrowed from Seán Ó Ríordáin); and Ronan Sheehan blends his reminiscences of an early meeting with Healy while offering insights into the story "Banished Misfortune" and a collaborative translation of Catullus.

Alannah Hopkin offers a split account of both her and Aidan Higgins's relationships with Healy, which traces, respectively, the elder writer's early mentorship, and Hopkin's account of Healy as mentor to her. Kevin Barry, alternatively, responds very specifically to chapter fourteen of *Long Time, No See* (2011), or more precisely, to the extraordinary strangeness that commands its pages, while Mike McCormack, similarly, marvels at the "shamanic intensity and electric charge" that he finds in the early collection *Banished Misfortune and Other Stories* (1982). More personally, Philip Ó Ceallaigh offers an account of a series of meetings with Healy, while mapping them against his own awakening as a writer; Danny Morrison recalls meeting Healy for the first time in Belfast, at the height of the Troubles; Glenn Patterson provides a glimpse of Healy via one mischievous encounter; and Roddy Doyle acknowledges him via a playful piece of dialogue redolent of Myles na Gopaleen. Brian Leyden and George O'Brien, separately but valuably, offer their insights and observations on the importance of Healy's editorship of *Force 10*, a journal which has acquired almost legendary status among Irish literary periodicals.

Acknowledgement of Healy's importance is registered too via several poems, including Michael Longley's two-line tribute, "Constellations," a kind of companion piece to Healy's own poem "The Plough," which we have placed alongside it. Harry Clifton's haunting poem takes its title from the date and place of

Healy's funeral—"Ballinfull, 3 July 2014"—while Kate Fagan's responsiveness to Healy extends far beyond the epigraph to her long poem sequence, "Song in the Grass." Fragments and echoes of Healy's voice are scattered like whispers throughout Fagan's poem, and his guiding presence is almost tangible. Included too are several *in memoriam* poems by Eoin McNamee, Caroline Bracken, Mary O'Malley, and Gerald Dawe, entitled, respectively, "The Eve of St John," "Form," "A Lift," and "Land of Dreams."

Several fellow-writers focus more specifically on the writing, as is the case with Colm Tóibín's critical response to Healy's poetry, which he describes as work "of stark images, dry wit, and a mild, amused, acceptance of things, including all their strangeness and sadness." Ranging widely across Healy's poetry collections, Tóibín writes of Healy's "astonishing gift as a poet, but also [his] poet's conscience, manifested in the way he will not wander into easy poetic spaces, or manipulate feeling, or strike a pose," but instead remains "reticent and eloquent, maintaining equilibrium between what is mysterious and what is material." Annie Proulx's response to *A Goat's Song*, Healy's "masterpiece," is clearly expressed in her concluding remarks: "Above all, there is fine writing in *A Goat's Song* of a quality that makes you rise up from your chair, go outside to look at the sky and give thanks." Molly McCloskey's response to Healy's memoir, *The Bend for Home*, similarly emphasises the singularity of Healy's prose and his sensitivity to the very act of turning life into language: "He knew language's pitfalls, its habit of falsifying, as well as its capacity to sanctify."

Switching focus, Nichola Bruce recounts her experience of directing Healy in her film version of Timothy O'Grady's *I Could Read the Sky* (1999), and observes how Healy brought "the strength of his own fragility and tenderness [...] and the wildness of the sea and wind" into the lead role. Alternatively, in an interview first published in 1999, Vincent Browne talks to Healy about the process behind *I Could Read the Sky*, and Healy explains how he drew on his own experiences of working on London building sites. Similarly, Garry Keane's account of his filming of *The Writing in the Sky* (2011)—ostensibly a documentary based on Healy's *A Fool's Errand* (2010), but in reality an elegant meditation on the writerly consciousness—is a fitting mix of reportage, memoir, and critical insight into Healy's career.

This collection of essays and observations also represents an attempt to establish the critical and academic foundations upon which future scholars can build. While there have been several important essays written on Healy's work in the past (by Golden, McCarthy, Hoffmann, Gefter, Wallace, amongst others), the overall body of focused critical work remains rather slim. Thus the fourteen critical essays in Section 2 of this volume represent an immediate and significant enlargement of the critical frame, with all of the major works receiving specific treatment. Seán Golden sees Healy's work as having an East Asian sense of proportion, "not as a figure dominating the foreground but as a contributory detail to the whole effect," and in this context offers a general overview of the fiction and poetry. Healy's former editor, Bill Swainson, mixes memoir with critical perspective and offers particular insights into *Banished Misfortune*, while also reflecting on the *oeuvre* in general. Thierry Robin, likewise, traces a series of patterns across the range of Healy's fiction, observing ultimately that "Healy's strength lies in his ability to convey the uncanny quality of ordinary human experience in simple effective terms."

Keith Hopper also considers the poetry alongside the novels and the memoir, and argues that Healy's abiding fascination with place is the cornerstone of his aesthetic and ethical sensibility: "Healy's overarching sense of place is not just epistemological but ontological: a way of thinking about one's self, one's place in the world, and the transient nature of one's existence." Flore Coulouma's focus on *Banished Misfortune and Other Stories* echoes Hopper's sense of Healy as a great writer of nature and landscape, and observes that the early stories already "display a singular and poetic vision of the world, on a par with the great Irish nature poets, Patrick Kavanagh and the Northern Irish poets."

Healy's debut novel, *Fighting with Shadows* (1984), is the focus of Jack Fennell's attention. Theoretically, Fennell draws on Foucault's heterotopic intersection of real and imaginary spaces as a means of exploring the uncanny boundaries and borders that define the novel in so many ways. *A Goat's Song* (1994), Healy's second novel, is considered from different perspectives by Gerry Smyth and Neil Murphy. Smyth explores the various ways in which Healy's work was influenced by music, and sees *A Goat's Song* as one of the finest expressions of Healy's "sound world"; Murphy, in a quite different reading, seeks to demonstrate a recurring obsession with the formal accommodation of reality in Healy's writings. In turn, Paul Fagan approaches Healy's third novel, the technically-innovative *Sudden Times* (1999), by stressing the way in which the tropes of guilt and loss, intertwined with its performance of narrative time, ultimately act as regenerative forces in the novel.

Both Dermot McCarthy and Catherine Hoffmann make strong critical cases for the central significance of *Long Time, No See* (2011) amongst all of Healy's fictions. McCarthy views the novel as an intense affirmation of human relationships, and sees in the "uncelebratory celebratory way of simple communal-social acts and manners" evidence of "his most finely balanced song of life." Hoffmann, on the other hand, concerns herself with the novel's "levelling of categories and abolition of boundaries," and discusses formal aspects such as the "typography, grammar, story world material, narrative discourse" and absence of narrative hierarchies. Like Molly McCloskey, Derek Hand engages with the sinewy complexity of Healy's memoir, *The Bend for Home*. Hand views it in the context of a "proliferation in the 1990s of autobiographical writing in Ireland" but, crucially, outlines how Healy "explored an alternative history, challenging and deconstructing some of the easier expectations of what Ireland was." It would seem that Healy's innovative spirit extends to autobiography, rendering the form much more fluid than other 'straight' autobiographies, and indicating a spirit of resistance to received forms beyond the fiction and poetry.

So too with his dramatic work which, according to Michelle C. Paull, "can be seen as part of his re-working of theatrical traditions" while simultaneously engaging with various marginalised and excluded groups—exiles, migrants, and the unemployed. In short, she argues, this fascination with alternative artistic forms, and the desire to urge silenced voices to find a way into speech, invites comparisons with modernist drama and, most obviously, with Beckett. The strong humanist impulse in Healy's work also finds expression in his poetry. Michael Cronin's situating of Healy's poetry within the deeply troubling context of the "Anthropocene" illustrates ways in which it resonates with perhaps the most urgent of all contemporary issues. *A Fool's Errand* (2010), in Cronin's view, pulls away "from the fragmented intransigence of the present to the long now of millennia," and this ultimately facilitates a more sophisticated sense of the interrelatedness of things. Furthermore, the "local connection," the here and now, is both itself and goes beyond itself and is intimately linked to "other parts of the world." As Cronin argues, this openness in Healy is significant, because it is always in "deep and lasting engagement with the particularities of place."

Overall, this volume of observations and essays serves both as a tribute and as a long-overdue critical response to a hugely significant body of work. Most of all, it suggests that Dermot Healy is not just a great Irish writer, but a writer of genuine international importance.

—Neil Murphy & Keith Hopper
Singapore and Oxford, 2016

Works Cited

Higgins, Aidan. "The Hollow and the Bitter and the Mirthless in Irish Writing." *Force 10* 13 (2008): 21–7. Print.

Keane, Garry. Dir. *The Writing in the Sky* [documentary on Dermot Healy]. Ireland: RTÉ, 2011. 54 mins. DVD.

O'Grady, Timothy. "Dermot Healy: An Interview." *Wasafiri* 25.2 (June 2010): 26-31. Print.

———. "Only myself, said Cúnla." *Dermot Healy: Writing the Sky: Observations and Essays on Dermot Healy*. Ed. Neil Murphy and Keith Hopper. Victoria: Dalkey Archive Press, 2016: 16–28. Print.

Proulx, Annie. "Dermot Healy's *A Goat's Song*: A Writer's Appreciation." *Litteraria Pragensia* 22.44 (Dec. 2012): 121–30. Print.

Acknowledgements

This volume was conceived prior to the untimely death of Dermot Healy in June 2014. It was initially motivated by its editors' desire to offer due recognition of an immense artistic achievement, and to simultaneously initiate a substantial body of criticism that might serve as a point of departure for scholars and readers new to Healy's work. In the wake of Healy's passing it was somewhat inevitable that a hint of the elegiac would enter the memoir-style pieces in particular; nonetheless, the initial motivation remains unchanged, except perhaps with a concomitant regret that Dermot did not get to see the finished product for himself. We hope that this collection is a fitting recognition of the tremendous significance of his work, and that its publication will, in some small way, serve as a tribute to his memory. We are very grateful to his family and friends for their encouragement and support in bringing this volume to fruition.

Immense gratitude and admiration are offered to Dermot's wife, Helen Gillard Healy, who was involved in this venture from the outset, during early discussions in Singapore and Sligo, and thereafter by phone, email and in person—none of this would have been possible without her help and commitment.

Special thanks too are offered to Neil Jordan, an old friend of Healy's, for kindly writing such a striking and memorable foreword.

Seán Golden's friendship with Healy spanned more than four decades, as did his familiarity with the intensely nuanced topography of the work—we have been extremely fortunate to find in Professor Golden a most helpful and gracious guide through the labyrinths of print and myth, at times almost on a daily basis. Brian Leyden has also been an invaluable presence for which we are, and continue to be, extremely grateful. Without the assistance of those who were familiar with Healy's life and career down through the years, our work would have been, at the very least, far more challenging.

Thanks too are offered to John O'Brien for his visionary Dalkey Archive Press, with sincere gratitude for his continued, steadfast support of this venture, and for his ongoing contribution to literature that matters.

We are very grateful to Dr Michelle Chiang, who offered much-needed support and dedication in preparing the text for publication, and to Cheryl Julia Lee whose insightful work on the final stages of the collection was of immense help. Dr Michelle Wang also made an enormous contribution to the preparation of the final manuscript, for which warm thanks are offered.

Thanks too to Tess Gallagher, Tim O'Grady, Pat McCabe, Bill Swainson, Molly McCloskey, Alannah Hopkin, Aidan Higgins, and Annie Proulx, all of whom significantly intersected with Healy's life and work, and who were all important sounding boards over the past few years. Anne Enright, Kevin Barry, Mike McCormack, Eoin McNamee, Vincent Browne, Nichola Bruce, and Philip Ó Ceallaigh—all longtime admirers of Healy's—have also been most supportive of this project from the outset, for which heartfelt thanks.

Many colleagues and friends have helped us out along the way, all of whom deserve our gratitude: Dr Derek Hand, Dr Gerry Smyth, Dr Jack Fennell, Dr Thierry Robin, Prof Michael Cronin, Dr Maurice Walsh, Prof Ondřej Pilný, Dr Louis de Paor, Prof Gerry Dawe, Senator Susan O'Keeffe, Declan Meade, Thomas Morris, Jonathan Creasy, Vincent Woods, Roz Dineen, Martin Finan, Katie Moriarty-Hopper, Alison Crosbie, Ellie Cummins, Brenda Rawn, and Pauline McLynn.

And to all of the contributors to the present volume, we wish to express our sincere appreciation for submitting such lively and engaging pieces.

Emma Wilcox, the English subject librarian at the School of Humanities and Social Sciences library, NTU, was extremely supportive. Thanks also to Prof Lance Pettitt, Dr Anne Goudsmit, Dr Michelle Paull, Donal McCay, and everyone in the Centre for Irish Studies at St Mary's University, Twickenham, for their encouragement and advice.

This work was completed with the assistance of a Singapore

MOE, ACRF Tier 1 grant, awarded to the editors in 2014, for which thanks and acknowledgement are registered.

Deepest gratitude, as always, is offered to Su Salim Murphy and Niamh Moriarty, for their constant support and encouragement.

A few of the poems and articles in this present volume previously appeared elsewhere. Acknowledgement is due to the following publishers for allowing us to reprint these pieces: Michael Longley, "Constellations" [poem], *The Stairwell* (London: Jonathan Cape; Winston-Salem, NC: Wake Forest University Press, 2014), p. 20, by kind permission of The Random House Group Ltd (UK) and Wake Forest University Press (USA). Michael Harding, "Dermot Healy was afflicted with an unruly mind," *Irish Times* (1 July 2014); Harry Clifton, "Ballinfull, 3 July 2014" [poem], *Irish Times* (2 August 2014); and Timothy O'Grady, "Only myself, said Cúnla," *Irish Times* (22 May 2015), all by kind permission of the *Irish Times*. Caroline Bracken, "Form" [poem], *WOW! Anthology* (Galway: Wordsonthestreet, 2015), p. 12, by kind permission of Wordsonthestreet (Galway). Neil Murphy, "Dermot Healy's *A Goat's Song*: 'To give some form to that which cannot be uttered,'" pp. 108–20, and Annie Proulx, "Dermot Healy and *A Goat's Song*: A Writer's Appreciation," pp. 121–30, both of which first appeared in *Litteraria Pragensia* 22.44 (December 2012), *Neglected Irish Fiction* issue, ed. Neil Murphy, Keith Hopper and Ondřej Pilný, by kind permission of *Litteraria Pragensia* (Prague).

Philip Ó Ceallaigh, "Anonymous is best," *The Stinging Fly* (10 September 2015), by kind permission of *The Stinging Fly*. Kevin Barry, "Sligo Occult: On Dermot Healy's Radical Style," *The Stinging Fly* (Winter 2014–15); this article first appeared in *The Stinging Fly* with the kind permission of Dalkey Archive Press. Vincent Browne, "Profile: Dermot Healy," *Film West* no. 37 (July 1999), pp. 16–18, by kind permission of *Film West*.

Dermot Healy, "The Plough" [poem], *The Travels of Sorrow* (Oldcastle: The Gallery Press, 2015), p. 18, is reprinted by kind permission of the Estate of Dermot Healy and The Gallery Press. We are especially grateful to Peter Fallon, Jean Barry, and The Gallery Press for granting our contributors the kind permission to quote from Dermot Healy's earlier collections of poetry: *A Fool's Errand* (Oldcastle: The Gallery Press, 2010); *The Reed Bed* (Oldcastle: The Gallery Press, 2001); *The Ballyconnell Colours* (Oldcastle: The Gallery Press, 2000); *What the Hammer* (Oldcastle: The Gallery Press, 1998). Go raibh maith agaibh.

SECTION I:
WRITERS AND ARTISTS ON THE WRITER

The Plough
Dermot Healy

The new plough in the sky
has moved to the sea side
of the house

to dig a white furrow
through the long acres of clouds
and star nests in the sky.

The old plough of the earth
has come to rest
at the gable,

to question the heavens,
with feet
and ribcage gone skeletal.

There the symbol sits rusting
under its new coat of blue
while the shape it once threw

moves on
along the lazy beds of the constellations,
like a letter in an old alphabet

whose sound is lost
to the tongue;
till, at daybreak, the work of the metaphor

is done.

Constellations
Michael Longley

Poem ending with a line of Dermot Healy

Thistledown and meteors are streaming
Along the lazybeds of the constellations.

Alone in a Landscape: The Poetry of Dermot Healy
Colm Tóibín

This is a poetry of stark images, dry wit, and a mild, amused, acceptance of things, including all their strangeness and sadness. Much is noticed, closely, almost wisely. The watcher is often alone in a landscape. The sky, the sea, the horizon play a central role, as do words of a single syllable placed at the end of a line or a stanza. While Dermot Healy is ready sometimes to let a line sing, he is more content on other occasions to create an awkward and surprising music that matches or indeed creates the mood of the poems which is often autumnal and filled with shadows. Death and the dead are entertained with sombre acceptance and grim watchfulness in these poems.

History for Healy is not replete with grand narratives or national questions, but rather animated by the wavering ones who have passed on, or seem to have, and by landscapes haunted by them. In "Rosses Point," he sees the dead:

> Each walks to the edge of the surf.
> One life for them was not enough.

In "The Next Room," he hears a cough at night in a house where he is alone. It comes from a space unoccupied, but filled nonetheless with resonance by the presence and the absence of those whom he has known:

> We take the next room
> With us everywhere, the unoccupied room
> Where they all live

In "I Catch Sight of Them as I Often Do," Healy contemplates the stars, "these settlements of light," aware of how long it has taken for that light to make its way to earth, and how the stars themselves may have faded. He then considers other humans in the past that have also stood in this place looking at the night sky, or who used the stars for navigation or direction. Their ghosts speak silently to him now:

> They too
> have gone out of existence,
> these sea-folk who stored stars
> in their heads for direction
> and prayer;
> the light from the stars
> that reached them reaches me,
> their existence shines down on my head
> though they are long dead.

In "Those Days," a poem of dark regret and self-accusation, he describes himself as "A ghost typing / in the spare room." In "The Hallway," he becomes a ghost of himself as he finds himself back in the house where he grew up as though time has frozen, or he has frozen, or memory has remained more powerful than present fact, and

> more often than not I am down in the hallway by the hall-stand
> where something is after happening.

This last line—"where something is after happening"—may seem simple, may appear to be a part of speech, casual, close to cliché, but by placing it where he does, by putting an aura of chill and ghostly wonder around it, Healy rescues it as a serious and powerful phrase with its own still music, its own foreboding, its way of catching the reader unawares, of hitting the nervous system without seeming to try.

In other poems, there are presences that fill silence and emptiness with their aura. "Footsteps," for example, begins with an image of the sound of a footstep in a place where the road has ended and the only possible human presence is that of the poet. Healy begins to imagine that other footsteps that occur in other places—Brixton, Dublin, Quito, Sligo—actually happen close by, within earshot. The problem he has, since he has evoked the ghostly sound that the living make, is how to end the poem, how to find an image that is conclusive, totalising, and also open-ended, suggestive, both ghostly and substantial. The final lines of "Footsteps" are an example of Healy at his most subtle and tactful. He allows the soft music of the poem to do most of the work, making the last line repeat the title of the poem, but having it sound like an echo, after a statement that is filled with implication:

> oh it will always be
> the plainsong
>
> of the ordinary
> that reduces whole cities out there
>
> to a step
> on a street
>
> and contains them all,
> all those footfalls.

Healy likes hushed statement, preferring to let his chiselled rhythms do the work. He writes at times like an Imagist let loose in an untamed landscape, or a writer of haikus who watches the Atlantic Ocean and the sky above it, and listens to the Sligo wind and weather. He likes the pure image itself, relishes charting what is visible and what can be witnessed and what can be found to be the case, using short lines and short stanzas and clear diction, moving towards a steely and deeply considered lyricism.

Thus a single stanza can read:

> Green-winged butterflies feed off
> The purples and mauves of May.

Or the opening poem in the volume *The Reed Bed*, a poem entitled

"A Ball of Starlings," has all the spare power of a Japanese painting:

> and suddenly over the lough
> a whispering ball of starlings
>
> rises into
> the blue night

Sometimes, Healy can be funny, as in:

> As we made love
> each of your previous lovers
> was present
>
> and all of mine
> strangely absent;
> they had better things to do,
>
> I suppose.

Or:

> I see you've finished
> *The Female Orgasm* -
> dare I ask
>
> what you're reading now.

He allows himself to be amused by the world and resigned to the way things happen. The last stanza of the three-stanza poem "After the Silence" has some of the shining clarity of late Patrick Kavanagh. It is close to ordinary speech, and then is moved effortlessly to the level of bleak and shivering truth:

> Oh there were happier times,
> There's no denying the fact,
> But they're over.
> It's done. That's that.

There is a feeling in many of the poems that much has happened before they were written. They come from a present that is filled with a notion of survival, of having found shelter, of having located a place of mild comfort from which the world can be observed, a haven where there is, as Healy beautifully puts it, "Enough light here to write by / Enough remorse to put it down."

In "Away with the Birds," he writes about a newly found rootedness:

> not like in the old days
> when I couldn't wait
> to enter
> the vast strangeness —

Like Melville and Emily Dickinson, and indeed J. M. Synge and Elizabeth Bishop, Healy views the sea as a place of danger, instability, death, but also richness, almost excitement, as it provides him with some of his most powerful images:

> I envy those
> Who live upriver
> At the quiet source.
> Here we are forever
>
> Stepping between
> The incoming roar
> Of life and the tides
> That carry death out.
>
> They are right
> Who had long ago
> The sense to collect
> In great numbers
>
> In sea-cities
> To protect themselves.

There is a sense that Healy has learned how to notice and connect things, but that it has taken time. He operates like a Metaphysical poet as he merges two aspects of the visible world into one narrative. Thus in "Neighbours' Lights," the land and the sky become indivisible, or the world has moved up into the skies:

> Killybegs and Ballyshannon
> Are villages open late
> In the heavens,
>
> And driving towards Easkey
> A fisherman's car
> Is a shooting star.

The weather is a figure in these poems, a wayward personality, someone to be watched. When in "Approaching Car" he looks to see who is coming, he finds instead of a person,

> The rain from the south-west
> driving past
>
> in a squall
> with no lights on

The sea becomes land in "July Storm":

> For three days the sea blooms
> in every crevice.

It becomes human in "Sea-sand":

> The splash grows closer
> till it's like someone
> turning in the bed
> beside you.

The sea evokes the complexity of the mind in "My House is Tiny":

> And yet the whole sea
> at my back
> can fit into
> the most frightened
>
> human mind.

In these poems, the moon takes precedence over the sun, which barely appears. Bird life is given more attention than the human presence. While there are some poems about London, the sea is evoked more sonorously and in more detail than towns or cities or the interiors of houses. This idea then of a poetry in which much is absent, in which the form of the poem itself and the tone are pared back and stripped down, in which the moon and the bird are allowed to hold centre stage, has much in common with the paintings of Joan Miró and Miró's spare and pointed iconography. The difference, of course, is wild wind and Northern light, which fill the psychic landscape of these poems as love or sadness might fill the work of another poet.

Healy can evoke images that will not ever appear in Miró's work. Firelight, or material to burn in the hearth in winter, for example. Healy in Sligo envies Philip Larkin in Hull:

> And yet I'd like to aspire
> to a centrally-heated library,
>
> like Larkin, in rooms where fires
> come on at a touch
>
> rather than flailing in the dark
> through a stack of turf

In "Coal Bags":

> The half-empty bags of Polish coal
> blow in a July wind
> like monks' cowls.

In "Fire," the hearth contains the soul as much as the fire:

> If you let the fire die
> the soul scurries across the field
> like a burning coal
> off to another hearth.

In "Tongs," Healy evokes a scenario from childhood in what could be read as homage to Seamus Heaney:

> My mother sits by the grate
> with a newspaper pressed
> like a sail sheet
> against the tall tongs.
>
> Behind, the fire whooshes
> as the draught ascends.

Healy wishes to evoke the spirit of the world, its shape, what it will look like in its own aftermath. (Of the geese in his book *A Fool's Errand*, he writes: "I like to look up / and see them / after they've gone.") A sort of animism nourishes his work. Something lurks within the landscape and within the lifespan much greater than what the facts might suggest. If there is a house, then there will be a room within it that is filled with spirit and can be evoked in a poem such as "The Thrashing Shadows" in which the poet seeks "the long room where souls gather to talk."

Towards the end of "The Beaten Sounds," Healy summons up a Yeatsian command as he ponders the connections between the dead and living:

> We speak in languages that carry
> messages from the dead and hand on
>
> our own into the silences that will never be read,
> but are known to you as you bend your head low
> and make the promises that time has kept.

While Healy's poems deal with regret and with love, and are open to joy and wonder, they are concerned mostly with mystery, with what lurks within the visible, what is hidden but might be revealed in the poem, in a phrase, a statement, a strange twist at the end of a poem, or moved into place by the right words so that something which was not previously known is now understood. Healy is a poet whose poetic diction does not reflect what has already been thought, but pulls thought with it, or is open enough to admit something never before considered.

It is interesting how much he uses images of the page itself, or language, or the alphabet, in the poems. The poem "Light" is just four lines long:

> Each scrap of daylight
> that crosses the sill
> is a blank page
> which I must fill.

In one of the sequences in "The Leavings" he compares the experience of walking and looking to reading a book, and then when the geese appear "it's as if you were turning down the leaf / of a book, so you might know where you stopped / reading that evening the geese shot out into the dark." In "The Words," a pane of glass is the page of a book, and thus when the rain starts slowly, it "took an age/ to run down a page." In another poem, the young geese fly "in the same script as the parent." In "The Wild Goose Chase," he sees "the writing in the sky." In another poem, the bird is "bringing news of a lost dialect."

In a marvellous image, he sees the flight of the geese as the completion of a sentence:

> to bring the prayer to rest,
> and carry the stop to the end of the sentence,
>
> the verb high
> over the rock
>
> and the noun
> down, quietly, into the nest.

In another poem from the same sequence, the geese, as they break over the sea, take "the vowel sounds / with them." Later:

> Out on Inishmurray[1]
> they nestle under St Molaise's stiff skirt, move the letters
>
> of the old alphabet on foot towards the monk's beehive hut.

Later, he invokes a bomb in Baghdad as it "cleared the old lettering off another page."

This use of metaphors of letters and language and print and the page points us to something essential and easy to miss in these poems. While many of them deal with the very edge of the world and study nature with some intensity, they are also, as artifacts, deliberate, self-conscious and highly crafted. In the ways he chooses and chisels an image and keeps his tone in check, in the clear-eyed tone of the poems, in the balance between the evocative, the spiritual, and the exact thing described by an exacting eye, Healy displays not only an astonishing gift as a poet, but also a poet's conscience, manifested in the way he will not wander into easy poetic spaces, or manipulate feeling, or strike a pose. Instead he will remain reticent and eloquent, maintaining equilibrium between what is mysterious and what is material. He is alone in the landscape, but he is alert to certain and uncertain forces in the air around him, blown in by the wind, that only the poem can find.

Works Cited

Healy, Dermot. *A Fool's Errand*. Oldcastle: The Gallery Press, 2010. Print.

———. *The Ballyconnell Colours*. Oldcastle: The Gallery Press, 2000. Print.

———. *The Reed Bed*. Oldcastle: The Gallery Press, 2001. Print.

———. *What the Hammer*. Oldcastle: The Gallery Press, 1998. Print.

---

1. Editors' note: In the original poem, "The Ebbing Song," from *A Fool's Errand* (Gallery Press, 92), Inishmurray is spelled Innishmurray. Tóibín has corrected this to reflect the most common local spelling of Inishmurray.

Ballinfull, 3 July 2014
Harry Clifton

Dermot Healy 1947–2014

It was like an eye opening,
An eye, or a space
Between nature and itself,
And through it poured the days,

The years, the mountain-shapes.
There was a smell of hay,
And swallows, elbowing a way
Between nothing and nothing,

Keeping the elements open wide
And summer at the full.
In the high corner of a field,
On this side of the wall,

A human crowd, a passing bell.
This being Ireland, sea in the distance,
Blue-grey skies, the changeable –
In short, existence

On the latch, or the hook,
Like a sashed country window,
An eyelid, or an inch of light
Propped open by a book.

"Only myself, said Cúnla"
Timothy O'Grady

The final act of his funeral was in the graveyard at Maugherow. The day started with the corpse being carried out of his home to the accompaniment of Mongolian throat-singers and ended in a whirling of shovels as the mourners took turns piling the earth on the coffin. They laboured until all that had been dug out to make the grave had been replaced, a local custom that had intrigued him. Around a thousand people had come to the little church at Maugherow, poets, carpenters, nurses, farmers, the President of Ireland, a poet himself. They were there in the graveyard as the earth flew and the priest prayed and the poet Theo Dorgan read out the poem "The Funeral."

>Twelve shovels
>dug the grave;
>
>the same twelve
>fill it in.
>
>It takes the length
>of a rosary.
>
>All together
>tap the dab,
>
>kick muck
>off a heel,
>
>toss old bones
>into a bag.

> The shovels
> work like oars
>
> rowing the dead man
> from this world
>
> to the next.
> Then the lights
>
> go back
> to the west.

Dermot had written this in memory of his friend and neighbour Jimmy Foley. Jimmy lived with a dog named Victor in a house filled with newspapers and in a condition of long bachelor neglect. It lacked electricity. He trapped lobsters in a device made of stones, played the accordion and lit a paraffin lamp in his window, by which Dermot knew when to call, which he did most days.

Dermot's house was just above on a rise at the end of the peninsula, back and sides to the Atlantic, a kind of cathedral-like chair looking out over land that some neighbours came to call Inishhealy. Wind stirred the grasses, clouds skimmed and churned, the sea beat on the cliffs and set the stones on the beach clattering. He set flowers and vegetables, built sea walls against winter storms, kept a donkey. He watched the geese fly over year after year and finally his thinking about them came out in the long, late poem *A Fool's Errand*, as Jimmy Foley did in Uncle Joejoe and the Blackbird in his final novel *Long Time, No See* and the sea and the wind and the sound of the stones in lines and phrases elsewhere. He talked to the postman, walked the lanes, provided feasts, listened to birds and tales of ghosts, watched the play of light, cooks' hands, glasses raised to lips, fingers moving over the buttons of a concertina and collected jokes, exclamations, sayings, idiomatic twists, shrugs, gestures, the way a thought or feeling broke into a face. You could feel when you were with him that it was all being stored and transformed and milled, the living world read as text, or something on the way to text. He seemed to be looking for the point where this living world would dissolve and reveal something truer and more mysterious beyond. It went on without cease. The act of writing was a taking down rather than a making up.

He became known for his silences because of two decade-long lapses between prose works, but in fact produced five works of fiction, a memoir, thirteen plays and five collections of poetry, constituting, in the reckoning of many, mine too, one of the greatest achievements in all of Irish literature. He also edited magazines, directed and ran writing workshops for convicts and the mentally ill, among others, wrote for newspapers and sat on innumerable committees. His heart stopped beating when he was just sixty-six.

I felt I heard him coming from a long way off. I met many young writers in Dublin when I was in my twenties, people in the main around the then just beginning Irish Writers' Co-op. They spoke of this one or that one, him or her, but when they spoke of Dermot it seemed to have a different tone, as if he could hear something others couldn't hear, work with tools they hadn't access to. It was as if what he did came not out of a mingling of erudition and ambition and a verbal skill and imagination, but rather out of some act of bestowal, an anointing, an almost chilling natural gift. He lived differently too. He left university after a year. He had red hair and wild practices and appetites, with a recklessness like someone from Dostoevsky. He worked on building sites, trawlers, a toilet seat factory and in Wallace Stevens's profession, insurance underwriting. He lived in unexpected places, neither urban nor romantically rural. One of the more expected was London, where he seemed to be interested in everything other than literary manoeuvring. He sought no agent, editor, network of connections or entrance to a club. He was ambitious for the text but not a career. It would remind you of the saying about the richest man being he with the least needs.

If there was an anointing there was also an education of his own making. He talked to everybody. He sought the far reaches of the consciousness, assisted and unassisted. He read Bashō, Nâzım Hikmet, Borges, Miroslav Holub, Lorca, Isaac Babel and Frank O'Connor among many others that included Joyce, someone whom he later claimed he once thought was a woman. Joyce, above all perhaps, for his ability to listen.

He wrote poems and Seamus Heaney published a selection, after calling him up to ask, "Do you know how good you are?" Stories began to appear in David Marcus's pages in the *Irish Press*. Aidan Higgins, judging the Hennessy Award, declared that first, second and third prizes should go to him for the single story "Banished Misfortune." Higgins and Neil Jordan told a young editor in London named Bill Swainson that the person writing the most interesting prose in Ireland was Dermot. Swainson wrote a letter. He heard nothing and wrote several more, all of them unanswered. "London at the time seemed so far away," said Dermot. Years later Swainson received a call and they met in a pub in Wandsworth. "The first thing that came out of it was that I was given the job of painting their office." Eventually, twelve stories collected under the title *Banished Misfortune* came out in 1982.

This was when I first encountered him on the page, as many years since I'd first heard of him as it would be until I met him in the flesh. I went first to the title story. I remember that the feeling of reading it was like throwing myself against a hedge. I'd read *Naked Lunch* and *Finnegans Wake* and some poems by Hart Crane by then, but still the mind seemed to move along tracks that expected order, sequence, meaning, identifiable people, and a mind in that condition could not meet this text. Yet you can be taught by the text how to read it, essentially by letting go and letting it happen to you. They are less stories than rendered sensations of consciousness. Time past and time present, space elsewhere and space here are brought together in this consciousness as radically sometimes as in Benjy's section in *The Sound and the Fury*. They are fields of language in the way that there are fields of music, the music of what happens you could say, meaning just itself. Not in each case. Sometimes there is symbol, or parable, or, rarely, conventional narrative, but mostly, it seems, he is trying to bring you intensified feeling. There is a lack of reference to a set of meanings, and no plot. Nor are there hierarchies. The sound of a bird or rushing water or the sight of the stretched leg of a hare can weigh the same as a kicking in a bank of snow or the wail of human loneliness.

The trick to experiencing *Finnegans Wake*, Joyce said, was to read it aloud. I think the trick with these stories is to read them twice. Then you can take them in as breath.

I took down the book again to read it in the days I am writing this. I've been struck by the intellect, the ambition about form, the honest rendering of feeling, the great, churning, Biblical cadences, such as—"For whatever reason the house might fall, the sleeping MacFarland would build again with a sense of adventure anywhere north of the lakes and in good time, son of Saul, master builder of Fermanagh country [sic] but by pneumonia put away while tended by his wife Olive, Glan woman and descendant of J. O'Reilly who danced once with flax in his trousers, and though nominally Christian died in foreign and pagan lands fighting an unjust war, but MacFarland sensing the lie of the land grew away from a sense of guilt or desire for power and prayed that the haphazard world would not destroy his family so well grounded among the moralities of chance and nature, if one could remain loyal to the nature of a people and not the people themselves, for whatever reason the house might fall"—and the delicacy of touch—"Soft Chinese music of the rain on glass and leaves, lightly touched cymbals, ducks crashing onto the waters, the primitive crane stretching her awkward wings in a lone high flight, the land below so cold and misty it looked as if a healing frost had settled." You can see Faulkner in the former of these sentences, Faulkner who went back to the Bible and forward to García Márquez, Ken Kesey, Cormac McCarthy, Toni Morrison and Dermot. I've been struck by the distress behind the stories, the sense of an aching, dislocated consciousness, of yearning for place or a woman or ease of mind, something smeared, unknowable about the self, a feeling of agony for the agony of others. The war in the North comes in, but as sensation rather than ideology. There is humour. A lonely and mordant columnist named Blake reviewing a collection of essays titles his review "Tin of Sardines" and declares of the author, "I think he has settled for the well-turned phrase, rather than exert the imagination, for what once ran cleanly through the ocean has been parboiled, salted, oiled and tinned, still it bears a very Christian label . . ." And finally I've been struck by the tremendous confidence in the rendering hand and a capacity to launch character into myth.

Neil Jordan once said to me, "He speaks out of a world I never knew existed—an extraordinarily alive, dangerous rural Irish world. I don't know how he makes this world mythical, but he does." Of course any writer would like to know how to make a mythical world. But there is no recipe.

I've wondered as I've read them what it must have been like to encounter them as they appeared, to sense the sudden arrival of this prose into a small island country so highly esteeming of the written word (still the case, it would seem, judging by his funeral and its coverage on the national news). I asked a few who pursued the same line of work. Anthony Cronin, who'd seen the generation of Flann O'Brien, Brendan Behan and Patrick Kavanagh come and go, said, "You need only read a sentence or two and you know you are in the presence of a natural writer. I don't mean by that a kind of naïve, accidental genius, for he's very sophisticated. I mean that he was always a writer. The first breaths he drew were writer's breaths. And what he did with it was to make something evanescent, almost unrealizable, as if he brought something into the realm of expression that was not previously there." Aidan Higgins, a friend and longtime sponsor of his, said, "What I like about him is that he doesn't put on airs. There's an honest throb there. And I admire that his idiomatic English is fuelled by the Gaelic. There is no guilt in Gaelic, no Freud. He seems to have bypassed all this and found a freedom of his own, to speak as he pleases."

Those who find the way to speak as they please often lift others to do the same. "When I first heard Elvis it was like I was busting out of jail," said Bob Dylan. Patrick McCabe, seven years his junior, said of the stories, "They were light-years ahead of anything else being done at the time. They came out of a naturalistic tradition we were all very familiar with, but they were shot through with another kind of sensibility of new music, new states of mind, new forms of expression that as usual were arriving later in Ireland than most other places. It was Patrick Kavanagh with a dash of mescaline. This was truly revolutionary work, and high literary art, unashamedly so."

I finally met him near the beginning of the 1990s on a night out in Maida Vale with Pat McCabe and Neil Jordan. It was pub to pub, drink to drink, as it often was when I saw him again, in Sligo or Andalusia or Prague, on to exhaustion or the stratospheric or the otherworldly. As his work was a storm, so was he. He was a large, unmissable, busy presence who remained watchful while commanding attention. His eyes conveyed intelligence, experience, mirth and pathos. He was often on the verge, or over it, of laughter. He could be obstreperous and petulant, bewilderingly so in a person so gracious, and he offended many at some point, but I never saw him wilfully cruel, arrogant, dismissive. He was a natural democrat. He sang. He did recitations. He could be transported all on his own into strange, abstract movement. Sometimes he forsook language and spoke as a bird. He told long and great stories. Often they started hesitantly, unpromisingly, and ended with something you'd never expect. He could carry gatherings for hours. You'd never know what would happen. I often thought it must take a lot of fuel to be him, and I mean energy rather than drink. He was kind to a rare degree. He visited the sick and feeble and lonely. He was an abettor of others. He was both rigorous and generous in observing the codes of hospitality. He listened. Large numbers of people loved him. When I met him he was in the late acts of *A Goat's Song*. It was a book that swelled to 740 pages at one time and then came down by around a third, through paring, excisions to avoid a lawsuit and finally a wild, fatalistic afternoon of butchery at his publisher's office when he took out two hundred pages in a few hours.

It began not as books generally do, from image or incident or some sense of a character, but rather from etymology—the *tragos*, or goat, and the *oide*, or song, that together make Tragedy. The goat song that he imagined was the cry of male to female over the water that separated them, a tragic cry, for goats can't swim. He imagined the tragedy as circular, appearing to move towards a happy ending the reader yearns for, but instead, through authorial trick, as in *Finnegans Wake*, returning in time to the beginning, a beginning we know will be a path of desolation. He gives to the man who moves along this path the name Jack Ferris, perhaps to suggest the fairground ride that is a wheel. He had behind him a story he had lived of love and loss, and he had a sense of an island country tragically riven, and he had, perhaps, even the connection between these two things, but he didn't have the book until he had the form of the circle.

The bad times are over at last, Jack Ferris tells himself in the opening sentence. Just when he thought she was gone forever he receives a letter. *I love you and want to be with you*, she writes. *Let's grow old and sober together. Meet me at the bridge some time Saturday afternoon.*

He watches sheep in a low field. He sees Christmas trees being hauled up Sean America Street. He talks with a bereaved man, goes into a paper shop, takes a lift out to her family home thinking he might have missed her, he sweeps and puts down a fire. Then he walks the miles back to the bridge, where he waits.

"I'm waiting for Catherine," he is compelled to say.

He enters a hotel yearning for a drink but instead takes coffee with a countryman who may be mad. He imagines her driving in her Lada to meet him, the music she'll play, what he will say to her. Dusk begins to fall. "The sand was a quiet phosphorescent carpet. Suds lay the landward side of the wrack." The night arrives and he walks the town with the beam from the Eagle lighthouse falling over him, steps back into the hotel and orders a brandy and *crème de menthe* before entering a vortex of drink and grief with a crowd of priests and waking the next day alone, sick and wracked with panic.

In the days that follow he walks the triangle that extends from his cottage to hers and down to the town. He makes increasingly bad-tempered calls to the theatre where she is rehearsing a play he has written. She won't come to the phone. He dreams of her and awakes weeping. He drinks through the day in the hope of dousing his virulent consciousness. He tries to get to Dublin to see her, the west of Ireland rushing at him like the roadside scenery in a video car chase game, but he collapses drunk in a bush in Ballina and is brought back to his reeking home with its starving animals by the Guards. What is the drink that will get him where he needs to go? He thinks each day. Gin? Brandy? The sherry he had put by as a surprise?

We get every twist and turn of this through forty-five pages, pieces of his being falling off as he travels the oblivious road, all of it relentlessly, brutally present, and rendered with care. This takes a long and vivid thought from a writer, and great patience in the telling.

Finally he is brought weeping in a car to an asylum to dry out, where to escape his self-loathing he takes down the stories of the mad and infirm around him. ". . . To give form to that which cannot be uttered," he'd read in the Bible in her cottage. Language had rotted in him in the days he walked and waited and drank—"He was no longer able to control the darkness. But *darkness* was too broad a word for what was overwhelming him, as was *overwhelming* the wrong word, as all words were the wrong words when they had not been lived in"—but in the asylum they become radiant, curative. In time he is let out of the gate, he makes his way back to his cottage and he takes down a notebook.

"Here it begins," he thinks, and begins to write.

What he writes is the remaining several hundred pages of the book we are holding in our hands, the story of his exhilarating and ruinous love for Catherine Adams, an attempt to transcend her by turning her into text. It is also the story of the Ireland of his time, and times beyond. It takes in the wild splendour of the West, bohemian Dublin, the bracing austerities of Northern Presbyterianism, rain-sodden Midland towns, the corrosiveness of Loyalist East Belfast, war, drink, madness and both the recoiling from and the yearning for impossible connections. Around and through it you hear the plaintive cry of the goat. It's hard to credit one man knowing such disparate things so well. But he'd lived them all.

There are two long migrations—that of Jonathan Adams, father of Catherine, a failed Presbyterian minister turned RUC man, into Gaelic Ireland at its geographical and mythical and psychological extremes, and that of Jack, a Catholic doctor's son from the Midlands, towards Catherine and through her into the heartland of Belfast Loyalism. They are like characters out of Beckett, crawling uncomprehendingly towards some dimly perceived light, some place or person where they hope to find completion, but then failing and falling back. The story of the love affair follows meeting, courtship, the brief and glorious mergence of their beings, the drink, the fights, chaos and loss until we are taken along a route that seems to be moving towards her again, towards salvation, the redemption of their love, when, at the end, we realize that we are at the bridge where we found him at the beginning, that the novel is a circle rimmed in black. It is the story of these people but it is also, as the writer Ronan Sheehan once said to me, of the country wishing to unite itself but being tragically unable to do so.

There have been Irish novels that were greatly ambitious about form and language—*At Swim-Two-Birds*, Máirtín Ó Cadhain's *Cré na Cille*, Joyce and Beckett, among which, I believe, *A Goat's Song* can live—but I know none as ambitious about comprising the island.

There are many things in this book you can find elsewhere in his work—the splendour of nature, the comedy of earnestness, the extraordinariness of the mundane, the sexual charge in the meeting of opposites, language that moves towards, and almost becomes, music, the act of writing itself. These are themes, tropes, literary garments of a kind. But there are two things at the root of this book, and I think in Dermot himself, that form the creation mythology of both, the "Big Bang," or Earth Diver or God's breathing into the clay in *Genesis*. These would be the act of breaking down and the act of recording the story of another, both of them forms of liberation from the oppressiveness and triviality and dullness of one's own consciousness. He filled notebooks with others' stories, as Jack Ferris did in the asylum, in buses, pubs, hospitals, kitchens, for plays or stories or the interviews he published in his magazine *Force 10* (someone should collect these). "I never wanted to be dominated by my own voice," he told me. "Writing is a hugely boring activity, the only boring thing that is truly wonderful. You can put in your honest day's work and each day get away from your own consciousness." Breaking down, far more hazardous of course, serves the same end. He had breakdowns large and small and seemed to seek them in everyday life, controlled detonations that worked as a release, a clearing away to allow things to be seen clear and fresh. One brought about his first story. He had a terrifying night among flying candles in a haunted room in Roscommon in which the concrete objects seemed to dissolve, and then wrote it. "When you break down you stop pretending," he said. "The force of your own personality works against your writing, but when you disintegrate it comes through."

•

His consciousness may have eased a little with time. He'd moved often, sometimes in restlessness and chaos, but then took the house at the end of Maugherow in 1989 and lived there with his wife Helen Gillard until he died. For the first three years they were lit only by candles, with the sea threatening to take down the cliff on which the house sat. The sea wall was reinforced, the three-room house extended southwards along the cliffline to comprise the outbuildings and they filled them with paintings and books. He built flowerbeds like tiny ring forts by the side of the road. One night a neighbour called on him to help dig a grave and they felt then as citizens of the place.

The work lightened. The poems were often of things he could see from his window and had the simplicity of Japanese ink drawings. They seemed to be happening in front of you as you read them. You felt the perceiving eye, the drawing hand and, with paradox, the thing itself. "May they live long lives, / The hares that afford us a break / From the language that would explain them," he wrote in a poem for his daughter.

He found an old diary from his youth and made the memoir *The Bend for Home*. The great floods of improvised language devolved at times to sentences of three single-syllable words. Humour and affection went into the ascendant. It would put you in mind of Patrick Kavanagh's later years, when he disavowed his earlier rage in favour of acceptance, with the "leafy-with-love banks and the green waters of the canal / Pouring redemption for me," or of so many others in art who move from the turbulent, the intricate, the assertive display of gifts, to simple, clear expression and the pleasure of small things.

He went straight on to a novel, building it from a story he'd taken down in an asylum, about a man moving with a severely attenuated consciousness through the streets of Sligo and London. It's a brutal tale, told with a light, comic touch. He called it *Sudden Times*, a phrase you can find on page one of a story he'd written twenty years earlier, "First Snow of the Year"—"Phildy stood under the gable again, surly looking, but of sudden times, nearly by inspiration, his full frame would relax, his face ruffle with silent laughter."

Laughter is the thing in his last work, *Long Time, No See*, though there was anxiety in the making of it. He'd taken by a long way the largest advance of his life from Faber for two unwritten books and then couldn't find them. He told me on the phone he was writing a book about a flood, but no such book appeared. His daughter Inor became seriously ill and they set up a care unit for her in the house. Later, the geese occupied him, and plays and community work. The advance sat heavily on him. He thought of sending it back. But then scenes began to accrue and he lined them up. He was hesitant to let it go but then finally did. As *A Goat's Song* is his Tragedy, this is his Comedy, a tale of human foibles and obsessions and misunderstandings told from an Olympian height, but with affection, amusement and a democratic embrace.

"It's all about getting out of the way," a painter once said to me. We were on a golf course in Las Vegas, and as it happened he was talking about the dynamics of the swing. But I thought, Yes, that's it, in life, in art, in relation to another or to one's own consciousness. Dermot told me he wanted to write a book that would be nearly all dialogue, in which he was all but absent, *out of the way*, and *Long Time, No See* came out like that. You hear the voices and just barely scent the faintest, powdery traces of him. That may be what he was always aiming for. To disappear.

Some time in these last years he told me that when he was seventeen he'd written down on a piece of paper a list of all the books he would one day write.

"What happened with them?" I asked.

"I've written them," he said.

I got a call on the morning of 30 June to tell me he'd died the previous night. I flew from Bydgoszcz in Poland to Dublin and then drove to Sligo. I got to the house after midnight. Helen was there, with neighbours and Dermot's sisters. In the room where he'd talked on the phone and conducted his feasts and taught his classes and read his books he was laid out in a coffin, impossibly small, I thought, impossibly inanimate, dressed in pale greens and browns, spectacles, pens and a leather book of old sacred verse about him. He didn't write about the small things of his life or make entertainments or finely cut jewelled ornaments whose purpose was to be admired or tailor what he did to make it more palatable. He reached beyond himself, spared neither himself nor his readers. No one asked him to do it, he did it because he wanted to, or had to, but there was nevertheless something of self-sacrifice about it, in the scale of what he had taken on and what he put himself through to do it.

There's a row of his books on my shelf, still but ready in a way that a corpse cannot be. On the title page of my copy of *A Goat's Song* he wrote "Only myself, said Cúnla." It's the single answer given each time to a series of questions put in a fourteenth-century Irish song, the person within a house asking the person without, "Oh who is that there knocking the ditches down . . . Who is that there tapping the windowpane . . . Who is that there raking the fire for me . . . Who is that there tickling the toes of me . . . Who is that there pulling the blanket from me . . . ?" "Only myself, said Cúnla." He disappears. He comes back.

Wings 2/6: Memories of Dermot Healy
Patrick McCabe

It is unlikely that the Co. Westmeath town of Finea in the year 1947 would have been considered a neo-Gallic orgiastic hotbed of concupiscence, philosophical expatiation, peyote ingestion and persistently riotous disputes of a theosophical and political nature. Or, indeed, celebrated for its tradition of late-night discussions in jasmine-scented cafés debating what Francis Stuart considered to be the absence of any counter-current to the main, shoddy stream of what passed for literature in these islands—tributaries of which were hailed every Sunday, with dreary predictability, in the literary supplements.

No, the midland village's main claim to international fame at that time was the fact that it had made an appearance in the Percy French song "Come Back Paddy Reilly To Ballyjamesduff," in which a local bridge is accorded pride of place—quite inappropriately as it transpires. For the truth of the matter is that you can't "turn left at the bridge of Finea." And if you happen to be wondering how I became privy to this extraordinary information, the answer is simple: Dermot Healy told me. "You can't turn left at the bridge of Finea—no matter how you try it, it can't be done," he said.

I don't know for sure what Dermot was doing in those days, but I imagine him hanging around parish halls selling tickets and collecting bottles while gathering intelligence on the habits of various local breeds of birds and dogs—travelling through their inscrutable irises, as he often put it.

1947 was the year he was born—the worst in living memory, or so they said. And never shut up saying, so far as I can remember. "When asses became sculptures of ice where they stood!" and "Petrified hares uttered the seven last words of Haydn before perishing." That last bit, as you probably know, I just made up. It reminds me of a technique that Dermot would sometimes use—when he would slyly permit his sentences to attain a certain mesmeric rhythm which he would then suddenly fracture, words springing out of nowhere like a sally rod during a quiet walk in the woods, whiplashing you with an almost shocking and unexpected image. These images in his fiction are as striking in their opulence as a Harry Clarke stained-glass window, and I always looked forward to them with delicious anticipation.

There are any number of these startling lines in the very first story of his that I read, "First Snow of the Year," which was eventually included in the collection *Banished Misfortune and Other Stories*, not long before I met him in Rathmines in 1975.

Salman Rushdie has written eloquently of Márquez's Macondo—his version of Faulkner's Yoknapatawpha County, R. K. Narayan's Malgudi, or Sherwood Anderson's Winesburg, Ohio. More specifically, Rushdie praises Márquez's approach to metaphor and rumour, so much a part of village life anywhere. There is a scene in *One Hundred Years of Solitude* where, in the aftermath of a pistol shot, a trickle of blood comes running out the door, crosses the living room out into the street, continues in a straight line across the uneven terraces, and trickles down some steps before passing along the Street of the Turks. Having turned a score of corners, it finally makes its way under a closed door to arrive at the feet of a woman breaking eggs and who cries out in alarm to her Almighty Father: "O Holy God!"

Looking back on it now, "First Snow of the Year"—in which a rural Cavan postman considers his retirement—possesses not only the same kinetic energy as *One Hundred Years Of Solitude* but the same seamless blend of trance and the quotidian. It was the world I lived in and one that I recognised—but it had never been approached like this before. I mean, I never found much of Borges in Patrick Kavanagh—but this! If he had read it, Francis Stuart would have perked up like a startled hare—pantheistic, unpatronising, the world's stained glass glimmering inside the eye of a dog.[1]

Did you ever notice in these writer's retreats all of these people going around thinking big thoughts? I know you probably haven't,

---

1. For Stuart's take on contemporary Irish writing, see Francis Stuart, "The Soft Centre of Irish Writing" (1976), repr. *Paddy No More: Modern Irish Short Stories*, ed. William Vorm, 1977; Dublin: Wolfhound, 1978: 5–9.

but it's true—for I've seen them. You'll come upon them staring fixedly out through windows, agonising over some particularly recondite chunk of "Sam"—no point telling these sepulchral souls that it was Behan, more than anyone, who took the anal grey whine out of Irish literature—before suddenly becoming alerted and staring at you in horror, like you've gone and snapped a Wordsworthian twig, and invaded a hallowed and sacred place. Such a look as they'd give you!

We discussed these fellows that very first night I met him—please don't take it to heart, fragile readers and poetasters, I'm merely being provocative—especially their tendency to cast certain types of people as representative of what he good-humouredly suggested might be the "native Irish." Dermot offered supporting evidence from the reaction to his extraordinary production, in those days, of *Waiting for Godot*, with the newly-minted local amateur drama troupe The Hacklers. My goodness, Beckett with Co. Cavan accents! And if that wasn't enough, along comes that book with the funny sideways yellow cottage on the front cover—*Banished Misfortune*!

Davora gavora! Jigs and reels! Subterranean inner-city London! Drugs mixed in with the Irish language! Old women smoking fags quoting Shakespeare and Laurel and Hardy! Why, it was for all the world like "Helter Skelter" played by The Dubliners, or Dolores Keane belting out "Raftery" in Sanskrit. The pre- and the post-lapsarian playing handball together, up against the gable of McCarren's sausage factory at lunchtime.

"How did someone like Dermot Healy come out of Cavan," I was once asked by a famous film director—and found that I could supply no adequate response. Not readily, at any rate. "I've always considered him," Seamus Heaney remarked in casual conversation, "sui generis, really."

A kind of tenuous assault on the citadel of language had begun in the early seventies—although, arguably, it had been originally conceived by the poet Patrick Kavanagh in all his grumpy belligerence and one-man war against the "thoroughgoing English-bred lie of the Irish renaissance." The torch passed subsequently, certainly in my apprehension of things, to the great Tom MacIntyre, who in his Faber short story collection *Dance the Dance* brazenly trapezed his way between Oblomov and Ó Bruadair; and then to his Monaghan neighbour, Eugene McCabe, whose colloquial abscissions continued along that same stretch of border—O land of sweet rolling hills and sulky, murderous milk churns—with their distinctive dum-dum projectiles of dialogue, most memorably in the stories "Heritage" and "Cancer."

Around that time, I also remember, Dermot was working on a piece about his friend Aidan Higgins—the two of them reminded me of Joyce and Beckett, I have to say, such was their dedication to their literary craft. Anyway, the piece concerned was an analysis of the language and imagery in the Kildare author's *Scenes from a Receding Past*—an episodic, impressionistic novel (and a most significant one), packed to the hilt with consecrated images and snaky, audacious rattling subjunctives. Higgins's writing made you feel that you hadn't so much fallen through some beautiful trapdoor but were being kicked stupid by opposing teams of extremely literate scholars from deep inside *The Third Policeman* darkness of a careering, vertiginous, outer-space Rubik cube.

We talked for hours about language and the importance of faith and place, with Dermot constantly referencing Babel and Higgins. And it occurs to me now how extraordinary that anthology of short stories edited by Aidan Higgins actually was—the one he had produced for Jonathan Cape entitled *A Century of Short Stories*—a compilation which, I daresay, in its breathtaking cheek and singular perception, would be pretty much close to unthinkable in these curiously conservative and commodified days.

Anyway, Dermot and me—now we were talking about the coppers—because he'd just been arrested. Looking like Catweazle—that magician-cum-medieval knight of the road who was so popular on TV in the early 1970s—they'd decided to take him in to cool off for the night. Macondo could play a part in Dermot's oral renditions and accounts as well, as his impressions alternated between the imaginary and the actual, weaving like coloured skeins in and out of one another, sometimes blending seamlessly into a new and startling pattern. When I looked out—I know, of course, that it's always so claimed in accounts such as this—the dawn was breaking. But in this case, it really was. He'd been telling me he was thinking of starting up a magazine. That became *The Drumlin*, a journal far ahead of its time. My mother wrote to him on my behalf—and I never forgave her. "My son is good at the writing," she told him. "Maybe you'd have room for one of his stories in your paper?" I never really got over the embarrassment. He used to come to the music sessions she ran. "The Halfpenny Loaf Fell Off the Dresser" was one of his party pieces. "The poor fellow. He might be able to write but he can't sing a note," I remember her saying. "That song—it's lovely. And he crucified it!"

He used to wear this silver tweed jacket—you can see it in his photo in the Wolfhound Press collection *Paddy No More*, in which he appears along with many of his peers—Neil Jordan, Desmond Hogan et al. Such a name for a story collection! It reminds me of the beat record—O my good Jesus now best forgotten—in which Dublin pop groups Orange Machine and Purple Pussycat, among many others, declare their mission to make Ireland safe for rock 'n' roll. Would you like to know what that was called? Yes—*Paddy is Dead and the Kids Know It!*

Not that Dermot Healy could ever be called hip, certainly not with that tweed jacket, which was the kind of thing—especially when paired with a pair of raggy old Levi's blue jeans—that your mother would put on you, if you happened to be 'going up the town.' Because no more than Bob Dylan, the words 'current' and 'contemporary' meant little to Dermot Healy. He straddled epochs, instinctively comprehending both puritan and cavalier, cornerboy and captain of industry. And nowhere is this more evident than in the pages both of *Force 10*, his journal of the North-West, and *The Drumlin*, where the 'ordinary five-eighths,' as they used to be called, are Falstaffian shadows—jaw-droppingly colossal against the sky of all time. Says Packie Clay to Joey Coyle: "Your man above is going to the scaffold." "Is that trapdoor safe?" he says to the hangman.

Conversation? Talk about Gogarty! One night I laughed so much I covered him in a mighty deluge of golden lager—Harp, as I recall. Of which we drank plenty. Once we were escorted out of a pub by the barman. It was the day of Live Aid, when the opinion might be advanced that rock 'n' roll—at least of the Jerry Lee Lewis kind—was consummately and publicly interred, never to recover. But anyone looking to give it another shot might arguably have discovered it in the car that day as we fell on the tarmac, and descried the assembly of our astonished hosts gazing through a bungalow window. As the door swung open, our host observed through gritted teeth: "This is it!" Not unexpectedly, we were given short shrift—perhaps because Dermot was talking to a bird. "Me man, the chaffinch," as I seem to recall being informed.

I left him a good way out the Granard Road, as no option remained but for the poet's thumb to be pressed into service. But he never made it, I discovered, having made his way back into the pub, bewilderingly persuading the same barman to cash a cheque for five pounds for the bus fare. "He said one day I'd be famous," he later told me. "He's going to frame it." And he wasn't joking, because it's still there in that Longford bar—I know, because I've been back to have a look. Not long after his funeral, in fact. "He was as good as a play," Flann O'Brien had written of the deceased Brendan Behan. "And he will not be replaced in a hurry—or at all. For there has been no Irishman quite like him." Before continuing: "I know it is probably only foolishness in my own head but there are streets in Dublin which seem strangely silent tonight."

I'm not suggesting that both writers have anything much in common, if anything at all, but that immediately came into my mind as I stood there admiring that neat and elegant signature, with its capital 'D' like a self-grooming, curtseying goose. And I'll tell you this—Flann O'Brien was right about that latter part, for I've never experienced such a loneliness 'up the town,' with this awful pang in my stomach as I reflected on the youthful, careering abandon of that day in Longford town—a near-delirium so often occasioned by time spent in Dermot Healy's company.

Once, in Brixton, he had inexplicably erupted, presumably having been inspired by some stray calypso beat and compelled towards a snaring of the local demotic by the hovering, colourful spirit of Haile Selassie. He caught me by the collar and leered into my face like a wax Luke Kelly melting in the heat, singing at the top of his voice: "Yuh always waahkin'! And yuh always always taahkin'!" Sang? He proceeded to subject me to the worst three minutes of torture ever inflicted on a human being. And which I had absolutely no hesitation in telling him. "No, I don't think Bob Marley would be likely to record it," I replied, on being informed that it was an original composition. He lit another Carroll's and his face contorted into that Catweazle crinkle-smile. "Ah well, bukkin' buk ye then!" I heard him say, before vanishing to talk to a Scottish communist about budgies.

Much is made these days, and rightly so, of the affection Irish people nurture for their poets and writers, and you can't catch a plane without the passenger next to you marvelling at how exceptional all of this is and how no other country, large or small, could consider itself so unique and fortunate in this regard. But, to be honest, when I was a young chap going about the place, writers were almost universally regarded as fruit-and-nut cases. Among the untamed souls I have in mind are Patrick Kavanagh—"That bowsy was at it again in the bus from Dublin, giving disgraceful guff to the driver!"—and Brendan Behan: "I seen him hitting a policeman a box outside McDaid's!" And it has to be admitted that, intermittently at least, during our travels over the years, myself and Dr Healy did little to disabuse the Irish populace of this traditional perception. I am thinking particularly of what might be considered a 'performance piece' involving a black leather coat draped, à la the old woman of the roads, over the head of the celebrated artificer as giddy ululations shrilly protesting "Moo! Moo! I'm a cow!" were heard to rend the startled air. And I'm also delighted to report that there were, on occasion, certain literary disputes, again in Brady's of Brixton High Road (which now, with its memories of donkey-jacketed men and duffle-coated students rattling tins in support of the miners, seems almost a lifetime ago). Anyway, quoting Kavanagh—and not for one moment suggesting the appraisal was original—I accused him, like Whitman, of "bullying his way to prophecy." This Olympian tendency to would-be profundity and self-mythologising was so at odds with the surgically incisive but concomitantly sincere flow of his unpoliced dam-bursting expression, which for me found its apotheosis in the chapter I consider to be nothing less than a masterpiece, "The Half-Day," included in his memoir *The Bend for Home*.

Is writing worth anything? I don't know. But no journalist ever chronicled postmen and bachelors and damaged drinkers with such gigantic, league-stepping inner lives, whether in the undramatic flatlands where the honeysuckle blooms, or the wild elemental slopes of the west, or the glum and unremarkable towns whose dreariness was legendary. When alchemised with that gentle filigree of language that characterises so much of *The Bend for Home*, then the wet streets might be moist from the paint of Monet, such is their arresting, made-new aesthetic wonder.

There are some memories that tend to wrench me more than others. Sometimes he'd call in out of nowhere—on his way to somewhere, on his way back from somewhere: Canada, Australia, maybe the South of France. On one particular occasion, *The Animals of Farthing Wood* was on TV—and he entered the mise-en-scène with aplomb, as I did myself. Its resident viewers, our two daughters, who would have been eight or nine at the time, were getting ready for school. "Do you know most of all what those ladies remind me of," I remember him saying about them, "they're like two sad poets." Before returning, with renewed enthusiasm, to his anthropomorphic mimicry of the characters on the screen. A year later we were out in Maugherow, enjoying the hospitality of Helen and himself in that little cottage-of-wonders by the sea, with Tiny the mongrel barking his head off. They were there again, pale, sitting in their wellies upon the dry stone wall. "Ah man!" he said. "Would you look at them—the Sad Poets!" Before observing, lest perhaps Tiny would feel uncherished: "You know, the dog's never happy till the donkey dies!"

Such a repast as that man could prepare! They say he had an unruly mind; well, such was the order and precise meticulousness that I noted that night—as I had on many other occasions—that I feel this appraisal must be hotly disputed. He hadn't licked it off the briars, of course, having learned it all in the regal halls of Milseanacht Breifne, the Healys' family-run café situated by the Farnham Arms Hotel in Cavan town, which had always been recommended by an uncle of my own, who consistently lauded the exclusivity of its fare: "fed and watered for 2/6 a skull!" And where the distorting concave mirror from *The Bend for Home* had reflected the protean nature of this enigmatic universe, one to which—just as soon as he stopped gallivanting and pretending to write books which never saw the light of day—we would soon be appending the word 'Healyesque.'

When I think of Dermot's road I see a highway of diamonds, a line of grey stones once again alchemised as otherwise drab exchanges began to approximate the climbing cadences of an orchestral sinfonia. There's stones on that road too, where I left him that day after the pub beyond Edgeworthstown that leads to Granard. But it's like a highway of diamonds, as Dylan wrote, with nobody on it. No one, that is, except Dermot Healy, "travelling into the interior," leafing through that black-bound notebook, trying to make sense of this orphan earth, this "Sciamachy Island," as he often called it—this elusive, shape-shifting place of shadows.

I was back in Macondo the other night. I'd been twisting and turning in my sleep and trying not to hear it—which of course is when you hear it. "Kill, kill, kill!" a voice said, as the blood of the dead man came rushing out into the square and away up past the Ulster Bank, past Maggie McClure's and down by Henchy's, skittering sideways by the Farnham Arms and up the side of the pebble-dashed building before becoming a curl of the bluest smoke, dawdling louchely in the hanging paw of Dermot Healy. "Kill!" he repeated in a neutral tone. I thought he was saying: "You killed me, didn't you? You had to—because you knew my early influence on your work was too strong. Kill. You had no option but to do it."

But that wasn't what he'd been saying at all. "Kill," he repeated, but not before adding with a smile: "Kilkenny was good. That was a really good day, wasn't it?"

And indeed it had been—in 2011, which was the last time the two of us shared a reading together, in that old Norman city, at the invitation of the novelist and critic Colm Tóibín, on behalf of the Arts Festival. It was good that a fellow writer had thought to put us together—I'll treasure that memory always. An old chap had come over to talk to him about donkeys, and before you knew it Dermot had launched into an impromptu series of arcane Irish ballads, tapping his toe in an old, long black coat. Then Dermot tapped me slyly on the ankle, without flinching, arching an impish eyebrow as he surreptitiously urged: "Look up, McCabe!" "Brrk!" burbled a rooster, camouflaged by a stack of encyclopaedias high on a shelf. And believe it or not, it kind of looked like him, sort of haughty and medieval. But the point is that he saw it straightaway— no one else did.

I dreamed of his return. Flanked on the Granard Road by the twin great compass legs of the zenith-poised midday sun. He was wearing a pair of dove-white wings, the tips of which came away down past his knees. "They're for Jimmy Foley," I heard him say. "Being from Cavan I got them cheap. I beat them down from three bob to two-and-six!"

So often in my mind the past acquires the primary-colour cast of an old Victorian penny gaff, with the players attaining such a sprightly and vivacious aspect that it is inconceivable they might ever have performed such a vulgar act as dying. But they had. O, they had all right.

I went back recently to the Granard Road. And after that, the hotel where we'd read for another arts festival long ago. Predictably enough, it was all boarded up. But there was enough energy remaining to take me back to that Sunday afternoon when an old priest had shaken the life out of his newspaper, on foot of a recital of "Awopbopaloopbopawopbamboom!" by the two Sad Poets, concealed behind a massive rubber plant in the foyer, squealing with toddleresque glee as the clergyman disappeared in a blood-busting fury.

"Only a Woman's Heart," the all-female folk sensation, had been popular at the time. Now I don't know whether it's true or not that only a woman's heart can know—but I do know this: that, in the words of Harold Pinter, "Ireland wasn't golden always but it was golden sometimes." And in Cootehill that year it surely was. With Footsbarn Theatre Company cartwheeling and carousing, and the maestro at the height of his powers.

I stood there awhile by the side of the old five-bar gate, in the very same place where I'd left him that day. Maybe there was a moorhen, a waxwing, a startled rabbit, or a party of geese like gentlemen and ladies at a wedding. I don't know. Like I say, I don't notice those things. But I do sometimes hear things, and, as a melody drifted from a nearby open window, it was hard not to construe it as a kind of aural Macondo river, freighting all sorts of memories as it passed, making its way under a bridge which, in the style of its Finea counterpart, could never have existed except within the realm of magic and false memory. Two phantom figures made their way along the riverbank, murmuring genially after the fashion of elderly clerics. Chatting, as such men do, of superior breeds in the sprinting world, along that worn and winding track. Before pausing where the children from Shell Corner—yes, for it is they, Dermot and Helen's multicultural troop of ecstatic, apprentice goose-herders all the way from the cottage-of-wonders—have gone to the trouble of erecting a sturdy little wooden stand, upon which they have placed the most beautiful pair of feathered appendages, all perfectly pressed and ironed. "Healy's wings!" I heard them peal excitedly, "Healy's wings! Now going cheap! Only two-and-six!"

And maybe, like Flann O'Brien, it was just another episode of that same disconsolate foolishness, because I don't suppose in all truthfulness it could be anything else. But on a recent visit to Longford Town, I sat in Eamon McKiernan's bar and as I looked northwards toward Granard I couldn't keep from thinking of those midland heavens opening up—not with rain or some natural catastrophe, but just another heave of those wicked, laughing shoulders, as he stooped down to give me one final, combative, affectionate Catweazle smile.

Song in the Grass
Kate Fagan

> One night the sea breaks up and you listen.
> —Dermot Healy

Today it's the butcherbird piping a vertical echo
Yesterday it was the blackbird rifling in leaves, waking
    my head like strong tea
The far distance of memory

I hear things in the places they happen, returning new
    as strangers

Wanting to say absolutely what uproots from soil
Moving no further than a stone hauled twice to a wall
    by different hands

Coral and shell bones held the rocks in balance,
    made them curve as ghosts
Dry chaffs of wheat tucked in
Plangent like a first word

Song in the Grass

The day is quiet now
I sit with a lamp, circled by pages
It's physical work to remain within this orbit and voyage
    as though my skull were oceans

Cliffs keeling
Neophytes dropping to ancestral floods

The gabions stave off the weather
It took years to pack them
Gale music is scored in rattling wire, a common song
    of oars lashed by rain
The erratic compass

I've stood on Treachery Head and heard what isn't there
Bodies emptied by sea and rowed to rest, floorboards
    primed with salt and tears

Electricity bumped aside
Thunder rolling in a dark room
The purest form of music

In her observatory were charts of constellations like crosswords
       and the snout of an antique telescope trained
       on the future
Intervals of seeing and being seen
Phantom hens, diluvian fish
The blue upstairs

Marginal things alter the scale of topography
It's a kind of veering

A novel trinity
Grandda, son and the holy bird
Is Joejoe Beckett, I asked and you said *yes*

A man steals a tree
A deer robs a donkey in plain sight

Clouds turn a corner
At the writer's house, conversation hops and jumps like a generator
    and you launch into Spancil Hill
The baby cries
He doesn't like that song
Good girl! She's honest

Collections of objects pass between states
Fuchsia petals, perfume bottles, a Brigid's cross from the shop
    at Gallarus Oratory

The stranger always teaches you something
The familiar is always strange

A word holds its history like a wall
Pages carry a lode of inheritance

A great unlocking
I scrawled out the scarp, its elevation and hanging swamps,
    the leaking rocks
Darwin might have peered at this one
Noted the infinite seeds

When you say the word 'moon' you're talking about four
    thousand years of moon
Sometimes when you look at the landscape you actually hear
    the unspoken words that are in your head
    that have been handed on to you

At the filling in of the moon
Beside the lake reeds

Beyond the dark is a kind of seeing
Time's experiment

The north easterlies whine
I'm drawn to the hill behind our shed where a giant gum
    wheels and lifts
For days I pinch out privet and blackberry
Fierce holly and hawksbeard
A lyrical index

Language falling from leaves: koel and spinebill, fan-tailed
    cuckoo, golden whistler

Water in a broken gutter
The instruments have turned into birds
The roof is an accordion with a 23-screw fingerboard
    and tin bellows

Dogs follow us into dreams
Under your cast the forgotten words appear like mackerel
    schooling in the deep

The errant broom
Dusty abdomen of a bee

The ocean pulls us from the mountain
Sifting in the bone tray we salvage owl pellets and the wings
    of a storm-bird
Yellow shells to ring the changes

A field newly cut
Gathering signs: a knock misheard, a knoll transferred,
    coat and shoes of a man found

Two men are stitched into the sky
One walks among trees while the other reclines on stars
    like needles

The second last time I saw my grandfather I said, *I will*
    come back and sing for you
Sing a song of sixpence
Hollow cheeks and sane eyes that return my look
    like a great mirror

I pick up the book again
Astounded by geometry

One sits, the other visits
One has nothing to confess
One shoots at his own image
One dies when the other is buried
Out of the corner of my eye I can see the dark approaching

Awake awake o drowsy sleeper
Birds fly in question marks and the dogs pelt about
    in mad loops

Closed eyes tell one story
Wide eyes another

Your spade fetches up sandy clods
We plant four maples and yank stones to pile around
    the trunks, towards and away
A map that will never be finished
The roots of a long argument

Song in the grass
You beside, alive in the words that came
    with the morning

Sea-strangeness: Memories of Dermot Healy
Tess Gallagher

I met Dermot Healy before I actually met him, as is often the way with writers in small literary arenas. We find each other on the pages of our books before life delivers us to each other in person.

I discovered Dermot's wonderful memoir *The Bend for Home*, about his father, and found it so compelling and true that I read it aloud to Josie Gray, my companion. It carried us movingly through every page.

My own father had been an alcoholic so I deeply connected with Dermot's story of his father who suffered from the same malady. The book is lyrical and moves into one at an effortless, truehearted level. One feels keenly and without sentimentality the deep affection, disappointment and general collapse of expectation a person suffers with such a father.

Josie and I both thought the book unforgettable, and when we learned Dermot lived in North Sligo with his wife Helen at Ballyconnell, we somehow formed the notion of visiting him. We must have been invited, for without intricate directions there would have been no way to find them on that far promontory above the lip of the Atlantic.

Josie drove us along the hedge-hugging narrow roads past Ellen's pub, Dermot's local, and other landmarks. We eventually arrived at a cosy cottage with add-ons of rooms and a huge stone fireplace at the centre. I recall Dermot backlit before the fire, his white hair and beard, his bluer-than-blue eyes flashing out as he moved, situating and resituating himself as he spoke—a bird-of-a-man in a checkered wool jacket.

Reading recently in the Yale anthology of translations of Seán Ó'Ríordáin's poetry I discovered the term "sea-strangeness"—*na mara oraibh*—in the poem "The Blaskets."

•

> Come drink with me
> You island men,
> With your sea-strangeness
> And boat-strangeness (trans. by Frank Sewell)

The notion of the sea entering one and working a strangeness on one's being suits my thoughts toward Dermot. He experienced the pounding and dashings of the Atlantic, while I took in the more Pacific tides of the Straits of Juan de Fuca below my Sky House in America. As if enacting a wave's encroachment towards land, Dermot often seemed on the verge of withdrawing at the same time he approached one. How could he be so welcoming and furtive at once, so genial and bedeviled? Sea-strangeness? I don't rightly know what it signifies, but perhaps that one has access to powers larger than one can compass—which can be as tormenting as it is empowering. Both of us were writers addicted to our seas—the way they roiled us, smoothed us out like stones; but also their overbearing, inexplicable inroads into our psyches. I suspect the sea's cargo of unknowns, of peril and bounty, emboldened our writing as much as it divided our presences, causing the furtiveness I mentioned earlier, as if one is accompanied by something pressing and unseen.

It's a great privilege to meet a friend in their habitation, for then you know the nest that holds them and from which they fly. Dermot, wanting more natural light in his cottage, had punched in skylights. The dashing of the sea in storm weather, night and day, had nearly driven him mad at times, he'd told me, but that was his element, the whiplash of wind, the buffeting and cuffing against the shore of his imagination.

He loved his place and gardened with seaweed for fertilizer and mulch on a patch beside the house. He took us down to the ancient lava-pour of black rocks, slick as the backs of seals, jutting out over the sea. There he told us stories of immigrant fishermen seeking to supplement their livelihoods with fish they caught from those very rocks, some of these men tragically washed away by rogue waves.

He took delight as we marvelled at his daring proximity to the sea, his closest neighbour. Josie would later paint Dermot's cottage from memory, as it was the kind of habitation able to hold its ground, yet follow after one imaginatively.

Dermot was a bit like a rogue wave himself in his sea-strangeness. His intensities were gripping when he told a story or listened to Josie offer one. I think he prized us for our own attentive listening—for he was dramatic, a natural performer, and the right audience compelled him to his best. But getting things written alone could be an agony, one guessed. I had the notion that he courted his muse with cunning and solitude, then dashed out to his friends like guilty play.

In Irish life my experience has been that one tends to know people in company—in couples or in a band of like-minded friends. To know a person one-on-one seems a thing of my youth when I was roving about Ireland with musicians and poets. I was used to meeting this one and that 'on their own.' Perhaps it's age that offers one the inclusive comfort of the hive.

Dermot and Helen soon led us to Sheila and Sean McSweeney. McSweeney had contributed a painting to the book of Dermot's poems I was carrying on that first visit to him. "I love this painting," I said. "Who's this Sean McSweeney?" Dermot immediately offered to help us meet his and Helen's close friends, who lived nearby.

That connection took hold and we became used to gathering several times a year as six friends at Sean's light-washed studio in a schoolhouse where his mother had attended primary school. Orna, Sean and Sheila's daughter, baked bread that they served with smoked salmon, cheeses, and fresh salad from the garden. There was always red wine and nonstop chat. The poet and novelist Leland Bardwell, another neighbour, would usually be there. Poems would be read; paintings of Josie's and Sean's would be gazed at and commented upon, or silently taken in. Sheila McSweeney's strong, inward-seeing photographs of Irish landscapes also came forward for admiration. Orna read Akhmatova's poems aloud, first in Russian, then in translation. Once I was asked to neigh for Orna's young son Hugh and his school pals—my prowess on that score having been touted by Josie who used me to call his horses when they were fields away. I also gave Raymond Carver's poems and my own, and sang the occasional aire.

Dermot would always be invited to these sessions, though Sean's quiet caveat was that 'he might not make it.' So when Dermot eventually dodged into the doorway, we always stopped everything for a welcome. At these studio lunches we buzzed and laughed, dipped in and out of each other's stories and lives.

Dermot admired my late husband, Raymond Carver's, stories and poems, but he also asked, on more than one occasion, about Ray's sobriety—how he came to it, how he kept it during those last productive ten years.

I volunteered some of Ray's touchstones for staying sober: leave any gathering early if the booze is flowing; give your drinking pals a wide berth; and the AA mantra for swerving off drink: HALT—"don't get too hungry, too angry, too lonely or too tired." He bowed his head and took it all in like a kind of verbal inoculation. That Ray had managed his escape was manna in the desert to many writers I met, both in America and Ireland, in search of peace from that particular demon.

"How'd he do it?" Dermot asked me. Ray would never take credit: "By grace," I said, adding that Ray wanted more than anything to live to write the next story or poem. Everything proceeded from that, I allowed—a true love of being alive, unencumbered by the soak of oblivion alcohol had brought to his former life. His last sober years really had been "gravy." Dermot leaned on these survival stories of Ray's. I had long ago come to understand that in Irish life, where one's local pub served also "as" a kind of church, such getaways were legend, and too often the road not taken.

It is easier to show a person's character by an action than to talk about it, so one story among several comes back to me in personal gratitude toward Dermot. Josie and I had been invited to spend the night, which saved the long nighttime journey back from N. Sligo to my Lough Arrow cottage near the Roscommon border. The evening could then be elastic into morning. Stories and poems would be given by the fireside at leisure.

That night Dermot read to us from his poems in manuscript. It was a feast, a bounty, an unforgettable rare pleasure. I asked to hear several poems more than once, the better to absorb them. Dermot obliged and seemed to experience his poems anew in our hearing.

It must have been three or four in the morning before it occurred to us to sleep. My dreams reverberated with the rhythms of his poems.

The following morning Josie, to my surprise, announced after breakfast that we were bound for Dowra in Co. Leitrim to a sheep mart. He needed directions. He had to meet a man with a truckload of lambs from the farm he and his eldest son managed.

Dermot realised immediately that I had not been figured into this errand. It was a delicate situation. He'd heard my poem about having bought lambs back before such sales and he knew well I couldn't abide watching a truck full of lambs being unloaded at a mart, thereafter to be sold for slaughter.

"I just can't go," I found myself exclaiming, like a bolt of lightning into the morning. "You could get stuck with me!" I laughed, apologising. Dermot didn't miss a beat.

"Don't worry, Tess. I'll drive you home!" he said. Helen delivered a plate of food to a widowed neighbour, then settled herself into the car with us. It was an hour and more to my cottage, but our journey passed quickly, relieved by our conversation.

To be understood at such a level with no defense necessary, was more than comforting. Dermot had rescued me without fuss, just in the normal graciousness of friendship, and had also managed not to make Josie uncomfortable at having to head off for Dowra without me.

Over the twenty years I knew Dermot, I recognised it was a natural inclination of his to rise to other people's occasions. I recall the beautiful, considered introduction he gave at the Yeats Centre when Josie's and my storybook *Barnacle Soup* was launched in Sligo. He'd taken time to write out well-considered remarks from which he spoke—so unlike the tossed off introductions of American book launches. It was one of his pleasures that he supported the work of others. When an opening was held for Josie's paintings at the Dock in Carrick on Shannon, he not only attended—he bought a painting.

Some of his students once told us, at an evening after a reading, what a marvellous teacher he was. I knew he'd travelled into the prisons with plays and poetry. His fine magazine *Force 10* gave many young Irish writers a leg up. His editing was passionate, a pure gift to his community.

On two memorable occasions Dermot visited me at my cottage. I had brought our three couples together there to celebrate having purchased the four-roomed cottage perched along the roadway near where I'd written my second book of poems, *Under Stars*. At this housewarming they all admired Josie's studio in a renovated garage. I served soup and salmon in the tiny entrance room. Then we gamboled on foot down to Ballindoon Abbey where Dermot began to take notes on a scrap of paper, jotting down names from the oldest gravestones inside the roofless abbey. He knew some of the history of the area since he said some of his people had originated not far from there.

As a housewarming gift, he had brought a stone he'd chosen for me from his shore, one that still rests on my mantle. How did he know I loved stones? But that's the way of friendship—a lot of ground is covered by an unspoken grasp of each other. You just know. And of course, he gave me something he loved.

During the filming of *The Writing in the Sky* Dermot arrived at my cottage with the cinematographer, and we sat together outside on the high deck above Josie's studio. Our backdrop was an expansive view of Abbey Ballindoon, the green shoulder of Jimmy Frazer's field, the tantalising blue of Lough Arrow and the distant ridges of the Bricklieve Mountains.

I read several of Dermot's poems aloud in the open air and remarked extemporaneously on them while the camera rolled. We chatted about the barnacle geese that came his way for winter respite each October and about which he'd written a moving sequence of poems. My own bird-watching in Ireland had been confined to my feeder—gold finches, coal tits, stonechats and blue tits, with magpies and the occasional flash of a pheasant in the field behind the cottage. Our lake swans were probably Mute swans, I joked with him, or Whoopers, but like many things Irish, I didn't actually know. I'd heard the cuckoo, but never seen it.

Dermot had a great knowledge of birds and wildlife. It fed his spirit and his poetry and made conversation with him, for a longtime interloper on Irish soil like myself, fascinating.

One final scene arises hauntingly when I think of times with Dermot: a small nighttime vignette—Josie, Sean, Sheila, Leland, myself and Dermot out under the stars on the roadway before the McSweeney house. Josie's jeep won't start. We mill about wishing for magic. The moon is overly bright. Electric. Sean starts to sing and do a little jig in the roadway. Dermot joins in. I'm laughing, but worrying about getting home. Two grown men are dancing and singing before the seeming corpse of our jeep.

Finally, we all gravitate back to the problem and study our case. Leland offers to push the jeep with her disproportionately small car. We decide it's safer if we push it ourselves—so there we go, all of us, with our shoulders to it. Josie's at the wheel—a catch and a jolt from the engine, then it shudders to life.

We shout our thanks as I jump aboard, waving at our moonstruck friends, who are in no hurry to close down the evening by going inside and leaving the festival of stars over their heads. When I look back they are still singing and dancing in the receding roadway. And that's where Dermot, lives still for me—that image of his childlike joy, his blessed, giddy uptake of the moment, his bright thievery of night-sky with friends.

Abbey Cottage, Ballindoon, February 13, 2015

Dermot Healy: A Cavan Antaeus
Ronan Sheehan

Dermot's sad death in the summer of 2014 brought my brother Garret and I across the country from Dublin to Sligo for his funeral. I had asked Dermot to translate three poems of Catullus for *The Irish Catullus or One Gentleman Of Verona*, which came out in 2010. He had done them well—of which more anon. The journey put me in mind of "Catullus 101," which my son Luke translated for that project:

> I've come through many crowds and over oceans
> to deliver this farewell to you, my brother.
> Sad to be speaking to you in death,
> to have to lay my pleas in passive ash,
> because the turning wheel has taken you
> from me—poor brother!—gone too soon and gone
> away from me. Now in our parents' name
> and in that ancient line that speaks to us,
> although they're sodden with a brother's tears
> and make a sorry gift, accept these words in passing
> Now and forever, hello and goodbye, oh my brother.

Thirty years previously, Garret and I had driven to a Cavan border town for the launch of *Fighting with Shadows*, also known by the Greek name for that idea: *Sciamachy*. Then Garret and I were both solicitors, I working in his firm in Thomas Street, Dublin. Now Garret was at my first meeting with Dermot, in 1974. We were photographed together at a reception for the Hennessy Literary Awards. That day we were both winners. If my calculations are correct, I was 21, and he 27. We both wore our hair long, as was the fashion for young men forty years ago. My story was called "Floating Structure, Drifting Part," and it was set in a London bar among

Irish emigrants, based on my experiences in the city in the summer of 1971. A world that Dermot was destined to know much better than I. Until recently I thought he had won the prize for "Banished Misfortune," the title story of his first collection of stories which appeared in 1982 and which, if I may make so bold as to say so, I recommended to be included in *The Field Day Anthology Of Irish Writing* ten years later. But in fact it was "First Snow of The Year," the first story in the collection, which won the prize (he won again for "Banished Misfortune" in 1976). We had a lot of fun that night and remained friends.

Apart from meeting Dermot, I have two memories of the awards ceremony. The judges were V. S. Pritchett and Edna O'Brien. Edna was strikingly beautiful with her red hair, peachy skin and black designer dress. The young men who worked for Hennessy's who were present gravitated towards her and she made their evening with her charming and witty conversation. Dermot and I did not begrudge them the moment. Was it Edna's fault I drank too much brandy? The prize, apart from some money, was a statuette of the Hennessy dog; a St. Bernard dog with a little barrel of brandy hanging from its neck; the kind of dog which finds you and saves your life when you are trapped by a blizzard in the Brenner Pass. Tim Pat Coogan, the editor of *The Irish Press*, presented me with the dog. I had too much brandy on board and promptly dropped the dog. To my embarrassment, its leg broke. For the photograph, Dermot grips my elbows, keeping me upright.

1974 was the year Seamus Heaney published *North*. I was studying English and Latin at UCD. The dominant figures in the English department were Denis Donoghue and Seamus Deane. The flavour was intellectual. Dermot did not go to university.

In my view, the source of his power as a writer is his direct apprehension of the physical presence of people, animals and objects in the natural world. Yeats wrote:

> John Synge, I and Augusta Gregory, thought
> All that we did, all that we said or sang
> Must come from contact with the soil, from that
> Contact everything Antaeus-like grew strong.

The *Oxford Classical Dictionary* tells us that Antaeus is a giant, son of Poseidon and Gaia, who lives in Libya. He compelled all comers to wrestle with him and killed them when overcome. He was made stronger when thrown into contact with his mother the earth. He was defeated and killed by Heracles, who suspended him in the air.

The title of the first story in *Banished Misfortune* presents a natural phenomenon: "First Snow of the Year." There is another feature of Dermot Healy's writing which is fundamental.

In Poe's essay "The Art of Fiction" he discloses his strategy in writing "The Fall of the House of Usher." He has to persuade the reader of the reality of a house sustained by evil. He introduces them to a real house, one with windows, doors, a garden, a roof. When the reader's belief in the real house has been won, he/she can be seduced into accepting the unreal house. Dermot does something like this: the first few lines of "First Snow of the Year" establish a credible character, then the language shifts into a visionary mode. We cross a threshold and enter the world of Dermot Healy:

> For a few bewildering seconds, Jim Philips, on the day of his retirement, queried late morning sounds he had not heard in years. Then his solitary sense of freedom began. He looked with leisure at the low pink boards that ran the length of the ceiling, yellowing at the fireplace, brightening at the window.
> Light was hammering on the broken shutter.
> Shadows darted across the mildewed embroidery of dogs and flowers.
> He cleared his womanless bed with a light heart, glad to have outgrown the ache in his smothered loins, outlived his job that he might die in a time of his own making.

The plot embraces a rural world—even underworld—which he does not explain to the outsider. If you are not in it, he pulls you in. At the end, you may not quite grasp what has happened. But you realise you have experienced something, bracing and vital, like a mountain stream, or a storm in a wood.

"Banished Misfortune," which I first read in *The Irish Press* forty odd years ago, continues to haunt me. The characters in the story endure a succession of problems. The epitome of these is the malaise recounted by Jimmy Cummins:

> I heard tonight a story when Furaisti played "Banish Misfortune." It happened back in the days when death wasn't an institution. Jimmy Cummins turned to me and said "Do you hear that? Well, there was a piper from Gurteen, a fine piper in his day who drank nothing but French wine and oddly enough just played once in a fine house. He'd mind that night if he were alive today. For there the gentry's daughter came away with him, a lightsome girl and the parents naturally enough with acres of turnips and cabbages for setting disowned her. There was no hue or cry and the Gurteen man took her on his short travels for money and baby clothes. For the girl was expecting a piper's baby and not long after she and the baby died in this town. The coffin was put up on a cart drawn by a dray horse and no-one following from the cobbles of the Spanish Arch. And the piper began a lament, not too slow or too quick on account of his losses, and the men in the fever hospital sweating from their labours counted four thousand mourners as they crossed Loch Ataila for Forthill graveyard. That's banished misfortune for you," said Jimmy Cummins.

This story, from history and folklore, from memory and from the racial unconscious, comes from the soil of Ireland. Dermot does not unravel its many layers. He dishes it out whole and you must swallow it that way. He went to live in rugged, beautiful Ballyconnell upon the Atlantic shore, which prompted the title for the magazine he edited: *Force 10*. He was always a great collaborator and I was delighted to work with him on two projects of mine that connected with mediaeval Sligo. "Colmcille and the Irish Copyright Tradition" explored the background to the oldest copyright case. The sixth-century dispute between Colmcille, Finnian and Diarmad comes to a head with the battle of Cuil Dreimthne in County Sligo. It is represented through a mural in the County Library. Sadly for me

Dermot never got to publish my essay in this connection because his magazine ran out of money.

The second attempt did materialise. It requires some background explanation: in 2002, I persuaded the Board of *Poetry Ireland* to protest at the closing of the Classics department in Queen's University. A project to affirm Ireland's tradition in the classics was required—a translation of Catullus into Irish, English and Ulster Scots by many hands: *The Irish Catullus*.

The Book of Ballymote (in County Sligo) was compiled in the late fourteenth century under the direction of Tomaltach Mac Donnchada. Among many texts we find the first ever translation of *The Aeneid* into a vernacular language: *Imtheachta Aeniasa*. In English, this work is known as *The Irish Aeneid*. It is the work of Solamh O'Droma, a bard from the Cavan/Fermanagh area who went to Sligo to work on *The Book of Ballymote*.

In the preface to *The Irish Catullus*, I said a few brief words about *The Irish Aeneid*. I condensed gleanings from various sources, especially George Calder's introduction to his edition of *The Irish Aeneid*:

> It reshapes Virgil's epic to suit the taste and values of the audience for whom it was intended. Poetry is rendered into prose. The time-scheme is reworked into a linear sequence. Some material—genealogies and speeches of the gods—is cut out. Some well-known passages from Irish literature are inserted. Aeneas in places resembles Cuchulain, for example when he first appears to Dido. The emotional and sensuous matter of *The Aeneid* is heightened: the beauty of the landscape, the pain of the defeated, jewellery, the sorrow of parting.[1]

Poets and writers in Irish and English were invited to translate Catullus in the spirit of *The Irish Aeneid*. Each was supplied with a literal translation—as not all were Latinists.

Dermot, like Solamh O'Droma before him, a Cavan bard transferred to Sligo on a writing mission, translated poems 108, 109, 110.

This is poem 110:
Aufillena, bonae semper laudantur amicae:
accipiunt pretium qui facere instituunt.
tu, quod promisti, mihi quod mentita inimica es,
quod nec das et fers saepe, facis facinus.
aut facere ingenuaest aut non promisse pudicae,
Aufillena, fuit: sed data corripere
fraudando officiis plus quam meretricis avaraest
quae sese toto corpore prostituit.

In the literal translation of F. W. Cornish:[2]
Aufillena, kind mistresses are always well-spoken of; they get their
price for what they purpose to do. In cruelly tricking me of that which
you promised, in continually taking and not giving, you are doing wrong.
To comply were handsome, not to have promised were chaste, Aufillena: but
to grab all you can get and cheat on the obligations exceeds the
conduct of a grasping harlot who prostitutes her self with all her body.

Dermot Healy:
Aufillena, a kind mistress
is well got; she names
her price and does what
he wants her to. Not you—

you took from the very beginning
and took all you could
without ever giving;
it was a wrong thing

to do. You broke your word.
And with every day
that passed
the mad debt grew.

To agree was comely
it could have been fun,
but if you had not promised
No harm was done.

Not to have made a pact
would have left us both
innocent. Are you
listening, Aufillena,

the bond, that oath
still stands, despite the promise
that turned to avarice,
and the arrogant demands

The whore would at least
have done her duty
but you exceeded
the harlot in all her art.

Obligation played no part—
as your very mind turned
to a gnarled knot
of theft. You took

all you could get, you slut,
and every time you sell
that dear body, you're
stealing from me yet.

Thus Dermot brings Aufillena to Cavan.

atque in perpetuum, frater, ave atque vale.
Now and forever, hello and goodbye, oh my brother.

Notes

1. *The Irish Catullus or One Gentleman of Verona*. ed. Ronan Sheehan. (Dublin: A. & A. Farmar, 2010), vi. The whole passage is from *The Irish Catullus* but there are two sentences that come from *The Irish Aeneid*, ed. Reverend George Calder (London Irish Texts Society, 1907/1995), beginning as follows: "Some material . . ."—and—"The emotional and sensuous matter . . ."

2. Citation: Harvard University Press/Loeb Classical Library, 1913.

The Bend for Healy
Roddy Doyle

—D'yeh read much?
—Wha'? Books?
—Yeah.
—Well, I do . . . I'd always read a few pages in the bed. War—I like books abou' war.
—Same as meself.
—Hitler an' tha'. I fall asleep every nigh' readin' abou' Hitler an' Stalin. Fuckin' gas, really.
—I read a bit of one last night. The wife is in a book club.
—Mine as well.
—What is a book club, exactly?
—Well—far as I can make ou'. Yeh go to a pal's house an' get fuckin' hammered. An' yeh bring a book with yeh, if yeh remember.
—Grand. Yeah, I thought tha', meself. Annyway, she was readin' one—*The Bend for Home*. An' she keeps sighin' and laughin'. Gettin' on me wick a bit. Cos I'm tryin' to read abou' the siege o' Stalingrad.
—I fuckin' love Stalingrad.
—Yeah—but, annyway. She goes ou' to the jacks an' I pick up the book. *The Bend for Home*, like. An' I read a bit—and, ah man—I'm tellin' yeh. Brilliant—fuckin' brilliant now. The bit I read—abou' a Thursday afternoon—in the town he grew up in, like. It was amazin'. You were there when yeh read it.
—Sounds good. Who wrote it?
—Dermot Healy.
—Played for Sligo Rovers back in the day.
—Tha' was Keely. Healy—Dermot Healy. So annyway, she said she was finished it an' I got dug in. "The doctor strolls into the bedroom and taps my mother's stomach."
—Tha' the start?
—Yeah.

—An' yeh remember it?

—Yeah. There's a photograph of him on the back . . .

—Ah, hang on, for fuck sake. Just cos we voted for the same-sex thing, doesn't mean yeh have to fall in love with him . . .

—Ah fuck off. Anyway—look it, it's the business—the book.

—Sounds great alrigh'.

—Will I pass it on to yeh when I'm finished?

—Is Hitler in it?

—No.

—G'wan then—okay.

A Song for Ireland
Danny Morrison

There he stood atop the pool table. Researching the effects of alcohol on vertigo.

Thirty or more years ago. Not as grey or frail or vulnerable as at the end when his heart died in Helen's arms, his body wracked, but there in Paddy Hyne's Bar, Falls Road, when things were still raw and Belfast was a very dark and dangerous place.

He stood on the pool table, a Commanding Officer of words, declaiming to an Officer Commanding the local IRA that he could beat any man in the bar at pool, challenging every and any man to a game. I was there to meet him for the first time and was a little late because there was a British army patrol in the area which might have hassled me. My then wife, and Dermot's partner, worked in the Belfast Rape Crisis centre together and I was told he was 'an interesting character' whom I would like.

The IRA OC said to me as I came in, "Who to fuck is this guy? He's mental. Just walked in and started."

I said that he was a loyalist paramilitary called Billy McQuade from Rathcoole, but then made it clear that I was joking!

"Oh, he's just a writer. He's all right. He's sound."

So I shouted, "Dermot! Dermot! Do you want a drink?" and he leaped off the table with the alacrity of a mountain goat and handed the cue to the nearest fella. We had never met but he recognised me from the newspapers and television and from the public profile I had as Bobby Sands's spokesperson during the hunger strike. Then he giggled, from the pit of his stomach that was his trademark. The hunched, accordion shoulders. A giggle that I was to hear many times throughout the times I knew him and which represented mischievousness, guilt and innocence. I was reminded of it again when—at his bequest—his funeral cortege paused outside his and Helen's open bedroom window while his favourite CD of Mongolian throat singing was played. The coffin shook and we all laughed and cried.

It might have been a G & T or a double G & T that he asked for. I can't remember. Later, we went to the off-licence for wine, Blue Nun or Black Tower the woeful vintage then in vogue, and went back to my house.

He gave me his book of short stories, *Banished Misfortune*. Later, the publisher Steve MacDonogh was to tell me that Dermot's *Fighting with Shadows* was one of the best novels to come out of the Troubles and would be read and admired for years to come. I liked the book but didn't agree with MacDonogh's opinion.

Dermot and I lost contact for a few years while I was in prison. One day the censor gave me a letter which turned out to be from him. Denied communication and cut off from the world of normal life, prisoners crave to be remembered, to be in someone's thoughts. A postcard will be put up on the cell wall for months, a letter treasured and re-read many times. Dermot wrote to me several times and we talked about life and love, how low he had at times become but that he was writing poems and a novel, a fated love story which would also cover the Troubles.

He also lifted my morale by telling me that Shane Connaughton (who had written the screenplay of Christy Brown's *My Left Foot*) was a big "fan" of mine and had praised *West Belfast* (my first novel) on BBC Radio 4.

In a letter around January 1991 he told me that he was moving into a cottage on a cliff overlooking the sea, a few miles outside Sligo town where he was working on an arts project. This was a reference to Maugherow and it would become his and Helen's Ballyconnell fastness, where he fought with the Atlantic waves as they tried to cut off the causeway to their cottage. He had a face for the cliffs and storms and the sea, the weather-beaten face of a boatman, the mane of a Viking but a Viking without violence or malice.

> *Living on your western shore,*
> *Saw summer sunsets, asked for more,*

> *I stood by your Atlantic Sea,*
> *And I sang a song for Ireland*
> ("Song for Ireland," Phil and June Colclough)

Despite winter springs and autumn summers, the cottage—the cottage he kept adding to; a room/a study here and there—drew many friends, writers, painters and poets and filmmakers towards it and the hospitality and kindness that was to be had within.

While I was in Long Kesh Dermot sent me a copy of his novel, *A Goat's Song*, which I read in a few sittings and which became one of the most loved and read novels in H-4. Parts of it were angry, raw and painful, depicting the love hurt madness of Jack Ferris, an addict, a man Under the Volcano, whose "hunger for hurt was insatiable."

But there were also many poetic, lyrical and beautiful passages like this description of two sisters by the shore: "When they emerged . . . the sun had given the mountains and sea a quality for which there are no words. The new hallucinating light that precedes the rainbow covered everything, killing all colours except the simple green that cannot be defined as colour only, but is a state of being that follows on the heels of summer rain."

It would be another five years before I saw Dermot. After my release he kindly invited me to the Scríobh festival in Sligo where I was reunited with my old friend Tim O'Grady. We stayed in the haggard beside the cottage. Late into the night we talked about books and Dermot read from the manuscript of his forthcoming autobiography *The Bend for Home*, which had us in stitches. What I learnt to appreciate over those few days with him was just how committed, conscientious and honest you have to be if you want to be a serious writer, which I was striving to become.

What was endearing and compelling about *The Bend for Home* is that the humanity of the writer surfaces again and again, almost against his own will, no matter how cruel and selfish he paints himself, particularly after his father's death when the tearaway teenager caused his mother much heartbreak with his drinking and when 'the horn' banjaxed his head.

Mortality punches you on the chin in one account of *young* Dermot, his father, an aunt and uncle, out fishing when they are caught in a storm, lose an oar and are in real danger for several hours before they touch land. *Old* Dermot suddenly concludes this passage with the words, "All in the boat, except me, are dead."

How we are immortalised through our children is demonstrated simply through the juxtaposition of two events separated by a generation which unites Dermot to his son Dallan. Dallan is jumping up and down on a giant inflatable and is advised by his father to concentrate and stop looking at him. Dallan ignores the advice, jumps higher, watching his father watching him throughout, misses his footing, and falling, strikes his head on the pavement. And suddenly Dermot remembers that when he was a child boxing a punch ball his father advised him to watch the punch ball and stop looking at him. Picking up Dallan, Dermot thinks: "I knew then that he too, like myself, was gripped by that awful condition of wanting to please."

The heroines in this book are his mother and his buxom Auntie Maisie who ran a thriving café and bakery in the market town of Cavan. His account of the descent into senility and the slow death of his mother is extremely moving, and haunting. His eighty-year-old mother once looked after the half-deaf Maisie, her senior, and resents that Maisie now gives out the advice. But the two old dames love each other, even in bedlam:

> You should eat for Dermot, Maisie says, raising her voice.
> Mind your own business, says my mother.
> What did she say? asks Maisie.

On another occasion Dermot is sitting with his mother:

> Your father never drank, she says and nips me.
> Yes, he did.
> No, he didn't. It's you are the guilty party.
> Mother, he did.
> Never, Never, *Never*. Nor did he smoke.
> He died of smoking, said Dermot.

In March 1996 I cycled through Leitrim and Sligo and phoned him to say that I was in the vicinity but was unfamiliar with the back roads, even though in the 1980s I had been to a caravan owned by my cousin and her husband, Eileen and Gordon Manly, not far from where Dermot was to buy his cottage. He told me to go to Ellen's Pub. We met. I was to follow his car on my bike. But first, said Dermot, you will be wanting a hot whiskey. It was three o'clock. It was four o'clock. It was five o'clock. It was six o'clock and Helen—the breadwinner who worked in a bank and had a *real* job—would be coming home soon and Dermot was to have her dinner ready.

"We have to go!" he said, jumped into the car and took off at high speed with me pedalling furiously behind. He only remembered me when he was a mile down the road and had to come back.

Dermot and Helen were married in 1997. Their party was one of the best I've ever been to. The reception was held in Lissadell Church of Ireland Hall where there was a banquet and dancing till all hours. It was like the extended wedding scene from *The Deer Hunter* except the war was over, there was no draft, and we had life to look forward to. I can't remember what time I crawled to bed in Leland Bardwell's house but recovery took several days and much medication.

Dermot could appear from nowhere. I remember him landing into my house in Belfast on one occasion with 5lbs of mussels, bread, a tub of double cream and a bottle of white wine.

"Dinner!" he giggled, shoulders shaking. I think it was before he was due to appear at the Elmwood Hall on stage with E. Annie Proulx.

Dermot played the part of 'the old man' in Nichola Bruce's impressionistic film adaptation of Tim O'Grady's novel *I Could Read the Sky* (in which I had a bit role), about a London Irish immigrant piecing together his fragmented, dislocated life. It also featured Stephen Rea, Maria Doyle Kennedy and Pat McCabe. Dermot was also the subject of a wonderfully mesmerising RTÉ portrait *The Writing in the Sky* which was filmed in Maugherow over a six-month period, the title referring to the annual migration of barnacle geese from Greenland to their winter habitat on an island near Dermot's home.

When I saw Dermot in his coffin, almost asleep, peaceful, I was taken aback because I thought to myself, I've seen him like this somewhere before. And then I realised that in the opening scene of *The Writing in the Sky* there is a shot of Dermot asleep in bed, peaceful, except that he gets to wake up and to continue to write his 'goose poem' as he so quaintly called *A Fool's Errand*.

A couple of times a year he would ring: always after nine at night.

Something would have been on the news about the North and he would have had a brainwave . . . or a Rioja or Sauvignon Blanc-wave.

"I've been thinking . . . sure, tell your man . . . they'll not be expecting it . . . think of the goodwill . . ." and he would propose some solution to whatever political crisis/stalemate was on the menu that day and I was to make sure 'your man' (Gerry Adams) got Dermot's advice! It usually involved Irish republicans making further gestures, being 'nice' to the unionists, and regardless how apolitical was his proposal you knew at least that he was still thinking about you, about things, and using his imagination and lateral thinking to come up with something Sinn Féin might have missed in its reckoning.

And now there shall be no more phone calls. No more advice. No letters. No sudden times. But there are the books, the poems, the films. And there is my wedding video! It includes him and Helen arriving at our house and later him on the floor in the Felons Club like a gazelle, Lord of The Dance—which he was in the early stages of creating and choreographing for Michael Flatley!

And, of course, there are the stories we will tell about him and the stories Dermot has left behind as our Dermot takes the bend for home.

"Anonymous is best . . ."[1]
Philip Ó Ceallaigh

I have a patch of land on a hillside, a few hours from the city where I live. No electricity, no running water, just a ruined house I've been slowly taking down by hand. It's an abandoned farm at the end of a valley, part of a village that emptied out decades ago, and at first I had to cut back the forest just to be able to walk around the house and have open space to clear back the debris from the demolition. I was there last summer, when I got a call; she was very sorry, but she'd been asked to pass on the news that a friend of mine had died. His name was Dermot Healy. I explained that we hadn't been close. In fact, I hadn't seen him for fifteen years, since I'd moved to Bucharest. I was standing in the open as I spoke, on the upper storey of the house, the roof and walls from the upper level gone and a clear view down the wooded valley.

I met Dermot Healy in Tigh Neachtain in Galway on an April morning in 1999. I stepped into the dim empty pub and wiped away the tears caused by the icy wind gusting in the street. The wind was what I was trying to get away from. The only other customer, standing at the bar, was a dishevelled bearded man who hadn't slept well and was trying to repair his guts with a brandy and port cure. "Let's hijack a car and go to Sligo," slurred the man with the beard. He was anxious to get home, but the logistics were looking tricky. I recognised him from the photograph on the back of one of his books. I was jobless at the time but I happened to have the keys to a borrowed car in my pocket. An hour later we were on the road, heading north.

I had turned thirty a couple of weeks before in a windowless unit in an industrial park outside Athlone, earning money by

---

[1]. This article first appeared on *The Stinging Fly* website on 10 September 2015: <www.stingingfly.org/anonymous-best>. We are grateful to the editors of *The Stinging Fly* for allowing us permission to reprint it.

participating in clinical trials for morphine sulphate. I'd spent a decade moving around, doing various jobs. And I'd been writing for about five years. I wrote stories in longhand and threw most of the pages away. I didn't own a computer. I never sought the company of writers, either the published or unpublished kinds, and probably Dermot Healy was the only writer I would have wanted to meet. The other ones who interested me were dead already or in foreign countries. Healy had written an extraordinary novel called *A Goat's Song*. I had read it twice. Its mood of strangeness and disorientation intrigued me. The central character was undergoing a mental breakdown, concurrent with the collapse of a relationship with a woman, and a lot of drink was mixed in. There were scenes of paranoia and jealousy set against the background of the sectarian hatred of Belfast, others against the landscape of the west coast of Ireland, familiar yet transfigured. And there was Healy's way with dialogue, idiomatic yet strange, fragmented and allusive. Lyrical, cunning writing that pushed you off-balance even as it drew you in. Healy ruled a space where another set of rules applied. This, I thought to myself as I read, is something that can't be taught.

We'd set off on our trip together as if it were the most natural thing, but as we drove out of Galway, me asking him questions about his work, he told me that he knew why it had happened. It was because I was a writer. I agreed I was, though I was unsure if this was true. I'd thought I'd offered to drive for him because I was a reader.

Through Sligo town, past Ben Bulben, past Lissadell—Dermot's house was the last one at the end of the road on a peninsula poking westwards into the Atlantic. He was a man who liked to lean into very strong wind. His home was an old cottage that he had renovated. He had to keep dumping truckloads of boulders on the shore because the Atlantic was taking chunks out of the land, advancing towards the house. He said he could feel the shock of the really big waves through the rock as he lay in bed.

A few hours later, we were back in Sligo, and Dermot delivered a few words at the opening of a friend's art exhibition. "Did I sound drunk?" he asked me, nervously, afterwards. He didn't enjoy public occasions. "You sounded fine," I said. I'd driven us between a number of pubs in the course of the day. But I hardly touched a drink until after the last one, on the home stretch back to Dermot's place. It was a bottle of rosé and very cold from being left in the car, and we passed the bottle back and forth and I took it very slowly down the quiet back roads in the slanting, lucid evening sunlight. We'd both done our jobs for the day and were in no hurry.

Dermot's wife Helen was back at the house and some local friends of theirs called around. He told people I was a writer, that we'd hijacked a car. We drank and talked and read poems—this was new to me—and I read a translation of an old anonymous Irish one that was wild and like a prayer, and I read it well. "Anonymous, he's the best," said Dermot. "Because he doesn't give a fuck."

The next morning I was away before Dermot was up. It was a clear morning and ahead of me was Ben Bulben, gleaming with frost and snow. At that point I had decided I was a writer.

I met Dermot on a couple of occasions after that. The last one was in early 2000, just before I left the country. I knew the time had come for me to settle down to work and that it was just a matter of getting a little room in one of the cheaper neighbourhoods of Bucharest and closing the door behind me. I had been working as a security guard on night shifts. It was a good way to save money because the hours were so long you had no time or energy to spend it. I worked through the winter and hardly saw daylight during those months. It was a ghostly sensation, like permanent jetlag; you're walking around but something is missing, perhaps your soul. In late January I quit the job and I hitched up to Sligo to see Dermot and Helen, and to say goodbye. A couple of weeks later I was on my way east. All I needed for my new life fitted in a sports bag. In the bag was a rock, a fossil Dermot picked up on the shore behind his house when we were walking. He gave it to me and I put it in my pocket. It's still on my work desk today. There were a few letters and phone-calls over the years, and Dermot talked of coming to Bucharest at one point, but we didn't meet again.

I tell people that my meeting with Dermot Healy changed me, but I don't mean that he encouraged my writing. I remember, in his living room that winter when I'd given up my life as a security guard, suggesting he read one of my stories. "I will not," he said gruffly.

"You'll only want me to like it." I remember the look on Helen's face—I think she felt bad for me. In fact it was probably Helen who had prodded him to invite me to visit, with something like: "For God's sake, Dermot, be nice to him. You can see he worships you." I'm sure that being somebody's hero was a job Dermot did not need.

About six years later my editor sent him an advance copy of my first book and he wrote back with more enthusiasm than I could have hoped for. But he had reservations about one aspect of the writing, and most of the letter was about that, and he didn't offer a blurb. I would have wanted Dermot's words on the cover of my book more than anyone's, but more than any blurb I appreciated that direct and workmanlike handwritten letter.

We drank and talked until late, on that night before I left the country, and—yes—read poems aloud. I had the pull-out bed in the living room. And just before he took his leave and went down the hall—I must have been talking about writing or getting published— he said, "Ah, it's all just a game of billiards."

I didn't understand. What he was telling me—it's obvious now— is that the little bit of sense you create in whatever holy cell you carve out for yourself will go forth and unite again with the great nonsense of the world, from whence it came. Out there, where everyone figures out the angles and the margins. And your desire to arrive, finally, as a writer—this sacred thing you had in your mind— will always recede away from you, as if in a dream, the harder you pursue it. It is something that will never be in the world. It will never be realer for me than the April morning I drove away from Dermot Healy's house, a little hungover and euphoric, thinking how I would tell my friends back in Galway what had happened to me, as though the transformation were a tangible thing—and Ben Bulben sharp and glinting white ahead of me, through the windshield of my borrowed car.

After the Event
Glenn Patterson

Two hours after the event I am still trying to work out how you did it, how you turned me interviewing you into you getting me to answer the questions I had asked you—There you are! you said, by way of encouragement, if not quite corroboration—how you went in a couple of glasses of complimentary cava in the white tent of a green room from co-conspirator to pure imp, when in through the door of the bar to which we have (me in greater need of it) repaired, walks a man in a hat. A man in a hat like the hat was the whole point of him, what he had been heading towards from the moment he left the ground.

Who wears a hat like that? Who wears a hat like that to a pub like this? Who insists on keeping it on all the way through his first pint standing at the bar? Who goes to the toilet still wearing it?

Who follows him?

Who comes out from the toilet in two shakes wearing the hat?

Who follows *him*? Who and whose mates, all rugby-sevens of them?

What follows that?

Not what in that first heated minute seemed inevitable.

What follows is an exchange of songs, the hat a kind of conch, bestowing—imposing—a voice on the wearer. (You conch the Sash out of me.)

Two years after the event I am still trying to work out how you did it, trying to work out too whether that really was the last time I saw you or whether it has just come to stand for all the other times, you orchestrating, risking a walk in another man's hat, seeing where it took you.

Like the books and the stories, the poems and the plays.

(Is that another question?

I think it is.

And?
I don't know. There could be something in it.
There you are!)

Dermot Healy: Newcomer, Mentor, Old Hand
Alannah Hopkin (& Aidan Higgins)

I

Dermot Healy and Aidan Higgins: Old Hand and Newcomer

Aidan Higgins sadly passed away in December 2015, and had not been well enough to write a piece about Dermot Healy, though he offered his sincere best wishes to this project. I have been Aidan's partner for the past 28 years, and a friend of Dermot's for about the same length of time.

I first read Dermot Healy in 1986 when Aidan gave me a copy of *Fighting with Shadows*, and told me Dermot was the best writer currently working in Ireland. This was confirmed by a quote from Aidan on its cover: "A terrific novel, bouncing off the ropes, the best novel to come out of Ireland since *Malone Dies*."

Aidan had discovered Dermot's work some ten years earlier, when he was judging the Hennessy Literary Awards for David Marcus. "Give all the prize money to Dermot Healy," Aidan told Marcus. "No one else comes near him."

When I first met Dermot he and Aidan were still very much mentor and protégé or rather, old hand and newcomer, neither of them having a hierarchical way of thinking. I immediately felt completely at home with Dermot. It was like having another version of Aidan to hand, closer to my own age, only two years older as opposed to 23.

Aidan was helped at the beginning of his career by Samuel Beckett, mentored, we would say nowadays, and he did what he could to encourage Dermot. "Write for nothing and yourself," Beckett advised Higgins in the first letter he wrote to him from

Paris: "In you already, with the beginner, there is the old hand"—words that were equally apt for Dermot.

Beckett recommended Aidan's work to his publisher, John Calder, who was a key supporter in the early years. In turn, Aidan recommended Dermot's work to the editor Bill Swainson, who had started his career in John Calder's office, and had moved on to Allison and Busby, the publisher of Dermot's first two books.

But just as important as practical help, were the hours that Dermot and Aidan spent walking around London, no doubt visiting the occasional pub, talking, exchanging ideas, sparking off each other. Like Aidan, Dermot was largely self-educated. Both were voracious readers, and most of the time both found American literature and literature in translation more interesting than the works of their English and Irish contemporaries. Aidan immediately recognised a kindred spirit in Dermot. He was impressed by the power of Dermot's imagination, his sure use of metaphor, and the way that he was pushing the boundaries of writing all the time. He found Dermot's work far more exciting and innovative than that of his own contemporaries—Francis Stuart, say, or John McGahern. This is from Aidan's 1986 review of *Fighting with Shadows*:

> The energy of Irish writing is dependent largely upon the vernacular and idiomatic; street language in *Ulysses*; the frequently forked-tongued natives found they had another hidden lingo at their disposal . . . And now Dermot Healy, who takes his rightful place in the first rank, a beady eye fixed on what's what in the here-and-now.[1]

Aidan's early stories were strange and unconventional, but the novel that followed—*Langrishe, Go Down*—has a relatively conventional narrative trajectory, locating it firmly in the tradition of the 'Big House novel.' It is very different in both style and content to his later works of fiction, especially *Balcony of Europe*, *Scenes from a Receding Past* and *Bornholm Night-Ferry*. Aidan is chiefly known for *Langrishe, Go Down*, but it is his least typical novel, and the one he likes least.

Aidan describes what happened when Samuel Beckett joined a gathering of friends in London one evening in 1966, shortly after the publication of *Langrishe*:

> My wife, Jill, somewhat importunate, pressed him for his candid opinion of *Langrishe*. He said he had only read half of it so far and didn't wish to give an opinion. When she still pressed him, wine speaking, Beckett in exasperation (feathers rising) finally burst out: "If you want to have my opinion I think it's literary shit and he knows it!"[2]

Aidan's next novel, *Balcony of Europe,* published eight years later, is a resounding rejection of the conventions of "literary shit." Dan Ruttle's obsessional affair with his friend's wife, set in Nerja in Andalusia, is a lightly fictionalised version of what was actually happening as the first draft was being written. The reader experiences Ruttle's daily life with unusual immediacy, unmediated by fine writing (literary shit). Instead you have a collage-like assembly of visual images, historical fact, dreams, anecdotes, lists, polyglot references, dialogue, embedded quotations from other writers and philosophers (both famous and obscure, their origins often unacknowledged), and detailed descriptions of physical surroundings so accurate that you smell the noisome Spanish latrine as vividly as you see the dance of sunlight on the Mediterranean.

In *Bornholm Night-Ferry*, love letters written between the author (again lightly fictionalised) and a Danish poet, are used apparently verbatim, so that rather than reading *about* the affair, the reader is plunged right *into* the affair, experiencing its progress firsthand. It is another novel totally devoid of literary shit.

Dermot learnt from reading Aidan's novels, but he followed his own project, taking the ball and running even further and faster with it, through *A Goat's Song*, to his novel-like memoir, *The Bend for Home* and *Sudden Times,* until he produced the painfully beautiful account of the daily life of Psyche and his neighbours, largely told in the vernacular, that is *Long Time, No See.*

Dermot and Aidan shared an instinctive conviction that writing should give an approximation of the experience being described, that reading about something should be as vivid and memorable as living it. By outlawing *telling*, and the rhetorical tropes that accompany the telling, you banish the authorial voice, and the writerly ego.

Both Aidan Higgins and Dermot Healy know what Samuel Beckett meant when he said that when you listen to the voice in your head it is not literature that you hear.

II

Healy as Mentor: "Go daft sometimes"

"The great Irish writer Dermot Healy was laid to rest yesterday in the company of poets and artists, musicians and singers and, above all, his neighbours." (*Irish Times*, July 4, 2014)

It would have been nice if they had called him a "great Irish writer" in print while he was still alive. He would have liked that, most likely he would have laughed, but he would have liked it. His greatness lay not only in the extraordinary body of work that he produced, but in his generosity and kindness to other writers, which I have experienced firsthand.

I published two novels with Hamish Hamilton (London) in my early thirties, and then got stuck in a loop with an impossible historical novel. After about ten years of rejections, I decided to write another contemporary novel, and I called it *The Wind that Shakes the Barley*.

No, not the film by Ken Loach about the fight against the Black and Tans in 1920; this was a contemporary novel named after a traditional air because the chorus was relevant to the story: "*Come home, come home, come home it sings / The wind that shakes the barley.*" Shortly after the typescript was sent out to prospective publishers, the news of the film broke. Apart from the horrible coincidence of the title, the film was being made on my doorstep; the whole of south County Cork was dotted with discreet little signposts for the film crew: WSB.

In a fit of pique I renamed the novel *Under the Weather*, a nod to Malcolm Lowry and to the wet Irish summer, and still nobody wanted to publish it. I started to think maybe there was something wrong with it. Dermot kindly volunteered to take a look at it. I posted him a bound typescript, and he sent it back to me with comments all over it in his strangely childlike handwriting, and a three-page, single-spaced typed letter, dated 8 April, 2005. Before the letter, there was a long phone call, to let me know as soon as he knew, that he liked it, a typically kind gesture. I remember he kept saying, "It has the ring of truth." That simple test has since become my most important criterion for judging a novel or a story: does it have the ring of truth?

Aidan once looked at some stories for me. His advice was to get rid of the all-knowing narrative voice, the voice telling the story, and let the story emerge through the speech and actions of the characters. Dermot's close textual advice echoed this, and could be summed up as an extreme version of the old adage, "Show, don't tell." Time and again he advises redrafting a scene in dialogue, increasing the use of direct speech, and cutting all explanations:

> "Keep a close eye on the dialogue. Go daft sometimes."
>
> "Give her plenty of dialogue, early on. In her dialogue we will learn who she is. Let the narrator stay quiet."
>
> "Let her voice speak out more often in inverted commas, and let the voices of the others speak out in inverted commas, and not have them trapped by the narrator in letters or journals."

"Go daft sometimes" was a brilliant way of getting rid of the censoring superego, and in my case, the journalist, who is compelled to explain everything. I have used Dermot's advice ever since when writing stories, especially the bit about going daft, and I believe it has made them much better.

Notes

1. Aidan Higgins. "Cantraps of Fermented Words," *Windy Arbours: Collected Criticism* (Normal: Dalkey Archive Press, 2006), 192.

2. Aidan Higgins, "On the Rack." Unpublished paper read at Cúirt, Galway. 24 April, 1999.

The Rogue Wave
Michael Harding

I tell a story sometimes that I heard from Dermot Healy. He went into an old bachelor one day. "Do you not be lonely sometimes?" Dermot wondered. To which the man replied, "No. Sure I know I'm always here."

It's a story with a universal truth; that in our sitting and solitude we are conscious of something beyond the narrow scope of the ego. A bigger mind inhabits us and observes our ego's passions rise and fall like the swell of the ocean.

It's the wisdom of Zen, but it is also to be found in the exuberance of Irish poets, from the minimalist luminosity of the 12th-century bards to the glory days of south Ulster poets such as Cathal Buí MacGiolla Ghunna, Art McCooey and many others, and right down to Patrick Kavanagh, who still carried the flickering lantern of those ancient muses in his poetry and lit the way for Dermot too. Dermot was afflicted with an unruly mind that could never quite attend to the mundane because of the sacred anarchy beneath the surface of everything, which drew him in and allowed him to write such viscerally beautiful poetry and prose.

I remember when I was fourteen going into a little cafe in Cavan, where he lived, to meet the twenty-year-old, who even then was acknowledged as a great poet. I was terrified. His mother said he wasn't out of bed, so I waited in the empty restaurant as sun broke in through the amber glass of a high window. He arrived with a big smile. It felt like I was being hugged when he looked at me.

One day he came to my mother's house to bring me out to dinner with some very important people. When I tried to get into the car there was a pot of curry on the passenger seat. "That's the dinner," he said. "They don't know we're coming yet."

Nobody knew if Dermot was coming or going. I remember drinking with him in Blessings Bar one night. At one stage he slipped out. I thought he was gone to the toilet. But he was over in the Farnham Arms having another life with someone else. When he appeared again I said, "You were a long time in the toilet." He said, "I'm across the road. Finish your drink and come over."

Dermot led people and people were glad to be led. But when it came to literature he was the hidden master in the Irish school, quietly encouraging other writers, masterfully critiquing their work, and pushing new boundaries in his beloved magazines, *Force 10* and *The Drumlin*.

Dermot took up where Liam O'Flaherty had left off, weaving into human stories the narratives of dogs, donkeys and other animals. In his work even the birds are held up in the sky, and they lift and swoop in an unpredictable weave of anarchy and love.

Love was the root of his books. And in his most famous work, *A Goat's Song*, he excelled himself in revealing the Irish male as the dreamer, the broken thing that a man becomes when the women have gone away.

So it was a joy to know he was safe in Sligo for so many years with a beautiful woman by his side, and the ocean throwing winter waves at him with the same unexpected roguery as his sentences followed one after another. He told me once it was hard to write in a beautiful place. "The waves," he said, "draw me in."

I saw him last December at a gig he organised to raise money for victims of weather in the Philippines. I saw him do an impromptu sean-nós dance on the floor as the band played. And he whispered in my ear. "The waves," he whispered. "Watch out for the rogue wave. It's waiting for all of us. It comes on your blind side. Just as you're casting."

I suppose the sea overcomes everything in the end. Movement overpowers words. Love destroys thinking. And the world is held in the loving embrace of its own form. I think that was the story at the heart of all his writing. And as such it was the most eloquent celebration of heaven in the ordinary that has come from his generation of writers.

He told me once that prose is poetry in the sense that a bird is still a bird when it sits still. And the last image he flung at me, with the glee of a Zen master, his eyes hugging me, his wisdom falling like rose petals from a teacher's hands was this: "If you want to break a dog's heart," he whispered, "throw a stone into the sea."

A Short History of *Force 10* (A Journal of the North-West)
Brian Leyden

Back in 1991, the All-Ireland *Fleadh Cheoil* was coming to Sligo for the third year running. In the offices of *Force 10*, the literary journal edited by Dermot Healy, we were working on a traditional Irish music special issue to coincide with the Fleadh and the centenary of the birth of the great South Sligo-born fiddle player Michael Coleman.

Dermot was assembling a longer than usual article on Coleman's life and legacy, and there was also an interview with Michael Coleman's daughter, Mary Coleman Hannon, born in the US in 1918 and back in Ireland only for the centenary commemorations. Ben Lennon, the celebrated Kiltyclogher-born North Leitrim fiddle player provided another hugely insightful interview where he talked about the '*neagh*' sound and how in your playing either you have it or you don't. So you have musicians with great technique but without the '*neagh*' who "take a tune like a dog catching a rabbit and shake the life out of it."

These interviews were an essential part of *Force 10*, conducted face-to-face and written in longhand. The aim was to encourage writers to listen. For as Dermot said, "The object you are trying to attain in writing is to describe the person outside you well." The process also allowed the subject time to reflect and elaborate in the pause while their answers were being transcribed. At the conclusion you could read back what had been written to verify its accuracy. The handwritten version of the interview might undergo further editing while being typed, with segments shortened or transposed, and the final result was an exceptionally true version of the subject's essential thoughts and voice with the interviewer removed.

Another unique feature of *Force 10* was its egalitarian approach to publishing established writers alongside up-and-coming new names. Many of us newcomers would go on to be published writers, including Martin Healy (posthumously), Ann P. Joyce, Noelle Vial,

Órfhlaith Ní Chonaill, Liam Browne, Ger Reidy, Neil Murphy and Molly McCloskey. But it gave everyone a boost to appear in print with the likes of M. J. Molloy, Francis Harvey, Leland Bardwell, Francis Stuart, Tom Morgan, Tom Kilroy, Patrick McCabe, Ciarán Carson, Michael Longley and Neil Jordan.

The generosity of better-known writers towards the journal and their faith in Dermot was exemplified by the appearance of twelve new poems from the "Squarings" sequence by Seamus Heaney; the original submission to *Force 10* containing hand-written corrections to several of the poems, including the final line in poem *xxxix* where Heaney changed the wording from "Beyond the range of possibility" to "Beyond the range you thought you'd settled for," as it would appear in *Seeing Things* (1991).

By giving equal standing to poetry, non-fiction, short stories, interviews, photography and the work of visual artists, *Force 10* was a publication Dermot believed "opened the door to other voices"; an approach prefigured by *The Drumlin* magazine he'd produced while living in Cavan.

Issue one of *Force 10* appeared in the winter of 1989, priced £3.95. The final issue, number thirteen, was published in 2008, priced €16. In 2007 there was a publication dedicated to the work of Cavan photographer Tom Hussey called *A Bar of Light* which carried the *Force 10* imprimatur. Over the years, editions were numbered or linked with the seasonal calendar but some have no clear date of publication.

The funding for the journal came largely through arts, community and local government organisations, especially the Borough of Sligo VEC and Jackie Lynch. The journal also carried advertising that today acts like a time-tunnel back to the old haunts of *Force 10*'s hometown. Throughout its existence, recouping money from sales bedevilled an endeavour with a publication history resembling the sun in west of Ireland skies, in that you never knew when it might appear but whenever it came out it was a welcome sight.

In the editorial written for issue one Dermot says *Force 10* came about thanks to his links with the writers' group who met in the Markievicz Centre for the Unemployed that stood opposite Clifford's Electrical Repairs on High Street. From the Markievicz

Writers' Group, and contacts established with other groups such as the Allingham Society in Ballyshannon, the Killybegs Writers' Co-Op, The Barrel-Store Arts Group in Carrick-on-Shannon, the Moylurg Writers' Group in Boyle and numerous individuals, Dermot came to believe there was "a style and energy in the North-West region which deserved recognition and publication."

Issue two saw a focus on spirituality and mental health; posing such questions as, "How do former mentally ill patients view themselves, and how do psychiatrists and psychologists view mental illness and the patients that suffer from it?" It was groundbreaking work at the time, and the reviews for issues one and two of *Force 10* were insightful and positive.

Presenter Mike Murphy from *The Arts Show* on RTÉ Radio 1 said, "The first issue I thought one of the best magazines to emerge in modern Ireland." Writer Nuala O'Faolain called *Force 10* "a magical production"—"I feel strongly that the extraordinary mix of both authors and subjects in *Force 10* is about the new Ireland." One of the journal's strongest champions, the Cork-based poet and reviewer Seán Dunne, captured the essential character of *Force 10* when he said of it: "The country is full of oddity, darkness, laughter and strangeness. It is also full of ordinary things and people. When you combine the two you end up with a marvel."

In some quarters, however, Dermot believed *Force 10* was negatively pigeonholed. By the time he came to writing the trenchantly-worded editorial for issue three he said, "There are many ambiguous lessons to be learnt from publishing a regional magazine; the first being that a regional magazine should learn not to call itself a regional magazine." The trouble being, "That *Force 10* is one of the few magazines in Ireland specifically publishing and promoting short stories and poetry by new writers and established writers from anywhere at all is straightaway overlooked."

Commenting too on the paucity of reviews in the national newspapers, he noted that when you reveal how the team compiling the magazine was funded by FÁS and therefore considered 'unemployed,' the publication immediately took on "the character of a charity." Dermot concluded: "If a magazine is to have national status these days it means being situated in Dublin."

Even so, Dermot could remind readers in the same editorial how the *Force 10* office on High Street now functioned as a mini-arts centre, with readings by *Force 10* contributors held in Killybegs, Belmullet, Castlebar, Sligo and Cavan; along with two Samuel Beckett plays which Dermot directed—*Krapp's Last Tape* and *Rockaby* with Des Braiden and Tani Bentis. Originally staged in the Trades Club, both productions were presented along with a photographic exhibition, "*Force 10* in the North-West."

For issue four, *Force 10* moved to County Mayo where Dermot had taken up the post of Writer-in-Residence: a job according to Dermot that "entails the same responsibilities a governess, or clerk with literary claims, might have who has clocked into work away from home with a strange family." It was in this issue of "*Force 10* in Mayo" that the notion the journal was somehow parochial was chillingly swept aside in a long interview Dermot conducted with John T. Reddington.

Originally a native of Mayo, Reddington described how he joined the Australian Royal King's Regiment to avoid a tax bill and ended up in Vietnam:

> An Australian officer took me in one day into the American camp. An American soldier was lying on the floor of the tent. He was all swollen up with what was called the Black Death . . . a venereal disease that the troops caught . . . the disease could not be treated. The Australian officer, who was my commanding officer, introduced me to an American officer that was there in the tent. The American officer put a .44 colt revolver into my hand. "Shoot him," he said, "and put him out of his agony." It was an American tradition that an American does not shoot an American. The reason he wanted the man shot was because it would take the soldier with Black Death a long time to die. It would be pure agony, lying there rotting away. It was easier and quicker to shoot him. So I shot him.

This astonishing interview ended with a characteristically Healyesque detail brought to light. Back in Ireland and looking after the 40 acre farm in Mayo where he was born, John T. Reddington's mother died. He told Dermot how,

> In her will she wrote: "I leave everything to my only son—the *real* and the *unreal*." I don't know what those words meant—"*real* and *unreal*"—but there they are written into the will. *Unreal* maybe means anything outside the farm. Memory probably. And *real* means what is there, the farm, money, the house, her handbag . . . But the *unreal* is beyond me . . .

After the Mayo edition, Dermot began to experience a personal renaissance, publishing novels, poetry collections, working in theatre and staying loyal to his writers' groups. He'd also married Helen Gillard and was living in Ballyconnell on the Sligo coast. In an interview I conducted at the time for *The Buzz* magazine in Sligo, edited by Keith Hopper, Dermot said:

> I feel at home here, and yet I'd be too superstitious to say, "I'll stay." If there is a magic you'll find it in yourself at last in a proper place. There is also the fact that the sea is reclaiming the headland I'm living on bit by bit. Coincidence brought me here, bad weather will drive me out. Maybe it's that security of owning a home and the insecurity of the elements combining to make a creative time in my life.

The upshot was that after working on the early issues of *Force 10*, and having my work published there regularly, Dermot asked me to guest edit issues seven and eight. With issue eight in particular an improvement in the print quality helped to highlight the work of the photographers who'd been so loyal to *Force 10*. You had the in-house photographers Jo Gray and Noel Kilgallon, and work by the likes of Mike Bunn, Nutan, David Knight, David Henry, Alec Foley and Rosalind Davies, and the exceptional generosity of John Minihan, pictured in issue eight by Hammond Journeaux embracing Stan Gebler Davies above John's own photo of Seamus Heaney and Joseph Brodsky with their arms around each other.

Issue nine would be guest edited by writer Molly McCloskey,

issue ten by filmmaker Bob Quinn, and issue eleven by broadcaster Frank Galligan. Dermot returned as editor for the Tom Hussey photography special issue twelve. Of which Dermot says,

> In every sense Tom Hussey saw that the moment was flying by fast. It was an eye opener to look at these photographs late into the night and to see how something small, off-centre, grew in stature, how nature and religion touched off each other, how the past goes down Main Street or up the Cock Hill or other directions, on swings in trees, or on violins at street corners where a girl is taking a first step into air.

At his own initiative Dermot produced issue thirteen with the backing of Sligo County Library. A projected issue fourteen never happened.

Now, after the passage of years, I confess I still feel a definite frisson whenever I open the original issue one of *Force 10* with the Seán McSweeney charcoal sketch on the cover. I am overtaken by the sense of surprise and strangeness Dermot himself registered when John T. Reddington's mother in her final will and testament bequeathed a gift of the real and the unreal; the passing on of values and of memories.

Works Cited

Healy, Dermot, ed. *Force 10*, Issues 1–13 (1989–2008): All. Print.
Leyden, Brian. "Headland: An Interview with Dermot Healy." *The Buzz* 10 (Jul.1994): 5. Print.
———. "The Place of Writing." *The Leitrim Guardian* 47 (2015): 20. Print.

Reading *Force 10*
George O'Brien

Whatever else about it, *Force 10* is not a small magazine. Even the look of it—its size reminiscent of one of those enviable Christmas annuals that our favourite comics used to issue—says so. But this is not only a matter of format, though cropping, spacing, juxtapositions and all the other compositorial niceties naturally play their part in creating the memorable, immersive place that each issue of *Force 10* is. And as with form, so with content. The heterogeneity and inclusiveness of poetry and prose, artists and storytellers, knowns and unknowns, pen portraits and snapshots, national figures and local interviewees—and the sense of a populace suggested thereby—are not small magazines' typical bill of fare. Openness and latitude are the editorial by-words. The result is more field than front room: Gráinne Yeats shown in concert plucking on her harp-strings, and in the picture alongside hers Pat Mahon of Skreen playing his flute on a street corner; Seamus Heaney's "Squarings" (xxxvii–xlviii) preceded by a piece called "Rainbow Warrior" by Lize ("I'm totally mind over matter"); an extract called "On the Skite" from Thomas Kilroy's novel *Quirke*—unpublished, as far as I know—with, like a tailpiece, a small poem entitled "The Anchor" by Breda Sullivan; the photo of local politician Tommy Higgins adorned with mayoral chain stepping out in a chorus line of little girls, ages four to seven . . .

This is just "A Journal of the North-West"; no echo of the familiar small magazine subtitle—*Horizon: A Review of Literature and Art*, say. Though *Force 10* is a title worth dwelling on, nobody would confuse it with another *Blast*. And there's no inverted snobbery either, no narrow localism, nothing glibly populist, no *faux* folksiness. The contributions of many an international name ensure there's none of the self-regard that narrows so many small magazines' appeal to vanishing point. The typical small magazine tends to pride itself on the assumption that it knows what matters. It has an agenda, it takes on subjects and sees through them, it wishes to lead, it speaks to an audience that already goes along with its line, it aims at a cultural intervention. It resembles the city—the capital, more often than not—that is its wellspring and climate. And that's fine. But in *Force 10* the reader encounters a publication that runs counter to all that. It doesn't even run. If it did, more critical essays would have been featured. Instead, it just takes its place, or I should say, it allows its contributors to take theirs. The contributors are no more than people willing to tell their stories, regardless of the form they put the stories in, a picture, a drawing, a memory, a sonnet; nothing more is required. "Sligonians . . . tell their story with candour and trust," as Dermot said in the first number's editorial, and these qualities are reflected throughout.

Not that the North-West is Sligo alone. Mention of it turns out to be a way of suggesting a zone, not a border. One of the most intriguing features of *Force 10* is how town and hinterland merge into each other, partly perhaps to suggest that the barriers thought to be between them are bogus (and as the contents in general declare—as though in one voice—down with barriers in whatever case). It may be that "uncharted waters," a phrase on which that first editorial concludes, are what Sligo lands you in. But that's true of all places and their people. Each has its unsuspected depths, a volatile and variegated current of being that underlies often unremarkable surfaces and unregarded appearances. Sligo is not a land of heart's desire but a place to start exploring, a point from which to open out. In this, too, being faithful to and accommodating the many layers, dimensions, angles, optics that inclusiveness signifies come across as fundamentals. In the title to his editorial for the inaugural number of *The Bell*, Seán Ó'Faoláin declared, "This is your magazine," and a good deal of good work was published as a result, much of it throwing light on dark corners of Irish experience—doing time and Northern attitudes among them. But *Force 10* is much more comprehensively in its contributors' hands. They are the reliable witnesses. Their trust in their own findings and perceptions is assumed. Their presence is unforced. There is something of an act of repossession in this work, an emergence from under the shadow of the metropolitan, a view of an undisputed territory. "A street you've nearly forgotten in the small town you grew up in will do," Dermot writes in "At the End of the Day" (*Force 10* 5, [Spring 1993]: 67). Something you know you can call your own.

Without stating any great ambition, though without not stating one either, just by being what its contributors made of it, *Force 10* became in time a landmark in a noteworthy turn of events in Irish life. From its contributors, the various workshops and communities of interests that they represent, the personalities and perspectives on whose behalf they speak and depict, their tastes, their reading, their culture, a good start may be made on getting a sense of what seems almost to be a writing or arts movement, a pilgrimage to silence and the white page, that a large number of people in Ireland began to embark on in or around the mid-1980s, and that grew into the extremely broad church of literary and artistic affirmers who continue to make their presence known. In this respect, the use of the word "journal" is evocative; *Force 10* is a kind of logbook of consciousness, an album of endeavours undertaken in private for all the world to see, including the intimate world of where the writer and the photographer and the inimitable interviewees who are the subjects of many of the most eye-opening pieces have spent their lives. And the people who put the thing together are part of this story too. To go back to that first editorial: "The title *Force 10* comes from a Sligo VEC [Vocational Education Committee] scheme for the unemployed." And while it is possible to find in the title resonances of weather, climate, atmospheric pressure, the unruly heavens to which all are subject, the calibration of an invisible element, it's also necessary not to lose sight of those whom, in one way or another the economy had no use for, and who found something to give there in the Markievicz Centre for the Unemployed. As Mr Kilgallon says to town-bound Ollie Ewing in *Sudden Times*: "Tell them we're still here" (41).

In the background of all this, there's the writer Dermot Healy. And as well as thinking about *Force 10* in itself, I began to wonder what connection there might be between it and those works of his, the prose in particular, that appeared after the journal was up and doing. To make a claim such as *Force 10*, seen in the light of *A Goat's*

Song, *Sudden Times*, *The Bend for Home* or *Long Time, No See*, or indeed the poems, amounts to an aesthetic would take elaborate and probably tedious teasing out. Just a few observations in passing, then. By its nature, *Force 10* has a multiple story structure. And that is also something there's a version of in *Fighting with Shadows*, which predates *Force 10*—the story of the deserter Corporal Wilson, the story of Mr and Mrs Moss. These and others seem departures from, as well as contributions to, the main interest. In the later novels, diversification of this type is looser, more net-like, more engaged with "[t]his wonderful sense of randomness" (*Sudden Times* 67) that appeals to Ollie Ewing. Along with such porosity, which is also a mode of transparency, the circular becomes much more a part of the narrative trajectory, a partner to the linear. And this effect is also sustained by the generally easier movement of the prose, helped by a greater stylistic informality, increasingly evident in *Sudden Times* and *Long Time, No See*. Every so often, the sentence is not enough and turns into some other kind of syntactical presence, something beyond the lapidary unit. The haul of those compendious trawling inventories in *The Bend for Home* are cases in point—the census of Cavan town closing for half-day; the rollcall of boarders in St. Patrick's; the congregation of Lenten mass-goers. In turn, the conventional sentence—pared back, more direct—has a simplicity that is a rhythm in itself and, in the overall scheme, a counter rhythm.

There's also the line in *The Bend for Home:* "surrealism is a conscious obliteration of unaesthetic effects. Someone is in control" (247). Being conscious in that sense means exercising control. The later works have no desire to be conscious in that manner, which in any case they realise cannot be maintained: consciousness ebbs and flows, is not to be typified. These works are against force. They're against the particular form of that force called politics. Instead of interpreting or framing or constraining, let consciousness keep faith with encountering, trusting, registering, abiding by. But then how best to have such a relation with a world, or a home ground, that is also adversarial and belittling? That's an especially difficult question for Jack Ferris, Ollie Ewing and Philip Feeney, who have been uprooted, who have to find out how to trust again and start over. The break and the repair of it are the dual themes; the strings of the net and the holes between them.

"This distance between my mind and my body has always remained and is insurmountable" (74), we're told in *The Bend for Home*. But perhaps as that work's title suggests, in its portraits of the physical Finea and the Finea of memory and imagination, the location both of finalised history and its interplay with unending need, place is where the question confronting those protagonists is enshrined and negotiated. As Healy's essay, "The Global Local," maintains, "place is always on the move" (185). Just like the mind. Place and mind—perhaps they replicate each other; place not fixed and out there, its location determined by known forces and precedents, but as an entity that is taken in and regarded differently over a succession of discontinuous meetings. We shape and are shaped. Hy-Brasil can be imagined, and it can be imagined imagining us (*The Bend for Home*). The shapes dissolve, are renewed in a different light. Reading is one version of the shaping, writing another. Absorbed but detached, we turn the page, remembering earlier pages, going on in the light of them. We add the sentence, make the paragraph, accretions and separations equally necessary. There are ways of making ourselves fit that we can dream up. Place proves that.

These glosses are no more than very rudimentary musings about Dermot Healy's prose in the years of *Force 10* and leading on from it. Those works' handling of time and space, of attachment and loss, of starting over and getting through would have changed in any case, whether the journal materialised or not. But an acknowledgement of the shifting nature of those dimensions, those shapers of seeing and being, does seem to have a prototype in the community of contrasts and combinations created in *Force 10*—a place (the North-West) and its spirit, or a place that can be represented in such a way as to evince a spirit. The journal is one version of the kind of gathering that place stands for, and it is an ideal of that gathering, where differences can do nothing but coexist, where the tingle of "the erotica of little things" (*Fighting with Shadows* 99) resonates unjudged, where everybody is an outsider—and nobody is. "I suppose writing, among many other skills, is an attempt to probe and celebrate the certainty and the uncertainty and, then the hard part, to negotiate the tension between the two" ("The Global Local" 188). In clearing a way to see the various levels of these antitheses, and in giving at least a formal model of negotiation, *Force 10* is an act of imagination not only by the nature of its presence but also in the very idea of it.

Works Cited

Healy, Dermot. *Fighting with Shadows*. 1984. London: Allison and Busby, 1986. Print.

———, ed. *Force 10*, Issues 1–13. (1989-2008): All. Print.

———. *Long Time, No See*. London: Faber and Faber, 2011. Print.

———. *Sudden Times*. London: Harvill Press, 1999. Print.

———. *The Bend for Home*. London: Harvill Press, 1996. Print.

———. "The Global Local". *Princeton University Library Chronicle* 72.1 (Autumn 2010): 185–97. Print.

Ó'Faoláin, Seán. "Gentile or Jew, Protestant or Catholic, priest or layman, Big House or Small House—*The Bell* is yours." *The Bell* 1.1 (Oct. 1940): 5–9. Print.

Form
Caroline Bracken

i.m. Dermot Healy

Send us a sign; a feather on the ground
    a page of a brand new book turned down
a text or email from an estranged friend
    a memory of an unknown land
a finding of a missing passport
    a tenner in an empty wallet
a horse-shaped branch of oak in a peat bog
    a wagging tail from a stranger's dog
a formation of geese in February
    a drenching wave on a tranquil day
a chipper open at midnight in Birr
    a grant from the Arts Council unasked for.
Fire up the engine of a burnt-out car
    just to let us know you are there and here.

Sligo Occult: On Dermot Healy's Radical Style
Kevin Barry

If you understand that the life of this island and its counties is permeated by strange sea-blown forces and occult shimmers, that in fact nine-tenths of the true life here lies beneath the surface of ordinary things and is utterly unexplainable, and thus beautiful, then you will understand that Dermot Healy's work feeds from this critical truth like nobody else's, and a close reading of it may help you break through to the stranger dimensions.

Witness chapter fourteen of the novel *Long Time, No See*, a sprightly twelve-page roundelay called "Sightseeing." It depicts a weekend night on the streets of Sligo town. Mister Psyche and his mother and father and the dog, Timmy, have driven in from their home on the coast. We understand this to be a ritual excursion. The father goes walkabout—I use the aboriginal term advisedly—and huddles in various doorways of the town as he watches the night's moves. Mister Psyche and the mother, meanwhile, sit darkly cocooned in the car down by the Tesco. They eat a few sweets and monitor the night also. It drifts in strange eddies and turns, as though on the drag of the moon. They occasionally break off from their quiet observations to have a mooch about the streets themselves. There are random bits of chat with recurring spacers. The récit busies along on very light feet—the style is honed and fine, the authorial voice is the merest whisper of a breeze across this night and world, but listen carefully and you will hear the steady beating of a clean narrative pulse. We are presented with the surface of things—a town that is simultaneously gaudy and drab—but only as an instruction that we should try to look beneath, that we should try to go deeper. Here is Mister Psyche, having a wander around a monastery in the town, and finding that it presents a vantage view:

I climbed the round steps up and looked down out of that V-shaped window. Underneath the souls in coats strolled in a medley. Even as they talked together, squinting to the person on their left, or right, they looked like animals entering new territory; and those who knew the place, and walked ahead through the dark with great confidence, were more alone than the strangers. I waved, but no one saw me.

Those most familiar with the terrain are most compromised by it. Great oddness might lurk in the shadows; pools of unknowable darkness might lie beyond the normal realm. But we are not going to get too het up about this; there is no hand-wringing, nor existential despair—Mister Psyche and the mother go and eat a crêpe outside the cinema. The father remains in the doorways, watching the town with the bead of a hawk, as if he didn't, it might disappear.

More night, more life:

The Hill was full of Northern bucks wrapped in shawls. Three girls, dressed as barbers, were singing in the Glazed Oven. Ma bought three slices of tongue, a bag of paprika, almond nuts and yes, sage, she said. At the monument a woman was screaming into her friend's mobile. Ma strolled over to Molloy's the drapers to see the style. She passed my father who was standing outside Currid's the chemists. She did not look at him, and he did not look at her.

Chronologically we are in the present tense but also we are in the future-medieval. It is impossible to situate this work in any canon. We are neither in the dreary kitchens of social realism nor in the heritage park of late modernism. Healy is something very unexpected and rare in the literature now: he is original.

Mister Psyche and the mother are back in the car. A young one stumbles against the car in the dark. Certainly she is half-cut and we suspect that she is on tablets. She has a huge pair of eyes on her. An exchange of unmarked dialogue lowers itself by careful holds down the rockface of the page:

We're waiting for my father.
Oh is he doing the shopping?
No.
Ah, I know, he's in the pub.
No.
It's kinda mad. What's he doing?
He's walking about, looking round him.
Oh. And you just like sit . . . like . . . here?
Is right, said Ma.
Yes, every Saturday night.
And Christmas Eve.
That's weird.
Is it?

The lines are pared to the quick and play queer music. The rhythm is not overly emphasised, being properly sprung. There is lightness, lightness on every page of the novel, and the pages turn as they should in a piece of natural art, as in the unchangeable sequence of a dream, but—ho-ho—a trap is all the while being set for the reader. What we are being given here in slow reveal is another tragedy, another goat-song.

Long Time, No See is also a repository of great strangenesses. An old stone wall is recovered from beneath the sea and Mister Psyche can sense the reverb of its ancient constructor's building rhythm. There is a virtuosic set piece on the cleaning of a big house's chimney. Time is not entirely fixed—it comes and goes with the Atlantic gusts. Half the time—as in life—you wouldn't know where you are nor when. The inanimate is often enlivened:

> An empty bucket went flying across the field . . . A heave of salt flew across . . .

Land and the weather will sometimes speak; the buildings of the towns and villages hardly ever shut up. Memory seeps into the stones of our places, and it leaves us in no doubt of its lingering.

The novel sifts its material and allows it to build in slow accumulation. Dunes of quiet prose form in scimitar drifts. The bird life is in every ounce and atom as important as the human; its music is our constant grace and fills the skies:

> A choir of starlings stood feeding on the seeds of the New Zealand flax that stood over my head in the next flower garden. Hallo, I called. Hallo, they called back. Then they began the flirty whistling. A stonechat spun by, then the wren, with a tipped-up tail, hopped along a branch of Olearia, keeping time to a questioning song she sang alone.

The book is utterly practical; also it is away with the faeries. Always, always it is pressing a palm lightly against the screen that shades us with a grey gauze from the Otherworld. The accent of a very particular sector of the Irish northwest is delineated with precision. We listen intently to what's not being said beneath the surface of the talk. There are constant silent tussles beneath the babble of talk. In *Long Time, No See,* whenever two Irishmen say hello to each other, one of them loses.

The power of the novel accumulates, too. Slowly but definitely, and gladly, we enter the world of the book; the accent quickens, life and the night happens, and quietly a great fiction writer is at his work; the mesmeric forces assert.

"Testing, said a voice. Testing, one two three..."
Mike McCormack

That summer I was at a fair in Achill when a man walked up to me. He wasn't young but apart from his NASA baseball cap there was nothing else setting him apart from all the other farmers milling around.

You're McCormack, am I right?

Yes.

I read your book.

Thank you.

It's very good.

I'm glad you liked it.

It's not as good as Healy's though.

Years later, Dermot had a good laugh when I told him this, that great husky laugh.

NASA, he marvelled.

Yes, that's what was on the cap.

That would explain a lot, wouldn't it?

Maybe.

The way he told it, the stories in *Banished Misfortune* were squeezed between his first instinct for poetry and the longer slog of the novel, *Fighting with Shadows*. He'd already had a few poems published in an anthology edited by Seamus Heaney, but David Marcus's "New Irish Writing" page in the *Irish Press* was a lively, beckoning forum for the young writers of his generation. He submitted a few stories and two of them won Hennessy Awards in 1974 and 1976.

Reading that collection now, from the perspective of his later work, what strikes is how tightly woven some of them are, a dense warp and weft of image and emotion, an ebb and flow closer to fugue than any narrative unspooling. Nowhere as yet is there evidence of those looser rhythms which drive those later novels, enabling them to breathe so easily in themselves. These stories are attentively detailed, lush ecologies in which it is easy to lose your way. "The Island and the Calves," "The Girl in the Muslin Dress" and the ringing final piece "Banished Misfortune," circle within themselves as if their truths would lend themselves only to a kind of spiralling embrace.

This being the early work it's easy to suppose that poet and fiction writer are still contending for supremacy within the same soul—the separation of powers has yet to be properly achieved. It might be more accurate to think of a young, open spirit tapping a shamanic, incantatory current, a broad imaginative attunement turning sentences like—"Towards the stones of the Dog Mountains, under the plural form of myths, they found refuge." Or, "History became the study of disappearing softness, for hardness always remained, the most accessible material of men."

> He stood in the middle of the room surrounded by other writers. He was suffering with backache and hadn't got a wink of sleep the night before. Margaret Atwood was tipping painkillers into his hand.
> Take one of these before going to sleep, she advised.
> I'll take four, he said, throwing them back on the spot.
> That was the first time I met him.

He spoke fondly of London. It was a second home to him during the sixties and seventies, a place of freedom and somewhere he could make a living; in all, he spent fifteen years there. He was in his mid-teens when he went there first to work on building sites and in hotels and off-licences. There was a spell working for Securicor also, transporting huge amounts of cash around north London, sweltering in the back of the van among the cash bags, stripped to his underpants. Then a period transporting gold bullion around Heathrow; he bought a typewriter with his first wages. These were the years when he might have been at UCD but a chronic bout of sinusitis at the end of his first year put an end to his academic ambitions. He loved the London years but admitted he would have loved also the scholarly journey that might have been his with the university experience.

So London, or a variation of it, bulks large in *Banished Misfortune and Other Stories*. Five of the twelve stories are set in a world where couples stumble through Sunday morning streets after the night before and weekends are spent drinking. Mad political prophets stalk the streets and lovers keep hopeless vigil outside the houses of the beloved. It is not a place of freedom and economic opportunity. Lives are lived on the margins and people's hearts are lightened by the absence of god. Women are fragile and contested—is it withdrawal or epilepsy which has Moody Alex so twitchy in "The Girl in the Muslin Dress." These are the stories of faith, all the things we believe in—love, politics and family—and all those things which menace them . . .

> *The following day, there was a good crowd in the backroom when he stood up to read. He looked rested but nervous. A copy of* A Goat's Song *lay on the table, that beautiful Harvill edition, glossy and tightly bound. He opened it in the middle and it sprang out of his hands, shot towards the roof, open-winged like a jackdaw. He clapped it between both hands and brought it down to rest on the lectern. The crowd clapped, breathed easier, and he went on to give one of those quiet readings which, sentence by sentence, draws a whole room into an electric intimacy.*

When we read them first in the eighties those of us who were casting around for new paradigms were baffled. The stories were difficult to discern—"The Island and the Calves," how does that unravel?—and reading them was a kind of teasing apart rather than following any point to point narrative progress. Nor, were they always willing to crystallise to a clear image—they had a blur and shift and the mind's eye had difficulty fixing them.

Those of us who wanted to bring the plot to the short story were thwarted; he admitted an open distrust of the device, in both its longer and shorter forms. If a story was plot driven it would eventually drive itself into a corner; better that randomness which is a more accurate reflection of life's wildness than that other clockwork causality.

But we would have agreed on exemplars—Joyce's "The Dead,"

Borges's "The South," Kafka's "Metamorphosis" and Gogol's "Overcoat." He was keen to remember all we forget when we read these stories—everyone remembers the sexual jealousy at the end of the Joyce masterpiece—but we have been at a party for a whole lot of pages up to that. And the longer we keep company with the beetle the more we forget his awful plight and find ourselves gazing with longing at the family life he has been cast out of. Life, he seemed to be saying, is played out against a large canvas of amnesia.

We should have focused on the voices which were so musical from the off. Listen to the old men eulogising all the variants of mashed potatoes in "First Snow of the Year"—"Ah, man dear." Years spent interviewing those men and women whose stories he transcribed for local journals stood to him. Here is the beginning of that patience which would enable his characters to go on at length and build up those oblique drifts of dialogue which slant through the late novels.

> *When I met him again he was holding himself delicately; his ribs were badly bruised. He'd fallen against a table at Neil Jordan's wedding.*
>
> *Playing air guitar, he explained.*
> *Who were you playing to?*
> *Buddy Holly or Chuck Berry, one of those. I always wanted to be a singer you know.*
> *I didn't know that.*
> *Ever since I was a child, but I can't sing at all.*
> *Who were your heroes, who did you want to be?*
> *Billy Fury, Halfway to Paradise.*

A few of those early pieces have an almost McGahernesque eye for the stifling intimacies of small-town Ireland. "The Curse" dwells on the same close, mean-spiritedness which so darkened *Nightlines*; "The Tenant," with its eye for rural hierarchies, covert sexuality and mortal fear of social embarrassment, could be one of the master's mid-period meditations. It's no coincidence that these two stories are the most linear and immediate of the entire collection.

And then the gap of almost twenty years between the collection and "Before the Off." This is an important piece and his longest short story. Published in 1999, it's tempting to see it as an overture to his final two novels. Here we finally see him pick up that patient lightness of touch which make his last novels so buoyant. Here is that sense of the author standing back and letting the characters have their say. However, its shifting scenes recall so many devices used in *Banished Misfortune and Other Stories*. Once again the eye is pulled along in a filmic survey of the town and the racetrack with its loudspeaker blaring out over the silence—"Testing, one two three"—before circling back to the two lads arguing at the bar like a married couple, the gypsies drinking warily in the corner . . . His last story "Images" (2013), a beautiful, intriguing piece, is unusual in being narrated in a woman's voice. Such an airy piece, so different in heft and balance from those early pieces.

He believed that concentrating on the novel pushed out the short story and he spoke of how he missed the genre, the neatness and beauty of it, how it begun here and ended there. But the commitment to the longer form would admit no short excursions, the odd poem now and again yes, but no short stories.

Not to worry. It is a marvellous thing to rediscover those wonderful wild pieces. With their shamanic intensity and electric charge they are more than enough to be getting on with.

The power in the small tent had cut and the singer was left high and dry, the electric guitar hanging lifeless on his hip; in the distance we could hear the band on the main stage. The whole place rested in darkness for a few minutes until a string of naked bulbs was found and plugged into a battery; they were left on the floor on one side as a kind of glowing nest.

His stride broken, the singer picked up his acoustic and strummed a few, slack chords.

Can anyone dance, he called, in a sudden inspiration. If I play will someone dance?

I'll dance, a young woman said, hopping onto the stage, but it's no use dancing alone.

I'll dance with you, a gravelly voice called. In one move he was beside her and had her pulled towards him.

If, by his own admission, there was no singer in him, there was no dancer either. It was a tango, of sorts, in which he kept to the one spot, both feet squarely planted. But he held the girl's hand high and she circled and pirouetted in a light which rose from the ground. She was elegant and he was her perfect foil. Together they were passionate and beautiful and they held the crowded tent together. They stopped, the electricity came back on, and light flooded in.

My wife reminded me of that one.

The Eve of St. John
Eoin McNamee

i.m. Dermot Healy

Midsummer night. The smoke of his fire hangs in the air
Between Tobar Eunan and Sliabh Liag.
The paths the geese follow must be lit for winter.

He stayed the night of the christening at McDermotts'.
The locals were upset.
Who was that man you brought among us?
We got rid of the old gods.
We don't want them back.

Stone thrown down and broken. Cry in the night.

He spent time with lesser angels.
They squabbled in the shadows.
He gave an ear to their disputes.

We saw him on Rockwood Parade outside St Bernadette's Chapel. Harried. Dissident. The network collapsing around him. He kept his head down, muttered something to us. Run you fools can you not see they are following.

Outside the church he put a coin in Kathleen's hand
And wished the child her fortune.

Silver in the hand. Foot in both camps. Lucky till his luck ran out.

This year he will not light the goosefields on midsummer. The geese broke clear and he broke with them.

St Bernadette. St Eunan. St John. Pray for us when we are gone.

A Goat's Song: A Writer's Appreciation
Annie Proulx

Dermot Healy's *A Goat's Song* is an exceptional novel, one of those rare books that permanently colour one's ideational map of place and human behaviour.[1] Its excellence raises the question of why it has not received more attention in the years since its publication. It is particularly rich in parts that encourage speculation and exegesis, examination of the quest for identity as old as human self-consciousness. It has been called a tragedy, for Jack Ferris loses his love, Catherine, but escaping an obsessive, destructive love spiralling toward insanity and hallucinatory drunkenness may be taken as a triumph.

A subtext of divisiveness pulls through the novel like an undertow, permeating it with a sense of malaise and breakage. Much has been made of the architecture of this novel, which, as some critics have noted, is unusual, as the beginning is the end and the end the beginning, the ancient uroboric symbol of the snake swallowing itself.[2] This technique (used by Homer in the *Iliad*) immediately excites the reader's curiosity and each backward-moving chapter is full of revelation. Readers have noticed the novel's momentum; it is the revelatory nature of the circular structure that impels the story. But at the same time the story is rigorously divided into four major parts and thirty-four chapters. We look at a map of Ireland and see the whole: yet it is politically and geographically divided; the cleavages of religion and language afflict its people; the characters in the story suffer divisions of identity and mind as they step in and out of their roles; the two lovers, Jack and Catherine, struggle to be together but are pulled apart. So wholeness and division tip back and forth. Dermot McCarthy sees this divisiveness more as duality: "*A Goat's Song* is a novel about 'the duality of things' or the way things are and the way they might have been. Tragic, romantic, melodramatic, it shimmers in the light of reading like the elusive salmon the quester lures to the surface."³

Jack Ferris is a Leitrim man of many parts, in his thirties, a Catholic, a failed medical student, a playwright, a small boat inshore fisherman who is suffering from a damaging love affair, suffering from longing for drink. Drink and loving Catherine are paired gnawing hungers. He lives in a remote hovel some miles from Belmullet in County Mayo, more than a little incommunicado from the rest of the world, but handy to the dock and the fishing boat *Blue Cormorant*. Later we learn that his father was a doctor and drove young Jack all over Ireland to compete in step-dance competitions, and that Jack himself enrolled in medical school. His mother expected him to do well and she is still distressed that he has become a fisherman. He is also a playwright, but that cannot erase the tang of fish.

On one level the novel concerns the lurching and ill-fated relationship between Jack Ferris and Catherine Adams, a singularly unsuited couple, though their irreconcilable differences become apparent only gradually as their story reels back to the beginning. No matter how desperately they try to love each other, promise fidelity and sobriety, it becomes painfully clear that their centre cannot hold. They have no chance.

As the book begins / ends Jack is expecting Catherine to come to him for the weekend. Catherine, an actress (as is her sister Sara), is rehearsing the lead role of Jack's play. (We learn only much later that the role is based on Catherine, that he has modelled the character in the play on the real woman who plays the part.) Catherine and Jack, who both drink heavily, quarrel, prove unfaithful and fall apart when they do so, have recently sworn to each other to remain sober and to love each other. But Catherine, on a visit to Belmullet, is informed by a man known only as "the gardener" that Jack is drinking. Jack has lied to her. It is the last straw. She does not come down to Belmullet, refuses to see him and when he persistently calls the theatre begging to talk to her he is refused. She ends their love affair, a situation Jack cannot accept. He begins to fray and shred.

Although Jack seems complete, he knows there is something very wrong with him. He is whipsawed by the existential question of who he is. Again and again, in drink and hangover, obsessive love and dreams, he is assaulted by the unbearable fact that he no longer knows who he is.

We first see this anxiety, which increases frighteningly as the days pass, when he gets on the bus to Ballina. He plans to catch the Dublin train and go to the theatre where Catherine is in rehearsal. He feels a sense of foreboding, feels diseased, feels his identity slip away:

> Reality had been a small window at the end of a dark corridor. Now a wall had gone up in front of the window. It was a skin-coloured wall. He had lived in his body and now it was the wrong body. . . . He was maddened by the other passengers, how their identities remained comfortable and intact while his careered around him. (25–26)

In Ballina he discovers it is "the type of day when anything might happen," that curious Ur-world of fiction into which a character may be slammed with the realisation of *all that could happen*. This moment is rarely one of benign enlightenment, but the instant when all the terrifying possibilities in life crash into the mind in a tangle and roar. And after a day of strange sights and drink Jack is driven home by a policeman whom he takes to be a New York taxi driver. The next day he makes it to Dublin and does not see Catherine. His friend the producer gives him some money and the advice to stay away from her.

Catherine is the younger of two daughters of Maisie and Jonathan Adams, the father a rigid-minded policeman with the Royal Ulster Constabulary (RUC) and a major pivot of the story. She is a blonde beauty, ambitious, romantically imaginative, highly sexual, headstrong with feminist leanings, a drinker. Her first sexual adventure was with a "stranger" and she is ever afterward drawn to strangers. She is Jack's "love object" (68).

The play opens and is a success, but Jack is not in attendance on opening night as he has made a nuisance of himself by repeatedly calling Catherine at the theatre while the play was in rehearsal. Jack goes to Dublin and lurks near the theatre until he finally sees Catherine in the street. They talk, briefly. Catherine is adamant, Jack hangdog. He goes back to his hovel. This brilliantly-drawn and complicated character Jack is the sum of his own problems—physical, religious, mental, cultural, regional, temporal, geographical and historical problems, to say nothing of fishing with illegal nets. Throughout the story Jack is troubled by who he really is, as he moves in and out of different minds and bodies.

When Catherine first meets Jack he appears to her as a handsome, older, sexually provocative working-class man. This is akin to the classic situation of the advantaged girl who falls in love with the good-looking fellow from a lower class background. She imagines Jack is an innocent, certainly less sophisticated, less experienced than she in sexual matters, but what she imagines him to be cannot stand the test of reality. Nor is she the ethereal maiden, but a hard-drinking faithless woman who promises more than she can give, and he, too, must depend on imagination to love her. Neither of them is accepted in their own identity by the other. Both are reshaped by the other's imagination. Small wonder Jack feels he has lost his identity when Catherine is wheeling from one stranger to another.

Because he feels diseased and lost, unsure whether he is an alcoholic or a schizophrenic, Jack asks his fishing mate Hugh, now the bartender at the Erris Hotel, to drive him to St John of God's hospital for the insane in Castlebar. He pins Catherine's photograph above his bed, an icon. His time at the hospital is almost a pleasant interlude; he wears pyjamas, he sleeps listening to the rain, he talks with other patients. He talks to the psychiatrist, a facile dodger: "You've had a nervous breakdown," the psychiatrist says, "and you can find out for yourself if you're an alcoholic. The only one who can tell you that is yourself" (49). Jack obsessively writes down the stories of the other patients at the hospital. He and the other Leitrim man talk often. The Leitrim man says "One minute . . . you're the one thing, the next, the other thing. How do you explain that?" (50).

In the hospital Jack has an interesting discussion with himself about Catherine and presence:

> She is not present. He cannot ask her to remain with him since she is not here. That is good. You are not present, whispered Jack.
> Now she can never return because they have misrepresented each other. He can never again exist as a possibility in her mind. That is good. He is not present where she is. (51)

Following this argument he is at least able to contemplate his life without her. He cannot love someone who isn't there. Not only are they mutually not present, but the ghost of absent presence is being laid. Absent presence has been graphically portrayed by the late landscape artist Robert Smithson who photographed a rock *in situ*, then removed the rock and photographed the cavity where it had rested: absent presence. Jack must fill in the hole Catherine has left behind.

He makes one more trip to Dublin. They speak uselessly and as he walks down Camden Street he thinks "the long drunkenness was nearly over. Now began the long insane journey into sobriety" (83). He realises too that "the role he'd written for her had released her from him," and that to free himself he must write about her, and that "once it became a story he would stop loving her" (79). Back in Belmullet he opens his notebook and begins to write the story of Catherine. As the child of Jonathan Adams her character is tied to her upbringing in his house.

Myths allow us entry into human psychology and behaviour. Much serious fiction is frosting atop mythological cake, the fiction enriched by the psychological values of ancient stories and wisdom. But Healy, as Melville with *Moby Dick*, made "mythologies themselves, as well as myths, part of his subject."[4] Two great myths dominate Healy's novel, the Greek myth of Dionysus (Bacchus), and the Irish myth of the Salmon of Knowledge.

The Salmon of Knowledge is a major myth of the Fenian Cycle concerning the magic fish who ate nine hazelnuts from the trees around the well of Wisdom and thereby became the bearer of the world's knowledge. In one of many versions of the myth, whoever first ate this salmon's flesh would absorb that wisdom. Aengus, the Irish Dionysus, the god of love, caught the fabulous salmon and told his helper Fionn to cook it but not to eat any. But Fionn, prising up a scale with his fingernail to see if the fish was done, got a concentrated drop of hot juice on his thumb and sucked it off. The knowledge of the salmon passed into Fionn. Another version says Fionn received only part of the Knowledge. One might think the longed-for Knowledge was a compendium of charms for success and fortune, but it was a very ancient wisdom that predated the Greeks—self-knowledge, self-identity—distilled into the concise philosophy "Know Thyself." All of the characters in *A Goat's Song* are pulled toward acquiring that knowledge.

Literary critic Dermot McCarthy focused on the Greek myth in his elegant essay "Recovering Dionysus." Among other apparent linkages, using several different versions of the myth, he equates Jonathan Adams with Aengus, and "helper" Matti Bonner with Fionn. In one version the salmon turns into a woman and breaks free before the hook is truly set. Here Jack Ferris is Aengus the Quester, and the salmon is Catherine.

In an interview with Timothy O'Grady Dermot Healy said,

> *A Goat's Song* comes from the word Tragedy; which came from a time whenever the wine harvest in Greece was poor the goat was slaughtered because he used to nibble at the vines. Then, after a while, instead of a live goat they had people dress up as goats and give the loud cry. The first actors had taken to the stage, and the drinking started, and people wandered the roads with horns on their heads and that is where the devil came from. So the festival of the goat is where theatre began; hence Dionysus; and why Jesus said the sheep would enter Heaven and not the goat. And there was another explanation: at night the farmers would put the he-goats on one island, and the she-goats on another, and at night the goats would raise a mournful cry, because goats can't swim.[5]

It is a myth particularly suited for this story in its oblique reference to the identity of a divided Ireland, but also because the Irish cherish the Atlantic salmon; the fish is a keystone in Ireland's identity. It remains today a magical creature, and in many places the first salmon of the year is still honoured at the table. Jack Ferris works as a fisherman on the *Blue Cormorant*, which sometimes fishes for turbot, then moves to the salmon grounds where the crew pull in drift or draft nets, now internationally illegal for their indiscriminate catch. Fishing has been a traditional following for millennia and continues as an economic mainstay in small Irish communities and ports. Jack's two occupations—fisherman and playwright—give him a kind of balance in practical and intellectual affairs. By intertwining mythological values, the dire love situation and Jack's employment, Healy inextricably knits mythologies into the story.

One of the most powerful parts of this novel is titled "Salmon of Knowledge," and concerns the story within the story of Jonathan Adams, his wife Maisie and his daughters Sara and Catherine. This is Jack's exorcism of Catherine through writing. His account of the events refers to the goat's song of the title. The scene shifts from the Mullet peninsula in the Republic, to the North.

The section opens with a shocking but somewhat stagy scene: thirteen-year-old Catherine Adams finds Matti Bonner, the friend and best man of Jonathan Adams, hanging from a birch tree between the Presbyterian and Catholic churches. Her untrustworthy memory and later dreams convince her that she saw the erect penis of the corpse. Embedded in the nested stories of the novel are numerous powerful dreams that throw the characters off balance: Catherine's dreams of Matti Bonner; Jack's dreams of Catherine's detached "frog" clitoris in his hand and his own severed penis; Jonathan Adams's dream of Catherine riding a goat along the edge of a cliff.

Jonathan Adams comes from a fervently Presbyterian family, and as a young man in the 1930s he attends several small seminaries with the plan of becoming an evangelical preacher. He has a strong scholarly bent. But when he graduates, and stands up on Sunday to preach for the first time he freezes up. He became "trapped in a set of thoughts which were denoted by the pronoun 'I.' 'I,' he said again and stopped . . . he suddenly realized: I know nothing of myself. To whom does this 'I' refer?" (99). And he could not go on. It was hopeless. He became a policeman as his father had been. As a policeman he was unyielding, a rigid stickler for the letter of the law and he hated Catholics, believed that Hitler's goal was to empower Catholicism in Europe. After the war he focused on the rampant smuggling between the Republic and the North. He began to keep a list of Fenians, and the list blossomed and grew into a massive annotated encyclopaedia of treasonous Catholics. The part-time police known as B-Specials began to filter up from the south. Adams, a paragon of paperwork, lived in the barracks in Fermanagh. His job was his narrow, scratchy life until he found eighteen-year-old Maisie Ruttle, "a gangly, fair-haired woman who was a Methodist, born and bred in the Free State. She had come north to work as a cook for Lord Brookborough" (107). They meet when a worker on a new estate road loses a finger to a winch. The man is Matti Bonner, a Catholic, and for Dermot McCarthy, both a scapegoat figure and a character from Healy's *The Bend for Home*.[6] Maisie bandaged the man and rode beside him in Adams's police car on the ride to the hospital. Adams and Matti exchanged no more than fifty words. He is twenty-five years older than she. A few days later, in one of literature's most awkward proposals, Adams said bluntly to Maisie, "Would you like to be buried with my people?" (108). Maisie persuades Adams to ask Matti Bonner to be his best man. Adams is shocked at the thought of having a Catholic for his best man, but he does so. Over the years Matti Bonner becomes his dependable helper and even, he thinks, a friend, despite his religion and origin in the south.

Jonathan Adams is one of the policemen involved in the 1968 protest march in Derry followed by the infamous Bogside riots. In a blind rage Adams loses control and passionately beats a man who has knocked off his hat, not realising television news cameras are trained on him. He is horrified to discover he has become a symbol of Protestant brutality as the scene appears on television screens again and again.

After this horror Adams is given three days leave and, at Maisie's pleading, he goes south with wife and daughters. They end up by chance on the Belmullet peninsula, and discover an idyllic place:

> They drove from Erris Head in Broad Haven Bay down to Blacksod in the south, amazed at the isolation, the white sandy roads that ran by the sea; the Inishkea Islands, holy, absolute; the wind-glazed violent cliffs; the meteorological station; the endless bogs, the rips and cracks through the huge dunes; the black curraghs; the lighthouse that sat perched on Eagle Island like a castle in a fairy story; the piers, the harbour, the sea. (119)

As the unrest intensifies in the North, the scent of fear is strong and omnipresent. Jonathan Adams is afraid, the police are afraid. Then Matti Bonner hangs himself, barefooted, his trousers torn by barbed wire, for he has run madly across the fields to his death. But why? There is no answer. Adams begins to see himself as an outsider in Northern Ireland and to look around for another place to live. Maisie, who misses the Republic, urges Adams to buy a house she fancies in Belmullet. Adams roars and protests but they buy the old lightkeeper's house. "It will be our summer home," says Maisie (141). The daughters are still young girls. It is the year Jack Ferris leaves college and comes to the fishing boats.

Jonathan Adams's character deepens as he settles into the Belmullet house. He begins to read history, hires tutors to teach the daughters Gaelic. Gradually his focus sharpens and he begins to write a history of Protestantism in Erris. Archaeology attracts his interest, the inscriptions on gravestones, stories, verses, old cures and curses, ruins, maps, all the flotsam and jetsam of past Protestant lives in the region find a place in his *The Mullet Ledger*. He believes it to be history. Finally he sends his collected source material to the National Museum, and when he hears nothing from that institution, he brings *The Mullet Ledger* to them. He comes back a thundercloud. "They took me for a figure of fun! I've picked my own out of their blood in a heap on the road and these Nationalists have the temerity to laugh at me!" (164). Wounded and insulted, he burns all his papers in the backyard.

One spring in Fermanagh Adams falls ill and after hospital tests knows his death is approaching. He insists they move to their lightkeeper's house in Belmullet which has been a place of refuge for the family for some years. There, in a gale-lashed springtime, in a morphine daze, he begins to read of Ireland's rivers until he becomes too ill. So a nurse, Sara, Catherine and Maisie read aloud to him all the versions of the Salmon of Knowledge—Aengus and Fionn, the silver hook, the salmon, its shadow on the rocks below, Fionn turning into a woman, a bird, love enchanting and elusive.

Readers who are not Irish bred and born often find themselves at a disadvantage in reading Irish fiction. In *A Goat's Song* the section on the years of the Troubles is, for outsider readers without a copy of, say, J. Bowyer Bell's *The Irish Troubles* at the elbow, a minefield of mysterious and mutable acronyms, nicknames, partisan newspapers, regional accents and expressions—RUC, RTE, UDR, Provos, Officials.[7] It is a truism that no one understands Irish ways except the Irish. And perhaps no one understands the complexities of Irish novels except Irish writers and readers. There is a scene in *A Goat's Song* that catches at the nature of the foreign reader's problem. Jack Ferris, who has sworn sobriety, is ruinously disappointed that his young and faithless lover Catherine does not come for a promised weekend. He has not received the many letters Catherine sent him since that promise, and in ignorance gets a ride to the Erris Hotel in Belmullet and drinks himself sodden in the hotel bar, wallowing in despair. A couple from Derry come in and sit at Jack's table. "Jack was glad they did because Northerners understood drunkenness" (22). As the Northerners understand drunkenness, so an Irish reader may understand the book. Even more importantly, countless strands of Irish history and mythology are threaded into this novel as with a hundred tiny needles, giving it the profundity and gravitas of Alan Paton's *Cry, the Beloved Country* and Chinua Achebe's *Things Fall Apart*. A lifetime backed by generations that have absorbed all that has happened in Ireland, that have heard and told the stories of invisibilities and twisting images of mythical heroes and fairies in the land may let the Irish reader more easily appreciate the most subtle intricacies of the novel; the rest of us can still be swept into it recognising it as a classic and wrenching human drama with universal meaning. When outsider readers approach the work of an Irish writer they may become aware of a curious in-country tendency to rank writers by their Irishness. Edna Longley refers to this sorting as "Irish, Irisher, Irishest" in an essay on nationalism, "From Cathleen to Anorexia: The Breakdown of Irelands."[8] Once recognised, this measuring is difficult to ignore, but *A Goat's Song*, through Healy's depth of insight into the human condition, Republican or the North, Catholic or Protestant, seems to rise above this report card mentality. Yet Jonathan Adams's gradual conversion to acceptance of, and fondness for, the South and the contrast of the Mullet peninsula with the hard and dangerous North tends to weight the novel on the Republican side.

Above all, there is fine writing in *A Goat's Song* of a quality that makes you rise up from your chair, go outside to look at the sky and give thanks. When Jack goes to Dublin to confront Catherine we see him in front of the theatre—"the bones of his forehead gleamed like horns" (36). Not only do we see the craggy supraorbital ridge but Pan, Bacchus, Dionysus, the goat, the devil. Healy's descriptions of place are vivid: "the sun worked a chisel through the clouds" (36); "there was a feeling that the dance music was issuing from a wireless where the hand had not quite found the station" (230); "on the beach the water crackled across the sand, then fizzled out" (241); "The hares . . . were leathery and brown and honey-eyed. With slow thrusts of their hips they moved off, then sat and listened. Then ran away a little, then stooped and squatted again. Their eyes were skilful and wild. Their coats weathered and grim" (254).

Dermot Healy is one of the best novelists of his time, with the virtuoso ability to tell a story through "the eerie language of the half-formed and the unsayable" (380). *A Goat's Song* is his masterpiece.

Notes

1. Dermot Healy, *A Goat's Song* (New York: Viking, 1995).

2. See Dermot McCarthy, "Recovering Dionysus: Dermot Healy's *A Goat's Song*," *New Hibernia Review* (Winter 2000): 148. McCarthy also points out many connections between *A Goat's Song* and Healy's memoir, *The Bend for Home* (London: Harvill Press, 1997).

3. McCarthy, "Recovering Dionysus," 149.

4. H. Bruce Franklin, *The Wake of the Gods: Melville's Mythology* (Stanford: Stanford University Press, 1963), viii.

5. Timothy O'Grady, "An Interview with Dermot Healy," *Wasafiri* 25.2 (June 2010): 5.

6. McCarthy, "Recovering Dionysus," 141, 145.

7. J. Bowyer Bell, *The Irish Troubles: A Generation of Violence 1967-1992* (Dublin: Gill and Macmillan, 1993).

8. Edna Longley, "From Cathleen to Anorexia: The Breakdown of Irelands" (1990), repr. *Irish Writing in the Twentieth Century: A Reader*, ed. David Pierce (Cork: Cork University Press, 2000), 1075.

Review Essay: Dermot Healy's *Sudden Times*
Annie Proulx

The Irish writer Dermot Healy has not yet attracted the international following his work merits, perhaps because his voice is strongly Irish, its wit and turn of language linked to place, the themes of his earlier books insular. But in *Sudden Times* he constructs a novel whose theme is both particular and general, starting with the common response of humans in situations they cannot control—they endure and get through—into the intimate story of a small-time carpenter and his moral suffering. The book invites comparison with Alan Paton's *Cry, the Beloved Country*, Ivo Andrić's *The Bridge on the Drina*, Chinua Achebe's *Things Fall Apart* in its power to pull the tragedy of contemporary political and social events into the story of a single life.

Sudden Times twists as a Möbius strip so that the character, Oliver Ewing, becomes the situation. The central events are revealed little by little through dialogue and narrative clips, the brief but interlocked scenes like cut film, a few frames, a few more until we see enough to catch the drift. In construction the novel is arranged in abrupt and odd angles, throwing light onto a floor which all at once becomes an abyss.

Ollie Ewing, a young Sligo man, has returned home following some undisclosed but terrible event in London where he has been working as a day labourer. He seems covertly blamed by those at home for what has happened there. We see him, edgy, paranoid, suffering nightmares in his attic, half mad with the noise in the street and the belief that men are after him, enduring certain glances and truncated conversations as he works at throwaway jobs, a little bartending, retrieving grocery carts at the market. That he does not maintain ordinary distances in daily affairs is revealed in several intense eye scenes: the "mirror image" passages where he believes a man is aping his every gesture, in a conversation about the flecks of colour in eye irises, flecks which may be tiny aliens from outer space, in the "child's eye" that he imagines in his forehead.

Through dialogue and narrative as minimal as a winter branch, Ollie's dread of confronting what has happened in London begins to colour the event as something half-real, half the black imagination rearing amid the frizzle of pop culture and day-to-day getting-on.

Suddenly—and that is part of it, for Ollie is someone to whom things happen suddenly—he decides to take a holiday "in Morocco." Liz, a young artist in his boarding house, asks to come along with him, but Ollie heads, not for Morocco, but back to London where the undisclosed events occurred and where his unforgiving father and vengeful men wait. At this point the story swerves back on itself and we are with Ollie (hammer in hand) arriving in London for the first time the year before.

He teams up with a friend, Marty Kilgallon, who is living in a trailer on an abandoned construction site. Ollie cannot get work as a carpenter, only as a day labourer. Gradually we see the labour infrastructure of the city as Irish, a loose network of men with shovels and watchmen's flashlights.

Things are pleasant enough in the trailer, Marty's photographs of Sligo on the wall, their food seasoned with a bottle of Chef Sauce that Ollie has brought from home. But the situation is menacingly surreal—the empty building site, a bucket of something dumped on Ollie by his fellow workers, Marty's mumbled hints that men involved in a construction extortion racket are after him. The name Silver John comes up. (We think of Long John Silver, later stand with Ollie at the junction of John and Silver streets in Luton, with him confront the silver paper on his burned brother.) And then Marty goes up north for a few days leaving Ollie in charge at their trailer site. During the anxious weeks when Marty does not return Ollie glimpses extraordinary urban secrets, dodges a sniper aiming down at him from a high building, sees and hears on a motorway overpass the "glass sprinkler," a diabolical machine that crushes glass and sprays it on London streets in the dark of night. Then Marty's acid-burned corpse is found in the back of his truck. His father, numb and off-balance, come to claim the body, says, while going through his murdered son's possessions, "These are sudden times."

He means that we live in a time when terrible things come at you with suddenness; the random sniper, the flung acid.

Ollie's half-confrontation and subsequent involvement with Silver John and his henchman, Scots Bob, show him as the reverse of the hard man; he is warped into a submissive relationship with those he fears, despises and suspects. He suffers a kind of *acedia*, a mortal and moral inertia. At the fatal party the confrontation he has unwittingly constructed flares violently, and in its aftermath come the varieties of guilt in the shades of grey that accompany sins of omission.

The long sixty-page section showing Ollie on the stand at the trial of Scots Bob is irksome in its length and for the hammering barrister who shapes Ollie Ewing's lack of action in life into sinister and political Irish plotting. This raging barrister is a kind of glass sprinkler and his slanted questions eventually awake in Ollie the inner barrier of the self. At a point the barrister sneers at Ollie's lame explanation of the random way in which things come together.

> Mr Ewing, are you telling the court that all that happened to you is based on chance?
> > Most things in life happen like that.
>
> Like what?
> > Like suddenly.

And there we have it, for "things in life" do fall on us like hard and unexpected rain, and most of us accept them with fatalism and stoicism.

Where *Sudden Times* vaults onto the large stage is back in Sligo at the goodbye party for the dead brother and the dead friend. All are there. There is unremitting music by the Not-So-Bads though no one is able to dance.

> Who's that over there?
> > Who were we at all?
> > We were members of the Where-The-Fuck-Are-We Tribe listening to the Not-So-Bads.

And, after all, the barrister was not so far off the mark, for it is all political, and we find ourselves examining the guilt of the "innocent" who stand uncommitted and uninvolved. We return to what seems to be a major theme in Healy's work, something cracked open, irremediably broken—a character's bruised heart, and the sense of identity and collective purpose.

On *The Bend for Home*
Molly McCloskey

I recall very clearly, in the way one does certain reading experiences, sitting in a threadbare armchair in the cottage in north Sligo where I was then living and reading a proof copy of *The Bend for Home*, Dermot Healy's idiosyncratic memoir. It was 1996, and though I may not have known exactly what made it so, I knew that I was reading something singular. I felt the sort of gratitude one can feel when in the presence of an affecting work—the recipient of a gift bestowed in the strange economy that exists between writer and reader.

In the years since, when I've gone back to the book, I've gone always to the final section, "It's Lilac Time Again," which struck me on first reading, and has ever after, as the memoir's most beautiful achievement. Healy describes here a period during which he is staying with his mother Winnie in Cootehill. It is the early 1990s, and Winnie, widowed years before, lives with her sister, Healy's Aunt Maisie. The two "dolls" are long since retired from the Breifne, the tea house they ran in Cavan Town. Winnie has Parkinson's and is succumbing to dementia. Maisie has her own age-related woes.

What I'd noticed on my first reading was the language: how, stripped down as it was, it managed to convey, in its tight rhythms and through the details on which it alighted, a rich emotional world, one riddled with faultlines and replete with tenderness. Recently, I assigned this section to a group of students in an Anglo-Irish literature module at University College Dublin. By then, I was interested in its preoccupations with home, not only as a physical location but as a psychic space from which one can become estranged. This sense of exile—from the self, from one's own past and present—is a recurring theme in Healy's work. In the final section of the memoir, with the house itself feeling like a "dream of unremembered objects," the writer's mother undergoes this process of splitting and estrangement in a quite explicit way: with her dementia accelerating, she becomes unmoored from her own history.

Lately, a different but related dimension of "Lilac Time" has struck me. It concerns the tension that every writer, and particularly the writer of memoir, must navigate if he or she is to produce work that is emotionally and psychologically rich and honest, and that yet avoids the taint of commodification. Writers are fond of decrying the marketplace's commodification of them; less often do we discuss our own acts of exploitation—our mining of other people's feelings and experiences to tell stories, stories we go on to sell, stories on which we build careers.

At one point Healy admits to a version of this: "I've stolen so many of Maisie's phrases over the years and inserted them into mouths and minds of fictional characters that she herself has become a work of the imagination." But the thieving of phrases and manners, even to the point where the actual person begins to feel to the writer a little less real in her own right, is not near as fraught as the sort of exposure Healy is really engaged in here—that is, his tracking of the degradations of ageing, incontinence and the loss of faculties that his mother is experiencing, and the turning inside-out for our inspection his own feelings for her.

I suspect that no writer who has ever taken seriously another person's privacies or the sanctity of intimate relationships—the sanctity of feeling itself, perhaps—has approached the sort of writing task Healy undertook without a measure of unease. This is as it should be. One is after all serving three masters—the human being who is the subject, the human being one is, and the work itself—and the three can exert very different, even mutually exclusive, demands.

It's a tension Roland Barthes states with beautiful economy in his book *Mourning Diary*, written in the aftermath of his own mother's death. Reflecting on the very activity in which he's engaged—the parsing of his grief, of his love for his mother, of her singular role in his life—he writes: "I don't want to talk about it, for fear of making literature out of it—or without being sure of not doing so—although as a matter of fact literature originates within these truths" (23).

What I find wonderful about this line is the way Barthes manages to pretend for a brief moment, or to pretend that he's pretending, that such a compartmentalisation of selves—his writing self and the self that was the loving, and is now the grieving, son—is possible, even desirable, before the pretence quickly collapses in upon itself, reminding the reader that to eschew the raw material of human emotion is to cut the legs from under art, and reminding the writer of the justification he needs to keep going. The self splits, or seems to, only to reunite in the act of commemoration, and in craft.

Healy touches, in various ways in *The Bend for Home*, on the splitting of the self, most explicitly when during his childhood the family gets a mirror in the house: "We learned faithlessness and duplicity from an early age. Always there were two of you there: the one in whom consciousness rested and the other, the body, which somehow didn't belong and was always at a certain remove."

It's an odd formulation. It seems backwards to me. For it is the mind that travels, *always at a certain remove*, while the body remains rooted to the spot, a prisoner of the present. But the point is clear: that the thinking, feeling self is the hidden self, and that one is guilty (faithless and duplicitous) simply by virtue of being a creature of a certain kind of consciousness—the sort of consciousness, in this case, that feels compelled to take notes as one's mother is losing her mind.

Philip Roth drafted *Patrimony* in real time as his father was dying, "in keeping with the unseemliness of my profession" (237). This unseemly remove poses not only a psychological and emotional dilemma, but also an ethical one. At one point Healy's mother remarks, with great lucidity: "You're spending a lot of time with the pen in your hand," and he realises that "while I've been watching her, she's been watching me." His mother's watchfulness niggles, as conscience niggles, reminding us that a writer who is dependent on his subject for raw material bears a special and complex responsibility to that subject.

And yet one cannot write as though being watched. So how does Healy navigate this tension? "It's Lilac Time Again" is to me one of the most moving passages in his entire body of work precisely because of the way he manages to be, all at once, at the service of the story, of literature, and of his mother's, Maisie's, and his own humanity.

How does he do this?

For starters, he doesn't flinch in the face of their indignities, for in order to be true to the dolls he must portray the range of act and feeling that comprise their lives—the moments of tenderness and beauty as well as the "ordinary shameful everyday." Only out of that contrast is a reader able to get a sense of what is being lost:

> *Once she was a very vain lady, now she'll turn aside at dinner and spit out meat she cannot chew onto the carpet.*
>
> *She fills her mouth at the table in such a manner that her small gorge cannot accommodate it, then up it comes, and she's on her feet to the door.*
>
> *Inside her bedroom door my mother is stretched out on her stomach. Her glasses are pressed into the carpet. She's shaking her legs like a stranded fish. Like a fish landed in a boat. We lift her together. She comes up straight as a plank and can't stand. The legs go backward and drag behind her.*

At one point, Maisie has a fit of retching due to a ruptured hernia. When she finally emerges from the bathroom, Healy asks if he should put the radio on.

> Yes, she says, at least let's have music.
>
> Then I go to clean the toilet. You'd be surprised how quick vomit sticks to porcelain. Why am I recording this? Because it's worthwhile telling that at the end of awfulness there's always a generous spirit who says: At least let's have music. The music would not mean what it does if we had not been in the bad places.

Similarly, the dignity would not be what it is had we not witnessed those assaults on it.

But any writer can record indignities, and looking squarely at the dolls' travails is only the start. What Healy does with the stuff of their days—the "human and domestic trivia"—is to treat it as seriously as he would any other matter. For a writer, this depth of attention and observation is the mark of deep respect. Having observed, Healy then translates what he sees and hears into art, through the exercise of style. Though the prose is fairly unadorned, the writing is in fact highly stylised. His rendering of Maisie as she emerges from the retching fit reads like Beckett (a writer Healy looked to and greatly admired), with Healy's interjections resembling stage directions:

> Now, oh. Her voice that of a young girl.
> She stops.
> Where is it? she says to herself.
> Goes on.
> Now see, she says.
> Stops.

Style is the tribute Healy pays to the women—this "making literature" that Barthes both chafed against and revelled in. The prose itself has dignity—care and seriousness and a lightness of touch—and thus restores to Winnie and Maisie, in their most difficult or degrading moments, a measure of dignity that age and infirmity are taking from them. One feels, on reading, not *this is what they suffer* but rather *this is what we suffer*, an erosion of the hard divide between subject and object that is enabled not only by style, but also—and this is the third way Healy navigates that tension between his writerly and human selves—by the writer's manner of implicating himself, occupying and giving voice to his own realm of unreality, just as his mother must occupy hers. He regards her condition as a state that is not so much alien to him as it is an exaggerated and heightened form of the fears and dislocations to which he himself is subject. When he writes, "We are trapped in what apparently is," or, "the mundane everyday feels like an illusion," he isn't camping it up, or piggybacking on his mother's dementia. It was his experience of the world, both rigorous and hallucinatory, a way of seeing that I imagine was the result of a mix of personal psychology, decades of excessive alcohol intake, and a fascination with illusion, reality, and fiction-making.

At one point his mother, following a bad fall that has left her eye a "mass of painful purple," looks across the room at her reflection in the mirror:

> The hurt is there, she said, in that person.
> She pointed over at herself.
> There, she said.

Her dissociation echoes Healy's own sense of the split self in the earlier mirror scene ("always there were two of you"), with the house, the home, now existing for them both as a place of slippage and rupture. Elsewhere he writes: "All those nights in the dark might never have happened." He is referring to the Magnet Cinema in Cavan Town, one of the dolls' ancient haunts, but it could serve as a summation of life as he himself experienced it: a dream state in which the real and the merely imagined are not easily differentiated.

This porousness to his mother's pain and confusion is a mark of what he refers to as a certain "telepathy" between them, an intimacy that is fleeting at best. ("Her genes have put in mine the same need to be away . . . and then with each departure, we're again embroiled in loss.") But it is also a prerequisite to the fourth element of Healy's writing I want to mention, which is perhaps a feature of all the best memoir-writing: the internalisation of the other.

> Today she is blissfully benign. She looks over at me and laughs while I make up things that never really happened, or if they did, happened to some other, some distant self that's been quietened by time, that never existed till words bring it again into being for further scrutiny. Then the inevitable happens. You come to a stop. The whole philosophizing sours. She even loses her earlier calm.

What strikes me about this passage is the way the point-of-view blurs early on—this "other distant self" to whom things may or may not have happened might be either or both of them; this "you" who comes to a stop might be any of us, as we come up against the limits of philosophy's consolations.

Eventually, Winnie must be prevented from leaving her bed at night. Healy rigs up an iron bed with a rail, and dresses her in nappies for the first time.

> She cried bitterly as the nappies were put on. I lay her down and closed the cage around her.
> I'm helpless now, she said. She watched me sadly from her cage and turned away.

I wouldn't suggest that Healy was being cheaply, or consciously, symbolic here, but it is hard not to see in the helplessness of this caged human being an echo of the subject who is at the mercy of the writer. What we also see, however, is Winnie turning her back on her son, in a bid perhaps to retain whatever remains of her autonomy, and some semblance of privacy. It is a turning-from that is a reminder of all that a writer will never quantify, record, or tell about another, because the other is always ultimately unknowable, and because language is only ever an approximation.

Healy knew this. He knew language's pitfalls, its habit of falsifying, as well as its capacity to sanctify. Like Barthes, he knew the "fear of making literature" out of mourning—that is, out of life itself—a fear that exists alongside a gratitude that such literature exists, that others before you knew that fear and proceeded, and that the results are your inheritance, as a writer and a human being.

At a certain point, in the living of such stories of loss, if we are sufficiently human in our dealings, something of the caged being in our care becomes internalised, so that what one reveals and withholds in the telling, and the manner and tone of revelation, begin to feel increasingly second nature. Healy's mother is watching him, half knowing, one assumes, that his note-taking may well concern the dramas of the day. Reading what has emerged from those notes, I get the sense that what oversight she might have imposed, he himself imposes—because of his love for her but also because of his respect for the act of making literature—so that what might have felt initially like constraints on his expression became, through that process of internalisation, more like intuition, just as the demands of craft itself become internalised, until they feel less like fetters and more like wisdom.

Works Cited

Barthes, Roland. *Mourning Diary*. New York: Hill and Wang/FSG, 2010. Print.

Healy, Dermot. *The Bend for Home*. London: Harvill Press, 1996. Print.

Roth, Philip. *Patrimony*. New York: Simon & Schuster, 1991. Print.

A Lift
Mary O'Malley

i.m. Dermot Healy

Tell me, is it all atomized energies
Or do the dead, as Baudelaire says, have bad hours?

The world goes on as wicked as before, or worse
Whatever history says. Because of us

We like to think. I'm not so sure. Remember
The time we said a decade of tunes in the car

To pass the time on the way to Derry, you giving
The first one, no stuttering allowed, me answering.

I'd like one more chat as we cross the border
Four packed in the back, faces solemn for the soldier.

Questions about fiddling styles, the long poem—
You were against it—where I stood on the bodhrán

And always the clouds parted and anything, statues
Soho strippers, homeless boys, a sinking cruise ship

Could appear there, out of nothing, like a flock
Of Maybirds because that's also how life is. Pure magic.

Remembering Dermot Healy and *I Could Read the Sky*
Nichola Bruce

I'm trying to remember the first time I met him. Somewhere in Dublin.
 We had rehearsals in hotel rooms. There were meetings in pubs. A mischievous innocent; there is a mischievous innocence in him, I thought. He was laughing in the pub; he said I was in two parts: the legs with a spring in them, and the top heavy.

London. We were filming for a week. He worked so hard that week he got ill. I think he emptied out. Acting in a vest in a chilly warehouse. Remembering the words. It was a lot of words to put meaning into, a lot of giving of himself.
 Seamus McGarvey was the cinematographer on that part of the journey. We kept to the hours and did three hundred slates. Early on, I had filmed many of the memory sequences for *I Could Read the Sky*: clouds and landscapes, graveyards, fallen houses. Owen McPolin filmed the remaining scenes on location in Wicklow at the home of the artist Pat Scott.
 The main character in the film never had a name. He was the Unknown Labourer. Dermot was cast for the part.
 I knew that the first time in most things carries a truth that is hard to regain when you have to repeat it. So everything we filmed was usually shot only once or twice. I asked that we record the first run-through on sound. A reading by Dermot of the whole script. Janine Marmot, the producer, along with co-producer Nicholas O'Neill, understood. So that's what we did and much of it stayed in the film.
 When I first heard Dermot saying the words, it was a strange moment. He knew his way around words after a thousand discussions with himself, out on the edge of a rocky outcrop in Sligo where he lived with the weather. Moving language around this

way and that, feeling the push and pull of his own tide. He could just say the words. He found the rhythm. Moments of tenderness, loss, redemption. The quiet spaces in between. It was all there. It was all there in Tim O'Grady's writing and in the way that the words were inside Dermot.

Tim had originally written the character as a man who was bald. I asked Dermot if he would shave his head. He looked at me with his head slightly to one side. Eyes that spend a long time looking out to sea; they move around a lot when he is uncertain and then fix you. The answer was no. If he did not have that windblown white-haired semblance of himself, we might go adrift.

I think Tim O'Grady and Steve Pyke had met Dermot when they were doing the book *I Could Read the Sky*. It is Steve's photograph of him in the pages of the book. This was the face I saw, as the book transformed from a large book of photographs with a foreword by Tim, into an eloquent story about a man recalling his past. The book seemed to grow into this story, with chapters of written words and chapters of photographs. As I moved the pages around on the kitchen table, helping to structure the layout for publishing, I could see the film in my mind and somehow Dermot was already imbedded. But I didn't realise this until later. He was quietly gazing out of the pages.

I had an archive of film that I began to reference. I wrote out a script following every word, just before the book went to print. Tim came to Hastings to read the script through. I filmed him reading it out loud, so I could understand how he meant it to be. I did drawings of how the film might flow, with images like words—separate but somehow rolling in to each other.

Tim had been listening to people's experiences as he travelled around writing, with Steve seeing and photographing. My mother tells me of the time she was drinking with my father in The Flowing Tide on the northside of Dublin with Tim and Steve, when a message came in that Tim's father had died in Chicago. So the book filled up with remembrance, loss, and the absence of a loved one. The distance between people in different parts of the world. Dermot became the man who would speak those words. Words that spoke about what it is to emigrate, to leave loved ones behind, to leave for work in a strange land. To grow up with ways of doing things like working the land that change their meaning when you end up working on roads and building sites.

Dermot asked me what I knew of this world. I told him about the year I spent working on building sites as a tosher, painting walls and ceilings. The nights spent behind the counter in the Tasty Tatty on Hornsey Road in North London, serving up baked potatoes spooned full of baked beans to the late night drinkers in muddy suits. The years spent in Kentish town in bars and pubs, trawling home in the early hours. The stories, the company, Brendan Shine on the jukebox. Also being alone in a room with the past swirling around my head; I knew something of that. But maybe it's not enough.

Was he interviewing me? This happens to me often.

The night before we begin filming we are sitting in a pub somewhere. Some pact made about total trust. He put his hand against my face in a fist shape. It wasn't like that, but it was too. Something about trust and not letting him down with the filming.

Opening night at the Edinburgh Film Festival. Everyone went into the cinema. We checked in with the projectionist. "Was everything okay?" "Yes," he replied. Then a few of us went off to have a drink and get back for the end. I was a wreck of nerves. Dermot went in to watch the film.

I got a phone call from him forty minutes in: "It's in the wrong reel order." My heart stops. We turn up back outside the cinema. Dermot is outside under the bright lights, moving about quickly. Saying how he was watching it, and that it wasn't making sense. I can't remember the rest. The night went blank. I remember feeling low for everyone who had put so much into it.

It turned out that this had been happening all week with the preview screenings for the press. The film was being shown in the wrong reel order. I don't know what it is about a film that you feel things so much. I still twitch thinking back on it.

Then the Galway Festival. The screening came with a standing ovation. I remember standing on the bridge near the cinema, just looking into the run of the river and thinking about that strange place of trust back in the pub and how you never know how anything is going to go.

Some time later, Steve Pyke, myself, and our two young boys, Jack and Duncan, travel over to Sligo. We meet Dermot at Ellen's pub—a long, pink-walled building with the name written outside in large black letters. He drives ahead along the winding roads to his home. The white-grey house set on a rise. A donkey looks over with its lip curling back as we park, a hee-hawing grin. The garden is heading towards winter, bursts of energy in rows, the end of things planted. I can't remember the month, but there was nothing coming up from the sea. Warm enough to go for a walk. But better to stay inside and have a drink. The boys need to get out of the car and run around. When I walk up to the house and around the side, there is a small cluster of empty wine bottles. Green plastic chairs tipped up against the table to keep the rain off the seats. The blue door with its net curtain pulled halfway across. I look in through a window, and see his computer crowding the desk, his papers scattered over, and his chair with a flattened cushion on it. Shelves line the room, filled with books. Newspaper cuttings, cards and family photos are pinned up on the wall. I wonder if he listens to anything when he is writing.

As we walk across the cliffs, he stops and points to a dark place set under the distant rockface with the sea crawling under it. "That's where the hermit used to live." We talked about the hermit and hermits generally. Dermot walks on his toes more than his heels. Maybe his name balances him. We stop. I sit down on the grass. We talk about the years of isolation the hermit had living away from people, gathering seafood off the rocks. What would it be like living in a cave and sleeping with the sea? Steve is balancing precariously on the edge of the cliff taking Dermot's picture. I am quieter with him now—a film set is so intense and now we are here, not in a big dark warehouse or the brawl of London, but out in the light. Dermot is sat where maybe he often sits. Just out of the wind, against a stony outcrop. Looking out.

When Dermot looked out like that, when we were filming, there was a faraway look in his eyes. These moments are not written in the script.

Jack and Duncan have run on ahead. I follow and tell them not to go near the edge. Then Dermot leads the way down, and we go looking for fossils amongst the dark rocks that splinter out to sea. White circles printed into the black shale. Further back on the grassy top we find sheep bones. Snail shells. We follow the thin pathways of rabbits.

Dermot is in his vest standing in the set built as a kitchen; he is over the sink, washing socks. There is a window with no glass that looks out onto a black wall running with pipes. Seamus McGarvey and I exchange looks; we can both see it. "Film him like this but quietly," I said. No slate, no "action!" or "running!" called. No concern with the clatter around us, of wood being hammered or props adjusted. Dermot sat in the chair wondering when would be the next chance for a cigarette, or who was feeding the dog in Sligo. Throughout the film we shot those quiet moments, often running the camera for just a few extra breaths, until Dermot himself broke out of the place he was speaking from. Those in-between moments carried with them a different intimacy.

At the house a small brown dog appears. It's Pat McCabe's dog. Dermot calls the dog "the spy," and says "he has a camera fitted in his arsehole." The dog skitters up the winding road towards us. He sniffs Dermot. Pat is not far behind, seafaring in his gait. I wonder what the dog would be spying on.

In rehearsal, we went through the script scene by scene: he would read it, and then we would talk it through and then work out the geography of movement. The emotional rise and fall of each mood. Putting in those words that he could find and place, and setting aside those that he couldn't. I had made drawings of the whole film, scene by scene. They helped make a shape.

Dermot's hotel room became the enclosed room in the film. He would be acting alone once we were on set. His conversations with other people, his moments of remembrance; all of these were in his head. We had filmed the memory sequences with the actors mostly in Dublin, but also some scenes in London. Now it was just Dermot for one week, under the lights, on set, performing in the present day to ghosts. A lad working on set volunteered to be the presence of others, to give Dermot a place to look at, so sometimes Dermot would say his words to him. Then there were the love scenes in the film. Helen, his wife, had come over to London to be with him. She stood at the edge of the film set with her coat on. He wanted her closer. She was shy about standing there. He said those loving words to her.

I drew up every scene again at the beginning of every day on set, as things inevitably shifted and scenes were pared back. Dermot fighting the shadows of his own memory and me seeing it become something else. Dermot talking to the walls, or lying down with his face pressed into the carpet. All these things leading to the inevitable breakdown in the film at the sheer incomprehensibility of the world.

Dermot understood the nature of the isolation, and the madness that can come with it. He brought the strength of his own fragility and tenderness into the film. I think we all emptied out, but Dermot brought some of the wildness of the sea and the wind with him.

30 June 2014: Sean O'Hagan calls me early in the morning, to tell me that Dermot has passed away. It was very unexpected. I haven't finished writing this article, and now I don't know how to.

Profile: Interview with Dermot Healy (1999)[1]
Vincent Browne

What Pyke and O'Grady have done is to read our imagination . . .

The above quote is taken from a review in *The Sunday Tribune* by Dermot Healy of the 1997 collaborative novel *I Could Read the Sky* by photographer Stephen Pyke and writer Timothy O'Grady. This book has now been adapted for film by director Nichola Bruce and features an astounding, show-stealing performance from Healy. Do we detect a faint whiff of nepotism here? Healy, with typical understatement, dismisses this out of hand:

> Ah no, it came about by pure chance really, it had nothing to do with me at all. It was Neil Jordan who suggested the whole thing to Tim. They were trying to cast it and were finding it difficult to get the right person. They phoned on a Sunday, I got the script on Monday, did the audition on Wednesday, and had the part that night. It wasn't on the cards for me at all before that.

This notwithstanding, Healy is, in many ways, the perfect person to play the role of an old Irish exile living alone in a darkened room in London, plaintively remembering significant people and events in his life. A poet and a novelist, with plenty of his own personal experience of emigration to draw on, Healy has always been interested in the individual voice and the ways that memory operates in people's lives. He founded *Force 10* magazine in Sligo in the late 1980s, a publication that grew out of the mix of the visual and the written—photographs and drawings with memoirs and interviews, short stories and poems—and it remains Ireland's

---

1. Vincent Browne, "Profile: Interview with Dermot Healy," *Film West* no. 37 (July 1999): 16–18.

most innovative literary journal today. Timothy O'Grady stayed in his house while writing some of *I Could Read the Sky*, and Healy's portrait appears in it as one of Pyke's "symbolically representative" photographs ("That had nothing to do with me . . . They just put it in . . . I don't know . . . I never asked them"). Excerpts from the book were originally published in *Force 10*. According to Healy, Tim liked the style of interviewing developed in *Force 10*:

> We would use a pen instead of a tape recorder which would make people repeat things that they had said. This way there would be three or four versions of what people are saying and you would get a kind of correspondence of the way people talk. Tim used this style to develop the character in the book.

Irish emigration in the middle years of the century reached such a level that there was hardly a family in the entire country that wasn't somehow affected by it. Is the experience of the poorer emigrant the last unexplored area of Irish life in the 1950s and 60s? "Well, it has been explored in literature by a few people but I don't think the Irish labourer has featured in film up to now," says Healy. "Often you need a distance from things to see them properly and someone taps into a vein of experience that's been there idling and the memory is then acknowledged."

Memory is *the* principal theme in the film and operates almost as an antagonist against which the archetypal character of "The Man" works. There is one scene that could serve as an emblematic motif for what the film is attempting to achieve. The main character visits his former neighbour, "The Tailor," to have a suit made for him. The tailor and his entire family have migrated to England, abandoned as he was by his customers in favour of the "shop." Healy, in a moment of understanding, looks into the camera and intones: "And then I see it—the absence of others draining the world."

This idea of absence in conjunction with memory runs throughout the film. Those who have left are always remembering those who remain, who in turn are missing those who are gone. Healy believes that memory can't be trusted, however: "The thing about memory is that it's always false. In *The Bend for Home* I tried to show the lies that memories make. You have to reinvent the whole thing and it's not the thing that happened."

Healy's performance in the film is nothing short of remarkable. The role demands that all of his acting is done straight to the camera as his character confronts the memories of his life. This is mixed in with voiceover scenes where he is watching the action from the outside, and so Healy's character is either on-screen or in voiceover throughout. The result is a brilliantly sustained tour-de-force that completely belies Healy's newcomer status. Equally remarkable is the fact that he hasn't seen the completed film yet, and a slightly absurd situation results whereby *he's asking me* about whether particular scenes are in the final cut or not:

> The filming was very strange as we shot the whole thing in London in five days and in that time I saw no other actor. I found it very frustrating not to have someone to sound off even though I was supposedly talking to other characters from my past, but there's no-one there. One day I had to call in a chippie to stand in for the Stephen Rea role, but it was okay, he was from the North so he was in character.

Healy lived in England for fifteen years in the sixties and seventies so he knew the society being depicted as well as anyone. This gave him a kind of empathy with this character that might not be available to many other actors, regardless of how much experience they may have had. He worked the building sites and factories every summer as a student, and moved there afterwards. This may also have helped him to appear so natural in the role, while he modestly claims that he was simply reading the text and hoping for the best. How does he look back on those days now?

> Well, all I remember is getting up in the morning, and building sites, and very long days. I wouldn't have been doing the full week. I would do two or three days to keep money coming in so that I could write. I wasn't depending on it outside of that. I was a day labourer and I would turn up in the morning and you would be picked or not by the

ganger. I would have no experience of being a good blockie or a chippie. The main memory I have is of coming home at six o'clock, having a pint, something to eat, and then being in bed by nine o'clock, exhausted.

Interestingly, Healy has a new book coming out in September which is set for the most part on the building sites in London. Called *Sudden Times*, it's about "a young fellah who goes over to London and everything goes horribly wrong for the next two years. There's a murder and he comes back completely bolloxed, totally brain-dead. It's based on a few stories that I heard. He's a kind of a dangerous paranoid." Healy went over to London to do some research for the book, and met a number of people who had given up on Ireland and had no intention of coming back:

> I went to a funeral of a cousin of mine a couple of years ago who worked on the Underground, and outside the church there were about thirty men I hadn't seen for twenty years, doffing their caps in respect. That was their life, they would trundle out, go back up to their room, watch TV, read newspapers, do crosswords, and that was it. They were all people who were there to stay. He wasn't going back—except in a box—and neither are they. They've fallen into the habit of life in the city and they couldn't break the routine, though some may have tried it with extended holidays. But they lost their way because [Ireland] is a very different country for them now. The film is very true to these people's experiences in that sense.

I ask him if there was any truth in the rumour that he would like to continue his acting career, a question he finds most amusing, laughing in the way that people do, when they know they've done something special and will probably get further offers. He also supplies *Film West* with an exclusive, and highlights the fact that the casting-couch culture is alive and well in Irish filmmaking:

> Well, I'll tell you the truth of it, the reason I got the part was that I slept with the producer [pause] . . . a "He" [laughs].

When I went up to meet Nicholas O'Neill, the audition was held in his flat. He booked me into a hotel on Baggot Street somewhere. I couldn't find it so I had to come back and spend the night with him . . . and that's how I got the part [more laughter].

He's still very cagey about his acting future though: "Well, you wouldn't say no, would ya? It makes a great change from sitting in a room on your own . . ."

As for the film, go and see it as a fine exercise in exploring histories that we already half-know, and realise that we have a duty to acknowledge the experience of people who, up to now, have been largely forgotten.

At the End of the Day
Garry Keane

i.m. of James B. Keane

"You're a masochist Garry Keane . . . you really are."
   "Ah now Helen . . . we planned all this."
   "Yeah, you and that mad eejit getting hypothermia over there! Nobody explained it to me . . . the pair of you are off your heads."
   "He'll be grand . . . it won't take long . . . I promise . . . and sure he can leave the sandals on . . ."
   I got the Helen look.
   "What's this all about anyway? What does this have to do with the story?"
   "I want him floating on his back in the sea as the geese fly over."
   "What! He has to stay in there till the geese fly over?"
   "God no . . . we'll add them in later."
   "Right."
   "It's Dermot's sea, Helen . . . he's going back to the womb!"

I couldn't keep a straight face and laughed, but I got that look again—stern but endearing. Helen was a woman who minded her man.

It was November 2010. Cameraman Michael O'Donovan and I were filming the final scenes for *The Writing in the Sky*, a documentary I was making on Dermot for RTÉ television. It was based on his poetry book, *A Fool's Errand*, about the barnacle geese who would arrive over from Greenland to winter on Inishmurray Island. They would fly over Dermot's house every morning for six months of the year:

> The same journey is made, again and again, by a wild goose,
>   tamed by centuries

of wind, which sets the hands on the clock, year after year,
   to map out remembrance and bring
  the unsure knowledge
to the door of the ruin on another island. (*A Fool's Errand*, 2010)

I first met Dermot in 1989. I had just returned to Ireland and was visiting my family in Donegal. Dad was heading up to Rosses Point to deliver the latest draft of a short story he'd written for "A wild man from Cavan," and he asked me to go along for the spin. Dermot had started the Markievicz Writers' Group, and they were busy putting together a collection for a new literary magazine called *Force 10*.

We pull up at a small whitewashed cottage in the middle of the coastal village.

It's windy.

Women with five hours work behind them, stomp the footpaths, arms flaying, faces scrunched, breathing deeply.

It's a Wednesday.

The angelus bells ring on the radio as we approach. Dad gives the door three loud knocks and we wait.

"He's not in."

"Ah, he's here all right."

One knock—pause—four quick successive knocks—pause—two more.

The familiar Irish knocking pattern brings me right back home. The code works and the door opens a crack.

"Ah Jim . . . come in."

We're led into the dark. I whack my head on the door leading to the sitting room, not thinking to bend. The pokey house smells of last night.

"Dermot . . . this is my son Garry. He's just back from London."

"Howiya."

He shakes my hand firmly and studies me properly.

"Don't worry, I have lots of London secrets too as well," he laughs wickedly and pulls away.

He moves around us slowly, opening curtains. He peers into the log basket for a long time. He picks up an A4 pad with scribbles on it, scans it and throws it down.

"Let me put some clothes on, boys . . . I'll be back in a minute."

"This fella's the real deal," Dad whispers, "he lives for writing. I'm glad you're here."

Dermot doesn't return for twenty minutes. While he's gone we sit quietly and look about. There's stuff everywhere: newspapers, drawings, paintings, handwritten notes, ashtrays, empty wine glasses, small clumps of tiny wild flowers, an old typewriter, a tape recorder buried under a mountain of traditional Irish tapes, and books—lots and lots of books: fiction, plays, biographies, history books, books on etymology, historic monuments, flora and fauna, books on Ireland—real stuff.

"What have ya got for me Jim?"

He reads, but mostly talks. He cooks us omelettes with fresh herbs carefully picked from a small terracotta pot on the window sill; we drink pots of good tea; we smoke; he observes unusual details and goes off on articulate, muddled tangents; he drifts into theatre-speak often; we spend a lot of time in the abstract, and time is never mentioned.

We arrive home well after six. I set about reading Dermot's books and I enjoy their company. I particularly love his language.

My Dad and Dermot meet each other often.

Family and career keeps me from seeing Dermot as much as I'd like to, but I keep in touch when I can.

Nearly twenty years after my first Dermot encounter, I pay a visit to him and Helen to see how they're doing. They're welcoming and smiling as usual.

I ask him what he's working on.

"I'm at a goose poem. I think I'm nearly there."

I keep a short silence as I wait for more . . . and it comes.

"I've been writing it for fifteen years or more. Probably ever since we first moved here. It stretches to over a hundred pages. I'm a bit obsessed by them I suppose."

Another thoughtful pause.

"I'm slow!"

There it was. The idea.

"Dermot—can I make a documentary with you on that?"

"You can if you want."

Dermot and Helen are living in Maugherow, in Sligo. Their cottage sits on the brink of a huge sea.

"We bought it in the dark, and struck the deal under the light of a match."

Dermot loves speaking about their house.

Their neighbour was a man called Jimmy Foley. Dermot loved being with Jimmy: "I'd sit with him night, noon and morning." Dermot speaks as he writes—in his own way. He would listen closely to Jimmy, noting stories and expressions in his head and would do whatever jobs were needed about the house. "I put a lot of things that Jimmy told me into me writing over the years," Dermot would tell me. "One time I asked him: do you ever get lonely?"

> I'm never lonely,
> said Jimmy Foley,
>
> I know that I'm here,
> that's all.
>
> I might sit up till two
> or three, happily.
>
> Lie down,
> get up again.
>
> A couple of hours
> On my back
>
> will do.
> Lonely? No.
>
> There's enough
> in my head
>
> to do me
> for a while longer.

After that
who knows?" ("Loneliness," *What the Hammer*, 1998)

I arrive up to a wild, blustery Maugherow at six in the morning to film the geese. They are all over the place as they fly in—ten or fifteen at a time. I have grown fascinated by them. The tea is on when I get up to the house after nine. Helen is at work in town. Dermot is on his own. Morning rituals are underway. Particular attention is being paid to the creation of fire. Country people are pyromaniacs by nature, but Dermot is fanatical. The grate is set with meticulous precision.

Pride registers when the kindling takes.

"Dermot, the sea looks big enough to get the shots I need. Can we do that today?"

"Okay . . . We better not get too close though—a stray one and we'll be gone."

We have a delicate breakfast and clamber over the rocks. The place is a treasure of fossils and personal visions of remote pasts always make their way into the conversation. Tiny the dog comes with us. He's lovely and is loved. He leads the way, tail wagging furiously. Tiny accompanies strangers across the rocks if he comes across them. He is kindhearted and knows the way.

I start filming, asking Dermot to do this and that. He moves slowly and is patient. He never questions or moans. A massive wave crashes a few feet away from us and I hug the camera to keep it dry. Dermot ducks and gets a little wet.

"I told ya!"

The sea was everywhere and everything. Dermot and Helen live with its thumping under their bed:

> *Meself and Helen often get up in the middle of the night, thinking someone is at the door but it'd just be a wave breaking out the shore. I've been in New York before and had this feeling like I'd lost something, or left something behind me. I'd be looking in my case, searching about the room wondering what is it?, what is it?, and then it'd dawn on me: it's the sound of the sea . . . That's what I missed.* (*The Writing in the Sky*, 2011)

Dermot calls a halt to the filming at exactly 5:45pm.

"Will we go up to Ellen's for one?"

"Aye, okay."

The prized local opens at six. Dermot sits at the end of the bar with his back to the partition wall. Without ordering, a pint of lager and a pinkish drink in a wine glass are placed in front of him. There are many comfortable silences. I ask Dermot if he fancies a bag of Tayto. He says no and eats most of mine. A few arrive—the writers Leland Bardwell and Brian Leyden, and Dermot's good friend, Seán Golden.

The geese have arrived too.

"They came back the other day, did you see them?"

"Yeah."

"What is it Mrs McGowan used to call it Leland? The writing in the sky, wasn't it?"

"Yeah. I used to think it looked like a cardiograph . . . I have that in a poem somewhere: the cardiograph in the sky."

"Go way."

"Every morning, every evening they come and go . . . things are sure, things are certain . . . they follow their season."

"I think the flock is getting bigger . . . I watched wave upon wave of them coming across the house this morning. I began thinking of them as flights of bombers." (*The Writing in the Sky*, 2011)

We go back to the house and after a home-cooked dinner, I ask Dermot can I do an interview with him. I want to talk about the geese.

About three thousand of them arrive over every October and they stick around until April. I must have filled over forty notebooks of writings on them—taking them out while they're here and putting them away for the six months that they're gone. They fly across the house five minutes after first light to feed, and fly back to the island five minutes before dark. They're like an ancient clock . . . and I suppose I've been trying all these years to wind the hands. (*The Writing in the Sky*, 2011)

Over the next few months, I take to the road to do other interviews for the film. People agree without hesitation and talk about Dermot easily.

> *He is the heir to Patrick Kavanagh. Kavanagh was the poet of the passionate transitory, bits and pieces of every day, snatched out of time. He was the poet of praise for these things. It isn't just nature poetry in Healy, it's gratitude for the whole gift of existence, and a complete accuracy of ear for the language.* (Seamus Heaney)

> *He wrote the finest memoir ever written in Ireland—well, in the last 50 years anyway. I think Dermot is kind of obsessed by the nature of memory, the tricks it plays and how language can attempt to capture it, throw a net around it, but it's nearly impossible . . . and he accepts that.* (Patrick McCabe)

> *When I said that I really meant it, that I did think he's Ireland's greatest writer.* (Roddy Doyle)

I'm back in Dermot and Helen's.

"Do you want to know what they said about you?"

"What? That I'm a bollix?"

"I meant about your writing."

"Nah, whatever they said, they said. It's none of my business . . . Did you go for a pint with Heaney? He's great company."

Mick Mahon gets Dermot completely and edits the film beautifully. We spend long nights, afternoons and mornings in a semi-darkened room together, alone with Dermot. We lament the comments and beautiful moments dropped to make duration. We dream of funding to edit a longer version, but it never comes.

Dermot did that: made you want more, made it hard for you to leave.

Or made it easy for you to stay.

"Don't you just hate the phrase, *At the end of the day*? What does that mean anyhow?" he would grumble. "I can't handle that one at all."

There is no end of the day Dermot.

Land of Dreams
Gerald Dawe

i.m. Dermot Healy

> *They passed the streams of Ocean, the White Rock, the Gates of the Sun and the Land of Dreams, and soon they came to the field of asphodel, where the souls, the phantoms of the dead, have their habitation.*

JJ snatches salmon on the Salmon Weir Bridge
    or the Claddagh, then, in newspaper folds
sells for what he can the shimmering fish.

    Matty Lydon's back—"I was schooled
in three universities but the best of the lot's
    Limerick: how are ye fixed for the rough touch?"

Render unto Caesar the things that are Caesar's
    young Matty recites as he dumps leaves over
the Bishop of Galway's palatial gates.

    The tourist guide on pony and trap
passes Moon's Corner as some kids sing
    "Oh Lord it's so hard to be humble."

"You'd not see the likes of that in Utopia," he quips.
    One bright spring day, the shopkeeper looks both ways:
"Fucking massive" is what he says.

    Nicholas, the dapper barman of Garavan's calls
"Last Orders"; aloft, red-lipped Una Taaffe,
    whelps at her stocking-less feet, sweeps all

before her as the Patrician Brass Band, caps
and instruments flood my room in waves of light.

SECTION II:
CRITICAL RESPONSES

"The small stone that no one sees gives all the balance": Unique Perspective and Personal Idiom in the Works of Dermot Healy
Seán Golden

He heeded things that others ignored. His poetry held pride of place in the *Soundings 2* anthology that Seamus Heaney edited in 1974. One of those early poems captured the importance of detail heeded and the significance of things absent, themes that would dominate his subsequent work (Heaney, *Soundings 2* 19):

> when the cat died
> of cat flu, the kitten
> looked round anxiously
> at night,
>
> waiting for the sneeze in the dark.

Another introduced an East Asian perspective and idiom (10):

> Li Po
> has circles
> under his eyes
> from the drink
>
> like the dark
> circles on stormy
> nights
>
> under the moon.

Li Bo 李白 (699-762) was the most celebrated poet of the Chinese classical tradition. He never succeeded in public life but was revered by the poets of his and later generations for the passion of his poetry. His best known poem celebrates life and company despite being completely alone and having drink to share by inviting the full moon and his moon-cast shadow to revel along with him. His lifelong friend was Du Fu 杜甫 (712–770), the acknowledged master of classical form, a public man and his advocate, whose dominion over form was more difficult to appreciate than the readily accessible emotional content of Li Bo (no mean master of form himself). They form a complementary pair at the pinnacle of Chinese poetic rhetoric: content and form, reception and production, aesthetics and poetics, readerly and writerly, *lecture* and écriture. Healy quoted Li He 李賀 (791–817), another master of the Chinese classical tradition, in the story "Jude and his mother" (66). Li He was reported to go riding inebriated, accompanied by a servant, and literally toss off disconnected verses on bits of script that the servant gathered behind him, to be harvested later and reworked into masterworks of poetry, anticipating the cut-up techniques of Tristan Tzara or William Burroughs or Brion Gysin. Healy did not do cut-ups, nor engage in chance operations, but he did accumulate in innumerable notebooks spoken phrases, quotidian incidents, that would serve later to weave into poems or narratives or theatre, details harvested then selected to furnish a unique setting, a kind of *bricolage*, like the bowerbird whose each constructed nest is decorated uniquely, competing with all others to attract a partner attuned to the originality of its taste (Golden, "Familiars in a Ruinstrewn Land" 428).

But in fact the style of Healy's short poems comes from Matsuo Bashō 松尾芭蕉 (1644–1694), the Japanese master of *haiku*, a *genre* in which the juxtaposition of carefully chosen homely details sparks a glimpse of an enormity that can be known but not expressed. He first read Bashō in the 1960s. Born Matsuo Kinsaku, Bashō is a pen name taken from the banana plant (*bashō* 芭蕉) some followers gave him for his garden. Healy was especially pleased to learn that Bashō chose for his name a symbol with connotations in Chinese and Japanese poetry for fragility in the face of storms and exceptionality for the climate. The short-circuit produced by *haiku* in the East Asian tradition does not work in the same way as the *epiphany* from the European tradition that James Joyce used to conjure a more explicit kind of revelation, though both evoke the recognition of something beyond what words can say.

That early metaphor of the kitten's loss introduces a deep-seated anxiety or apprehension for something gone or almost there, for the absence that is as important as presence, that haunts Healy's work, as does the use of a unique perspective and a personal idiom to express them. His affinity for an East Asian perspective was intuitive, not based on study, but an informed understanding of East Asian perspective can enrich the appreciation of his work, as I will try to show in this study.

The classical Confucian text 中庸 *Zhongyong* states a paradox that is common to many aspects of traditional East Asian thought: 莫見乎隱，莫顯乎微 *mo jian hu yin, mo xian hu wei*, nothing is more visible than something hidden, nothing more overwhelming than something minute. Daoism and Zen Buddhism give the paradox another twist, as Wallace Stevens—who did study Zen art—frames it in "The Snow Man" (Qian 92–93):

> For the listener, who listens in the snow,
> And, nothing himself, beholds
> Nothing that is not there and the nothing that is.

Zhuangzi 莊子 (369–286 B.C.E.), perhaps the most interesting of ancient Chinese thinkers, calls for 齊物 *qiwu* treating everything equally, giving no one thing any importance, or what is the same, giving the same importance to every single thing, as a way of avoiding discrimination of any kind, since discrimination leads inevitably to the injustice of disputable priorities. He uses the example of 天籟 *tianlai* the pipes of the sky, bamboo pipes of varying lengths pegged into the ground so the wind blowing across them would play musical notes, like blowing across the mouth of a bottle (the term could also be translated as the flutes of the sky), like the murmuring of the reed bed or the ornithomancy of an augur who could read the sky, the writing in the sky (perhaps a wild goose chase, a fool's errand). This seemed to be a form of divination, allowing the ancestors to express their will musically, calling upon diviners to interpret their music.

Zhuangzi asked why we should give more importance to the musical notes produced deliberately by a human flautist than to the musical notes produced by chance by nature, the kind of question Marcel Duchamp and my mentor John Cage would ask in the 20th century. Healy's unique perspective also gives each thing its weight, avoids privileging one aspect over another, leaving the reader free to weigh things up rather than telling him/her what each should weigh. As a result, his work tends to escape the confines of conventional *genres* and readers' expectations, producing an idiom, a literary idiolect, so personal it becomes inimitable.

Perspective in East Asian landscape painting works differently to that of European perspectives. In European art things converge on a vantage point vanishing perhaps over the horizon. A mountain viewed from the base dwindles toward a point in the sky, distorting the view of the summit. In East Asian landscape painting we see the mountain from a stack of perspectives. Each height of the mountain is present at eye level to the spectator, who thus ascends it virtually in the act of viewing it. The same is true in classical Chinese poetry set in the mountains. To understand the scene being painted by the words the reader must assume the poet's perspective, a perspective that adjusts itself to each height of the mountain, not discriminating one view from another nor privileging one perspective over another. The role of the human in East Asian landscape painting is reduced to a minimum as well, letting the observation-representation lend all of the elements composing the scene an equal weight. Empty, unpainted space makes palpable something not physically present, suggesting clouds or mist. Absence becomes presence, like the cat's missing sneeze in the dark.

In *What the Hammer* the cat appears under various guises, including "Death, the Cat," (20):

> It pitied me as I turned my mind to other things
> and began to think of finishing the wall on the beach.
>
> I counted the number of books I needed to write
> before I'd feel worthwhile.
>
> I thought of those I'd known who've died.
> Soon I was down on the actual beach

> building a wall I knew would be taken away
> in a January storm.

The building of actual walls will also take on added significance in his work (and in the conclusion of this study). The paradox of the missing voice of the cat and the resulting anxiety returns in *The Reed Bed* in "The Cat" (63).

> The cat who has lost her voice
> is the cat that calls out loudest.
>
> So it is when the muse goes
> into the terrible silence.

And "Joe Donlon" (*What the Hammer* 22) tells how the silence can be more existential, more than a writer's block, how words can be inadequate inevitably, how there are things unsayable, not out of some difficulty in finding adequate words, but because there are things that cannot be said. (Can they then be known?)

> We seem then to flounder,
> the dog and the house and myself,
> towards what I cannot name.

There was a skit by the famous German clown Karl Valentin, searching on stage the circle of ground lighted by a street lamp. A policeman enters, observes, joins the search; pauses, asks the purpose of the search—lost house key, continues; stops in frustration: "Are you sure you lost it here?" "Oh no—I lost it over there," indicating an area obscured by the darkness. "Then why look for it here!?" "Because there is no light over there" (*Dilemma of Modern Belief* 58–59). Dermot Healy explored the obscurity, the neglected darkened wings of an otherwise well-lighted contemporary scene.

Sometimes silence, or the lack of light, leads to disorientation, to *jamais vu* or *presque vu*, where the familiar becomes strange or we see-saw on the cusp of understanding, as when Owen goes astray through otherwise familiar bogs in the first published version of "First Snow of the Year," running the risk of falling into a boghole, and must take off his jacket, turn it inside out and put it on again, the traditional remedy to heighten the shock of unfamiliarity in order to facilitate recovery of the recognition of the already known (7). Or like the disorientation of "After the Silence":

> The moon stood
> Like a drunk
> Looking up the street
> Wondering,
>
> Is this the street,
> Is this the town,
> What happened,
> And who did I meet? (43)

Or "The Reed Bed":

> and then I start
> wondering what is it I lost,
>
> what was that thing,
> that important thing,
>
> I left behind me
> on the dreaming road? (29)

Sometimes the silence, or the lack of words, can be a relief, can put things in their place, à la Zhuangzi, like "The Hares on Oyster Island," where natural rhythms became a refuge:

> May they have long lives,
> The hares that afford us a break
> From the language that would explain them. (48)

The epigraph to *The Ballyconnell Colours*, taken from Federico García Lorca, of whose play *Blood Wedding* Healy would make a version, states the gap between understanding and expression, the unattainable bend for home:

> *Although I know the road*
> *I will never reach Córdoba.*

Circumstances alter cases. Landscapes make a difference. Nature itself is subject to point of view in "Two Moons":

> The moon above Sligo
> Is not
> The moon above Mayo. (55)

Octavio Paz wrote, "*El sol que canta el poema azteca es distinto al sol del himno egipcio, aunque el astro sea el mismo*" ["the sun the Aztec poem sings is different from the sun of the Egyptian hymn, though it be the same star"] (2). Jorge Luis Borges, whose story "*El Sur*" ("The South") was one of Healy's favourites, wrote, "*La luna de Bengala no es igual a la luna del Yemen, pero se deja describir con las mismas voces,*" the moon of Bengal is not the same as the moon of Yemen, though they allow themselves to be described with the same terms (81).

But language insists. In the epigraph to "An Open Letter" Seamus Heaney quoted Gaston Bachelard: "What is the source of our first suffering? It lies in the fact that we hesitated to speak. It was born in the moment when we accumulated silent things within us" (*On Poetic Imagination*, xxxvii). Samuel Beckett's four certainties included his inability for reasons unknown and unknowable to stay silent. He wrote of "the obligation to express" ("Three Dialogues" 139). Still, the narrative voice in Healy's work, in concert with the varying forms he evolved, tries to bridge the gap. There is a notable urge toward aphorism in his early work, the *persona* of the narrator or the poet proposing some kind of existential conclusion on the basis of narrated detail, as in "The Island and the Calves":

> He appraised the tension trembling in the hare's back, the jump withheld in the joints of its knees; Jim had interrupted a joyous fling around the wild apple trees . . .
>
> And even though this was an emotional, fundamental fashion of discovery, yet when the wind died down (no west wind ever blew) and passion departed, when passion departed and reason returned to the branches of a tree separating the heavens and the earth, when he stood bewildered by the strange simplicity of the sorrowful day that follows the joyous day, when man's heart might take that agile journey towards always discovering anew, still the points of that compass held firm . . .
>
> For at last he had authenticated the outside world, and each part was now sustained by itself and no longer needed a deity or an interpreter for a tiring audience. (17–20)

But the urge toward aphorism of Healy's narrators avoids any confirmation of received wisdom. Their unique personal idioms produce what ne'er was thought, but oft so well expressed, to invert Alexander Pope's formulation. The wit of Irish conversation when carried to the level of a contact sport depends upon one's ability to vary a commonplace expression, not on the recourse to clichés. Such parody requires a shared repertoire of stock phrases that lend themselves to variation. Language teachers and students are familiar with the cloze test, wherein certain words are deleted from an authentic oration, to be supplied by the student. The cloze test requires native or near native fluency to supply the correct words, that is to say, the words a native speaker would expect to hear in a given context. Myles na gCopaleen, with the invaluable and unerring help of the Plain People of Ireland, worked this technique to perfection when skewering the catechism of clichés used by politicians and the communications media. The aphorisms that Healy's narrators try to formulate defy the equivalent of any such cloze test based on established literary conventions.

This tendency gives way in the later work to an exterior polyphony of voices and descriptive details, a palimpsest the far side of interior monologue. Healy's greatest strength as a writer consists in this ability to create and sustain a unique and complex style. He invented a new grammatical category—the narrative mood. In *Banished Misfortune*, his first collection of stories, he demonstrated an innovative ability to restructure narrative and to sustain an intense mood, as I have suggested elsewhere ("Traditional Irish Music" 21–23). In *Fighting with Shadows* he built upon and expanded his earlier experiments while achieving a remarkable degree of control and consistency (Golden, "Oriental Sense of the Border" 18). The works that followed each sought its own new form. There would be no repetition, no predictability. While true to his own originality, he did wink at experiments of the Master. *Sudden Times* renews the use of headlines from the "Aeolus" chapter of *Ulysses* and the *ricorso* of a circular narrative that structured *Finnegans Wake* is renewed in *A Goat's Song*. I seem to recall it having been said that James Joyce could have turned out bestsellers on a regular basis had he wanted to but chose not to because he abhorred the repetition of form. Thomas Hardy told Robert Graves, "All we can do is to write on the old themes in the old styles, but to try to do a little better than those who went before us" (*Goodbye to All That* 251). Joyce told Arthur Power, "The important thing is not what we write, but how we write, and in my opinion the modern writer must be an adventurer above all, willing to take every risk, and be prepared to founder in his effort if need be. In other words we must write dangerously" (*Conversations with James Joyce* 110). Samuel Beckett spoke "of an art turning from [the plane of the feasible] in disgust, weary of its puny exploits, weary of pretending to be able, of being able, of doing a little better the same old thing, of going a little further along a dreary road" ("Three Dialogues" 139; Golden, "Post- Traditional English Literature" 16).

More must be said about his style, the single most noticeable and pervasive element of his work. No one else writes like Healy, nor could. The Dermot who was capable of capturing half-closing day in Cavan town shares this trait, this originality, this unpredictability, with the Dylan Thomas who wrote *Under Milk Wood*, or his namesake, Bob Dylan. His stylistic approach to the problems of narrative makes discussion of plot, characterisation, dialogue, exposition, the traditional tools of the novelist, almost irrelevant. His novels have characters and tell stories. The characters live as memorable individuals but not as flashily individualised stock types. His approach to characterisation creates the effect of a hand-tinted monochrome, a vision of a set of individuals objectified in intimate relation with their environment. The narrative voice of a *persona* intermingles with the thoughts and words of the characters to such an extent that it could as well be said that the characters live to contribute to the creation of that narrative voice, which, unspecified, avoiding the embodiment of an "I," shares their lives at the same time that it creates and comments on them. It also creates the living world around them. Healy understood well Frank O'Connor's call for narration to "[ring] with the tone of a man's voice speaking," the oral tradition of the *seanchaí* that Healy himself embodied (not to mention his affinity for O'Connor's "submerged population group"; *The Lonely Voice* 29). Healy's narrative voices weave in and out and among the dialogue, plot, description and exposition, adjusting their points of view to each moment, like the spectator's point of view weaves in and out of the scene of an East Asian landscape painting, raising and lowering its vantage of a mountain as each of the levels demands.

Healy's work has this East Asian sense of proportion, of man's place in the world, not as a figure dominating the foreground but as a contributory detail to the whole effect. Background and foreground merge. Style replaces character and plot as the key element of his work. It is vivid and flexible, an elliptical complex of acute and apt observation, aphorism, wit, hilarity, poetic image, musical phrase, word play, and verbatim dabs of local idiom which dapple the text with authenticity. He composes phrase by phrase, juxtaposing and accumulating observations and details, avoiding authorial intrusion or belaboured transitions, leaving gaps to be filled by intuition. Quantum leaps of energy from phrase to phrase, shift of perspective to further shift, image to aphorism, make reading the text an experience of the text—and that experience justifies the text. The strength of his work rests on unique perspective and a very personal narrative idiom. His work has been faulted for those very strengths because it defies conventional categorisation, but his work successfully tackles problems of contemporary life in Ireland that have foundered more conventional treatments.

As a result, he has been called "a writer's writer." Writers seem to agree, and see this as a merit. Some critics have doubted the accessibility of his writerly style to the "ordinary" reader. This apparent antinomy bears further reflection. Ezra Pound was called "a poet's poet" and many readers of poetry were perplexed by the importance other poets gave to his dominion over poetic technique (for T. S. Eliot, himself the darling of literary critics, Pound was *il miglior fabbro*, by analogy with Dante's admiration for Guido Cavalcanti, though he placed him in Hell). My mentor, Louis Zukofksy, was called "a poet's poet's poet." The idea that Healy is a writer's writer, perhaps *the* writer's writer in Ireland today, merits further analysis (although he would pay tribute to Aidan Higgins and Tom MacIntyre). Why does his work fascinate other writers and why are some readers perplexed by it? That being the case, let writers speak on his behalf. Beckett praised Jack B. Yeats for "this unparalleled strangeness which renders irrelevant the usual tracing of a heritage, whether national or other" and affirmed that "[t]he artist that stakes his being comes from nowhere. And he has no brothers" ("Homage to Jack B. Yeats" xi). Gertrude Stein quoted Picasso on the cost of originality, on the cost of creating something outside the confines of convention and established taste:

> Picasso said once that he who created a thing is forced to make it ugly. In the effort to create the intensity and the struggle to create this intensity, the result always produces a certain ugliness, those who follow can make of this thing a beautiful thing because they know what they are doing, the thing having already been invented, but the inventor because he does not know what he is going to invent inevitably the thing he makes must have its ugliness. (9)

Arnold Schoenberg defended the right of the individual artist (himself) to explore beyond the confines of established taste of the majority:

> That is my situation: I find myself in a minority . . . It would be inconceivable to attack the heroes who make daring flights over the ocean or to the North Pole, for their achievement is obvious to everyone. But although experience has shown that many a pioneer trod his path with absolute certainty at a time when he was still held to be wandering half-demented, most people invariably turn against those who strike out into unknown regions of the spirit . . . New music is never beautiful on first acquaintance . . . The reason is simply this: one can only like what one remembers; and with all new music that is very difficult. (226–7)

In the face of outright originality, Beckett eschewed comparison or explanation or justification in favour of marvel:

> Shall I embellish? There is neither place nor time for reassuring notes on these desperately immediate images. On this violence of need which not only unleashes them but disrupts them beyond their vanishing lines. On this great internal reality which incorporates into a single witness dead and living spirits, nature and void, everything that will cease and everything that will never be. And finally on this supreme master who submits to what cannot be mastered, and trembles.
>
> No.
>
> One can simply bow, wonder-struck.
> ("Homage to Jack B. Yeats" xi)

The conventions of literary genre that configure a literary tradition also shape conventional taste and readers' expectations. Originality, unique perspective, and a personal idiom have to make their own way, establish new tastes. The situation is paradoxical. As Zhang Longxi points out, the creative genius defined by Immanuel Kant is at once exemplary and inimitable; exemplary for setting a standard that subsequent artists would aspire to; inimitable because the canon of originality decries mere repetition. For Kant, there are categories that organise one's ability to understand the perceived world, categories that are prior to taste. What then of works not constructed within such categories?

> In Kant's third critique . . . An aesthetic judgment is faced with the contradiction between its private, individual nature and its implied universality; for an aesthetic judgment, though not without reasonable ground, is a judgment based on personal taste and therefore unlikely to be universally applicable . . . To find a way out of that dilemma, one must base a judgment of taste on something that is not a concept but that can validate aesthetic judgment, and one must find someone who has the special capacity of going beyond the two sides of the opposition. Both of these are proposed by Kant as solution to the antinomy, and both are found in his idea of genius; for genius, says Kant, has the special talent to represent "aesthetic ideas" which transcend all concepts while still providing necessary grounds for the validation of aesthetic judgment . . . In creating a work of art, genius is not only above the rule but is itself the rule . . . It produces things for which there can be no determinate rule, hence its *originality*; and it gives art the rule that it may be followed but not reproduced by others, hence its *exemplariness* . . . Concerned with the validity of aesthetic judgment, Kant puts more emphasis on taste than genius, insisting that genius needs to be guided and curbed by good taste, which "clips its wings, and makes it civilized, or polished," and that in case of a conflict which calls for sacrificing one of the two, then the sacrifice "should rather be on the side of genius." . . . As a kind of *sensus communis,* aesthetic taste is the power that makes the work of genius accessible to others, that allows it to be shared by the community. (6–7)

Classical *rhetoric* distinguishes between *poetics* and *aesthetics* based on a set repertoire of rhetorical devices. The same devices serve to construct a text meant to persuade (poetics) as to deconstruct a text in order to identify its strategies of persuasion (aesthetics). Production and reception are separate and different activities. A writer's writer invents new forms of production, new strategies based on new devices. This fascinates other "makers," who are weary of doing a little better the same old thing, but may perplex readers who expect tried and true strategies and devices, who want the old themes in the old styles, done a little better than before. Not having heard them before, some readers and critics know not how to appreciate them whereas writers can profit from them.

In "Blake's Column" an embittered literary critic savages conventional work:

> Mr Humphrie's *Selected Essays*, which will certainly recommend him on Judgment Day to the Creator, may not succeed so well in our more petty habitation. I think he has settled for the well-turned phrase, rather than exert the imagination, so that what once ran cleanly through the ocean has been parboiled, salted, oiled and tinned, still it bears a very fine Christian label.
>
> We have need of such lies to sustain us through our drab inferiority . . .
>
> [Blake] tried as best he could to avoid the new journalistic successes, female and male, who sat perched by their typewriters, sounding like daft parrots, as they whittled away at their self-infatuation, till they too might end up like him, rearranging the editor's words in his ears. (*Banished Misfortune* 28, 40)

The philosopher Donald L. Hall and the Sinologist Roger T. Ames have called attention to the difference between two kinds of *order*, the *rational* or *logical* order that dominates post-Socratic thought, and the *aesthetic* order that dominates Confucian thought.

> Two fundamental understandings of order are possible: one requires that order be achieved by application to a given

situation of an antecedent pattern of relatedness. This we might call "rational" or "logical" . . . order. A second meaning of order is fundamentally aesthetic. Aesthetic order is achieved by the creation of novel patterns . . . (16)

The distinctive feature of aesthetic order is that, whereas rational order permits one to abstract from the concrete particularities of the elements of the order and to treat these elements indifferently, aesthetic order is constituted by just those particularities . . . (134)

The concepts of aesthetic and logical order are inversely related. Aesthetic order presses in the direction of particularity and uniqueness; logical order toward generality and absolute substitutability . . . (136)

The contrast of what we are calling logical and aesthetic orders is one that has, surprisingly, been little stressed within the Anglo-European tradition. This is, perhaps, due in large measure to the fact that paradigm instances of order have been drawn from notions of "the created order" or from "the order of nature." With regard to such notions we are more concerned to account for uniformities than irregularities. Thus we seek causal laws or patterns of meaning that normatively measure our natural world. (137–138)

The writer's writer creates a new aesthetic order that is not amenable to antecedent patterns of relatedness. The poet's poet Ezra Pound identified three essential elements of poetry—*phanopoeia* (image), *melopoeia* (prosody) and *logopoeia*:

"the dance of the intellect among words," that is to say, it employs words not only for their direct meaning, but it takes count in a special way of habits of usage, of the context we *expect* to find with the word, its usual concomitants, of its known acceptances, and of ironical play. It holds the aesthetic content which is peculiarly the domain of verbal manifestation, and cannot possibly be contained in plastic or in music. ("How to Read" 25)

T. S. Eliot identified two essential elements, the auditory imagination and the objective correlative.

> What I call "auditory imagination" is the feeling for syllable and rhythm, penetrating far below the conscious levels of thought and feeling, invigorating every word; sinking to the most primitive and forgotten, returning to the origin and bringing something back, seeking the beginning and the end. It works through meanings, certainly, or not without meanings in the ordinary sense, and fuses the old and obliterated and the trite, the current, and the new and surprising, the most ancient and the most civilized mentality. ("Matthew Arnold" 118–19)

> The only way of expressing emotion in the form of art is by finding an "objective correlative"; in other words, a set of objects, a situation, a chain of events which shall be the formula of that *particular* emotion; such that when the external facts, which terminate in sensory experience, are given, the emotion is immediately invoked. ("Hamlet and His Problems" 100)

In Healy's case, his personal idiom penetrates below the conscious levels of thought and invigorates every word, while the unique point of view of the narrative becomes itself an objective correlative. In *Long Time, No See* the narrative strips away all semblance of an interior monologue in favour of an exterior polyphony. No stream of consciousness, no dreams. It may well be his most experimental work. It certainly brings to maturity his personal repertoire of new rhetorical devices and strategies. Let the actual building of walls, fragments shored against ruins, serve as our objective correlative in this study, though they be washed away by a January storm.

In life, and by force of circumstances, living on an alt, a raised headland slowly being consumed by the sea, he built two kinds of walls. On dry land he built drystone walls meant to stand, to resist, fitting himself into a tradition of master wall builders and menders. On the shore he innovated, building gabions, cages filled with smaller stones, stacked to build bulwarks against the tide, meant to stand but not to resist, wherein freedom of movement allows the stones to absorb the force of a tide that would annihilate resistance, and showed the way to a new tradition. Both kinds of wall figure in his work, as in "The Task":

> Go down into the dab with the rock,
> I'm told, go down into the dab,
>
> right down into the blue dab
> is the job,
>
> it's there you'll find
> purchase for a wall,
>
> man dear,
> *again' the say.*
>
> I'm down in the dab for hours
> before I take a break to see
>
> how far there is to go. Right
> round the alt and on forever,
>
> and I realise he's set me
> a task for a lifetime, that man,
>
> that man who sent me
> down into the dab
>
> to hoke
> again' the ocean . . . (*The Reed Bed* 34)

Or in "Walls":

> . . . and sometimes
> I panic in the windy
> open spaces,
> and often rest
>
> where there
> was nothing before,
> and think, well,
> the wall under me may lack
>
> the Donlon touch,
> the finish of mason and fiddlemaker,
> saddler, farmer.
> A poor type of man
>
> I am to follow them
> who built battery walls
> and turned the earth
> around to face
>
> the north-west.
> So be it.
> I look back,
> pleased with myself,
>
> as if I'd just climbed
> Everest
> and was waiting for
> the others to arrive. (*The Reed Bed* 55–6)

And yet "The Wall I Built" confirms the futility of this necessary effort:

> The wall I built
> the sea took.

> "The small stone that no one sees gives all the balance"   177

> The stones I gathered
> the sea scattered . . . (*The Reed Bed* 57)

The gabions become a leitmotif of *A Fool's Errand*:

> While they're away I work on the beach, according to advice
> I got from a man whose name I can't remember.
> . . .
> I lean over to throw
> stones in a cage.
> . . .
> You have to be there
> in the actual place
> listening to what can never be heard till the next time
> . . .
> and here they are—not ambitions
> or works of wonder, not even chores,
> but plain dear labour I took on
>
> to shore up the beach
> against the storms; but the wall I built
>
> to keep the sea out is keeping me in
> amongst the pounding diction.
> . . .
> Behind me the stones
> are finding their place, and are sitting on their own weight
>   at last.
> . . .
> Down on the beach the gabions in the middle of the night
> give a faraway groan as they sweep through the empty
>   stations. . . .
> (19, 25, 28, 35, 45).

In *Long Time, No See* Mr Psyche transfers a drystone wall, stone by stone:

> All that Thursday and Friday afternoon I worked the wall, pushing the wheelbarrow to and fro, lifting; looking; standing back and then heading off again. I was trying to get the curve right. The curve had to be gradual. The thing was to let each stone find its place; this was the rule that went through my head. Every time I lifted a rock I heard the command from somewhere in the past—let the rock find its own balance, let it sit on its own weight, and when it does, only then push in the slanted stones to right the position.
> I have rules for everything.
> If the rock does not fit, wait; every rock will find its place in the wall. No stone shall be proud; and stand out from the rest.
> It is the small stone that no one sees gives all the balance . . .
>
> I was trying to repeat the pattern of the old stone work in the new wall. (242)

And meanwhile grows the palimpsest of meanings stacking up around the activity of being in the moment, of being in the world, of acting in harmony with the world, of giving every thing its due equal place. Not for nothing did Michael Harding, himself well-acquainted with Buddhism, call Healy and Sean McSweeney, a neighbour, the painter who immersed his work in those environs and whose artwork adorns the books of poems, two Zen masters perched on the edge of the Atlantic ("The War Is Over" 11).

> The wall grew along the curve. A choir of starlings stood feeding on the seeds of the New Zealand flax that stood over my head in the next flower garden. Hallo, I called. Hallo, they called back. Then they began the flirty whistling. A stonechat spun by, then the wren, with a tipped-up tail, hopped along a branch of olearia, keeping time to a questioning song she sang alone.
> There was no reply.
> Then Timmy appeared, and started pulling himself to and from against a low tough hanging branch of olearia, all for a

scratch on the back. I thought of the two sailors heading up the road as I saw the Lithuanians make their way with their fishing rods along the beach. Then along came the Japanese fisherman who always parked his motor bicycle in our drive. A year ago he'd asked for permission, and some days he'd arrive, shout a greeting, and drop out of sight behind the alt. The gulls were thrashing around Tingle's boat as it sped outside the bar. Beyond that a trawler was headed toward the island.

The thing was to lift, put in place, let it sit.

Then gather.

Push.

Wait, while across from me, the clothes that Ma had hung out that morning on the washing line blew like the front line of an army of empty ghosts. The sea thrift was losing its white leaves. The heads of the sea pinks had faded to grey. (*Long Time, No See* 242–3)

As Beckett said of the work of Jack B. Yeats there is no need for reassuring notes to embellish these immediate images that incorporate into a single witness dead and living spirits, nature and void, everything that will cease and everything that will never be. Contemplating the work of the supreme master Healy who submits to what cannot be mastered, and trembles, one can simply bow, wonder-struck.

Works Cited

Bachelard, Gaston. *On Poetic Imagination: Selections from the Works of Gaston Bachelard*. New York: Bobbs Merrill, 1971. xxxvii. Print.

Beckett, Samuel. "Homage to Jack B. Yeats." *Jack B. Yeats. The Late Paintings*. Ed. T.G. Rosenthal. London: André Deutsch, 1993. xi. Print.

———. "Three Dialogues." *Disjecta: Miscellaneous Writings and a Dramatic Fragment*. Ed. Ruby Cohn. New York: Grove, 1984: 138–45. Print.

Borges, Jorge Luis. "La busca de Averroes." *Ficciones. El Aleph. El informe de Brodie*. Buenos Aires: Emecé, 1982. 77–87. Print.

Eliot, T.S. "Matthew Arnold." *The Use of Poetry and the Use of Criticism.* London: Faber and Faber, 1964. Print.

———. "Hamlet and His Problems." *The Sacred Wood: Essays on Poetry and Criticism.* London: Methuen, 1921. 95–103. Print.

Golden, Seán. "Familiars in a Ruinstrewn Land: *Endgame* as a Political Allegory." *Contemporary Literature* 22.4 (1981): 425–55. Print.

———. "Oriental Sense of the Border." *Fortnight* 210 (3–16 Dec. 1984): 18. Print.

———. "Post-Traditional English Literature: A Polemic." *The Crane Bag: A Journal of Irish Studies* 3.2 (1979): 7–18. Print.

———. "Traditional Irish Music in Contemporary Irish Literature." *MOSAIC: A Quarterly Journal for the Comparative Study of Literature & Ideas* 12.3 (Summer 1979): 1–24. Print.

Graves, Robert. *Goodbye to All That.* Hammondsworth: Penguin, 1960. Print.

Hall, Donald L., and Roger T. Ames. *Thinking through Confucius.* Albany: State University of New York Press, 1987. Print.

Harding, Michael. "The War Is Over. Feral Boys Are Everywhere." *The Irish Times* 20 Aug. 2013: 11. Print.

Healy, Dermot. *A Fool's Errand.* Oldcastle: The Gallery Press, 2010. Print.

———. *Banished Misfortune.* London and New York: Allison and Busby; Dingle: Brandon Book Publishers, 1982. Print.

———. *Fighting with Shadows.* London and New York: Allison and Busby; Dingle: Brandon Book Publishers, 1984. Print.

———. "First Snow of the Year." *The Irish Press* 11 Aug. 1973: 7. Print.

———. "Jude and his mother." *Paddy No More.* Ed. William Vorm. Dublin: Wolfhound Press, 1982. 63–73. Print.

———. *Long Time, No See.* London: Faber and Faber, 2011. Print.

———. *Sudden Times.* London: Harvill Press, 1999. Print.

———. *The Ballyconnell Colours.* Oldcastle: The Gallery Press, 1992. Print.

———. *The Bend for Home.* London: Harvill Press, 1996. Print.

———. *The Reed Bed.* Oldcastle: The Gallery Press, 2001. Print.

———. *What the Hammer.* Oldcastle: The Gallery Press, 1998. Print.

Heaney, Seamus, ed. *Soundings 2. An annual anthology of new Irish poetry.* Belfast: Blackstaff Press, 1974. Print.

———. "An Open Letter." Dublin: Field Day Publications, 1983. Print.

Miller, Samuel H. *The Dilemma of Modern Belief: The Lyman Beecher Lectures*. London: Hodder and Stoughton, 1964. Print.

O'Connor, Frank. *The Lonely Voice: A Study of the Short Story*. Cleveland: World, 1962. Print.

Paz, Octavio. *Traducción: literatura y literalidad*. Barcelona: Tusquets, 1971. Print.

Pound, Ezra. "How to Read." *Literary Essays of Ezra Pound*. New York: New Directions, 1968. 15–40. Print.

Power, Arthur. *Conversations with James Joyce*. Dublin: Lilliput Press, 1999. Print.

Qian, Zhaoming. *The Modernist Response to Chinese Art: Pound, Moore, Stevens*. Charlottesville: University of Virginia Press, 2003. Print.

Schoenberg, Arnold. "On the Individual and the Majority." *A Schoenberg Reader: Documents of a Life*. Ed. Joseph Aune. New Haven: Yale University Press, 2003. Print.

Stein, Gertrude. *Picasso*. London: B.T. Batsford, 1938; New York: Dover, 1984. Print.

Zhang, Longxi. *The Tao and the Logos. Literary Hermeneutics, East and West*. Durham: Duke University Press, 1992. Print.

Dermot Healy—Art into Life: Life into Art
Bill Swainson

"What could you give the young if they were barricaded from the present by our lyrical, stifling past?"
("Banished Misfortune," 1974)

In 1978 I was a tyro editor when John Calder asked me to go to Dublin to launch Aidan Higgins's novel *Scenes from a Receding Past*. I had already met Aidan at John Calder's cramped offices above Lina Stores at 18 Brewer Street, Soho, from which address he published Samuel Beckett, William Burroughs, Marguerite Duras, Henry Miller and Alain Robbe-Grillet, among many other leading writers of the post-war period.

One of my editorial duties had been to type up certain passages of *Scenes from a Receding Past* to make a clean typescript ready to go into production. There is, perhaps, no better way to really begin to understand a writer's work and style than to type up a fair copy of several much corrected and amended paragraphs, word for word, comma for comma, line for line, and paragraph for paragraph. (Only translation is likely to lead to closer scrutiny of a text.) It proved to be a master class that I would appreciate again and again in my subsequent work as an editor.

> My father holds me in his arms at the window, pointing to the wonders of the world without. A goat in a tree, flying fish over a meadow, sailing boats disappearing into clouds. I fidget in his arms, turning like a top, always missing the sailing boat hidden in clouds, the goat hidden in the leaves, the flying fish hidden in the meadow. All I see are clouds, cowslip in the meadow, a tree quivering. (Higgins 12)

For me this work was as precious as copying out and learning passages of poetry by heart, a habit that I had learnt at school and carried on at university. This way you hear the sound of the writer's words in your head, and Higgins, the arch stylist, was like Samuel Beckett before him, and Dermot Healy after him, a writer acutely aware of rhythm.

I managed to make the expedition to Dublin coincide with a holiday on the Dingle Peninsula. On my return I was definitely not the same young man who had left. Once you've been to the West, careened around that Kerry peninsula on a hired pushbike and looked out from the Garullus Oratory at the shimmering sea and the silhouettes of the Blasket Islands beyond, how could you be?

On the evening of the launch I went to Rosita Sweetman's house in Rathmines and although I do not now remember everyone who was there, I do remember meeting Rosita, of course, Patrick Gallagher of RTÉ, and Steve MacDonogh, who was shortly to start Brandon Publishing. At that time he was obsessed with Antonin Artaud and *Pour en finir avec le jugement de dieu*. But the person I found myself talking to longest that evening was Neil Jordan. His story collection *Night in Tunisia* had just been published by the Irish Writers' Co-operative, and it was Neil, standing in a temporary polythene-covered conservatory built for the occasion by Cathal Goulding—a structure that made Aidan nervous—who told me on that wet and windy night about a writer who Higgins also admired and to whom he had presented a Hennessy Award in 1974 for a story with the enigmatic title *Banished Misfortune*. Aidan and Neil talked with a mixture of enthusiasm, affection and awe about Healy's writing and his use of metaphor.

I asked Neil whether he could introduce me, but he smiled and said that Healy was not in Dublin, he was away in the country, living in County Cavan. But he did give me the address and so I wrote an enthusiastic letter to Dermot saying how much I would like to read his work. Meanwhile, I set about tracking down everything I could find, which turned out to be five stories: "Banished Misfortune," "The Island and the Calves," "A Family and a Future," "First Snow of the Year" and to my inexperienced but eager eyes a wonderfully strange piece called "Jude and His Mother."

Two years later Dermot answered my letter with a phone call and invited me to meet him at a TV studio in Wandsworth, where he was helping a friend on a media course direct a TV play, and where he was calling the shots and camera angles as if he had been doing it all his life. It was his first time in a TV studio, he said, but the confidence was undeniable and seemed to inspire everyone there. He said a cheerful hello and went back to his work. He later told me that he had been part of a Cavan theatre company called the Hacklers (still going strong to this day) for whom he had directed a production of *Waiting for Godot* that won the Esso Award at the 1980 Drama All-Ireland Amateur Festival. Playwriting, poetry, magazine editing, publishing and community involvement, were and would continue to be essential components of Dermot's conception and practice of the writer's life alongside the prose that had caught my imagination.

When the studio work was over, Dermot led the way to the bar of the Spread Eagle pub and there we were able to talk properly. I was struck by his confident manner, as a group including Maura O'Brien—very pretty, with dark auburn hair, and heavily pregnant with their daughter Inor—gathered round him. I would see that confidence again when he took a lead role in a play at the ICA, and so be surprised when I first heard him read his own work a few years later by the shy, hesitant, countryman's shuffle to the stage, head down, an embarrassed smile on his lips, his voice just audible. He inspired confidence in others and showed it in his role as mentor, encourager, writing group leader, but never seemed to me to show it when reading his own work, though he had every reason to.

Soon afterwards I visited the sparsely furnished housing association flat in Caldwell Street, Stockwell, on the corner of Liberty Street in South London where Dermot and Maura lived, not far from his great friend Mick Murphy and others who had shared a squat in Pimlico in the mid-70s.

In the kitchen, which was also the living room, there were a few upright chairs and a table just big enough for six people. The television was usually on in the background and you were always made welcome—another role to be confident in. The young couple hadn't two pins to rub together, but Dermot was a natural host in so far as a host with nothing much in his larder can be, yet the cup of tea or meal was carefully made and offered with humorous ceremony. Perhaps this professional courtesy came from watching his mother Winnie and his aunt Maisie at work in the café called the Breifne that they ran in Cavan Town.

In the flat in Caldwell Street, Dermot showed me poems he'd written, including a set of twelve that had been chosen by Seamus Heaney for an issue of *Soundings* published by the Blackstaff Press in Belfast in 1974, and a long poem, whose title was, I think, "The Stonemason," that was dense and allusive.

For Dermot Irish poetry and literature seemed to be one continuum, a river into which he could dive at will and which he seemed to me to know intimately, whether he was talking about Brian Friel's story collection *The Saucer of Larks*, Maria Edgeworth, or the blind Irish poet Raftery. And behind his writing was a sense of a richer, more allusive language than English—Irish. I remember him saying to me in an attempt to characterise the difference: "In Irish you are not in love with someone; the love is on you." He loved the word *grá* (desire) for instance. He loved the difference between English and Irish, although it also frustrated him, and when much later we were working on *A Goat's Song* he lamented through one of his characters, a teacher of Irish, "My trouble is I wrote a book in Irish. In Irish it was spare and true. Now they want it in English, and in English I've added things I've never seen" (189).

Yet at the same time as being steeped in Irish poetry, he was extremely well read generally, not only in British and Irish fiction, but in fiction from Europe and the Americas and would become more so as time went by. In 1980 when I first met him, he was reading *The Autumn of the Patriarch* by Gabriel García Márquez and this was an influence he had to absorb and then expel, or at least all that he could not use. I remember that in an early draft of *Fighting with Shadows* (then called *Sciamachy* or *A Fight with Shadows*) there was a chapter called "The City of the Swallows and the City of the Swifts" that owed a lot to the Colombian master, but being undigested did not make the final cut, nor did the opening sentence of *The Autumn of the Patriarch* survive as the epigraph it had once been destined to be ("Over the weekend the vultures got into the presidential palace by pecking through the screens on the balcony windows . . ."). On the other hand, the Márquezian influence can be seen most clearly in the attempt to generalise by elevating the particular to an almost mythic level. You can sense it in "Banished Misfortune" and see it at its most fully developed in *Fighting with Shadows*.

But for all that, his work was grounded in Joyce (of course, *Ulysses*, but also *Dubliners*), in Beckett (especially the plays) and perhaps, above all, in the poetry and prose of Patrick Kavanagh. The Monaghan poet's sonnet "Epic"[1] might have been Healy's credo if he had ever believed in such things. He would talk about Cavan's local paper, the *Anglo-Celt*, that to my eye seemed curiously old-fashioned, looking more like *The Times* before photos appeared on its front page in the 1960s, with real affection; its concern with the local and particular showed itself in his approach to journal editing in *The Drumlin* and later *Force 10*, where apparently small-scale stories took on a larger dimension.

He recommended to me the stories, novels and prose of Brian Friel, Leland Bardwell, Frank O'Connor, Peadar O'Donnell, Patrick Boyle, Seumas O'Kelly, Patrick Kavanagh and Flann O'Brien, amongst many others. (I think he may have already decided that if he was going to be stuck with an English editor, it might as well be one who knew the literary world that was already his home.) He talked about Dylan Thomas's *A Portrait of the Artist as a Young Dog* and *Adventures in the Skin Trade* with real affection, as he would later talk of Oliver Goldsmith's *The Vicar of Wakefield* (see *The Bend for Home*), and later still when I was at Harvill and we were working on *A Goat's Song* we would talk about Franz Kafka and Raymond Carver (another favourite), whose *Uncollected Prose* and *Collected Poems* I was then editing. Anyone who visited Dermot's home knew from his bookshelves that his reading was voracious and wide-ranging, but I mention these books and authors here because they were among his touchstones.

Healy was born in the village of Finea in Co. Westmeath, but moved to Cavan as a young boy when his father, an RIC policeman, was stationed there—a disruption that disturbed his young life and can be sensed in all his fiction. However widely he read, and however broad the influences he absorbed, it was the drumlin country of Co. Cavan and Patrick Kavanagh's neighbouring Co. Monaghan that infused his first book of stories, *Banished Misfortune*, and his first novel, *Fighting with Shadows*. In the mid-1980s I remember going to Dublin to see Patrick Kavanagh's *The Great Hunger* in a stage version devised by Tom MacIntyre and staged at the Peacock, in which Dermot was very much involved; he spoke highly of MacIntyre's stories, *The Harper's Turn*, and would have liked to have seen them published in London.

•

So what kind of world was I plunged into on reading those early stories written by Dermot in his twenties, some of which went into the collection *Banished Misfortune*? Three of them stand out.

"First Snow of the Year" was selected by the discerning David Marcus, who edited a young writers' short story series for *The Irish Press*. It was written when Dermot was in his early twenties and first published in 1972. This engaging story, which appears at first as if it is going to be a simple domestic tale about a village postman's first day of retirement, builds up layer upon realistically described layer until a portrait of a village emerges within which a love triangle resolves itself.

> "This round is on me," said O'Grady without enthusiasm. In honour of Jim Philips, postman, recently retired. O'Grady set up an electric kettle on a stout crate and dropped a measure of cloves and sugar into each glass. His wife was throwing darts with the boys in the bar. The light was right for drinking by. Elephants from a circus roared from a nearby town. The radio said: "Walton's, your weekly reminder of the grace and beauties that lie—"
> "I'll have a woman above in the house in no time, true as God," spoke Jim.
> "Smell that," said Phildy.
> Phildy went into the lounge and took a cue off some of the young lads playing there . . . (3)

What was striking about it was how the traditional narrative voice of the opening rapidly became polyphonic so that, for example, the reader hears the voices in the village bar unmediated by the narrator. Then, just as we have taken on board this adjustment, and think we know where we are, the jilted lover Phildy erupts into the narrative with—at least at this stage—unexplained malevolence. Here was the enthralling ability to evoke a whole world and the forces and emotions at work within it.

Then there was "Jude and His Mother," a flawed story I admired greatly, which first appeared in the anthology *Paddy No More*. What makes this such a fascinating piece is that it depicts the urban world of the Irish migrant labourer, but is not satisfied with portraying simply that tough reality. The narrator has both an accurate eye and a large-hearted, generous spirit that animates the world around him; this is one of the key features of Dermot's writing throughout his life. The story may have failed—he certainly decided not to include it in *Banished Misfortune*—and yet it contains a powerful desire to understand and to explain, to celebrate life through description, to connect contemporary experience to the more familiar world of Irish music and literature:

> The factory is near Wood Green, opposite the bookies, a grey half mile from the Underground. I stand by my own furnace, clamp down the shape of the toilet bowl, the rubber recoils under the heavy heat, my great gloves hold the flame. Keep the clamp in position, lean on it, the machine shivers, and then I withdraw the design. The burnt rubber is doused with water. The ends cut off with a knife. The threads inspected. Sometimes they hang askew, as when the strings of a harp are held aside to permit the passage of a sweeter note. Pop music is played all day, the supervisor remembers happier tunes of Music While You Work. The walls and galvanized roofs burn, and the ladies love to daunder in the cooler air of the finishing evening, hesitate within the gates a minute longer than necessary to facilitate a more blissful entrance into the streets. (65)

I was particularly struck by the sharp description of work (we see this throughout Healy's writing), the surprising comparison of the threads of the toilet seat and the harp, the pop music and the foreman's nostalgia for "Music While You Work," the "ladies'" enjoyment of "daundering in the cooler air" after the heat of the factory before heading into the streets and home.

Finally, and wonderfully, from among these early stories there is "Banished Misfortune." Recently Tim O'Grady read the following paragraph-long sentence of this story on RTÉ radio; it made several points beautifully. It displayed the circular, musical form that Dermot used again and again in his work, at first in "Banished Misfortune" (as described by Seán Golden in his fascinating late-'70s essay "Traditional Irish Music in Contemporary Irish Literature") and later notably in the structure of *A Goat's Song* and *Sudden Times*, and it showed an ambition to generalise from the particular:

> For whatever reason the house might fall, the sleeping McFarland would build again with a sense of adventure anywhere north of the lakes and in good time, son of Saul, master builder of Fermanagh county but by pneumonia put away while tended by his wife Olive, Glan woman and descendant of J. O'Reilly who danced once with flax in his trousers, and though nominally Christian died in foreign and pagan lands fighting an unjust war, but McFarland sensing the lie of the land grew away from a sense of guilt or desire for power and prayed that the haphazard world would not destroy his family so well grounded among the moralities of chance and nature, if one could remain loyal to the nature of a people and not to the people themselves, for whatever reason the house might fall. (97)

After hearing the story of the tune "Banish Misfortune," Judy the wife of McFarland the musician, lies in bed in a Galway boarding house thinking:

> She heard him in a drunken vulgar way, accessible still for all his various frailties, but she was silent for in her heart of hearts she feared he was softening, losing his sense of justice,

merely protesting that erratic comedy of life. Fear was so addictive, consuming all of a body's time and she wanted to share this vigil with him in Fermanagh but what could you give the young if they were barricaded from the present by our lyrical, stifling past? She said nothing, knowing she shared this empty ecstasy with a thousand others who had let their laziness go on too long. (110)

And here is where we come to what is for me a defining feature of Dermot's writing, "[. . .] what could you give the young if they were barricaded from the present by our lyrical, stifling past?" I would argue that all of Dermot's fiction was an attempt to take down those barricades and to engage with reality, and here's the irony, with lyricism the main weapon in his literary arsenal. But each book Dermot wrote after *Banished Misfortune* and *Fighting with Shadows* was an attempt, not to be anti-lyrical, but to simplify his language so as not to stifle the book or his reader.

•

Dermot seemed to know the books he was going to write in his lifetime far ahead of their actual publication. When I first met him he knew there would be a story collection called *Banished Misfortune*, though by 1980 only half of it was written; the same was true of his first novel *Fighting with Shadows* or *Sciamachy*. I remember an early draft that was barely 160 typescript pages long. But more remarkable still were books in embryo like *The Poverty of Localities* that became *A Goat's Song*, and later still *The Bend for Home* that began life as a prose piece about Westmeath commissioned by Robin Robertson for a photographic essay by Donovan Wylie, but which had an earlier existence still as a novel to be called *The Seven-Arched Bridge*, of which the landscape and some themes went into the memoir, while other themes, but not the landscape, went into *A Goat's Song*, and *Sudden Times*, that had its genesis in a piece Dermot wrote for Leland Bardwell's magazine *Cyphers 31* in 1989, but whose terrain if not mood was already sketched in "Jude and His Mother," drawing on Dermot's experiences living and labouring in London in the late '60s and early '70s.

This is not to say that all was predetermined. It was more that I think Dermot knew what he wanted to explore and that some of the elements were already circling. For instance, there was his family, to whom he was very loyal and from whom he drew many of the stories that ended up in his books. As he said himself in *The Bend for Home*, "I've stolen so many of Maisie's phrases over the years and inserted them into the minds and mouths of fictional characters that she has herself become a work of the imagination" (241).

In *Fighting with Shadows*, which originally had a three-part structure that was to be "The Village"—"The Town"—"The City," the city never materialised and perhaps was later absorbed into *Sudden Times* and parts of *A Goat's Song*; certainly the death of Pop (the grandfather) in *Fighting with Shadows* brings matters to a close at the end of Part II, which is also the end of the published novel. When the paperback was published two years after the hardback by Allison and Busby, Dermot wanted the novel to be split into two parts: "The South" and "The North," but for lack of pages (the book was already exactly 288 pages long, an even working) we had to leave out this two-part division.

More pertinently, in the first draft of a mere 160 pages or so, the novel began with the laying out and washing of a corpse, an episode that moved forward and backwards as the writing progressed until, in the final draft, the ritual preparations had gone, but the identity of the corpse was now known: it was Frank Allen, father of Joseph, whose story the book tells. His death provides one of the novel's most dramatic moments:

> It was evening. The mountains moved over the village like great war-clouds. The lakes were covered in mist. Frank was drinking whiskey by the window. He read out a story to Pop from the local paper and began a short letter to George [his brother]. There was little to tell. Things in the country had been bad for a while. Then he answered the door to a man with a gun who shot him three times through the head. (115)

The burial of the corpse could only find its place in the novel once the identity of the dead man was known, but it had been there from the beginning.

It is, perhaps, in *A Goat's Song* that we can see the coming together of the ur-novel and the published work, the imagined plan and the lived life, most clearly. This was to be a novel set mainly in an Irish seaside landscape, beautifully evoked in a prefatory piece of natural description at the end of which was the phrase, "Something happened here." What happened would be a love story that would provide a way for Dermot to explore the differences between Protestant and Catholic worlds. This was something that had concerned him before he went to live in Belfast for several years, and that continued to concern him long after he had made his home in Ballyconnell, Co. Sligo.

The novel has a circular structure that begins with the protagonist Jack Ferris standing on a bridge waiting for his lover, Catherine, to return to him after a break-up—"The bad times were over at last"—and it ends at a moment just before that point with the brief sentence "The bark of a dog flew by." Inside that "commodius vicus of recirculation" a love story is called into existence by the power of imagination that will explore "the tension between the Catholic and Protestant imaginations, and the sense of psychological distance between the Republic and the violently contested state on the other side of the Irish border," as Sean O'Hagan eloquently described it in his *Guardian* obituary of Dermot.

The barriers of the "lyrical and stifling past" are taken down in bare, simple, direct prose so that the reality of love and the worlds the lovers come from can be explored. The story takes us from waiting on the bridge to Jack Ferris's breakdown followed by a spell in hospital, until "language like a nurse" (to quote one of the poems in *The Ballyconnell Colours*) provides an entry into worlds and experiences as different as work on fishing boats off the Mayo coast or violence on the streets of Belfast.

While Dermot was writing this novel, I remember a moment when his progress had been stymied for a while. Where he wanted to get to was the far side of a barricade he could not breach. But then one day a brown envelope arrived at the Harvill office, bearing Healy's distinctive handwriting, with its mixture of upper and lowercase letters, and containing a new chapter called "The News at Six." This was the chapter that connected Ireland's recent troubled past to the present in which the novel was taking place. Jonathan Adams, the old RUC sergeant and father of Catherine with whom fisherman and playwright Jack Ferris will one day fall in love, is called up with many other country policemen to police the civil rights march in Derry on 5 October 1968. Jonathan loses his hat and his temper in the melée and is caught on camera "hatless" belabouring "a middle-aged man who was already pouring blood" (121).

> In the light of day he had become the author of his own misfortune. Jonathan Adams cursed the cameraman. He cursed the police that had used him and his stupidity. He remembered going up together with other policemen in the minibus from Fermanagh on the fatal day. They stopped off at a seaside town for dinner at a hotel. All the talk that day was of how they would put a stop to Rome. We'll show them! Hey! Now he felt that the same policemen had thrown him to the lions. After he turned on Saunderson for mentioning that escapade, his appearance on the TV was never mentioned. But sometimes, out of the corner of his eye, he caught them smiling. There was no escape.
>
> The whole of the world had seen him.
>
> Because someone had knocked off his hat, Jonathan Adams had started a war. (123)

This passage was inspired directly by well-known newsreel footage of that Derry march in which you can see happening what Dermot describes in his novel, but by merging actual documented history with his fiction he achieved an imaginative breakthrough that unlocked the rest of the book. Jonathan Adams is that older policeman caught on camera and yet, portrayed by Dermot with deep empathy, is a genuine fictional creation too.

It was not only imaginative risks Dermot took in order to get through to the truth of things. He took real, serious risks too. In the back of taxis when he lived in East Belfast he would start up conversations with the driver, never knowing who or what they were, determined to talk about how things were rather than pretend that all was well with the world. It could be hair-raising when you were with him; it worried his friends and it did not always achieve the breakthrough he was after, though it had its funny side too. One day he had been to the baker's to buy a roll for his breakfast and had then left it in the newsagents when picking up a copy of the *Belfast Newsletter*. The next time he visited the newsagent he was handed the roll in the brown paper bag on which was written simply "The Irishman." This, too, found its way, slightly transformed, into the novel (282).

In the same way that he used his extraordinary imagination to push his writing to the limits, he lived his life for real, pushing it to the limits too with a sense of almost reckless responsibility to get beyond whatever barrier might be in his path and report back.

In the year he published *Sudden Times*, he also took the lead role (an Irish migrant labourer as an old man) in Nichola Bruce's film of Tim O'Grady and Steve Pyke's photographic novel, *I Could Read the Sky*. The film was released in November 1999, and I remember that at the first screening, which Aidan Higgins also attended, we all went for drinks afterwards at Jury's Hotel in the Angel, where Dermot and Aidan were staying. Dermot had been pushing himself to the limit all that year and much of the previous one too, using the main character of *Sudden Times*, Ollie Ewing, who returns to England after previous bad times in London to face his demons, in order to get at the character in the film and, I suspect, vice versa. By the time of the screening and the celebrations afterwards, with much drink taken, he had gone beyond Ollie and the old labourer, and by the end of the evening had gone, too, beyond what that night his friend Aidan could tolerate. When I spoke with Aidan the next day, however unsettling Dermot's behaviour under the influence had been—it was almost shamanistic—we both acknowledged that he demanded of his writing and his writing in turn demanded of him that he took these appalling risks.

As his editor, and as his friend, I admired Dermot Healy for the beauty of his writing, for never being satisfied with repeating what he knew he could do, for always pushing on to a new place whatever the risks. We his readers are the beneficiaries of his sometimes precipitate courage.

Works Cited

"Dermot Healy: A consideration of his writing and literary work." *Arts Tonight*. RTÉ Radio. 18 May 2015. Radio.

Golden, Seán. "Traditional Irish Music in Contemporary Irish Literature." *MOSAIC: A Quarterly Journal for The Comparative Study of Literature & Ideas* 12 (1979): 1–24. Print.

Healy, Dermot. *A Goat's Song*. London: Collins Harvill Press, 1994. Print.

———. *Banished Misfortune*. London: Allison and Busby, 1982. Print.

———. *Fighting with Shadows*. London: Allison and Busby, 1984. Print.

———. "Jude and His Mother." *Paddy No More: Modern Irish Short Stories*. Ed. William Vorm. Nantucket: Longship Press, 1977. Print.

———. *Sudden Times*. London: Harvill Press, 1998. Print.

———. *The Bend for Home*. London: Harvill Press, 1996. Print.

Higgins, Aidan. *Scenes from a Receding Past*. Normal: Dalkey Archive Press, (1978) 2005. Print.

Kavanagh, Patrick. "Epic." *The New Oxford Book of Irish Verse*. Ed. Thomas Kinsella. Oxford: Oxford University Press, 1986: 334–5.

MacIntyre, Tom. *The Harper's Turn*. Oldcastle: The Gallery Press, 1982. Print.

O'Grady, Timothy, and Steve Pyke. *I Could Read the Sky*. London: Harvill Press, 1998. Print.

O'Hagan, Sean. "Dermot Healy Obituary." *Guardian* 30 June 2014. Web. 7 Aug. 2014.

Wylie, Donovan. *32 Counties*. London: Secker and Warburg, 1989. Print.

Notes

1. "Epic" by Patrick Kavanagh (1960)
    I have lived in important places, times
    When great events were decided, who owned
    That half a rood of rock, a no-man's land
    Surrounded by our pitchfork-armed claims.

I heard the Duffys shouting "Damn your soul!"
And old McCabe stripped to the waist, seen
Step the plot defying blue cast-steel—
"Here is the march along these iron stones."
That was the year of the Munich bother. Which
Was more important? I inclined
To lose my faith in Ballyrush and Gortin
Till Homer's ghost came whispering to my mind.
He said: I made the Iliad from such
A local row. Gods make their own importance.

The Importance of Being Dermot: Healy's Idiosyncrasies
Thierry Robin

Who are you? he asked.
I'm Dermot Healy, I said.
I'm Dermot Burke, he replied.
There can't be three Dermots, I said. (*The Bend for Home* 35)

Dermot Healy is a singular writer in more senses than one. His poetry often turns out to be a celebration of nature and a recognition that humble details in everyday life are rich with unexpected poetic qualities. His novels, however, seldom create this sense of tranquility. *Long Time, No See* (2011), for example, though serene on the surface, can be read as a disturbing parable of the silent frustrations of routine lives in the West of Ireland and, more generally, of the inescapable mental collapse inherent to the human condition. These darker nuances may be due to the episodic structure of this particular novel, but also to the novelistic genre as a whole. A novel is often more compatible with dynamic narrative processes, and it usually addresses problems through complex reasoning and careful plotting. However, Healy's novels frequently demonstrate that their main interest lies beyond plot. This essay intends to show that what makes Healy's creative world so unique is the way in which he deals with ubiquitous uncertainties; moreover, I will also suggest that Healy's writings function as a kind of literature of healing. To paraphrase a key sentence from *A Goat's Song* (5, 99–100, 202), his work manages "to give a form to what cannot be uttered."[1]

Healy's literary endeavours often prove *apophatic* by doing precisely what they denied in the first place. According to the *Merriam-Webster Dictionary*, apophasis is a rhetorical strategy which consists in "the raising of an issue by claiming not to mention it." When reading Healy, one is constantly reminded that no global coherence is to be expected from life or its representations. The meandering and anticlimactic destinies of his male anti-heroes all point towards the same *anti*-revelation. Yet throughout his novels, whilst giving a form to formlessness, Healy also provides a key to help transform that absence of shape into the most meaningful patterns. By tackling guilt, the sense of belonging (somewhere or nowhere at all), the very (im)possibility of sincere love, the notion of (un)stable identity, death and mortality, the seeming absence of causality (as if things were only happening "suddenly"), Healy's work exorcises—in an almost shaman-like manner—the difficulties of existence. His writing provides a form and a scenario to shapeless strings of events, the bits-and-pieces which make up everybody's existence.

Three themes stand out in Healy's novels: loneliness, near insanity, and the problematic perception of how reality is mediated through language. Jack Ferris in *A Goat's Song* (1994), Ollie Ewing in *Sudden Times* (1999), Philip Feeney (a.k.a. "Mr Psyche") and his granduncle Joejoe in *Long Time, No See* (2011)—not to mention Healy himself in *The Bend for Home* (1996)—are all contemplative figures, frantically grappling with reality, temporality, language and causality. Accordingly, this essay will first address the notion of loneliness as a symptom of the idiotic singularity of reality identified by the contemporary French philosopher Clément Rosset. It will then proceed to show how narrative temporality and apparent nonsense are mutually constructed in Healy's work through the absence of formal closure, drawing on Frank Kermode's *The Sense of an Ending*. Finally, the eeriness of language will be briefly scrutinised in two aspects: its Irish dimension and its acute awareness of the unfathomable aspects of reality.

As I have pointed out elsewhere, Clément Rosset's philosophy comes in handy to account both for the notion of idiosyncrasy in a given author's work and for the notion of idiosyncrasy in reality itself.[2] According to Rosset, in his *Reality: A Treatise on Idiocy* (1977), reality is precisely what cannot ever be duplicated.[3] What stems from this thesis is that something real is doomed to be singular and unique, for representation and copy—which are mere secondary constructs, not to be confused with the original reality—

engender, in turn, new and singular entities. Therefore reality, including historical reality, is "idiotic" so to speak: so hermetically unique in its origins and causes—as well as in its finality and goals—that it does not make obvious sense (except perhaps through the simplifying prism of retrospective reconstruction known as History).

This notion of retrospective reconstruction is useful for thinking about Healy's work. In *The Bend for Home*, ostensibly a memoir, the boundaries between fact and fiction are blurred from the outset:

> At three in the morning the midwife delivers the child. [. . .] As for the child, it did not grow up to be me, although till recently I believed this was how I was born. Family stories were told so often that I always thought I was there. In fact, all this took place in a neighbour's house up the road, and it was my mother, not Mary Sheridan, arrived on her bike to lend a hand. It's in a neighbour's house fiction begins. (3)

Fiction and tales are emphasised right from the start as being central in one's life. Healy was not born where he thinks he was. Displacement onto the fringe and into the neighbour's house allows the author-narrator to recount the impossible story of his own birth. Comical deflation presides over the birth. His mother is not exactly where she ought to be—"it was my mother, not Mary Sheridan, arrived on her bike"—and his elder brother reacts unexpectedly to the news of Dermot's birth after their father told him there was a surprise awaiting him at home: "In [my brother's] mind's eye, he saw a black Raleigh bike [. . .] He was sent ahead into the kitchen. He approached the pram. In disbelief and disappointment, he looked in and saw me" (4).

Disbelief, disappointment and fiction characterise the author's fictional birth. Healy also underlines his individuality by evoking an unlikely doppelgänger—his own cousin Dermot Kinane: "By the time he was three Dermot had come to despise the sound of his own name because it called to his mind his alter ego in Finea. He was tormented. It was Dermot Healy this and Dermot Healy that till he was sick of me" (5). This comic emphasis on impossible doubles underlines the traps of representation. Language allows you to create illusory doubles, but there is no such thing in real life. There may be three or four Dermots on the paper but each is unique outside the page. Much of Healy's inventive prose lurks in that gap between language and things.

This concern with reality as deeply solipsistic and problematic in terms of representation brings about two consequences: first, and throughout Healy's work, History (with a capital H) is a story that can never be taken for granted. Events which are only graspable through language are forever shifting. As a consequence, language and facts seldom go together but sometimes act as foils to each other. Second, there is a constant fear of personal alienation, especially when language proves unable to render things sensible.

Both of these epistemological consequences come into play in *A Goat's Song*. Jack Ferris, who happens to be a writer and playwright (just like Dermot Healy), finds refuge in pure fiction after his disastrous love affair with Catherine Adams. As Neil Murphy comments on this escapist *mise-en-abyme* strategy:

> Healy's novel is a bogus analeptic text in the sense that we do not technically return to the actual beginning or experience a *temporally* second narrative. Rather, it is an *imagined* second narrative. Technically, the account that we experience from section II onwards is an imaginative invention rather than a tale told about events from a different temporal zone based in the actual past. (116)

The reader knows that parts II, III and IV are imagined by Jack Ferris. The key to this is given in section I when Jack says to himself: "the only way I can free myself is to imagine her, not as herself, but as someone else, someone different, for then I can think of her without resenting her. And then he realized what she had done; she had saved them from each other" (83). Fiction is then a remedy to reality. And the very moment when fictional therapy prevails is foregrounded at the end of section I:

> For a moment it could have begun all over, but it didn't. She had struggled against the disillusionment. She had seen

what was coming. Now he [Jack] had to live on in a different world. To transcend. To enter a new story. She had to be imagined. He opened a spiral-bound notebook and thought, here it begins. (84)

The whole novel reads like a memoir, probably due to its true-to-life depiction of the Northern Irish historical background, but it simultaneously emphasises its own fictional status. Ferris reinvents his existence and sorts out the mess of his love life by rewriting it as a story within the story. This original structure, which interweaves different diegetic levels, creates a fictional loop. The final reinvented passage echoes and reproduces the first couple of pages. The end is in the beginning, i.e. the same love letter written by Catherine fills Jack with joy: "Jack, [. . .] I love you and want to be with you. We have a break this weekend. [. . .] We know we want to be with each other; let's grow old and sober together" (exact same passage, 3–4 and 409). However, the second mention here is hypodiegetic or metafictional. It is *what-if* History, a fancy that may allow Jack a way to soothe his loneliness.

Writing in this context sounds like the "life-scripts" theorised by Eric Berne in his insightful study *Transactional Analysis in Psychotherapy* (1961). Berne insists that sense in one's life derives from a more or less conscious life plan that ideally implies order, chronology and purpose. If one's life-script is faulty for some reason, Berne, as a psychotherapist, believes that this script may be altered, reprocessed or simply improved. Or as Jack Ferris—who ends up in a psychiatric ward in hospital—puts it: "Each man's story must be written down" (63). *A Goat's Song* is thus a story of a person writing themselves back to mental health through the very act of *fiction* itself.

Throughout *A Goat's Song*, the reader encounters characters on the brink of mental collapse. Even Jonathan Adams—a potential figure of authority and stability as a would-be priest and then father and policeman—"was possessed of such a feeling of disorientation that his chin and wrists shook uncontrollably. Words refused to come to him. Meaning departed. [. . .] To say 'I' implied a thinking subject, and yet he suddenly realized: I know nothing of myself. To whom does this 'I' refer?" (99). Similarly, Jack Ferris, an alcoholic, is uncomfortably aware of that disconnection between sense and words in real life: "There are a few private moments of truth that can't be said. They stay outside the reach of language" (51). Once, on a coach, Ferris "was maddened by the other passengers, how their identities remained comfortable and intact while his careered around him. [. . .] Suddenly, Jack was swept into a panic of non-being. [. . .] He felt all his actions were false masks behind which he imitated and observed normality. That meant he was false, playing to an audience" (28). For Jack, reality cannot be real: "He thought he was living through a nightmare that would soon end, like all the others did. But it didn't" (27). Language becomes a barrier rather than a medium: "all the words were the wrong words" (27), and eventually this realisation contaminates Jack's relationship with his own body:

> Everything, in fact, was happening in lurid technicolour. The wall that separated him from everyone was growing higher and more impenetrable. Reality had been a small window at the end of a dark corridor. Now a wall had gone up in front of the window. It was a skin-coloured wall. He had lived in his body and now it was the wrong body. His body, errant and sickly, was what controlled his mind [. . .]. (27)

Jack dissociates himself from his body while reality slowly disintegrates "from being a small window at the end of a dark corridor" to a walled-up window the colour of skin. Here, Healy shows great skill in depicting these sufferings as the signs of schizophrenia, a mental disorder whose symptoms range from false beliefs, confused thinking, auditory hallucinations, and a failure to recognise what is real. More specifically, Jack Ferris seems to suffer from depersonalisation disorder or DPD, defined as an anomaly of self-awareness which consists of the feeling of watching oneself act while having no control over a situation.[4] To Jack, the world has become vague, dreamlike, and lacking in significance, as if it were a movie: "Eventually, in the fourth pub, he found that someone he was searching for. That someone who was no one. [. . .] The old feeling of being a camera returned. [. . .] It's a B-movie, that's what my subconscious is" (32–3).

This linguistic blockage, this idiocy of reality, affects all of the male protagonists in Healy's novels at some stage. For instance, Ollie Ewing in *Sudden Times* goes through the same process when he is locked up in his mind, with no words to connect him with the outside world. A revealing episode takes place when Ollie shares a drink with his father in a pub called "The Town Crier":

> [My dad] ordered a drink and out of habit slipped some of the change into a slot machine. I stood behind him to watch the fruits spin. There it was again. I lost my place and began to panic. [. . .] I was in a world of signs. I don't know how long I stood there [. . .]. (136)

Sudden Times reads as a twisted Irish immigrant version of *Crime and Punishment*, as Ollie, a young Irish carpenter working in London, tries to figure out what has happened to his friend Marty Kilgallon. Eventually Ollie goes insane, after finding Marty's dead body burned by acid in the back of a lorry without any clear culprit being identified. Consequently, voices, silence, and absurd signs alternate, and language itself is dislocated. Ollie suffers from fits of aphasia and begins to stutter mentally. Several sections are devoted to the description of this phenomenon. The first is aptly entitled "The mental stutter," with short sentences such as "Givadaint," "Tatat!," "Ilostthekeysiddahise," "Istaso so?," "In my case, I say, itslossingonhoses," "Hosesorry," "Snags, I explain. Bluednags" (91–2).

Interestingly, when asked in an interview if Ollie's character was inspired from real people Healy may have met while working in London, he answered:

> Maybe. You pick bits and pieces up along the way. But, you know, I would have been a bit that way myself. Picking up the voices now and again. I've experienced the odd hallucination of reality: out of nowhere comes the car that hits the bike. The feeling of: did that just happen? Or the bits

of conversation that play in your head like a snatch of an old pop song that you can't get rid of. Hangovers can give you that feeling of an altered reality. And, maybe life [. . .] is one big hangover. (Healy, qtd. in O'Hagan)

Life may be one big hangover, yet Healy's prose is far more faithful to the sense of unreality experienced by most people than the cosmetic style offered by more realist works. He carries on the experimental tradition initiated by the great modernist and post-modernist writers, from Joyce and Woolf and their stream of consciousness techniques, to Flann O'Brien's wild, tongue-in-cheek treatment of structure and language.

In *The Sense of an Ending: Studies in the Theory of Fiction* (1967), Frank Kermode observes that all novels have to lie: "The novel provides a reduction of the world different from that of the treatise. It has to lie. Words, thoughts, patterns of word and thought, are enemies of truth, if you identify that with what may be had by phenomenological reductions" (140). In Healy's novels, however, the general pattern is reversed. Most of the time, the main protagonist deliberately acknowledges his own spurious or false nature. In other words, the novel doesn't lie about its limited, lying nature. In Healy's aesthetics, truth is to be found in dreams or in non-reality, as Jack Ferris illustrates: "All he could think was that a false author dwelt within him. In his dreams the true author existed, unhampered by reality" (66). Similarly, in *Sudden Times*, reality is best expressed through dreams right from the start, or as Ollie simply states: "It always happens in the first dream. If you can get by that you're away" (3). Thus *pure* mimetic fiction is disowned by Healy since reality is inadequately rendered—maimed by memory which, in the long run, is the only thing that remains.

Healy's fiction is primarily about that sense of loss that characterises human existence. This probably accounts for the peculiar structure often visible in the novels. In *Long Time, No See*, for instance, which unfolds sluggishly without even trying to comply with the traditional idea of a central plot, the long perspective is given prominence in the sense advocated by Frank Kermode:

> The books which seal off the long perspectives, which sever us from our losses, which represent the world of potency as a world of act, these are the books which, when the drug wears off, go on to the dump with the other empty bottles. Those that continue to interest us move through time to an end, an end we must sense even if we cannot know it [. . .]. (179)

This is why there is no simplistic teleology in Healy's novels. As he admits, *Long Time, No See* is "a bit of a curved mystery" (Healy, qtd. in O'Hagan). This is also true of *The Bend for Home*, which lays bare Healy's aesthetic and ethical literary agenda:

> It is hard for me to remember my first lie, since I've told so many. And now I'm at it again. Can I lie here and sidestep some memory I'd rather not entertain, and then let fiction take care of it elsewhere, because that is sometimes what fiction does? It becomes the receptacle for those truths we would rather not allow into our tales of the self. (57)

Of course, "Can I lie here?" is a rhetorical question asked by a desperately sincere but unreliable narrator who later, when asked about his real age and his future plans after leaving a nightclub, confesses that he always tells lies: "Yes I said, it was what my father taught me—always tell lies" (207). This mock-candid confession is typical of Healy's style: revealing both its earnest and counterfeit qualities, as when the narrator remembers watching a BBC anthropological documentary in a cinema in which African villagers are performing fertility rites "lobbing their mickeys and breasts to and fro" (100). The same narrator immediately acknowledges: "By Monday the story had gone round the town. [. . .] And we exaggerated all we'd seen. As I am doing here, and not for the first time" (101). Memory is the great deceiver in such cases: "What awfulness do we leave out as memory defends its terrain? What images are locked away that only imagination can release? [. . .] They are the mundane everyday that memory does not espouse" (100).

Long Time, No See also presents us with several bizarre distortions of memory and reality. The plot itself is flimsy. A bullet shot through one of the windowpanes in the house belonging to Joejoe, the narrator's granduncle, constitutes the original mystery in the novel (which will remain unsolved amongst the multiplicity of daily routines and mundane details). The narrator's father, when contemplating interrogating one of Joejoe's friends about the incident, says: "Do you know what reality is—it's a joke" (53). Joejoe himself has a slightly different take, remarking that "it's a strange world," while throwing sticks into the fire (55). Later, the Blackbird—another of Joejoe's friends—declares, "It is extraordinary how ordinary life is" (80). And again, during a bizarre exchange on the art of flirting between the narrator's girlfriend and his mother, the latter says to the narrator in French, "la réalité et toi, vous ne vous entendez pas, n'est-ce pas?"—"You and reality do not get on, do you?" (107). The critic Terry Eagleton has suggested a convincing explanation for this odd atmosphere: "The border between sanity and madness constantly wavers. [. . .] There is no plot and no evolving narrative, just a montage of episodes. Life in this forsaken corner is not heading anywhere in particular, and neither is the novel" (23).

The whole novel is rife with dialogues which sound Beckettian. Take, for instance, the following extract, where Joejoe laments the fact that he is not living in the midst of trees. No particular element is in itself outlandish; rather, it is the whole combination of cues and ideas which sounds faintly—and quaintly—disturbing:

> A beaten tree is a sad sight. I wanted trees, but there again if
>   I was surrounded by
>   trees I would not be here.
> You would not.
> I'd be living somewhere else.
> You would.
> Still and all I'd like a tree to look at.
> Will we go in? asked my father, and Joejoe immediately said:
>   Will you do me a
>   favour?
> I will if I can.
> Bring us for a spin to the woods. (214–5)

The Importance of Being Dermot: Healy's Idiosyncrasies

Part of the charm in Healy's work may derive from its Irish dimension. Healy sometimes overdoes the stage-Irishman act on purpose as when he has his narrator, Philip Feeney, confirm that everyone in Ireland is known by their nickname: "We are all rechristened in this part of the world" (434). But one should not restrict Healy's singularity to this picturesque or parochial Irish aspect. Take the scene, for instance, where Philip—a.k.a. "Mr Psyche"—builds a dry stone wall at the back of the farmhouse:

> He drew the stone from the coral beach by ass and cart to the spot I was taking them from. As he built alongside me, I was pulling his work down. As he dropped a stone into place, I lifted it and carried it away. He built towards me, and I built away from him. I could feel the way he carried himself. (128)

According to Terry Eagleton (commenting on this same scene), "Thoughts like these are only ambiguously Psyche's own. He cannot really carry them off without the author's unobtrusive assistance" (24). However, what really matters here is what immediately precedes this moment, which is not about authorial intrusiveness at all:

> Sometimes I'd be building walls in my dreams. Some of the stones I used had come inland in storms. But today I started to haul from an old ruin on the bank overlooking the sea. I got an awful bad feeling as I pulled the rocks out of the ruin. I had to tell myself over and over that they were going back into another wall. The ruin was supposed to have been a henhouse way back, but it was the strongest henhouse I ever came across. There were massive stones in her. I could have been demolishing a small church, and sometimes I thought I was. (128)

To my mind, this is the most earnest passage in the book. It offers a vision of History as an anxious and simultaneous process of construction and deconstruction, one which transcends all notions of causality, teleology and temporality. All of these dimensions merge into the text. Just as Ollie the carpenter haunts building sites in *Sudden Times*, or Jack Ferris anatomises his failed love story with Catherine Adams in *A Goat's Song*, Healy's work is about that singular, inescapable, and elusive process of reality construction. Healy's strength lies in his ability to convey the uncanny quality of ordinary human experience in simple effective terms. Life is all about (de-)constructing stories. As Ollie says in *Sudden Times*: "*This is all a front*. Life is pretending to be normal. But I'll adapt" (50).

Works Cited

American Psychiatric Association. *Diagnostic and Statistical Manual of Mental Disorders DSM-IV-TR* (Text Revision). New York: American Psychiatric Publishing, 2004. Print.

Eagleton, Terry. "An Octopus at my Window." Rev. of *Long Time, No See*, by Dermot Healy. *London Review of Books* 33.10 (19 May 2011): 23–4. Print.

Healy, Dermot. *A Goat's Song*. New York: Harcourt, 1994. Print.

———. *Long Time, No See*. London: Faber and Faber, 2011. Print.

———. *Sudden Times*. New York: Harcourt, 1999. Print.

———. *The Bend for Home*. New York: Harcourt, 1996. Print.

Hoffmann, Catherine. "Dancing to Ollie's Tunes: The Rhetoric of Narrative Stutter." *Style* 43.3 (Fall 2009): 357–72. Print.

Kermode, Frank. *The Sense of an Ending: Studies in the Theory of Fiction*. New York: Oxford University Press, 1967. Print.

Murphy, Neil. "Dermot Healy's *A Goat's Song*: 'To give some form to that which cannot be uttered.'" *Litteraria Pragensia* 22.44 (Dec. 2012): 108–20. Print.

Robin, Thierry. "Representation as a Hollow Form, or the Paradoxical Magic of Idiocy and Skepticism in Flann O'Brien's Works." *Flann O'Brien: Centenary Essays*. Spec. issue of *Review of Contemporary Fiction* 31.2 (Nov. 2011): 33–48. Print.

O'Hagan, Sean. "Dermot Healy: 'I try to stay out of it and let the reader take over.'" Interview with Dermot Healy. *The Observer* 3 Apr. 2011. Web. 15 Feb. 2015.

Rosset, Clément. *Le Réel Traité de l'idiotie*. Paris: les Editions de Minuit, 1977. Print.

———. *Le Réel et son double*. Paris: Gallimard, 1984. Print.

Notes

1. For further discussion of this key phrase, see Neil Murphy, "Dermot Healy's A Goat's Song: 'To give some form to that which cannot be uttered,'" *Neglected Irish Fiction* issue, *Litteraria Pragensia* 22.44 (Dec. 2012): 108–20, ed. Neil Murphy, Keith Hopper and Ondřej Pilný.

2. See my "Representation as a Hollow Form, or the Paradoxical Magic of Idiocy and Skepticism in Flann O'Brien's Works," *Flann O'Brien: Centenary Essays, Review of Contemporary Fiction* 31.2 (Nov. 2011): 33–48, ed. Neil Murphy and Keith Hopper.

3. *Reality: A Treatise on Idiocy* is my own translation from the French *Le Réel Traité de l'idiotie*.

4. See DSM IV, *Diagnostic and Statistical Manual of Mental Disorders* DSM-IV-TR. New York: American Psychiatric Publishing, 2004.

"The Passionate Transitory":
Dermot Healy and the Sense of Place
Keith Hopper

> It is this feeling, assenting, equable marriage between the geographical country and the country of the mind, whether that country of the mind takes its tone unconsciously from a shared oral inherited culture, or from a consciously savoured literary culture, or of both, it is this marriage that constitutes the sense of place in its richest possible manifestation. (Seamus Heaney, "The Sense of Place" 132)

In the 2011 RTÉ documentary about Dermot Healy, *The Writing in the Sky* (dir. Garry Keane), Seamus Heaney hailed his former protégé as the poetic heir to Patrick Kavanagh: "Kavanagh was the poet of, as he said, 'the passionate transitory,' bits and pieces of the everyday snatched out of time. He was the poet of praise for those things. It isn't just nature poetry, it's gratitude for the whole gift of existence in Healy."[1] Heaney's shrewd comparison is more than just rhetorical: like Heaney himself, both Kavanagh and Healy share a powerful sense of place, which is rooted in the practical rather than the picturesque; both revel in the rhythms of colloquial speech as well as the rhythms of seasonal labour; and both transform a tarnished system of faith into a fragile poetics of transcendental humanism.

In Healy's first collection of poetry, *The Ballyconnell Colours* (1992), Kavanagh's early poem "A Prayer for Faith" (1933)—"O give me faith / That I may be / Alive when April's / Ecstasy / Dances in every / White-thorn tree" (*The Complete Poems* 8)—is echoed in Healy's "Prayer," where contingent matter is gradually stripped away until the poem becomes a meditation on the nature of prayer itself:

> I search the words for it
> And would break out
> Into prayer,
> If I could.
>
> Or if I knew
> One prayer to the sea
> I'd say it. Instead
> I remember
>
> Your definition
> Of prayer—
> To wish another well.
> This is all we can do. (*The Ballyconnell Colours* 65–6)

Conscious that this reverence for ordinary things can easily slip into earnestness, Healy counterbalances the drift towards mysticism with a series of ironic palinodes, as in his three-line imagistic squib, "Two Moons": "The moon above Sligo / Is not / The moon above Mayo" (*The Ballyconnell Colours* 55). However, this dry mischievousness did not always appeal to Healy's early critics, some of whom found its zen-like wit a little too flippant. Richard Hayes in *The Poetry Ireland Review*, for instance, felt that some of the poems in the volume "seem unaware of themselves as reductions, distillations of some greater noise. Significantly, many of the poems in the book take 'place' in the 'cracks between worlds,' perhaps in a vain attempt to deny themselves presence." For Hayes, "The 'real' in Healy's book seems to be what happens before the book is opened and after it is closed" (119). Similarly, in *Books Ireland*, Fred Johnston argued that "Poem try-outs such as 'Two Moons' [. . .] have a Durcanesque wink-and-nod quality to them and shouldn't have been included in this collection. They outsmart themselves." For Johnston, "That is the problem with so many of these poems, however well-constructed and emotionally engineered. They are about the known (to Healy), the familiar, the poet's home ground. They do not rise above this ground, merely describe it" (137).

To my mind, though, the problem with a poem like "Two Moons" is not that it fails to rise above the familiar, but rather that it remains a static snapshot of an abstract thought. At his best, Healy is a maker of moving images, in both senses of the phrase: his images are poignant, often weighed down with melancholy, but they are also deeply rooted in the real (however unknowable that 'real' may be) and constantly in motion, moving tentatively towards some ineffable future. Or as he says in his conclusion to the title poem of *The Ballyconnell Colours*:

> Trying to find
> Space for it all—
> Yourself, the silence of gales,
> The unyielding stars,
> And the white seal pup on the rocks
> Thrown up here,
> Like myself,
>
> In a storm. (74–5)

This cinematic quality greatly enlivens Healy's fourth and penultimate collection, *A Fool's Errand* (2010), a linked sequence of eighty-nine sonnets which centres on the annual migration and return of the barnacle geese near Healy's home in Ballyconnell, Co. Sligo. Every October the geese make the journey from Greenland, and for the next six months they nest on Inishmurray Island, five miles off the Sligo coast. Every morning, five minutes after first light, they fly over Healy's house to their feeding grounds, and every evening they return to Inishmurray, five minutes before dark: "They're like an ancient clock," Healy says in *The Writing in the Sky*, "and I've been trying all these years to learn to wind the hands."

The migration of the wild geese is a familiar theme in Irish poetry, but part of what distinguishes this collection is its tight formal structure: each sonnet is presented in a strict 2-2-3-3-2-2 pattern, mirroring the V-shape of the flock in flight. This ceremonial elegance allows for repetition and variation, which stays true to the cyclical nature of the phenomenon described, but it also enables the poet to speak about time, memory and loss in a way that is rarely sentimental or self-pitying, as in the final sonnet of the collection, where the geese are preparing to migrate once again:

> Today
> they've grown tidy,
>
> the wave of the line is perfect,
> the cries
>
> are not fearful, they know
> where they are going:
> the weather is right.
>
> What more could you ask for?
> And when they hit the sea
> the chorus stops.
>
> We do not hear them.
> They take their song with them.
>
> This is the one certainty—
> that ebbing song. (*A Fool's Errand* 97)

As the critic Colin Graham perceptively observed,

> What Healy describes, in the final phrase [. . .] as an "ebbing song" is this book [itself], one that is alive to the sounds and mysteries of natural phenomena. And Healy is wise enough never to think that his metaphors or his poetry can turn the flow of the natural world into anything other than [what he calls] "unsure knowledge" (n. pag.).

For the purposes of this essay, I wish to consider this seemingly paradoxical notion of "unsure knowledge," especially in relation to Healy's complex and abiding sense of place. Of course, every writer comes from somewhere and has to live somewhere, and inevitably those originary and circumstantial places will worm their way into the artistic work as a backdrop or setting. However, what I want to argue here is that Healy's sense of place is absolutely central to his understanding of the world, and that it functions as the cornerstone of his aesthetic and ethical sensibility. Like Patrick Kavanagh, Healy is interested in the parochial rather than the provincial, and throughout his work there is a fascination with local habitats, dialects, customs and codes of behaviour. And it is this close attention to the particularities (and the peculiarities) of place that makes Healy such an engaging and organic writer, or as Kavanagh himself insisted: "To be parochial a man needs the right kind of sensitive courage and the right kind of sensitive humility. Parochialism is universal; it deals with the fundamentals" ("The Parish and the Universe" 205).

Throughout Healy's writings, and especially his novels, this more fundamental relationship between word and world manifests itself in three overlapping ways. First, at the most basic level of content, Healy's sense of place is social as well as personal, with an almost anthropological appreciation for the whole life of a community. Place, from this perspective, is not just a convenient site for locating a work of fiction but something much more vital and intrinsic, what the French sociologist Pierre Bourdieu calls *habitus*: "a sense of one's (and others') place and role in the world of one's lived experience" (Hillier and Rooksby 5). As Cheryl Herr describes this rich and suggestive concept:

> Bourdieu took the term "habitus" most immediately from Erwin Panofsky's *Gothic Architecture and Scholasticism* (1951). For Panofsky, the concept signifies the ideological categories and assumptions that human beings embody without articulating, possibly without being able to make explicit. This aspect of reality is behavioural rather than intellectual, everyday rather than extraordinary, structural rather than idiosyncratic. [. . .] The habitus always stands in dialogue with the often strategic, improvisational, fluid behaviour of individuals who perform tasks not only in space but also over time. (Herr 32)

Second, I want to think about how this more dynamic sense of place is reproduced in Healy's writings on a formal level. While this formal aspect is easier to discern in poetry—the typographical V-shape and the seasonal sequencing of the poems in *A Fool's Errand*, for example—the topography of the habitus is continually experienced in Healy's fiction through fluctuating and multiple points of view, unexpected shifts in time and space, and in defamiliarising metaphors and rhythmic motifs which cut across the sequential narrative and plot. All of these devices help to 'make strange' the lived environment, and allow us to perceive the extraordinary complexity of ordinary places, people and things.

Finally, I also wish to consider Healy's sense of place from a more broadly philosophical perspective, and think about how the depiction of the habitus frequently becomes a meditation on the nature of Being or, more specifically, on what Martin Heidegger calls "Being-in-the-world."[2] As the philosopher Michael Wheeler notes:

> The Being-in dimension of Being-in-the-world cannot be thought of as a merely spatial relation in some sense that might be determined by a GPS device [. . .]. Heidegger sometimes uses the term *dwelling* to capture the distinctive manner in which *Dasein* [being there; presence] is in the world. To dwell in a house is not merely to be inside it spatially [. . .]. Rather, it is to belong there, to have a familiar place there. It is in this sense that Dasein is (essentially) in the world. (n. pag.)[3]

In all of his novels, Healy is deeply concerned with the problem of representation, and with the vexed question of how to adequately register the protean flux of the world beyond the static and fossilised conventions of realism. However, Healy's overarching sense of place is not just epistemological but ontological: a way of thinking about one's self, one's place in the world, and the transient nature of one's existence. Or as Seamus Heaney phrased it: "We are dwellers, we are namers, we are lovers, we make homes and search for our histories. And when we look for the history of our sensibilities [...], it is to the stable element, the land itself, that we must look for continuity" (148–9).

Dermot Healy was born in Finea, Co. Westmeath, but grew up in Cavan town near the border with Northern Ireland. Following various stints in London and Dublin, Healy returned to Cavan in the late 1970s where he co-founded the Hacklers Theatre Group and edited the regional magazine *The Drumlin* (1978–1980), a forerunner to *Force 10: A Journal of the North-West* (the very titles of which attest to his enduring interest in place). After leading a somewhat peripatetic existence, he eventually settled down in Ballyconnell, Co. Sligo, about thirteen miles northwest of Sligo town. In an interview with Brian Leyden for *The Buzz* magazine (Sligo) in 1994, Healy remarked:

> Arriving in Sligo was like arriving home, and eventually I reached Ballyconnell. […] I wasn't conscious that my four grandparents came from Sligo when I moved here. I only got to know that afterwards, but the telling point is that I feel at home here, and yet I'd be too superstitious to say, "I'll stay." […] The whole landscape of Maugherow [in Co. Sligo] has flooded the poetry, the fiction and the playwrighting that I do. In a few short years its landscape has provided me with half the poems in *The Ballyconnell Colours* and some of the hidden figures in *A Goat's Song*. I'm immensely grateful for that. If there is a magic you'll find it in yourself at last in a proper place. (Leyden 5)

Throughout his career, Healy remained fascinated by borderlands and liminal states of mind, and he frequently transgressed the formal boundaries between poetry, fiction and drama, while also foregrounding the gap between representation and reality. In his memoir *The Bend for Home* (1996), for example, he describes his birth on the opening page, but by the end of the passage he owns up to the Shandyesque lie:

> As for the child, it did not grow up to be me, although till recently I believed this was how I was born. Family stories

were told so often that I always thought I was there. In fact, all of this took place in a neighbour's house up the road [...]. It's in a neighbour's house fiction begins. (3)

This self-conscious awareness of the performative power of storytelling extends to a keen understanding of how place is intertextually inscribed within (and through) popular and literary culture. In chapter two, for instance, the songwriter Percy French is wryly taken to task for misplacing "the bridge of Finea" in "Come Back Paddy Reilly to Ballyjamesduff": "It's a cod. For the sake of a song Percy French got his geography amiss. Even road-engineers are capable of giving wrong directions in order to get a couplet true. And that's how I found out writers not only make up things, but get things wrong as well" (10). Similarly, in chapter three, Healy speculates why James Joyce in *Ulysses* might have sent Milly Bloom to Mullingar, the capital of Westmeath: "He must have thought that County Westmeath had about it that sense of separation, of inwardness, of dullness even, that was necessary to portray a guilt over unfinished things. For it is the halfway house between the magic realism of the West and the bustling consciousness of the East" (15). And in chapter eighteen, he recalls a priest in Cavan who once "devoted an entire sermon to Beckett's *Waiting for Godot*; he'd gone to see a performance in London. We all wait for the message, he said. We wait, despite the fact that no one comes" (107).

In one of the most moving passages in *The Bend for Home*, Healy recalls keeping vigil over his dying mother. As he sits beside her in the family home in Cavan, hungover, he daydreams of his own home in Sligo, and of the mythical island of Hy Brazil.[4] According to legend, Hy Brazil is located somewhere off the northwest coast of Ireland, and every seven years it rises up out of the Atlantic before disappearing again: "If I close my eyes I think I can see Hy Brazil, a little beyond Inishmurray Island, not exactly land, not even someplace eternal, but a place imagined by people long before me that I must imagine in my turn. Imagination hands on a duty to those who come after" (267). Throughout the scene, his mind freely drifts between Hy Brazil, his cottage in Ballyconnell, his early childhood in Finea, his mother's living room in Cavan, and, finally, the troubled world outside. One of the most remarkable things about this sequence is the way that the images and rhythms perfectly capture the ebb and flow of the imagination as it weaves in and out of memory and sense perception, while remaining fitfully aware of other subjectivities and other realities:

> By thinking of Hy Brazil I get homesick for my cottage in Sligo. I sit there thinking of the cottage in the same way I used think of Finea before sleep. I go up the road that was taken away in the storm. The asses roar. The sea is thumping on the rocks. Beside me my mother sleeps with a cooing song. She—despite infirmity, spasms and weakness—is on her own Hy Brazil. Next door Maisie calls for green grapes. On the TV, 7000 people gather in the Shankill Road in Belfast to mourn nine out of ten killed in a fishmonger's shop.
> The tenth they will not mourn.
> He planted the bomb. (268)

The slipperiness of memory and the bonds of community and place are common themes in Healy's fiction, but there is often a darker thread to these preoccupations. As Catriona Crowe remarked, "With writers such as Eugene McCabe, Tom MacIntyre and Michael Harding, [Healy] shares a commitment to local territories of the imagination and their distinct idioms [. . .]. They all deal in an oblique way with the ever-present darkness of Northern Ireland; living close to the Border provides special insights into that intractable situation" (25).

Healy's debut novel, *Fighting with Shadows* (1984; reissued 2015), is a good example of this borderland imagination. The novel is essentially structured in two parts, each part mirroring or shadowing the other. The first part is set in the border village of Fanacross in Co. Fermanagh, and follows the fortunes (and misfortunes) of the Allen family at the height of the Northern Irish Troubles in the 1970s. In the second part, several of the characters move across the border for refuge and work, in what appears to be a fictional version of Cavan town. Thus the world of the novel is literally divided by the political border between North and South, but Healy also explores the deeper divisions—social, sectarian and sexual—which simmer away beneath the surface: "They talked politics out of fear, taking their vengeance on names out there in the real world for what happened here in their own" (80).

In an interesting postmodern take on the ancient Irish idea of *dinnseanchas* ("the lore of places"), place names become part of the wider struggle for meaning within a fiercely divided culture. As Neil Murphy and I noted in our brief "Glossary of Irish Terms" for the Dalkey Archive Press edition of *Fighting with Shadows* (2015):

> The etymology of the name of the fictional village, Fanacross, is explained differently on two occasions in the novel: first by Frank Allen: "Fanacross. *Fan ocras*, the end of hunger, surely" (9); and then, towards the end of the book, a police interrogator says to George, Frank's twin brother: "'Fanacross,' he says, '*Fánaí na coise*, the slopes of the bank'" (352). Both etymologies are imprecise and this may be deliberate on Healy's part, implying a kind of ignorance of place that is a result of not knowing the language properly. (xxiii)[5]

Midway through *Fighting with Shadows*, this brooding obsession with *dinnseanchas* finds its fullest expression in a strange and uncanny funeral sequence. Following the brutal and unexpected murder of Frank Allen (hitherto one of the main characters), his family bring his body to an island graveyard on a lake near Fanacross, where generations of the Allens are buried. In a moment reminiscent of Healy's groundbreaking short story "Banished Misfortune" (1975),[6] the naturalistic flow of the primary mimetic narrative is suddenly interrupted—without signpost or warning—by a diegetic digression, as if history itself seems determined to have its say beyond the characters or the exigencies of plot:

> Seabirds' droppings, white as shingle, covered the other Allen graves. Geraldine, and around her the recent deaths buttressed with stone, and beyond that, the unmarked grave from the Famine. For when the lazy beds failed and the first

> boatloads of skeletons took to the sea looking for grain, the villagers were too tired to bring any new corpses up to the old burial ground at the deserted village in the mountains. [. . .] So they turned their funeral boats up the river, across the freshwater lake to the Island. (149)

This dramatic slippage into the dark Famine past continues on for another two pages. Then, just as suddenly—and again without signpost or warning—the primary mimetic narrative begins to reassert itself, mid-sentence: "And when another of their clan fell dead from starvation they oared to the Island just as the Allens did, over the same water, knowing nothing of who came after" (150). Briefly, for another few beats, the narrative lapses back into a kind of continuous past, before finally flickering back to the present moment, and to Frank's distraught father, Pop:

> Water-lilies lifted up like a mat before the cut of the boat.
> The black depths followed them.
> Two weeks later the [coastguard] cutter passed again. This time they had biscuits, Indian meal and salt. Again they had been saved. They cursed the dead for not having hung on just one day longer. So Pop took leave of his son. (150–1)

It is difficult to locate with any real certainty the source of the diegetic narrative voice: is it simply an authorial amplification of Pop's grief-stricken imagination, or some kind of collective unconscious channelling itself through Pop and the other mourners? Or is it, perhaps, the melancholy voice of the island itself—a ghostly enunciation of past traumas coming back to haunt? In any case, it is a bold and unsettling moment, one where the habitus itself seems to bear witness to the memories and desires of a troubled people, and to the terrible burden of Irish history.

This modernist concern with memory and desire finds its objective correlative in Healy's 1994 novel, *A Goat's Song*. As the author noted in his 1994 interview with Brian Leyden, the novel had a long gestation period, and its sense of place gradually shifted and evolved over time:

I started *A Goat's Song* in Donegal in 1984. By the time I'd ended the book it was set in Mayo. The change came about because of the year I spent as Writer in Residence in Mayo in 1992. Another thing is that Synge's *The Playboy of the Western World* is set in Belmullet, and I'd toured Ireland in a version by Seven Woods [Theatre Company]. I loved where the playboy used to shine her shoes—which is what Jack Ferris does in the book. He cleans Catherine's underthings, like someone who is going to save her.

One of the reasons we get so many tragic books is because the writer begins to make his stories suit his condition of being alone by a desk. You get this sadness for yourself. You must forget the condition of writing to achieve dialogue out there. The object you are trying to attain in writing is to describe the person outside you well. The hardest thing to achieve is the celebration of the world outside yourself, with all its flaws inherent. (5)

Set largely in the west of Ireland (but with some terrifying sorties into the heart of sectarian Belfast), *A Goat's Song* charts the conflict between Jack, a Catholic playwright from the South, and his lover Catherine, a Protestant actress from the North. Driven apart by dreadful alcoholic rows, the playwright tries to recreate their broken relationship in his imagination, and this act of creative contrition becomes a sustained meditation on the vexed relationship between longing and belonging in a divided country. The allegorical conceit is striking but never feels contrived, and Healy's ability to empathise with his characters is superb. For example, when the Northern Protestant family at the heart of the novel cross the Irish border for the first time, the landscape itself—dynamically perceived through the windows of a moving car—mirrors their individual fear and excitement:

> They drove from Erris Head in Broad Haven Bay down to Blacksod in the south, amazed at the isolation, the white sandy roads that ran by the sea; the Inishkea Islands, holy, absolute; the wind-glazed violent cliffs; the meteorological

stations; the endless bogs; the rips and cracks through the huge dunes; the black curraghs; the lighthouse that sat perched on Eagle Island like a castle in a fairy story; the piers, the harbour, the sea. (119)

Sudden Times, Healy's 1999 novel, is a variation on this borderland format, focussing on a young man, Ollie Ewing, who has returned home to Sligo from England. Ollie exists in a twilight zone of casual labour and drunkenness, traumatised by the memory of what happened to him on the building sites of London. Ollie's solipsist confusion and almost schizophrenic estrangement from reality is reflected in the sequencing and shape of the narrative—constantly jumping forwards and backwards in time, all the while circling around the unspoken and unspeakable horror of what happened (we eventually learn that Ollie's brother, Redmond, and his best friend, Marty, were brutally murdered after having crossed some violent criminals in London).

As in Healy's previous novels, the ear for regional dialogue is finely tuned and the description of place is pungent and authentic. However, the description of the world is filtered through the unstable perspective of a highly unreliable protagonist, and so the various streetscapes, though realistically rendered and geographically accurate, take on an expressionistic quality as well. In the opening pages, for instance, Ollie is living in a cramped attic room in the centre of Sligo town. Gazing out through the window, he conveys the sights and sounds of his alien new home:

> You crouched and looked out and saw what you saw— every jackdaw in town croaking, monks in white ascending to Harmony Hill, the roofs over High Street, shoppers, newspaper vans.
>
> It was a light everyday melody, cheerful even. It would not do your head in.
>
> But by night it was something else.
>
> It's like this.
>
> If you left the fucking window open it turned into a loudspeaker through which a town in turmoil screeched its wares.

> Every sound travelled straight up from the street—drunks, women screaming, church bells, taxis, skinheads. Some frantic demon seemed to grip the folk once darkness fell. At night the whole town bedded down with me. It was a ward of the insane. (6)

As the narrative progresses, it becomes more and more apparent that Ollie's sense of dislocation will not easily be overcome. In chapter twelve, he tells us that "I went back to London" (85), but given his heightened state of existential displacement it is impossible to say with any certainty whether he has literally returned to the scene of the crime, or if he is just imagining this scenario and replaying past events in his head. Either way, Ollie is unable to cope with the sheer uncanniness of the material world, which is both familiar and unfamiliar at the same time:

> I catch a glimpse of a vague place I once was daily. The vagueness hurts. It has no name. I try the streets and smells that lead there, but they taper off. [. . .] I search for a familiar place, a place I'd be most days. I have to try very hard. No one's there but ghosts, fast-receding ghosts. Voices recede, nothing really except for the briefest knowledge that I was once there, wherever that is. (86)

At the end of the novel, Ollie attends a party in Sligo held in memory of Marty and Redmond. In the final lines, he hears his father's accusing voice (again, it's unclear whether this voice is inside or outside of Ollie's head, or both): "I don't forgive you, I heard him saying again. *I don't forgive you*" (133). Finally, in a typically audacious move, the last unpunctuated line of the text deliberately evokes the famous ending of Joyce's *Finnegans Wake*:

> I pulled the hood of my sweater over my head and sat on the bed waiting until the listening stopped (331)

If *Finnegans Wake* is the model here, then it suggests an endlessly circular narrative where the ending brings us back to the beginning, and to Ollie's lonely attic room in Sligo town. Place, Healy seems to imply, is the most grounding thing in a person's life—but once that ground is lost it proves difficult to recover.

In many ways, Healy's final novel, *Long Time, No See* (2011), is a subtle variation on the themes and tonal patterns of *Sudden Times*, but one which shows how a more secure sense of place can help to restore a damaged and distressed psyche. The story is set in the coastal townland of Ballintra in the northwest of Ireland, and is told from the point-of-view of Philip Feeney, a young school-leaver suffering from an unspoken trauma (the death of a friend in a car crash, which remains unspecified for most of the novel). Philip—known locally as "Mister Psyche"—awaits the results of his Leaving Cert exam and an uncertain future, and spends most of his time doing odd-jobs and looking after his granduncle, Joejoe, and Joejoe's best friend The Blackbird, both of whom are beginning to show signs of senility. The action, which takes place over the months of August and September, is deliberately muted and low-key, a direct consequence of Philip's gentle but raddled perspective, and the addled reminiscences of his elderly companions.

Synopsis is quite difficult here because nothing much seems to happen, which is all part of its aesthetic design. However, the plot, such as it is, is more straightforward than the hyperactive Faber blurb suggests, with its *grand guignol* rhetoric and vague hints of impending violence, more redolent of the kind of black pastoral practised by Patrick McCabe and Martin McDonagh:[7]

> *Hanging out with men some fifty-plus years his senior proves hazardous for Mister Psyche when the appearance of a bullet-hole in Uncle Joe-Joe's* [sic] *window draws him into a series of (mis)adventures which unsettle and bemuse. Perhaps The Blackbird is losing it? Or perhaps The General has decided to act on a decades-old grudge? Whichever way, as the paranoia grabs a creeping hold of Uncle Joe-Joe* [sic]*, his fragile world threatens to collapse. And it is Mister Psyche who must digest this and acknowledge the new world taking shape in the old.*

It is not that the blurb is untrue exactly, but rather that it underplays the idiomatic texture of the novel, and the subtle interiority which underlies it. Instead of a structured plot, the narrative is constructed around a series of patterned set pieces: building a dry stone wall, digging gardens, sweeping chimneys, hosting a Station Mass, attending wakes. Although the novel is set in 2006, towards the end of the ill-fated Celtic Tiger era, Healy seems keen to record some of these more archaic rituals for posterity. Above all, Healy cherishes the communal activities of a predominantly rural people, who prefer to define themselves through work and love rather than through politics, religion or consumerism. As Joejoe says, after a memorable Sunday dinner with his family, "We forget what we owe to what we've forgotten till we encounter it again out of the corner of the eye, in passing" (132).

Although the narrative structure is deliberately (and deceptively) loose and baggy, the montage of set pieces and vignettes allow Healy's various gifts as a dramatist, storyteller and poet to shine. He has a pitch-perfect ear not just for the cadences of individual speech but for the interwoven rhythms of conversation, what Patrick Kavanagh in "Inniskeen Road" (1935) called the "half-talk code of mysteries / And the wink-and-elbow language of delight" (*The Complete Poems* 18). As in *Sudden Times*, Healy's dialogue is stripped of intrusive quotation marks and dashes, but despite the lack of visual signposts the reader never loses their way. Take, for example, the playful and cagey encounter between Philip and Joejoe on the opening page:

> I took the handle and slid through with a couple of newspapers under my arm. He stepped back as I stepped in, the table cloth rose, Timmy the dog done a turn and I swung the door shut. Joejoe studied me with his back against the shaking panels.
> I was expecting my dear neighbour Mister Blackbird.
> Sorry about that.
> And I said to myself that's him.
> And it was me.
> It was you, but it was his knock, you see a knock can carry anyone's signature on a day like that. I could have sworn. You know what it is son—memory is a stranger who comes to call less and less.
> Aye. (3)

Similes are used sparingly—"Grass from a mown lawn [. . .] lifted and fell like sympathy cards among the graves" (289); "away in the distance the mountain looked like a dark circus tent" (289)—in favour of describing the thing-in-itself, and Healy takes great pleasure in detailing simple rituals, such as the lighting of a fire:

> All the news—the traffic congestion, business and financial affairs, houses for sale, wage and pension increases, obituaries, racing and soccer pages—shot up the chimney. We sat back and watched the flames, and then when the fire was at full tempo, he set the oil lamp on the window and studied the storm. He sang the song of the dog. Rain pounded the asbestos roof. We stepped out, slamming the door behind us, and he took the rusted spade to dig up some onions. The stalks were bent low and swinging in a frenzy of wind. (6)

Throughout the novel, everyday chores and familial obligations are elevated to the level of epiphany; as the elderly scion of the local Big House, Miss Jilly, says, "It's extraordinary how ordinary life is" (80). Indeed, at the end of the story, it is the accumulation of these ordinary things, punctuated by sanctifying rituals of the habitus, which allow Philip the chance to break out of his traumatic narrative loop. In the final lines, as Philip heads off to attend Joejoe's wake, there is a quiet sense of reawakening through his easy and sure-footed negotiation of the familiar terrain:

> I said goodnight, and went out and took the Bog road, and started the walk, with the torch, through the smell of dung, back down through the cut fields, past the rushes and whins and grey shuffling reeds, to the Wake. (438)

Significantly, the word "Wake" is capitalised, drawing attention to the importance of this particular wake for Philip, but also evoking—as in *Sudden Times*—Joyce's *Finnegans Wake*, and its endlessly repeating cycle of life. Unlike Ollie Ewing though, Philip chooses to take comfort in the habitus, and allows himself to be guided by the memory of those who came before him. At its core,

Long Time, No See is a quiet hymn to the troubled ecstasy of life on the Atlantic seaboard, and a celebration of the whole gift of existence. Above all, that fragile and transitory sense of existence is firmly rooted in Healy's extraordinary sense of place—in those ordinary bogs, fields, rushes, whins and "grey shuffling reeds." Like his poetical progenitor Patrick Kavanagh, Dermot Healy is a "king / Of banks and stones and every blooming thing" ("Inniskeen Road," *The Complete Poems* 19).

Works Cited

Crowe, Catriona. "Dark Shoes on a Doorstep." Rev. of *The Bend for Home*, by Dermot Healy. *London Review of Books* 19.15 (31 July 1997): 25–6. Print.

Foster, John Wilson. "Dermot Healy" [Headnote]. "Irish Fiction 1965–1990." *The Field Day Anthology of Irish Writing*, vol. 3. Ed. Seamus Deane. Derry: Field Day, 1992: 1093. Print.

Graham, Colin. "Words on the Wing." Rev. of *A Fool's Errand*, by Dermot Healy. *The Irish Times* 20 Nov. 2010. Web. 7 July 2015.

Grene, Nicholas. "Black Pastoral: 1990s Images of Ireland" (2000). Repr. *After History*. Ed. Martin Procházka. Prague: *Litteraria Pragensia*, 2006. 243–55. Print.

Hayes, Richard. "A Place Called Fruitfulness, a Space Called Silence." Rev. of *The Ballyconnell Colours*, by Dermot Healy. *The Poetry Ireland Review* 37 (Winter 1992/1993): 115–21. Print.

Healy, Dermot. *A Fool's Errand*. Oldcastle: The Gallery Press, 2010. Print.

———. *A Goat's Song*. 1994. London: Flamingo, 1995. Print.

———. *The Ballyconnell Colours*. Oldcastle: The Gallery Press, 1992. Print.

———. *The Bend for Home: A Memoir*. London: Harvill Press, 1996. Print.

———. *Fighting with Shadows*. 1984. Victoria/London/Dublin: Dalkey Archive Press, 2015. Print.

———. *Long Time, No See*. London: Faber and Faber, 2011. Print.

———. *Sudden Times*. London: Harvill Press, 1999. Print.

Heaney, Seamus. "The Sense of Place." 1977. Repr. *Preoccupations:*

Selected Prose 1968–1978. London and Boston: Faber and Faber, 1980. 131–49. Print.

Heidegger, Martin. *Being and Time*. 1927. Trans. J. Macquarrie and E. Robinson. Oxford: Basil Blackwell, 1962. Print.

Herr, Cheryl. *The Field. Ireland into Film* series. Ed. Keith Hopper (text) and Gráinne Humphreys (images). Cork: Cork University Press /Film Institute of Ireland, 2002. Print.

Hillier, Jean, and Emma Rooksby, eds. Introduction. *Habitus: A Sense of Place*. Aldershot: Ashgate, 2002. 3–26. Print.

Hopper, Keith, and Neil Murphy, eds. "Editors' Introduction: Making it New." *The Collected Short Stories*. By Dermot Healy. Victoria/London/Dublin: Dalkey Archive Press, 2015. xi–xxv. Print.

Johnston, Fred. "Innocence and Angst." Rev. of *The Ballyconnell Colours*, by Dermot Healy. *Books Ireland* 169 (Summer 1993): 136–8. Print.

Joyce, James. *Finnegans Wake*. 1939. London: Faber and Faber, 1975. Print.

Kavanagh, Patrick. *The Complete Poems*. Ed. Peter Kavanagh. 1972. Newbridge: Goldsmith Press, 1984. Print.

———. "The Parish and the Universe." 1952. Repr. *Poetry and Ireland Since 1800: A Source Book*. Ed. Mark Storey, London: Routledge, 1988. 204–6. Print.

Keane, Garry. Dir. *The Writing in the Sky* [documentary on Dermot Healy]. Ireland: RTÉ, 2011. 54 mins. DVD.

Leyden, Brian. "Headland: An Interview with Dermot Healy." *The Buzz* [Sligo] no. 10 (July 1994). Ed. Keith Hopper: 5. Print.

Lynch, Sean. "Preliminary Sketches for the Reappearance of Hy Brazil." *Utopian Studies* 21.1 (2010): 5–15. Print.

Murphy, Neil, and Keith Hopper, eds. "Glossary of Irish Terms." *Fighting with Shadows*. By Dermot Healy. Victoria/London/Dublin: Dalkey Archive Press, 2015. xxiii. Print.

Wheeler, Michael. "Martin Heidegger." *The Stanford Encyclopedia of Philosophy* (Fall 2015 Edition). Ed. Edward N. Zalta. Web. 7 July 2015.

Notes

1. Though left uncited in the documentary, the phrase "the passionate

transitory" comes from Kavanagh's poem "The Hospital" (1955): "Naming these things is the love-act and its pledge; / For we must record love's mystery without claptrap, / Snatch out of time the passionate transitory" (Kavanagh 280).

2. As Martin Heidegger wrote: "It is not the case that man 'is' and then has, by way of an extra, a relationship-of-Being towards the 'world'—a world with which he provides himself occasionally. [. . .] Taking up relationships towards the world is possible only because Dasein, as Being-in-the-world, is as it is. This state of Being does not arise just because some entity is present-at-hand outside of Dasein and meets up with it. Such an entity can 'meet up with' Dasein only insofar as it can, of its own accord, show itself within a world" (*Being and Time* 84).

3. As Neil Murphy and I noted in our introduction to *The Collected Short Stories* (2015), Healy's stories often centre around the idea of house and dwelling spaces—both occupied and abandoned—as indexes of cultural continuity and generational change, and as self-reflexive metaphors for the act of writing itself (xiii).

4. For a good overview of the legend of Hy Brazil, see Sean Lynch, "Preliminary Sketches for the Reappearance of Hy Brazil," in *Utopian Studies* 21.1 (2010): 5–15.

5. It is possible to discern a deliberate mischievousness in these misrepresentations of the etymological roots of Fanacross: "fan" (wait), "fán" (slope), and "fánaí" (wanderer), plus "coise" instead of "croise" (of the cross[roads]). Implicit in this Joycean wordplay is a subtle statement about cultural disconnectedness, one which speaks of waiting, wandering, and a terrible sense of loss in the lives of the Irish people. See Murphy and Hopper, "Glossary of Irish Terms," *Fighting with Shadows*, xxiii. Thanks to Dr Seosamh Mac Muirí and Dr Guinevere Barlow for their Irish-language expertise.

6. In "Banished Misfortune" the narrative cross-cuts between multiple viewpoints, but it also flickers backwards and forwards in time and space, and as the critic John Wilson Foster remarked, "The journey through history and geography becomes a form of meditation on Ireland's violent present and broken past" (Foster 1093). At the end of the story—which, like *Fighting with Shadows*, is set on both sides of the Irish border in the 1970s—the narrative abruptly and unexpectedly shifts back in time to 1910. For further discussion of this formal strategy, see Keith Hopper

and Neil Murphy, "Editors' Introduction: Making it New," *The Collected Short Stories*, xix–xxi.

7. Nicholas Grene coined the term "black pastoral" to describe various texts from the 1990s—such as Martin McDonagh's *The Beauty Queen of Leenane* and Patrick McCabe's *The Butcher Boy*—which "turn the green idyll of Ireland into a black dystopia" (243).

Reveries of the Solitary Self in *Banished Misfortune*
Flore Coulouma

When Dermot Healy sought a publisher for his first collection of short stories, a curious thing happened. "I rang up this publisher and they asked me what I was doing at the time," Healy recalled, in an interview with the *Guardian* journalist John O'Mahony. "I told them I was a house painter, so first of all they had me come round and paint the place. Only later did they consider my work and *Banished Misfortune* was published." Thus Healy put the finishing touches to his publisher's abode before he could put out his stories of solitary longing for home. Healy was living in London at the time, doing a variety of jobs from night watchman to building site labourer. Throughout the fifteen years Healy spent in the city, he drifted from house to house yet still managed to feel at home in exile: "I lived for two years in a squat in Brixton. There was a big hole in the ceiling but it was home and I enjoyed it" (O'Mahony). Making a place one's home is what is at stake here. The house-painting episode is a significant anecdote given that Healy's writing, and indeed his early collection of stories, are imbued with a poetic reflection on place and displacement, on making a home, and more generally, they express their characters' longing for "authenticating the outside world" (Healy 20) and finding their place in it. Healy was a painter of houses as he paints the world, in these stories, a hazy shade of dreamy nostalgia.

Banished Misfortune came out in 1982. At that time, Healy was largely unknown to the public, despite having published many poems and stories in literary magazines, being the editor of Cavan literary magazine *The Drumlin*, and having received two Hennessy Literary Awards, in 1974 (for "First Love") and 1976 (for "Banished Misfortune"). His untimely death in June 2014 prompted many a tribute both in Ireland and abroad, yet his work still has not reached a wider audience, despite the unqualified admiration professed by

Seamus Heaney—who called Healy the heir to Patrick Kavanagh—and Patrick McCabe and Roddy Doyle, amongst others. Anne Enright famously declared that "among the Irish, Dermot Healy is the writer's writer. He is the man" (O'Hagan). Healy's first published book, *Banished Misfortune*, is long out of print and no longer features in the publisher's catalogue, which shows how crucially underrated Healy's talent still is (although the publication of Healy's *Collected Short Stories* in 2015 should help rectify this gap in the oeuvre). However, the purpose of this article is not to claim for Healy a place in the pantheon of Irish literary greats—this is already being done successfully at an international level—but, more modestly, to present Healy's early stories and examine their grounding themes and structure as they offer a first glimpse into a singular and poetical depiction of the natural world.

Healy had started writing early on as a teenager, but he remained fully immersed in the world of manual labour and physical craftsmanship throughout his life, which perhaps enabled him to approach writing as a tangible, physical endeavour. His writing is imbued with a sensual depth that has not gone unnoticed, with journalist John O'Mahony remarking in 2000 that:

> If there is a single strain running through [Healy's] work, from the early collections of stories and poems to his novels *A Goat's Song* and *Sudden Times*, it would be that [. . .] notion of bristling physicality, not just of the Sligo landscapes that fill his books or even the punishing daily graft of the London building sites he often conjures up, but the essential physicality of language.

In the stories, such physicality translates as a form of poetic prose that summons all the senses to evoke the overwhelming vastness and protean shape of the outside world. In *Banished Misfortune*, Healy posits his solitary characters as the recorders of the sounds and sights of the physical world, turning their nostalgic musings into a poetic evocation where language reaches out to hazy, dreamlike visions and resounding echoes. Characters reflect on their own sense of longing while their movements in space and time map out Healy's complex representation of the exilic self, torn between a keen sense of loss and a near transcendent "delight in nature" (Healy 17). This pervasive mix of restlessness and quietude finally leads us back to the question of home and finding one's place in the natural world.

Sights and Sounds:
A Synesthetic Representation of the Outside World

The first story in the collection, "First Snow of the Year," opens with music and light:

> For a few bewildering seconds, Jim Philips, on the day of his retirement, queried late morning sounds he had not heard in years. Then his solitary sense of freedom began. He looked with leisure at the low pink boards that ran the length of the ceiling, yellowing at the fireplace, brightening by the window.
> Light was hammering on the broken shutter.
> Shadows darted across the mildewed embroidery of dogs and flowers. (1)

Healy lays out the tone and dissonant themes of his collection: loneliness and serenity, light and dark, stillness and movement, the passing of time and the decaying permanence of home. As the retired postman surveys his room, we are drawn into a symphony of colour and sound in which the hammering light marks the rhythm of life, while the mildewed wallpaper reminds us that texture and smell are no less crucial in the picture. The "embroidery of dogs and flowers" meets the dance of light and shadows, bringing together the movements of nature and the work of man.

While this and most of the other stories in the collection draw a critical picture of (rural) Irish society and social interaction in the late 1970s, nature and place play the greatest part in Healy's poetic storytelling. "First Snow of the Year" is set in a rural part of County Roscommon and features several characters brought together or against each other by their acute sense of solitude. When Jim comes out of his house to inspect the fields around his house, it again translates through a chorus of sights and sounds:

"He shattered the surface water of the well, and from where Jim stood, the earth was on its side, reflected in every piece of ice, the wind sounding through the gulleys and drains like a concert flute" (1). While Jim's fragmented vision of the field creates an unsettling dizziness and takes in character and readers alike, it is also a source of wonder, as the observer's gaze is a distorting force that topples the earth. In the same scene, Jim's silent friend behind him betrays the more desperate helplessness of man in nature, as he huddles against the wall, "out of the wind, looking at the earth, humourless and uncertain" (1).

The initial scenes of this first story sets the tone for the collection as a whole and takes us through the sometimes cacophonous music of the world and into the blurred visions of Healy's dreamy characters. "First Snow of the Year" follows Jim, Phildy and Owen through a winter's day, from the morning funeral of Owen's mother to the gathering of mourners at the village pub and Owen's silent walk back to his lover's house. Throughout the story, the music of man and nature signals the passing of time and puts main observers Jim and Owen through their contemplative, melancholy pace: "'For one bright sovereign sold my life away,' a cockfighter was singing" (6). Songs and sounds echo one another until the story reaches its conclusion at the end of the day, with the return of a gypsy couple to their home: "Soon John Cawley and Margaret Cawley came over the rocks singing dead verse" (9). The mysterious wandering of the gypsies and their cryptic singing make them one with the movements of nature, and this deeply evocative story, based on poetic synaesthesia rather than plot, paves the way for the rest of the collection. While Heaney called Healy the heir of Patrick Kavanagh for his depiction of the Irish rural landscape, here, Healy's stories are rather reminiscent of Baudelaire, whose poem "Correspondences" famously presents his theory of poetic synaesthesia in bringing together colours, sounds and scents:

> Nature is a temple, where the living
> Columns sometimes breathe confusing speech; [. . .]
> As the long echoes, shadowy, profound,
> Heard from afar, blend in a unity,

Vast as the night, as sunlight's clarity,
So perfumes, colours, sounds may correspond.
(Baudelaire 19)

Healy expresses his near mystical sensitivity in a similar vein throughout the collection. In "The Island and the Calves," human singing echoes the sounds of nature to reveal that "the spiritual world [is] ecstatic and sensual" (16), and again, Healy brings together sight and sound: "In the deep pool of water, the edges of the purple pines sharpened towards sunset. Winds channelled through the woods with a low hum" (16). Here, the sounds of the outside world find their counterpart in the "deep bass music, The Seven Last Words of Jesus Christ on the Cross by Haydn," and later, the "sudden mad screech of the geese rising with a chorus of screams" parallels "Haydn's [. . .] final celebration" (18). In "The Island and the Calves," the physical sounds of music express the spiritual union of body and soul as the characters read from The Song of Songs. Healy's insistence on the echoing sounds of life and nature lays out a three-dimensional universe and balances his blurry and slanted visions. The recurring imagery of pools, lakes and water reflections is also surprisingly reminiscent of the early baroque aesthetic of mirrors, distorted visions and dreams. At the same time, Healy's references to recognisable songs, poems and tunes bring us back to the realm of language and discourse, thus anchoring his dreamy depictions to a concrete sense of historical and political relevance.

"The Girl in the Muslin Dress" opens with a young woman "singing 'Under Milk Wood' to an old Welsh air she had learned from her grandfather" (43). As she and the first-person narrator drift through the streets of early morning London, her song, and later, a passerby "humming a number of ancient concert-hall tunes," ground them in a concrete moment of historical time and provide a counterpoint to the universality and atemporality of meteorological cycles. *Under Milk Wood*, Dylan Thomas's 1954 radio drama, is doubly significant here; Healy pays tribute to one of his most crucial influences during his own time as a drifting expatriate in London. As Sean O'Hagan notes in his obituary for Healy, "For two years he worked as a security guard in empty factories near Heathrow airport, where he helped pass the long hours on the night shifts by reading Dylan Thomas" (O'Hagan). Healy's reference also operates a reflexive *mise-en-abyme* of his interior journeys into the minds and dreams of his characters, emulating the narrative structure of Thomas's *Under Milk Wood*. Here, the old song and "ancient concert-hall tunes" also introduce a sense of temporal and spatial disruption in the main characters, two destitute city drifters exiled from their Welsh and Irish homelands, and who are painfully aware of the passing of time and the foreignness of their surroundings. Significantly, in "The Island and the Calves," expatriate Catholic priest Edward sings 1964 hit song "Under the Boardwalk, Down by the Sea," by American band The Drifters.

Singing is mostly a solitary activity in the stories, even in the eponymous "Banished Misfortune," in which a professional fiddler and his family leave the violence of their Northern hometown and find temporary relief in Galway. The main character McFarland plays music with his Galway friends to escape the fear and tension of his hometown:

> "Politics is the last thing in the world I want to hear about," said McFarland in a pub where he was the centre of attraction as he laid his fiddle down. "The very last thing."
> "Give us a slow air," someone interrupted in Salthill as they went from "Toss the Feathers" to "The Flowers of Spring." And the Bank manager danced to the tune. (106)

Despite the company of his friends, McFarland is alone with his nostalgic recollections of the past, "when death wasn't an institution" (109), and his melancholy reflection on the traditional Irish tune "Banish Misfortune." The past is lost and McFarland has forgotten the sounds of his childhood: "There must be a thousand stories and songs about my own place that I hardly know" (109–10), he says to his sleeping wife. Music is no remedy for the characters' solitary nostalgia as they strive to reclaim a sense of place in their ancestral home. Here and throughout the collection, Healy makes music and sounds the instruments of his sensual evocation of place while his characters come to terms with their "solitary sense of freedom" (1). Let us now examine the solitary observers of Healy's melancholy universe.

Reveries of a Solitary Observer

In *Banished Misfortune*, sounds and sights are experienced by solitary subjects. Although many of the stories depict social interaction and feature characters in pairs and couples, the overall impression is one of pervading loneliness. Families, couples and friends meet and part, yet there is no true understanding, save in "The Island and the Calves," where Healy's third-person narrator only hints at the depth of his characters' bond: "it would be unfair to show how much they loved each other, that would be to invade them; let their occupations this day speak for them" (17). This disingenuous refusal to invade his characters' privacy contrasts with Healy's stream-of-consciousness narratives throughout the collection, and this hesitation between restraint and scrutiny feeds the melancholy thoughtfulness of Healy's characters, as well as his first-person narrators in stories such as "A Family and a Future," "The Curse" and "The Girl in the Muslin Dress." The posture of the solitary observer, reminiscent of Rousseau's bittersweet *Reveries,* ushers the reader into a drifting narrative where the nomadic self is a singular entity at once apart from his fellow men and strongly empathetic towards his natural surroundings. In "First Snow of the Year," recently bereaved Owen walks back to his house as in a dream: "He walked across a new planet, journeying inwards, without thought of his fellows" (8). The characters' sense of apartness pervades the very structure of dialogic interaction with perfunctory, uninformative and disconnected utterances interrupting the characters' inner thoughts at irregular intervals:

> "What are you thinking about?" asked Jim.
> "Nothing. There's no change."
> "We'll look down from the hill."
> Phildy did not answer, but mumbled, with a hint of anger was it, in his voice. (2)

This exchange, the first in the collection, sets the tone for Healy's pared-down dialogues. Words are part of the general soundscape of the characters' lives, but the rare verbal interactions serve to emphasise the overall sense of apartness and solitude of Healy's mournful observer-characters.

Dialogue is a treacherous pretence used as deceitful manipulation or to smoothen out the obligatory human interactions of daily life. "The Curse" displays the falsity of friendly conversation and points to the ultimate violence of language. The young first-person narrator agrees to run an unusual errand for the local Anglo-Irish "horse-racing man" against the elusive promise of a job:

> "I want you to go up to [the bar maid] and say, 'You rotting cunting bitch,' then clear off out of there." [. . .]
> "Yes," says I, "and when do I get to ride the ponies?" (25)

The naïve narrator soon realises that his newly-found friends are nothing but bullies who "go on drinking as if they didn't notice me" after the job is done. The narrator finds his revenge when he turns the curse back against his former allies: "At last, I turn one foot into the hall, open the outside door, and shout backward to all there, 'You dirty fat English gets,' and clear off up the street diagonally, thinking, if it comes to it, I can run forever" (26). The story ends with another non-communicative dialogue when the boy follows the Dean in the street, "pretending, for today at least, to be other than I am, and much more besides, while he, thinking he knows me, talks of superior breeds in the sprinting world" (27). In this story of class divide and prejudice, Healy shows the impossibility of communication and exposes the radical solitude of his characters.

In "Blake's Column," the failure of communication takes on another dimension with the depiction of a newspaper columnist locked in his solipsistic world and unable to relate to the people around him: "like all others of his creed he was superficially hardened toward unhelpful criticism, but especially anxious over praise which he had not earned" (29). While Blake fails to make casual conversation with his neighbourhood acquaintants and lives alone, separated from his wife, he has become a recorder of his town's events: "He now lived in the cottage alone, taking his morning walk at cock-crow, with the collar of his coat up to his ears and taking in all he heard" (33). Yet this solitary observer is not a benevolent onlooker, and his scathing column becomes an alienating force further separating him from the rest of the world. The violence of language, here, rests on the force of the written word and echoes the young boy's insults in "The Curse." Blake only finds solace in the contemplation of the calves grazing in the field outside his cottage, thus bringing us back to the original purpose of the solitary *flâneur*.

Stories of love and friendship similarly display the failure of perfect communion through language. In "Kelly," two expatriate drifters strike up a friendship in London, but their intimacy cannot survive their individual fates of madness and loss: "Darcy was shocked by the mad lifeless gleam in the Pole's eyes. It reminded him of the night his eyes had remained open while he slept, like cracks that opened to nowhere" (64). Darcy's realisation that his friend is lost throws him back to his own inability to make sense of the world: "The previous year had been composed of two sounds for Darcy, lake-sound and city-sound, and as time passed the shadows merged but did not strengthen into something articulate and real" (53). Darcy recognises the power of true dialogue to make the world real and break his dream-like detachment, yet there is no way out as communication breaks down and Darcy finally mourns the end of his friendship: "what saddened him most was the personal defence mechanism that destroyed a relationship so newly born" (65).

Like friendship, love fails to fulfil the characters' longing for togetherness. In "The Girl in the Muslin Dress," the first-person narrator reflects about the end of love: "she made me promise never to let her go because she knew that was what I wanted to hear. Now, back in normality, no dreams come, the future separates us" (50). Even the act of love cannot mend the narrator's loneliness, as "moonless night exhaustion and relief [. . .] finally coax[es] both of us away, worlds apart" (44). In "Reprieve," an Irish couple who has travelled to Birmingham for an abortion are breaking apart: "'There is still time to go back on this,' he repeated. She held her silence" (51). Relief comes with the doctor's "spectacular shot in the arm" but there is no reprieve in the woman's temporary slip from consciousness, and no mending of the rift that has opened between them. In "Betrayal," Healy gives us a brief glimpse into the bitter-sweet epiphany of a man and woman meeting for love: "Their situation, outside of these few moments together, appeared impossible" (67). In *Banished Misfortune*, love is at best a shared illusion, at worst a false game of make-believe. Finally, in the poignant story "Love," young apprentice Jimmy spends nights waiting for a girl to come out of her house and join him, yet we soon realise that his feeling is unrequited: "He looked at the door, willing it to open. The door did not open" (68).

As Jimmy witnesses his sister's relationship of convenience with a man she does not love, he is faced with his own loneliness: "The sight of them together looked so false that a feeling of nervous sickness attacked Jimmy's stomach and he sought to escape, with that desperate knowledge that all ways led back here, among relationships he had no place in" (77). Healy magnifies the poignant intensity of Jimmy's longing only to underline the impossibility of human understanding.

Only in "The Island and the Calves" does Healy suggest the existence of deep, untainted love between his characters, yet the observation of nature and understanding of transcendent realities remains a quintessentially solitary experience. By the end of the collection, Healy has drawn a complex picture of the human condition; his characters hover between the solace and pain of their "solitary freedom," while the pervasive feeling of the impossibility of love is occasionally broken up by epiphanic moments of communion. *Banished Misfortune* delves into the utopian motif of finding oneself through the contemplation of nature; its necessary counterpart is alienation from the social world. The recurring themes of solitary wandering, resignation and withdrawal make up the structuring tropes of this dialectic movement: finding one's true—interior—self can only be achieved through renouncing the Other, and such melancholic renouncement reaches towards a deeply utopian hope for a new, better condition. The title of the collection, *Banished Misfortune*, underlines this hopeful reversal, thus tying Healy's mystical utopia to the concrete reality of the Irish experience. As Healy's solitary, brooding characters pace through poetic landscapes of blurred visions and sounds, they strive to find their place in the world; movement and stillness finally come together into Healy's poetic longing for home.

Finding One's Place

Healy's representation of the natural world through the visions of his pensive drifters brings us to his central concerns of place and home. Home is the common thread to *Banished Misfortune*'s twelve stories, whether they are set in rural Ireland or in the urban maze of London. Healy expresses his characters' sense of place and longing for home through the recurring opposition between drifters, travellers and immigrants, on the one hand, and the imagery of houses and dwellings rooted in timeless landscapes, on the other hand. While the uncertain status of the drifter translates in the nostalgic longing for a home real or imagined, Healy also depicts movements in space and time as reflections of the cosmic motion of the universe. His contemplative, wandering subject finds wholeness in nature and transcends his exilic sense of place to reach a universal sense of home. Healy thus moves beyond the social and historical context of Irish oppression and deprivation—with economic underdevelopment and emigration still a defining trait of 1970s Ireland—to draw an allegorical picture bringing national and political concerns into his universalist sense of home.

"Kelly" and "The Girl in the Muslin Dress" feature characters exiled from home and drifting through a place that they cannot make their own. The Polish migrant Kelly—whose Irish-sounding nickname translates his status as an outsider—ends up in a London psychiatric hospital, and his Irish immigrant friend eventually realises that the root cause of the trauma was the destruction of his original home: "This Christmas five years ago my neighbours were gunned down in the shipyards of Gdynia. I pray for them now" (65), Kelly writes to his friend. Kelly's reference to the 1970 protests against the ruling Polish Communist Party in Gdynia parallels his friend's own political angst about the onset of the Northern Irish

Troubles. The relevance of political violence in Healy's stories is directly related to the question of home; in "Banished Misfortune," the McFarlands briefly escape the Northern tensions, only to yearn for home from the safety of their Galway hotel. In this story, travelling and home make up the conscious identity of the main character, Irish fiddler McFarland, son of wandering man Saul: "And McFarland, reared amongst a series of foreign and local escapades, took everywhere his copies of the Arctic and Antarctic voyages" (99). Now McFarland and his family live in the house built by his father who settled down after a life of travelling and planted roots by the river Erne: "They gathered the red limestone rocks from the hills and fine washed stones from the Erne, the broached flagstones from Sliabh Buadh [. . .] and the gypsies carried cartloads of rocks up the hillside and sat under the chestnut tree smoking and drinking while it rained" (110).

The figure of the gypsy is significant here as a paradoxical symbol of grounded uprootedness: in *Banished Misfortune*, the nomadic gypsies represent the soul of the rural Irish countryside and are an integral part of nature's timeless history. The mysterious combination of movement and stillness of the "grimy gypsies" (110), a recurring feature in Healy's stories, suggests a romantic influence both homegrown—Healy's ubiquitous "gypsies" are reminiscent of Celtic Twilight romanticism and Synge's *The Tinker's Wedding*—and continental, with Baudelairean echoes of "that ardent eyed people" resonating throughout the hazy visions of gypsy camps in *Banished Misfortune* (Baudelaire 33).

In "First Snow of the Year," gypsies are the first people that main character Jim Philips sees after he comes out of his house to inspect the fields around him: "He saw John and Margaret Cawley, the gypsies, stealing through the yellow gorse with rotten turf. Their children moved from clownish tree to clownish tree out of the wind" (1). Healy's houseless gypsies mirror his recurring obsession with building one's own house and laying claim to a place as one's home. In "The Tenant," newcomer Mr Franklin, who has taken up rooms at the "colonial hotel" as he begins his new position at the local bank, meets Mr Johnson, a returned immigrant who has "built [his] two-storey house himself, plastering the porch with seashells" (82). This is another tale of misunderstanding and solitude in which the stranger is ultimately rejected by Mr Johnson and his wife, because Mr Franklin's solitary independence and seeming detachment threaten their idea of a stable homelife. While Healy draws an ironical portrait of provincial small-mindedness and social resentment in this particular story, his social depiction relies on the crucial questions of time and space. Melancholy arises from Mr Franklin's failure to make himself at home in his new surroundings, and from the ineluctability of the passing of time. The hotel's name, Swann's Hotel, provides an ironic echo to Proust's *In Search of Lost Time* and reminds us that the solitary wanderer's reveries are prompted as much by his awareness of his own mortality as by his ataraxic delight in nature. Space and time, then, follow the cyclical laws of nature's binding force, and Healy's characters only find peace when they yield to the cosmic movement of the seasons.

"The Island and the Calves" takes place in the Sussex countryside. Jim and Edward are both expatriates, yet theirs is an experience in ecstatic communion with nature, an acquiescence to the passing of time and the cyclical renewal of life: "They have, for old time's sake, erected an aerial off a high tree to pick up the Mass in Irish from Radio Éireann, to allow the chants from Jim's home country to permeate the house"; those chants join the "mad screech of the geese rising with a chorus of screams" as "emigration has begun" (17–18). As Jim's gaze follows the slanted flight of the geese and comes to rest on the calves in his field, he draws his balance from the movements of nature:

> Now Jim knew the four points of the compass from the wind and the calves, the corners of that elementary field he extended onto the lake to find direction from there. [. . .] And what was permanent, what stood still, would always point in a different direction to the man or the bird always moving, recognizing and turning, lifted on a current of air. (19)

Blurred visions, sharp sounds and a melancholy acquiescence to the movements of space and the passing of time, such is the landscape that emerges through Healy's bittersweet stories of solitary characters in search of solace. This dreamy "journeying inwards" of his reflective characters is what ultimately enables them to embrace the outside world and reach their epiphanic contemplation of nature.

Dermot Healy has been called one of the finest contemporary writers of Irish rural life. Yet his early short stories, while rooted in places symbolic of the Irish experience at home and abroad in the late twentieth century (rural Ireland, Belfast, London), are steeped in a poetic tradition beyond these spatial and historical borders. Early reviewers of the stories deemed them promising but unequal, and remarked that their distinct poetic style—making them at times inscrutable pieces of prose poetry—sometimes missed the mark (see, for instance, the *Kirkus Review*). My reading, however, is that these early stories display a singular and poetic vision of the world, on a par with the great Irish nature poets, Patrick Kavanagh and the Northern Irish poets. Yet Healy's melancholy does not compare to Kavanagh's fatalistic despair, nor does it arise from the sectarian divides depicted in the Northern poets' vision of nature. Healy's dreamy representation of time, space and the natural world harks back to Rousseauist visions and the melancholic longings of the Baudelairean *flâneur*. *Banished Misfortune* thus paves the way for Healy's later work both as a poet and novelist, and lays out the significant images of his natural landscapes, in a movement at once singular and universal: bird flight, lakes and ponds, the passing of the seasons, looking for home across a field.

Works Cited

Anon. "*Banished Misfortune* by Dermot Healy." *Kirkus Review* 21 Nov. 1982. Web. 20 Nov. 2014.

Baudelaire, Charles. *The Flowers of Evil.* Oxford: Oxford World's Classics, 1993. Print.

Healy, Dermot. *Banished Misfortune.* London: Allison and Busby, 1982. Print.

Jarman, Anthony Mark. "A Brilliant Return for Dermot Healy." *The*

Globe and Mail 8 July 2011. Web. 20 Nov. 2014.

O'Hagan, Sean. "Dermot Healy Obituary." *Guardian* 30 June 2014. Web. 20 Nov. 2014.

O'Mahony, John. "Let the West of the World go by." *Guardian* 3 June 2000. Web. 20 Nov. 2014.

Dermot Healy's Heterotopias:
Fanacross and Northern Ireland in *Fighting with Shadows*
Jack Fennell

Fighting with Shadows is set sometime during the 1970s in Fanacross, County Fermanagh, a fictional village whose hinterlands, as hinted at by its name, bleed over (or "fan across") the border between the Republic and the North. Squeezed between a prolonged drought to the South and war in the North, generally ignored by Westminster, Stormont and Dublin, the village's only noteworthy feature is a bridge connecting the two countries, which is demolished by the British Army in the course of the story. Against this backdrop, the novel focuses on the Allens, an average and mostly unremarkable family.

Indeed, the setting and its characters could all be reasonably described as 'average' and 'unremarkable'—at one point, Frank Allen even describes himself as "a strong-bodied man with average intelligence" (11). Healy describes in detail the everyday routines of thoroughly average people with no great achievements, ambitions or past glories to speak of. In the background, of course, the Troubles are looming, and while Fanacross is depicted as a politically isolated backwater to a large extent, the characters are well aware that there is no escaping the coming violence.

The ordinariness of the setting serves to heighten the sense of an approaching threat: these are everyday people in an unremarkable village, about to be caught up in the bloodshed and murder reported in news broadcasts. The full force of this contrast is felt in the short, matter-of-fact sequence describing Frank's murder. While the Allens' married life is not a picture of domestic bliss, Frank and Helen have settled into a peaceful, somewhat banal pattern since moving into the family home with Frank's father. Then, one evening, while sipping whiskey and writing a letter to his brother George, "[Frank] answered the door to a man with a gun who shot him three times in the head" (115).

The juxtaposition of prosaic characters and settings with bloody murder is not subtle; paradoxically, despite its 'ordinariness,' there is very little subtlety to this novel at all, whether in imagery (the bridge), plot (Frank is murdered because he has been mistaken for his identical twin George, a member of the IRA) or even the title—to drive the point home, *Fighting with Shadows* is subtitled *Sciamachy*, a Greek term for mock-combat, or fighting with a nonexistent enemy. Healy quite rightly eschews equivocation as much as the sensationalism of Troubles-set thrillers, derided elsewhere as "action-packed near pornography" (Golden 18). The effect is to enhance the realism of the literary depiction of murder by removing it from the entertainment or ideological contexts that would otherwise lessen or alter its impact. At the time of the novel's publication, however, there were some who objected to this technique.

In a piece for the *Linenhall Review*, Peter Brooke dismisses *Fighting with Shadows* as "woefully pessimistic and badly written." The main problem, Brooke says, is a lack of the "spiritual self-confidence" characteristic of the work of Canon Sheehan; Healy is Sheehan's antithesis, and seems to regard Catholic Ireland as "a great, diseased void," while the characters who inhabit that setting are all "uniformly stupid, passive and are only driven out of complete, self-enclosed introspection by the need to fondle each other and be loved." His castigation of the novel comes to a remarkable climax: "[Healy] is unable to believe in the superiority of Catholic Irish culture over British culture and so is left, like Milton's vision of the fate of Evil after the Last Judgement, self-consuming and self-consumed" (Brooke 19).

Brooke's review is an interesting artefact in its own right, because his objections to the novel are so clearly coded in moralistic and nationalistic terms—there is a dichotomy between Irish/Catholic and British/Protestant, as though only those particular combinations were possible, and there is an accusation that Healy is letting 'his side' down: "[Healy] hates the Brits and the Prods," Brooke asserts, but "can find nothing admirable in the culture that is counterposed to the Brits and the Prods." It is also rather telling that Brooke objects to the characters' interest in fondling each other, since elsewhere in the same review he argues that the novel is symptomatic of

> [. . .] a serious problem that is at present afflicting Irish Catholic culture. We might have called it "alienation," were it not that Mr. Healy comes from Cavan, in that part of Ireland free from foreign domination. A much better word would be the sense of "futility"—the collapse of all values. (Brooke 19)

No less hyperbolic, though taking the opposing view, is Aubrey Dillon-Malone's *Books Ireland* review from the same time. Initially horrified at the prospect of "another, aaarrrgh, novel about [. . .] the North," Dillon-Malone goes on to praise *Fighting with Shadows* as being "like no other novel about the North. In fact it is like no other novel." The experience of reading it is a "mindfuck" and the reviewer compares it to Joyce, since "it's meant to be re-read rather than read." Dillon-Malone notes, a little mistakenly, that there is no clear thematic or narrative thread in the novel, but nevertheless manages to work himself up into a breathless, surreal climax, proclaiming "the talent behind it is voluminous, great whores [sic] of meaning unfurling themselves like the layers of an onion" (233).

In another review, Seán Golden states that "[i]n many ways Healy's characters' lives of quiet frustration could transpire anywhere, but they happen to transpire on the border between North and South in Ireland" (Golden). To my mind, this skips over one of the most interesting aspects of *Fighting with Shadows*, and I would argue that conceptions of space are fundamental to understanding this work.

Edward Soja argues convincingly that:

> [t]he structure of organised space is not a separate structure with its own autonomous laws of construction and transformation, nor is it simply an expression of the class structure emerging from social [. . .] relations of production. It represents, instead, a dialectically defined component of the general relations of production, relations which are simultaneously social and spatial. (Soja 78)

Countries and national boundaries are perfect examples of this kind of organised space. They are not natural phenomena, but are produced dialectically; the social construction of space acts upon and within physical geography to create these political entities. Ireland is a particularly apt specimen of this sort of dialectical arrangement, with the physical 'fact' of the island containing two socially-constructed countries—partition itself thus highlights the imaginary nature of both nation-states, though they are no less real for it. This overlap of natural and man-made boundaries, material reality and cultural imagination, is a fundamental aspect of Northern Irish identity, as outlined by Seamus Heaney:

> The fountainhead of the Unionist's myth springs in the Crown of England, but he has to hold his own in the island of Ireland. The fountainhead of the Nationalist's myth lies in the idea of an integral Ireland, but he too lives in an exile from his ideal place. Yet while he has to concede that he is a citizen of the partitioned British state, the Nationalist can hold to the physical fact of his presence upon the Irish island, just as the Unionist can affirm the reality of the political realm of the United Kingdom even as he recognizes the geographical fact that Ireland is his insular home. (Heaney 5)

This messy overlap of geography, politics and society suggests that Northern Ireland could be usefully interpreted as a number of intersecting Foucauldian heterotopias, a 'heterotopia' being "a sort of place that lies outside all places and yet is actually localizable" (352).

Graveyards, Margins and Other Spaces

One example Foucault gives of a heterotopia is the cemetery: once situated almost in the centre of the city, nowadays cemeteries mostly exist on the edges, or out in the suburbs. Foucault links this relocation to a decline in belief in the immortality of the soul—as the continuation of the personality into the afterlife became increasingly uncertain, physical death assumed more and more importance. Thus, death became explicitly linked with sickness rather than salvation, and therefore it had to be kept at a safe remove from the city centre (353–4). Foucault argues that any element that cannot be spatially ordered is similarly pushed to the peripheries, an argument with striking similarities to actual trends from Northern Irish history.

Joep Leerssen argues that "[t]he extent and spatial outlines of a community, a polity, are defined by the reach of its laws," and so communities conceive of themselves as 'spheres of law and order': "within that sphere, one plays by rules and the individual has a defined place in the order of things; outside, it's a dog-eat-dog world" (Leerssen 1–2). Those who challenge the state's legitimacy, particularly the legitimacy of the state's monopoly on violence, "become, symbolically if not spatially, external enemies rather than internal offenders" (2). This was, of course, precisely how Catholics had historically been perceived in the North, and for much of the twentieth century it was clear that the Northern Irish polity was being spatially ordered to place Catholics outside the legal and political sphere.

One of the principal arguments of Northern Irish civil rights campaigners was that infrastructural planning in the North was being conducted in such a way as to marginalise Catholics, in a very literal spatial/geographical sense. Aside from the endemic gerrymandering, peculiarities in town planning (such as inadequate provision for the construction of Catholic primary schools) were interpreted by Catholics as "fortress unionism," a bid to discourage Catholics from living and working in the province's urban centres. There was also discrimination in higher education, most notably in one case where Coleraine (in the 'Protestant' eastern half of the country) was chosen as the site for a new university, at a time when Derry (in the 'Catholic' west) was hoping for funds to expand its already existing third-level facilities (Coogan 41–3).

Theoretical and critical resonances abound in this spatial ordering of Northern Ireland. We hear echoes of Giorgio Agamben, who, using the ancient Roman legal figure of the 'sacred man' (*homo sacer*, a citizen who can be killed with impunity), argues that "[t]he banishment of sacred life is the sovereign *nomos* that conditions every rule, the originary spatialization that governs and makes possible every localization and every territorialization"

(Agamben 66). A more visceral comparison can be made to Julia Kristeva's description of the 'abject,' the unsettling other "ejected beyond the scope of the possible, the tolerable, the thinkable" (Kristeva 1), encompassing all that "I permanently thrust aside in order to live"; the abject evokes revulsion and fascination at the same time, and it has a spatial component in that the 'ordinary' processes of life are not possible in its presence—as in Kristeva's example of the human corpse, which must be ritualistically removed from the spaces of everyday life before that everyday life can continue (3). As Kristeva explains, the abjected thing can also be a person or group of people, as in the case of the Jews, who are for anti-Semites "an object of hatred and desire, of threat and aggressivity [sic], of envy and domination" (178).

The Northern Irish conflict has always been, to a certain extent, a territorial one, a contest for space in both material and symbolic terms; thus, it is fitting that literature arising out of it should focus on the liminal, the abjected and the heterotopian.

Foucault in Fermanagh

Fanacross, the main setting of *Fighting with Shadows,* presents with many of the characteristics of a heterotopia as described by Foucault. First and foremost, it suggests a problematic intersection of real and imaginary spaces:

> [Heterotopias] have, in relation to the rest of space, a function that takes place between two opposite poles. On the one hand they perform the task of creating a space of illusion that reveals how all of real space is more illusory, all the locations within which life is fragmented. On the other, they have the function of forming another space, another real space, as perfect, meticulous and well-arranged as ours is disordered, ill-conceived and in a sketchy state. (356)

As much as partition does, the existence of a townland that spans a national divide highlights the fact that countries, states and national boundaries are all socially constructed, as demonstrated by their permeable nature: we are told that as well as routinely bringing pigs south to be slaughtered, the locals also move cattle back and forth across the border in order to claim multiple grants (9), a scam which relies on the perpetrators being able to claim sole residence in both countries—rather than keeping two polities separated, in this case the border has actually provided an incentive for people to cross it regularly.

The other function Foucault describes, that of forming a "perfect, meticulous, well-arranged" space to contrast against the apparent chaos of our own, is revealed in the way Fanacross village has a utopian resonance for many of the characters: this is summed up by Frank when he gives the original Irish place-name as *Fan Ocras*, which he translates as "the end of hunger" (11). While Frank and Helen are living in the South, their son Joseph wants nothing more than to return to Fanacross, and he soon learns a harsh lesson on the sometimes dispiriting nature of utopian longing. Frank's sister-in-law Geraldine comes to visit and takes Joe on a walk while Helen and Frank are fighting; as they wander aimlessly around the countryside, Geraldine tells Joe that the light in a distant farmhouse window is hers and George's house. Joe insists on walking to it and Geraldine has to trick him into doubling back on his tracks, bringing him back to his parents' caravan. Tired and dejected, the boy climbs into bed, and Geraldine says, "Now . . . he knows all he need ever know about Fanacross" (17–19). Joseph's longed-for home village is to all intents and purposes a literal utopia, a 'no-place' that can be hoped for but never reached. As an adult, Joseph channels this longing into his dreams, where he can eat his fill, his father is still alive, and he can "know by times the honesty of his mother." He is reluctant to leave this dream-state, and in order to maintain it he develops an addiction to sleeping tablets (233–4). Herein lies one of the probable reasons for Brooke's abhorrence of the novel, and his reading of the characters as "uniformly stupid," passive and introspective: it is not so much the abandonment of Catholic morals that he finds offensive, but the denial of hope, and with it all possibility of redemption. Joseph epitomises this pessimism (which Brooke interprets as a lack of "spiritual self-confidence") in that he regards himself as a "man without a soul" (233); following the death of his father, he also enacts a strange ritual that seems to parody Catholic symbolism, repeatedly arranging stones and tractor parts into the shape of a crucifix at the door of the house (137). In *Fighting with Shadows*, Healy gives his characters glimpses of potential utopias, only to reveal that the whole notion of utopia is a sham.

In the overlap of utopia and heterotopia lies the mirror, "allowing me to look at myself where I do not exist: utopia of the mirror. At the same time, we are dealing with a heterotopia. The mirror really exists and has a kind of come-back effect on the place that I occupy, starting from it, in fact" (Foucault 352). *Fighting with Shadows* is full of mirror-images, symmetry and mimicry, most obviously in the characters of Frank and George: we are told that, as babies, George would laugh when Frank was tickled, and it appears that the UDR gunman mistakes Frank for George because Frank has allowed his beard to grow out (114). Distorted reflections make up another recurring theme: Helen sees "a distorted image of herself in her husband's eye" that foretells the onset of marital difficulty (12), while the South is described as "a distorting mirror" when Joseph crosses the border to work for his uncle Tom (137). Sometimes, the distinction between the person and the warped reflection is not entirely clear, and the former starts to take on characteristics of the latter. At Frank's funeral, a group of strangers appear and drape a tricolour over his coffin, despite the fact that Frank had no involvement with any paramilitary organisation (118), and at the graveside, Pop calls him "Proinsias" (the Gaelic form of Francis) in an oddly pointed and derisive way (119); it is as though being mistaken for George not only cost Frank his life, but has erased his identity in death. Later, we witness something similar happening to his son: in the midst of a sequence set during the 1981 Fermanagh and South Tyrone by-election, we are told that "[Joseph] was going to nothing. He wanted to become lightweight" (234), unconsciously mimicking the Republican hunger-striker Bobby Sands, who was elected to the House of Commons in that by-election.

One recurring criticism of the novel is that Healy's prose is sometimes difficult to follow, a difficulty heightened by the novel's nonlinear chronology and vague temporal setting. The reader understands that the story is set sometime during the 1970s, though this is sometimes unclear: the reviewer Marianne Koenig, for example, writes of finding a character gambling with pre-decimal money "in what by my reckoning ought to have been about 1980" (Koenig 112). As the story goes on, the chronological oddities become more pronounced: Frank's burial in an old graveyard on a lake island segues into a flashback to the Famine, complete with images of starving locals begging for food and grinding Indian meal. These images are intertwined with the account of the burial to the extent that Pop's angry graveside rant could be directed at the Famine dead as much as Frank, just as those who survived the Famine "cursed the dead for not having hung on just one day longer" (119). In describing Tom's hotel, the Cove Inn, Healy gives us a brief outline of the building's history that culminates in a flashback to the original construction, led by "a roving band of Protestant lads with slanty eyes and blond, spoon-shaped faces" directing a "token group of ethnic Irish labourers"; the flashback goes beyond generalised imagery by including the story of an overburdened dray horse which "disappeared with a sad look, as if to say, Why does all this happen to me?, into a sudden collapse of earth, dragging after him sufficient debris to cover his own grave" (140).

This calls to mind another characteristic of the Foucauldian heterotopia, namely the confusion or breakdown of the normal passage of time: "Heterotopias are linked for the most part to bits and pieces of time . . . The heterotopia enters fully into function when men find themselves in a sort of total breach of their traditional time" (354). Those heterotopias that are explicitly linked to time include libraries and museums, "in which time does not cease to accumulate, perching, so to speak, on its own summit" (355). In this respect, Fanacross could be considered a heterotopia by virtue of its bridge alone—partition has changed it from an innocuous structure to a dangerous anachronism. In 1970, the British Army attempt to blow up the bridge, but a crowd of Southern protesters break through the Garda cordon south of the border and swarm onto the bridge, refusing to budge. While the Army is distracted with arresting the protesters (and fishing one of them out of the river), Frank dives into the river and swims to the bridge, inspiring dozens of others to do likewise. He is arrested and returns home a few days later. While in custody, Frank was subjected to torture: he says that they threw something in his eyes that burned him (19–21).

The Fanacross bridge is in fact the weakest and most simplistic element of the novel, though bridges carry a counterintuitive symbolism that works well in a heterotopian context. The use of bridges as symbols or metaphors in the context of divided communities, while satisfying on a superficial level, overlooks the fact that bridges do not actually bring the banks they touch any closer together. In fact, the argument could be made that bridges actually emphasise the material reality of separation even as they connect, bringing two opposing realities into a state of non-contradiction. Echoes of this strange simultaneity can be detected throughout the novel in the ambiguous relationship between the Allens and the South; though the Allens regard the South as a refuge of some kind, a place to seek work, keep their son safe and eventually escape to, their interactions with southerners reaffirm the differences between them: we are told that people from the Midlands hate the Northerners on account of the fighting (9), and they refer to Frank as a "gruff murdering Northerner" (11).

The biggest indicator by far of Northern Ireland's heterotopian nature is the neither-here-nor-there legal measures enacted to counter paramilitary violence. Leerssen argues that the biggest contributor to the Northern Irish 'Gordian knot' was "[. . .] the fact that the crown authorities have for centuries vacillated in their estimation as to whether Ireland was part of their inner polity, or a neighbouring country, and have accordingly applied mutually incompatible registers of government policy" (4). This ambiguity was reflected in criminal legislation, often with fatal consequences.

Between 1969 and 1988, 270 individuals were killed by the Northern Irish security services, at least 155 of whom were 'civilians' (Jennings 104)—'civilians' defined by the Irish Information Partnership as people "without manifest connection with paramilitaries, security forces, police or prison services" (128 n3). Anthony Jennings concluded in 1988 that the security forces had effectively "been granted the power to decide the guilt or innocence of suspected Republican activists without recourse to the courts" (105). The situation was compounded by legal ambiguities pertaining to suspects who resisted arrest: in cases where the suspect offered physical resistance or assaulted the arresting officer, that officer was allowed to respond under the common law understanding of reasonable self-defence; if a suspect fled but offered no resistance, however, the situation came under Section 3(1) of the Criminal Law (Northern Ireland) Act 1967, which basically stipulated that the use of lethal force was justified in cases where it might prevent the commission of a 'greater evil.' The use of deadly force was also considered acceptable if the suspect was considered to be dangerous (106–7). The result of these legal ambiguities was the emergence of a 'shoot to kill' policy, whereby the security forces would deliberately engage known or suspected Republican activists in armed confrontation in order to justify killing them. In *Fighting with Shadows*, this policy appears to be a major contributing factor in Frank Allen's killing.

Towards the end of the novel, a part-time UDR soldier named Norman McCreedy finally appears before a court to confess to the murder. McCreedy describes himself as a church-going man, not very well educated but determined to do his duty, "to protect the people of this province." He repeatedly apologises for what happened, and reveals that his own family has suffered too: one of his children was born without eyes, the consequence of drugs given to his wife during pregnancy (272–3). He claims that he identified himself as a UDR officer, and that he saw Frank reaching for something after the door was opened (275); thus, his actions were consistent with a legal standard established by the 1967 Criminal Law Act.

During a break in the proceedings, Helen is offered £10,000 to prevent the trial for compensation, but she refuses (274). She eventually receives £40,000 compensation for the death of her husband, and the money is used to move the family south of the border (284–6). There are still a number of ambiguities, however. McCreedy is apparently contradicting the testimonies of several of his fellow officers, none of whom personally witnessed or heard the shooting (275–6). Locals have testified to seeing his jeep parked near the village on the night of the killing, and he makes a number of suspiciously specific statements to the effect that he was not coerced into confessing, that he wanted to clear his conscience and that he is not a member of the UVF (276–7). The Allens do not get a straightforward happy ending, and it is heavily implied that the truth behind Frank's death will never emerge: there is no such thing as perfect knowledge in a heterotopia.

Conclusion

Healy gives us a milieu wherein identities are malleable, time does not flow in a straight line and images from the past are superimposed on the present like the ghostly artefacts of double-exposure. He was writing about a place that was simultaneously a country and a province, where space was re-organised in response to the growth of the Catholic population, where adults who could not afford houses of their own were recorded as 'children' on the electoral register if they continued to live in the family home, and where business and property votes were still counted, though they had been abolished elsewhere in the UK (Coogan 29). These practices all involved nonsensical breaches of natural time and space: districts changed shape between elections, anachronism abounded, adults were legally recorded as children and business owners effectively became two people at election time, if their place of business was situated in another district. These peculiarities were all largely done away with when the Parliament of Northern Ireland was suspended in 1972, but direct rule from Westminster was no more coherent or comprehensible: since 1969, the British Army had been deployed in the North as a peacekeeping force, highlighting the confusion Leerssen diagnoses about whether the Troubles constituted an internal or an external problem for the UK. Healy depicts the everyday lives of everyday people, but he fractures this normality with nonlinear narratives and ambiguous spaces.

Given the spatially ambiguous, ambivalent and sometimes self-contradictory nature of *Fighting with Shadows*, it is not difficult to see why Aubrey Dillon-Malone characterised this novel as a "mindfuck." When the chaos of heterotopian life in Northern Ireland is taken into account, however, with human lives abjected and pushed beyond the sphere of law and order, only a mindfuck will do.

Works Cited

Agamben, Giorgio. *Homo Sacer: Sovereign Power and Bare Life*. Trans. Daniel Heller-Roazen. Stanford: Stanford University Press, 1995.

Brooke, Peter. Rev. of *Fighting with Shadows*, by Dermot Healy. *The Linenhall Review* 1.4 (Winter 1984/85): 19. Print.

Coogan, Tim Pat. *The Troubles: Ireland's Ordeal 1966-1995 and the Search for Peace*. London: Hutchinson, 1995.

Dillon-Malone, Aubrey. "Vim and Vinegar." Rev. of *Fighting with Shadows*, by Dermot Healy. *Books Ireland* 89 (Dec. 1984): 232–3. Print.

Foucault, Michel. "Of Other Spaces: Utopias and Heterotopias." *Rethinking Architecture: A Reader in Cultural Theory*. Ed. Neil Leach. London: Routledge, 1997. 350–6. Print.

Golden, Seán. "Oriental Sense of the Border." *Fortnight* 210 (3–16 December 1984): 18. Print.

Healy, Dermot. *Fighting with Shadows*. Dingle: Brandon Books, 1984. Print.

Heaney, Seamus. *Place and Displacement*. Grasmere: Trustees of Dove Cottage, 1985. Print.

Jennings, Anthony, ed.. "Shoot to Kill: The Final Courts of Justice" (1988). *Justice Under Fire: The Abuse of Civil Liberties in Northern Ireland*. 2nd edition. London: Pluto Press, 1990. 104–30. Print.

Koenig, Marianne. Rev. of *Fighting With Shadows*, by Dermot Healy. *Irish University Review* 15.1 (Spring 1985): 112–15. Print.

Kristeva, Julia. *Powers of Horror: An Essay in Abjection*. 1980. Trans. Leon S. Roudiez. New York: Columbia University Press, 1982. Print.

Leerssen, Joep. "Law and Border (How and Where We Draw the Line)." *The Irish Review* 24 (Autumn 1999): 1–8. Print.

Soja, Edward. *Postmodern Geographies: The Reassertion of Space in Critical Social Theory*. London: Verso, 1989. Print.

"The orchestra of memory":
Music, Sound and Silence in *A Goat's Song*
Gerry Smyth

[. . .] A sister is a honk in the void

as the orchestra of memory
takes to the air.
—Dermot Healy, *A Fool's Errand*

I

Before his untimely death in 2014, Dermot Healy had established a reputation as a penetrating and powerful chronicler of contemporary rural Ireland in all its emotional, cultural and moral complexity.[1] He did so, moreover, across a variety of literary forms—poetry, drama, self-writing and fiction—and with reference to a number of recurring devices and motifs. One of the most potent motifs or devices permeating the canon of Healy's work is that of sound: from the early short stories to the late poetry and the final novel, Healy's Ireland is a noisy place, full of human and natural sounds, many of which are musical, all of which may be observed to engage with the developing narrative in complex ways.[2]

The creative writer's concern with (musical) sound registers across a range of contemporary critical discourses and disciplines. One of my own long-term interests, for example, lies in what I have described elsewhere as "the musical novel"—narratives in which music features as a distinctive element at both/either a formal and/or a conceptual level.[3] Healy's invocation of a wide range of musical styles and references situates him within a genealogy of Irish writing going back at least as far as Joyce (and arguably much earlier) in which music, with all its social and psychological resonances, functions as an important index of Irish identity.[4]

Another area of potential interest concerns a concept known to disciplines such as ethnomusicology and communications studies as "ubiquitous music." As defined in the subtitle of a recent book on the subject, this term refers to "the everyday sounds that we don't always notice." The premise here is that music pervades modern life in every aspect of its private and public experience. This ubiquitous music has escaped serious attention, however, because it obviates the kind of serious, focused listening upon which the traditional discipline of musicology was founded and developed. Very few people 'hear' the music of everyday life in the way that traditional musicology imagines the ideal musical text-to-be-studied is heard—in isolation, with focus, understanding and alertness. Ubiquitous music, rather, refers to "those musical events that take place alongside other activities" (Quiñones, Kassabian and Boschi 7)—driving, queuing, eating, working, shopping, etc.—and as part of a much wider "orchestra" of social sounds: conversation, traffic, wind, bird-song, and so on.

Such a concept resonates strongly with the work produced across the thirty years or so of Healy's publishing career. His work is full of overheard music, drifting in from another room or a car radio.[5] It's certainly the case that music-making or music-listening sometimes takes centre stage in the narrative; in this regard, Healy was fully attuned to the seminal role played in modern Irish rural life by a wide range of music styles. Such practices tend to be only one element of a much wider sonic array in which society at large is implicated, however. From the evidence of the writing, Healy did not share Joyce's concern to integrate music as part of a self-conscious aesthetic philosophy; he did, however, share Joyce's passion for the fabric of ordinary everyday Irish life in which music—however fragmentary, however incidental—plays a seminal role.

These two concepts (the musical novel and ubiquitous music) overlap significantly with a final theory I want to mention in this context: sound worlds. As described by one of its foremost practitioners, this notion refers to the ways in which "sound figures in bodily ways of knowing and being in the world." Such a project, moreover, is located at a significant anthropological intersection, one where the phrase "sound worlds" conjoins its dual possibilities, namely "worlds of sound," and "sounds of the world." The idea of the former, of "worlds of sound," instantly denotes the multiplicity of distinctively local environmental soundscapes mapping the globe, and the complex ways their distinctiveness blurs as they change through space and time. Likewise, "sounds of the world" equally denotes the diversity of human musical practices both in their most distinct and their most amalgamated forms. Together the two ideas imply that sound worlds are entities both distinct and cumulative, built up from the interaction of diverse communities, diverse acoustic environments, diverse languages and musics. In short, the idea of sound worlds is that social formations are indexed in sonic histories and sonic geographies. (Feld 173–4)

In this essay I want to consider what an appropriately sensitised reader, equipped with the array of theoretical concepts briefly introduced above, might make of Dermot Healy's writing. More specifically, I want to try to describe Healy's typical "sound world" as represented in his celebrated 1994 novel *A Goat's Song*. My contention is that as we approach an understanding of this particular author's "sound world," we shall simultaneously approach a better understanding of Ireland itself during a crucial phase of its modern history.

II

Despite its title, *A Goat's Song* is not easily recognisable as a "musical novel"; although music of various kinds is invoked throughout the narrative, none of it is foregrounded as being of especial narrative significance. This contrasts with the work of contemporary Irish novelists such as Roddy Doyle or Patrick McCabe, for each of whom music tends to embody or articulate an array of potential meanings which resonate in relation to the ongoing narrative (Smyth, *Music in Irish Cultural History* 65–83, 119–21). We observe this quite clearly in McCabe's *Breakfast on Pluto* (1998), for example, the title of which references *a* particular song which, if the reader knows it, reflects ironically on the life and experiences of its main protagonist. The same is true of Doyle's *The Commitments* (1987), the story of *a* (fictional) band purveying *a* specific style of music which, if the reader is familiar with it, affords a telling insight on a particular moment in modern Irish history.

Healy's invocation of music tends to operate somewhat differently. *A Goat's Song* tells the story of an ill-fated relationship between a Northern Protestant woman and a Southern Catholic man against the backdrop of late twentieth-century Irish history. In chapter nineteen (entitled "Oh No, Don't Stop the Carnival") the sisters Sara and Catherine Adams attend a folk festival in a field near the Mayo townland where they have a holiday home. There they run into the enigmatic playwright/fisherman Jack Ferris, whom they had first met as teenagers during earlier visits to the area, and to whom each woman is at this stage attracted. The episode represents an important moment in the developing relationship between Catherine and Jack, as the reader is enabled to observe elements of their personality and habits which will continue to grow in significance over the course of the narrative.

Part of that significance lies in the setting: a folk festival in the west of Ireland sometime in the mid-1970s. Four principal kinds of music are described throughout the episode, each of which resonates in particular ways in relation to the various characters and to the wider community in which they are invoked. The first is 'folk' music, represented here by festival headliners, Planxty. The latter were a 'super group' comprised of four leading figures from the traditional music revival which had been growing in scope and influence since the previous decade. In terms of their age, their virtuosity, their repertoire and their iconography, Planxty embodied what might be described as the *progressive* wing of the *traditional* revival—and this is interesting in the context of a story which is in part about the ways in which the past continues to warp the present.[6] It's also interesting that Healy invokes the music without ever attempting to describe or reproduce what it actually sounds like:

Inside, the new generation were screaming for Planxty. The musicians must have come on because a great roar arose. Over the speakers came the bodhran and the mandolin, the bazooki and the Uilleann pipes. Then Andy Irvine began singing "A Blacksmith Courted Me" (243).

Now, some of Healy's readers may be familiar with Planxty's version of this song, others may not; it's interesting to observe, however, that the author does not attempt to transpose that version into some form of literary discourse by using metaphors or other figures to try to integrate the (necessarily absent) musical discourse into the present narrative. It's true that the title of the song is suggestive, offering an ironic commentary on the evolving affair between Jack (associated in part, like the blacksmith, with manual labour) and "me." But the music itself remains curiously de-emphasised, unlike in the work of McCabe or Doyle; it's simply there, one element amongst many within this community's complex soundscape.

The musical taste of this "new generation" is set against the three other forms of music invoked in the episode:

> In a white suit a crooner from the fifties sang Walter Glynn's version of "Where My Caravan is Resting," then came a local fiddle band who played too fast to dance to, then a long-retired country-and-western showband from Castlebar who looked into each other's eyes as they swept through old popular airs. (239)[7]

Each of these styles embodies characteristics and connotations located at some remove from that embraced by "the new generation" who have come to worship at the feet of Planxty. In this context, crooning, *céilí* and showband music are linked by a sentimental regard for the past, expressed across a continuum running between nostalgia on the one hand and 'the craic' (that mythical Irish version of enjoyment) on the other. The music of Planxty, however, seems future-orientated, impelled by a regard for authenticity and an evolving 'scene.' All these styles and traditions have met temporarily at the folk festival, in the fictional 'present' of Healy's narrative, where they form part of the sonic backdrop against which the story unfolds.

These four styles of music recur throughout the novel, where they are joined by others (including jazz and classical) and where they continue to assume important—although not defining—roles in relation to the narrative. Rock music grows in significance during Jack's Belfast sojourn, as do the three playback formats which in large part facilitated the success of rock as a popular form during the period covered in the story itself (that is, the 1950s to the 1980s): the vinyl record, the cassette tape and the transistor radio. Chapters such as "Madame George" (295–305, named for a much-loved Van Morrison song) and "Popular Songs" (391–8), as well as sections such as "The Musical Bridge" (319–408), signal the fact that music is a central part of the society in which this particular tragedy plays itself out, a seminal form of popular culture through which the characters engage with themselves, with each other, and with the community at large.

Much of this music, moreover, is of the kind described above as "ubiquitous"; and much of it does not appear to merit (or to receive) the kind of intense listening demanded in (popular) musicological discourse. It is, rather, casual, incidental, a vague contributing element to the sonic backdrop but one lacking the presence or the attention to solidify into a significant symbol: piped music in pubs (32); Christmas music in the streets of Dublin (36); the unidentified hymn overheard by Catherine as she gazes upon Matti Bonner's hanged body (87); the unnamed tune hummed by a nervous Jack during a meeting with Catherine (226); and so on. Alongside the songs and artists self-consciously invoked throughout the text, these examples evade the narrative's interpretive sonar; they are present, but we're not sure why or what they contribute. Neither are we at all sure how the presence (or more intriguingly the potential absence) of these musics might be affecting the texture, and thus the meaning, of this imaginary world. It's a testament to the incredible subtlety of Healy's art that he manages to evoke a musical landscape which, in its vagueness as well as its precision, so accurately reflects the sonic texture of lived experience.

So, music of various kinds and significance features throughout *A Goat's Song*. Above and beyond this level of engagement, however, any consideration of the text as a musical novel would have to take cognisance of its formal structure. It's interesting, for example, that the first section of the *narrative*, entitled "Christmas Day in the Workhouse" (3–84), is actually the final section of the *story*, and that the general thrust of the narrative is as a consequence belied by the reader's knowledge, gained during that opening section, of the ultimate failure of the relationship and its breakdown into alienation and alcoholism. Thus, the story ends (on page 84) with Jack getting ready to write the story of his relationship with Catherine and everything that has led up to this point.[8] This unusual format clearly relates in some respects to the artistic discourse which constitutes one of the text's principal reference points: Athenian tragedy, in which the audience knows the fate awaiting the unsuspecting protagonist. But it's also interesting to consider it in musical terms, as a sort of overture, embodying notions of return and reprise. Indeed, such an anti- or counter-narrative gesture invokes the supremely musical effect in which the present contains within itself both its own past as well as the future towards which it is inevitably tending.[9]

Another musical effect adopted by Healy is the *leitmotif*. Particularly associated with Wagnerian opera, the *leitmotif* is a short musical phrase intended to represent a particular presence—whether character, object or idea—within the developing action of the story. As deployed in literary discourse, it is (according to an early scholar of the musical novel) "a verbal formula which is deliberately repeated, which is easily recognised at each recurrence, and which serves, by means of this recognition, to link the context in which the repetition occurs with earlier contexts in which the motive had appeared" (Brown 211). Now, every writer has peculiar 'tics' which characterise their style (Healy's "used" instead of "used to"—found throughout his work—is one example); but there are certain usages beyond this which qualify as *leitmotifs* in this context. The ubiquitous wind and the roaring sea of the Mullet peninsula seems two obvious examples, and important ones (as we shall see) given their status as crucial elements of that community's particular sound world.

Rather less obvious would be a word such as "galvanize," which occurs on thirteen occasions throughout the novel.[10] The process of galvanization (whereby a protective coat of zinc is applied to iron or steel fixtures in order to prevent rusting) is commonly associated with the various milieux featured in the novel (farm, sea-board and war-torn city). "To galvanise" also means to rouse or to stir into activity, something which might be regarded ironically in the light of Jack's increasing inertia. The word's repeated usage throughout the novel, however, seems to perform no specific task other than to refer back to previous occurrences and forward to future ones. And yet, as those usages recur and as the instances mount up, some other process seems to be at work. Healy, like Joyce before him, doesn't waste words; once the reader is properly sensitised, what might appear to be a 'tic' or even laziness emerges as a kind of *leitmotif*, suggesting potential resonances between various characters and contexts—resonances of which the text itself, apparently, is hardly aware. In literary terms such an effect may appear obviously poetic; like poetry, meaning is created at least partially through repeated words and images, some of them organised in relation to a semiotic (including a sonic) rather than a semantic function. The derivation of such an effect, however, is undoubtedly musical, linked to that field's unique ability to provide interpretive possibilities for the listener through subtle patterns of resonance and repetition.

I suggest that any consideration of *A Goat's Song* as a musical novel would progress along these lines, examining specific musical references (both deliberately symbolic as well as "ubiquitous") at the level of the plot while also remaining alert to formal features that rely on or invoke musical discourse in some or other fashion. Besides this, however, Healy is (as suggested above) a writer who is in some senses paradoxically at odds with the written word, and for whom sound rather than sight represents the pre-eminent mode of sensory engagement with the world. He is a writer constantly listening for and trying to transcribe into literary terms what, in his penultimate poetry collection *A Fool's Errand*, he referred to as "the orchestra of memory."

III

The various kinds of music encountered thus far qualify as "sounds of the world" in the terms described by Feld. *Céilí*, ballad, showband, country and western, rock, and so on—these denote (as quoted above) "the diversity of human musical practices both in their most distinct and their most amalgamated forms": "distinct," in the sense that this particular sonic array could only have emerged in Ireland during a specific phase of late twentieth-century history; "amalgamated," in the sense that each of these musical forms is implicitly dialogic in Bakhtinian terms—less a 'place' where Irish identity dwells than a 'space' in which Irish identity encounters a variety of 'others' and attempts to remake itself in sonic form.

Equally important for any consideration of Healy's work in general, and for *A Goat's Song* in particular, is the construction of a "sound world" through which the author attempts to encapsulate the fabric of lived experience in various Irish contexts during this period. Let's return to "Oh No, Don't Stop the Carnival" and note some of the many sonic elements which combine to form that world.

It is St John's Eve, the summer solstice, and as the Adams sisters drive from the Mullet peninsula towards the folk festival at Barnatra (a few miles inland) they see bonfires all along the coast. This level of engagement is soon accompanied by the introduction of sonic elements which offset the scopic pleasure afforded by mere sight. These sounds tend to be of three principal types: 1) human-generated; 2) non-human-generated (including animal, machine and object), although with the inference of human agency; and 3) natural.

Besides the basic inference of sound implicit in the literary convention of dialogue, examples of human-generated sound in this section (237–43) include the barking of orders to stewards; the shouting by car drivers at passing women; the exaggerated cheers and raucous applause of the audience; aggressive roars of laughter; shrieks and screams; an odd roar from outside; the clamouring of drunken outsiders; a huge cheer of nostalgia and mirth and lust; the voices of couples. At one point a stray terrier wanders into the dance tent and begins "barking furiously at the band" (240); coming so soon after the previous (metaphorical) usage, the effect of this "barking" is to suggest the proximity of the human and the animal rather than the distance between the two. The festival represents a coming together of individuals into a crowd, and it's interesting to observe in this list the description of sounds generated by the group rather than by any particular individual: cheers, applause, roars, clamour. Each of these sounds, in other words, concerns humanity above and beyond the level of the single unit; this is the community generating noise and listening to itself. This is the "sonic world" within which Jack and Catherine take a decisive step closer to their tragic *affaire*.

Another family of sounds contributing to this particular "orchestra" is created by the interaction of humans with objects of various kinds: in the present context, a generator hums, bicycle tyres lisp, engines moan, and footsteps clatter across a makeshift dancefloor. Besides the voice with which the species has been endowed by evolution—that exquisitely subtle instrument which bequeathed us language and endowed us with such an evolutionary advantage *vis-à-vis* the other life forms with which we share the planet—humans, it seem, generate inordinate amounts of noise, especially when they cluster together in large groups. Much of this noise is an effect of our reliance on technology—as in the list above: fire, bicycles, engines, generators, and the built environment (however temporary).

Besides the human voice and the sounds generated by human interaction with technology, the consistently dominant element in Healy's sound world is the wind. It is present throughout the section under discussion, in the "fierce" wind that makes the marquee billow and shake, and the "gusts" that assail the sisters as they walk from their car; it causes the sparks to "whoosh" from the bonfires; it "whips" the canvas, "charges" through the entrance, and threatens to carry off paper money. As Jack emerges from the toilet tent towards the end of the evening he hears the wind entering into crazy harmony with the human voices and technological noises described above, and this provides an apt and enduring soundtrack for his growing infatuation with Catherine Adams.

Healy's fascination with the sound of the wind resonates with the work of another west-coast writer, the cartographer and folklorist Tim Robinson. In *Listening to the Wind* (2006), the first volume of his *Connemara Trilogy*, Robinson recruits the ubiquitous wind of the Atlantic seaboard as a metaphor for the ways in which both the landscape and the past constantly impress themselves upon the world of the living. Like the "indefinite but enormous noises [which] are part of Connemara" (1), he writes, history also "has rhythms, tunes and even harmonies . . . the sound of the past is an agonistic multiplicity" (2). This is the analogue of Healy's "orchestra of memory"—the complex harmonic sound world produced by the interaction of the human subject with the sounds of the past and the sounds of the landscape within which he dwells.

All these concerns come together in these paragraphs from "Oh No, Don't Stop the Carnival":

> And there was a feeling that the dance music was issuing from a wireless where the hand had not quite found the station; it was a music gone back in time; other timeless conversations kept breaking in—arguments, the mock grunts of men wrestling, women screeching; it was something dangerous, something pagan; winds from the sea blew the tunes around, loudspeakers seemed to pick up one instrument only—and all this sound woven brashly together travelled across to where a small herd of cattle watched ears-up over a ditch.
>
> It reached the old men who stood for a moment outside the houses on the outskirts of Barnatra watching the bonfires the children had lit. It reached a woman making her way home to her daughter's. I remember those tunes, she thought. It was a small insignificant human sound, carried this way, carried that way. Sometimes not heard at all even if you listened keenly for it. (241)

The image of a badly tuned wireless brilliantly encapsulates the way in which the past constantly evades the focus of the listener in the present; at the same time, this "music gone back in time" is the "world of sound" created by the community as it continually makes and remakes itself. It is a world full of human sounds—grunting men, screeching women—but one also full of the ubiquitous wind, that insistent sonic backdrop to everything that is said or done or thought in this world. All these sounds weave together to form the orchestra of memory, the music of which may seem "insignificant," but which is in fact keyed into something "pagan" and "dangerous," something deeply embedded within the landscape. It is the sound world of this particular community; ever-present yet audible only on occasion, and then only by those who are properly attuned to its music. In the second paragraph, focus zooms in to anonymous, "insignificant" (in terms of the narrative) members of that community whom we observe catching little snatches of the sound world as they go about their business in the present. And the passage ends on an ominous note: sometimes, one cannot hear the orchestra of memory no matter how hard one listens; sometimes (and this may describe the condition awaiting Jack Ferris) one becomes desensitised to the music of the past and the music of the community. Sometimes, most terrifyingly, the past may simply refuse to speak.

IV

This last possibility haunts Jack throughout the text—a silence representing not peace or respite, but loneliness, isolation and death. This possibility also reminds us of the fact that amongst all its other signifying capacities, the phenomenon of sound—including the organised instances of sound that we call 'music'—registers in human affairs in relation to its own recent or impending absence. The celebrated Israeli conductor Daniel Barenboim has described music as being in "a permanent, constant and unavoidable relation with silence . . . the beginning, the first sound, is already in relation to the silence that precedes it . . . the note dies," he goes on, "[and] this is the beginning of the tragic element in music" (2006). The reference to tragedy brings us back to *A Goat's Song*, the title of which (as Jack explains to Catherine during the course of the narrative, 227) refers to the ancient Greek myth concerning the birth of tragedy.[11]

Silence recurs at strategic points throughout the text; it operates, indeed, as a kind of *leitmotif*, although one characterised by the absence rather than the presence of a recognisable sound. Over the course of the narrative, moreover, it emerges that silence is multifarious and multi-accented—each instance of silence functions differently in relation to the sounds which surround it, bestowing and receiving its meaning in relation to those sounds. Silence, in short, makes a crucial contribution to the orchestra of memory.

We observe this particularly in relation to the friendship between Jonathan Adams, the failed Presbyterian minister turned Northern Irish policeman, and his Catholic neighbour, Matti Bonner. In the context of Northern Ireland's sectarian history, their relationship poses in essence a question about the validity of the voice, the right to speak, and the meaning of silence in relation to both that right and that voice. The silence maintained by Jonathan and Matti on a long drive south (when Matti will stand as Best Man at Jonathan's wedding) is a positive rejoinder to the tradition of sectarian denigration (96); on another occasion, however, Jonathan hears Matti's silence as blame for his own documented Protestant aggression (134). The "fatalistic silence" (97) that assails Jonathan at Matti's graveside resonates meaningfully in relation to modern history and to his own experience, as Jonathan's entire life is in some senses an attempt to overcome the "long embarrassing silence" (100) that ruins his career as a preacher. Finally, after Matti's suicide, Jonathan comes to regard "the silence of the labourer [as] one long note of defiance" (135).

As much as their relationship is characterised and indeed organised in relation to the array of sonic practices described in earlier sections of this essay, Jack and Catherine are in some senses the inheritors of this silence. And insofar as they represent or symbolise modern Ireland, in fact, the silence of previous generations is embedded within each, waiting to assert itself as a crucial, ineluctable element with the community's sound world.

Jack follows Catherine to Belfast, where issues of "voice" and "silence" become politically charged, and where personal and public pressures combine to lead his always fragile personality into crisis. As his alcoholism takes hold, Jack experiences "a sound he could not place running through his head. It was like the static across the trawler's radio at sea" (306). This noise is augmented by a company of internal voices—"his own crazy thoughts raging in his ears": these voices articulate feelings (guilt, self-recrimination, self-cleansing) which he attempts to repress over the course of the day by means of alcohol consumption. So insistent is the resulting cacophony, however, that it threatens to destabilise Jack entirely; only when Catherine appears does "the silence mysteriously [return and the] furies [depart]" (307).

Silence is not benign in itself, however; its significance is a function of its relationship—contextual and contingent—with sound. Just before his breakdown (towards the end of the story although at the beginning of the text, pp. 11-2) Jack is haunted by an ominous silence: he stands by a road accompanied by three silent dogs; "the violent sea [makes] no sound" and "the surf [rises] silently"; a passing man makes no reply to Jack's salutation. This "alarming silence" is all the more uncanny because of the presence of actual sounds—tractor engines and Irish-speaking girls spilling out of a nearby house. It is "alarming" precisely because Jack perceives it so; under pressure from alcoholism and intense emotion he is losing his place within the community and, as a consequence, losing his sensitivity towards that community's sound world.

Another form of silence emerges as a response to the unanswerable questions Jack asks of himself (60). As (his) understanding approaches the realm of the unsayable, language thickens, slows down and then stops altogether, leaving in its place a silence pregnant with one very particular meaning, a first cause, a "word": alcoholism. Jack intuits this word, although at this stage he cannot or will not countenance it. Later (in the text, although once again earlier in the story), after Catherine has committed herself to the affair, she lies waiting for Jack to return from a fishing trip:

> From her bed she heard someone passing over the gravel. She waited but no knock came. Then she thought, I've let myself down. Someone went over the gravel again, and even when she knew it made no sense, she listened on.

If the gate stirred in the wind her heart flitted. If the wind blew a can down the road she listened for the silence that would come and bear his step (261).

Here we find distilled many of the sonic practices which inform the particular sound world created by Healy in this text: the anonymous human 'noises off,' the intense listening, the ubiquitous wind, the inanimate objects resonating in response to human desire; and the silence which envelops and punctuates everything—the silence that was present before the emergence of this sonic community and which will still be there after that community has ceased to reverberate.

V

Of course, Ireland in the 1970s and 1980s was awash with questions to which nobody seemed able or willing to supply a credible answer; but if "alcoholism" is the implicit response to all Jack's questions, then what might it be for the question of late twentieth-century Irish experience? Sectarianism? Revisionism? Post-colonialism? Post-nationalism? Late capitalism?

One should not turn to Healy's work (or indeed the work of any artist) to discover the truth (or otherwise) of these potential responses. What one does find there, however, is a portrait of a country undergoing profound change, desperately attempting to calculate the moral, emotional and psychological debts of the past in relation to the demands of the present and the hopes of the future. Of course, this dauntingly complex equation faces every artist and every community; but part of Healy's achievement was to recognise that, for very particular historical and social reasons, the experience of change is registered most sensitively and most revealingly in this particular community's unique sound world. It is a calculation brilliantly encapsulated in the image of an "orchestra of memory"—a collection of sounds, natural and human, in which the complex "harmonies" of the past (pleasing or dissonant as they be) resonate in the present. These sounds provide an array of signifying practices through which both the community at large and its component members can approach a sense of identity—who they are, where they come from, what they want.

Healy's extraordinary achievement was to enable us to hear Ireland listening to itself.

Works Cited

Barenboim, Daniel. "In the Beginning Was Sound." *Reith Lectures* 1 (7 Apr. 2006). Web. 3 June 2015.

Bauerle, Ruth H. *The James Joyce Songbook*. New York: Garland, 1982. Print.

———, ed. *Picking up Airs: Hearing the Music in Joyce's Text*. Urbana: University of Illinois Press, 1993. Print.

Bowen, Zack. *Musical Allusions in the Works of James Joyce: Early Poetry through Ulysses*. Albany: State University of New York Press, 1974. Print.

Brown, Calvin S. *Music and Literature: A Comparison of the Arts*. Athens: University of Georgia Press, 1948. Print.

Bucknell, Brad. *Literary Modernism and Musical Aesthetics: Pater, Pound, Joyce, and Stein*. Cambridge: Cambridge University Press, 2001. Print.

Doyle, Roddy. *The Commitments* (1987). Vol. I of *The Barrytown Trilogy*. London: Minerva, 1992. Print.

Farrell, Antony, Vivienne Guinness, and Julian Lloyd, eds. *My Generation: Rock 'n' Roll Remembered*. Dublin: Lilliput Press, 1996. Print.

Feld, Steven. "Sound Worlds." *Sound*. Ed. Patricia Kruth and Henry Stobart. Cambridge: Cambridge University Press, 2000. 173–200. Print.

Healy, Dermot. *A Fool's Errand*. Oldcastle: The Gallery Press, 2010. Print.

———. *A Goat's Song*. 1994. London: Flamingo, 1995. Print.

———. *Long Time, No See*. 2011. London: Faber and Faber, 2012. Print.

———. *Sudden Times*. 1999. London: Harvill Press, 2000. Print.

———. *The Bend for Home*. London: Harvill Press, 1996. Print.

Knowles, Sebastian D. G. *Bronze by Gold: The Music of James Joyce*. New York: Garland, 1999. Print.

MacLaverty, Bernard. *Grace Notes*. 1997. London: Vintage, 1998. Print.

McCabe, Patrick. *Breakfast on Pluto*. London: Picador, 1998. Print.

Nietzsche, Friedrich. *The Birth of Tragedy from the Spirit of Music* (1872) and *The Genealogy of Morals* (1887). Trans. Francis Golffing. New York: Doubleday Anchor, 1956. Print.

Quiñones, Marta Garcia, Anahid Kassabian, and Elena Boschi, eds. *Ubiquitous Musics: The Everyday Sounds That We Don't Always Hear*. Farnham: Ashgate, 2013. Print.

Robinson, Tim. *Connemara: Listening to the Wind*. 2006. London: Penguin, 2007. Print.

Smyth, Gerry. *Listening to the Novel: Music in Contemporary British Fiction*. Basingstoke: Palgrave, 2008. Print.

———. *Music in Irish Cultural History*. London and Dublin: Irish Academic Press, 2009. Print.

———. *Noisy Island: A Short History of Irish Popular Music*. Cork: Cork University Press, 2005. Print.

Vico, Giambattista. *The New Science*. Trans. Thomas Goddard Bergin and Max Harold Fisch. 3rd ed. New York: Anchor Books, 1961. Print.

Weaver, Jack W. *Joyce's Music and Noise: Theme and Variation in His Writings*. Gainesville: University Press of Florida, 1998. Print.

Notes

1. The word which recurs most frequently in the reviews cited at the outset of *A Goat's Song* is "powerful."

2. In 1996 Healy wrote (along with many other contemporary Irish writers and public figures) about his musical tastes and memories in a short piece included in *My Generation: Rock 'n' Roll Remembered*, ed. Antony Farrell, Vivienne Guinness and Julian Lloyd, pp. 151–3.

3. See my *Listening to the Novel: Music in Contemporary British Fiction* (2008), pp. 1–11. For the Irish context see the chapter "Listening to the Novel: The Role and Representation of Traditional Music in Contemporary Irish Fiction" in my *Music in Irish Cultural History* (2009), 102–23.

4. The critical literature on Joyce's musical concerns is vast; the most influential contributions in the present context include Bauerle (1982, 1993), Bowen (1974), Bucknell (2001), Knowles (1999), and Weaver (1998).

5. The radio features particularly strongly in Healy's celebrated memoir *The Bend for Home* (1996), and also in his novels *Sudden Times* (1999) and *Long Time, No See* (2011).

6. On the development of Irish traditional music during this period see my *Noisy Island* (2005), pp. 18–24; on Planxty in particular see pp. 67–8 of the same volume.

7. Healy misquotes the title of "Where My Caravan Has Rested" a 'Romany' song first published in 1910, with music by Hermann Löhr and words by Edward Teschemacher. In the piece for *My Generation* already referenced, he wrongly attributes "Here Comes the Sun" from *Abbey Road* (1969) by the Beatles to *Sgt. Pepper's Lonely Hearts Club Band* (1967). I make this point not to expose Healy's deficient musical knowledge but to emphasise that his engagement with music is, like that of his characters, non-systematic and quotidian, that of a casual user rather than a committed aficionado.

8. For another example of an unusually structured Irish novel in which music features see Bernard MacLaverty's *Grace Notes* (1997), and my analysis of it (Smyth, *Music in Irish Cultural History*, pp. 141–57).

9. The conjunction of music and Greek tragedy in this context invokes the inevitable presence of Nietzsche, for whom the satyr chorus, with its goatish associations, provides the audience with an opportunity to assume its role as "the Dionysiac multitude" (54). For an alternative account of the association of goats with the emergence of tragedy see Vico (277–8). Each of these theories contrasts with Jack Ferris's story of male goats in ancient Greece crying for females from which they have been separated (227).

10. Variants appear on pp. 11, 91, 99, 110, 187, 210, 213, 249, 252, 261, 370, 393 and 394.

11. See Note 9 above.

Dermot Healy's *A Goat's Song*: "To give some form to that which cannot be uttered"
Neil Murphy

> All he could think was that a false author dwelt within him. In his dreams the true author existed, unhampered by reality.
> —Dermot Healy, *A Goat's Song* (66)

Dermot Healy's *A Goat's Song* (1994) occupies a curiously ambivalent position in the recent history of Irish writing. Timothy O'Grady claims that it is Ireland's "most ambitious novel since Beckett's *Trilogy*" (26), while Pat McCabe considers Healy's fiction, in general, to be "truly revolutionary work, and high literary art" (qtd. in O'Grady 26), but his work has also been consistently overlooked for the major literary prizes and, possibly as a result of this, he hasn't received due international acknowledgement for an accomplished, ambitious and unique body of work in drama, fiction and poetry. Part of the reason for this neglect may be linked to a quality that Aidan Higgins has praised in Healy: "[F]ew [other] Irish writers in the generation that came after me have profited from *Ulysses* and *Finnegans Wake*," implicitly alluding to the technical achievements of Joyce (qtd. in O'Grady 26). More specifically, Healy, like Joyce in all of his novels, has explicitly foregrounded the complex problem of locating suitable fictive forms that might adequately express the complexity of lived experience, and in the case of several of his protagonists, that lived experience is even more complex being infused with alcoholism (Jack Ferris, *A Goat's Song*) and mental instability (Ollie Ewing, *Sudden Times*); and lived experience is enormously complex in Healy—reality shape-shifts, small-town life is explosively layered with its own particular energy, and in a way that may render it quite alien to those possessed of an imagination forged in metropolitan centres. Furthermore, the majority of critics who have written about *A Goat's Song* have largely responded to the social and political implications of a novel partially set in Northern Ireland that features troubled relationships between its Northern Irish characters and Southern Irish Catholic population. But the lives of the characters are also imprinted with a persistent anxiety at their inability to fully grasp the lived texture of their lives, irrespective of their religious or political allegiances.

In fact, several of the critics who respond to the material realities of the plot also exhibit an awareness of the complex narrative shape that contains and shapes its subject matter. Kim Wallace, for example, focuses on the political difficulties of identity formation but also acknowledges the complex implications of how reality is subjectivised in the novel: "It transfigures the world of Ireland, but also examines the problematic of remaking 'reality,' exploring the dialectic between the 'world of action' and the 'world of the text'" (122). Ultimately, however, the material 'reality' of Irish politics is Wallace's primary consideration. Similarly, while Roberta Gefter acknowledges the centrality of the transformative power of the imagination in the novel, especially as it pertains to Jack's task of trying to "re-create her [Catherine] through the imagination," her primary focus is on the implications of a cross-border narrative (71). Healy's work is certainly deeply-rooted in its largely Irish contexts and the fascination with his subjects is everywhere in the work but, as with Joyce, there is also an overwhelming sense in which the subject matter, the material reality with which the work is engaged, is only ultimately accessible via the forms of art. In all of Healy's novels we witness a perpetual negotiation between the complex lives of the characters and events, and the clear desire to erect a form that might coherently speak of the richness of these lives. The overt imaginative reconfiguration of the lives of the characters is evident in all of the novels primarily because the technical experiment is so unique, and so too is the persistent acknowledgement of how reality is deeply interwoven with what we call fiction, far more frequently and resolutely than is usually acknowledged in more static, fictive storyworlds.

From the outset, Healy sought ways to address the complex problem of assigning fictional narrated forms to the human experience, or to reflect a sense of how that experience is imbued with the fictional as a matter of fact. This tendency, or what Barry Sloan calls "the seamless merger that takes place between memory and imagination," even finds expression in the autobiography, *The Bend for Home* (1996) (221). As Healy puts it, "[w]hat happened is a wonder [. . .] memory is always incomplete, like a map with pieces missing. But it's all right, it's entered the imagination, and nothing is ever the same" (Healy, *BFH* 33). In the fiction, rather than employ overt self-reflexive commentary like that used by his near-contemporaries, John Banville, Neil Jordan and, in his later work, Aidan Higgins, Healy's narrative constructions themselves reveal a variety of attempts to both reflect the imaginative multiplicity of both the interior and exterior lives of the characters, and to artistically create fluid narrative systems that might generate a sense of that multiplicity. In his first novel, *Fighting with Shadows* (1984), there is a constant shift in narratorial focus, between first and third person while, on occasion, the primary narrative voice is removed altogether and is replaced by direct speech from the characters for a few pages, as when we are, variously, offered direct commentary by Helen, Peter, the soldiers, and Pop, without explicit narratorial anchoring (132). Alternatively, at certain intervals the characters are omitted from the narrative, and images of landscape, or local historical data, momentarily disrupt the plot sequence (133–5). A direct contrast to this is also used in chapter thirty-three, when the epistolary mode replaces the primary narrator with a sequence of loosely connected letters between Margaret, Helen and Joseph. All such variations are indicative of a desire to escape from a single, authoritative narrative voice and, by extension, the implicit suggestion of the value of a single perspective and the notion of the world as a monotone, knowable space. *Fighting with Shadows* repeatedly resists such easy formulations. The constant, unannounced time-shifts, for example, have the effect of introducing a thickening background context to our perspective on the characters, not with the intention of rendering them more comprehensible, but largely to remind us of the endless unknowable depths to the lives of people. More information doesn't necessarily clarify. And these depths, as elsewhere in Healy, are a complex amalgam of the material substances of daily struggle and the imaginative re-making of these struggles: "The night air was ripe with the smell of the local tannery. Calves with their hooves stiffened into the air had been hauled over the ditches. 'It looks,' whispered Geraldine, 'like we are only imagining all this'" (18). The fusion of the real and the imaginary is later more directly insisted upon by Frank: "'There is nothing,' said Frank, 'in your imagination cannot happen in reality'" (33).

The hybrid nature of the real and the imaginary, if such a blunt distinction is even possible, is even more emphatically registered in Healy's second novel, *A Goat's Song*, in which the compelling, multifaceted character, Jack Ferris, whose capacity to 'imagine' his world as a knowable, coherent, shape is deeply compromised, which defines the narrative impulse of the novel and motivates Jack's own ultimate narrative recreation of his time with Catherine, her childhood and her father, Jonathan Adams's life. Most of the novel is constructed as a quasi-analeptic narrative but also as an embedded, framing narrative, within Jack's primary telling. While the implications of this will be considered more fully hereafter, the shaping of such a complex narrative system was, by his third novel, becoming a characteristic artistic attribute. *A Goat's Song* frequently foregrounds, within the various strands of narration, the perpetual problem of assigning words to things, of bringing the imagination into some kind of harmony with the "incorrigibly plural" world, as Louis MacNeice has it (86). While *A Goat's Song* openly addresses this problem in numerous ways—to be considered presently—Healy's work by now could be seen to be deeply concerned with the tormented problem of finding ways to speak that might begin to approach the complexity of existence, and a simultaneous refusal to simply endorse linear, or monological narrative systems.

Healy's third novel, *Sudden Times*, offers further evidence of a deeply innovative technical spirit, in which Ollie Ewing's consciousness is an often-tortured fusion of fragments of real conversations in his head, guilt-driven nightmares and a deeply compromised capacity to gain access to the communal sense of the real that most other characters in the novel inhabit. Most unsettling, perhaps, is his fluid sense of time and space, even when he is living in Sligo: "I went back to the crossword. Then some word made me step down off a train in France. One word and I'm away. For a long period I walked the docks listening to the sailors . . . After a long trip through the fields of wheat, I bed down for the night in Montmartre" (116). In fact, within two pages we shift from Sligo to France to London, and back to Sligo, with the barest of narrative transitions evident (116–7). Catherine Hoffmann argues that, in *Sudden Times*, "indeterminacy characterizes the narrator's temporal and spatial location in relation to the Sligo period" (359), but as the novel progresses, particularly during the London section, his temporal position "vanishes completely as a point of reference" (361). Healy's challenge, in his second novel, was to find a form that would serve to imaginatively encompass Ollie's fractured consciousness rather than simply represent him as a deranged character. His incapacity to distinguish between distinctions in time and space, as well as to establish in his mind any causation factors for what happens is striking, for example, in the way that he repeatedly insists in court that things just happened, "suddenly," as though each moment in life is disconnected from a causative pattern (295, 311). Similarly, and this is a recurring tendency in several of Healy's novels, words take leave of their moorings, and the signifier/signified relationship is ruptured, leaving Ollie rudderless in his communicative wilderness: "Then the things with the words happened. The words for things escaped me" (329). While the obvious comparison in Irish contemporary fiction is Pat McCabe's *The Butcher Boy*, the unrelenting technical evocation of a mind that is disconnected from the events of his context that we find in *Sudden Times* produces a far more technically complex and uncompromising novel than McCabe's. While the first person narrator, Francie Brady, in *The Butcher Boy*, is also a terrifying figure, Healy's Ollie is encased in a narratorial frame that, as Hoffmann puts it, "both consciously records the effects on the diegetic level, of Ollie's mental derangement, and integrates them, at the level of narration, as a dynamic factor in the narrating process" (358). This dual feature ensures that we glimpse at the chaotic rendering within Ollie's private consciousness and then witness that consciousness mediate the ordinary realities of Sligo and London life until they become haunted, nightmarish landscapes. Ultimately, of course, the inner nightmares meet external monsters to match them in the grim underworld of London criminal life.

Healy's last novel, *Long Time, No See* (2011), further extends the search for a narrative form that might fit the endlessly complex, and ordinary, world of small-town Ireland of the last decade. He largely dispenses with the formal device of a primary narrative voice: "'When I was writing,' he says, 'I was trying to let the dialogue kick in the way it is spoken where the novel is set, which is just out of Sligo a bit on the verge of Donegal. In a way, I was trying to stay out of it and let the reader take over and run with it. So I would often put the meaning of a passage in, then take it out again'"(qtd. in O'Hagan). The fluid form of the novel is largely constructed out of sequences of dialogue between local characters, various passersby, and immigrants, and while many of the local characters are adorned with characteristically (for rural Irish towns and villages) exotic names (Mister Psyche, the Judge, the Bird, the Blackbird, Mr Awesome, Mister John, Mrs Puff, etc.—everyone seems to have a nickname in small-town Ireland), the ordinary, but imaginatively exaggerated, spectacles of their lives are what dictate the movement of the novel. *Long Time, No See* ensures that everyday lives, with their dramas, conflicts and private crises are witnessed in rich detail, refracted through oceans of dialogue and commonplace stories. But what is again artistically striking is the commitment to a unique formal system, built largely from fragments of dialogue, usually expressed in local dialect, and which largely removes the guiding hand of the narrative voice.

One of the consequences of such a narrative form is the absence of a fixed central designator of reality and we are instead offered a polyphony of voices each competing with the other to mark out their senses of the "real"—and these are frequently insecure and/or highly charged by an infusion of the imaginative lives of the characters. It is as though the world cannot be fixed with singular designations so he invents narratives of movement, fluidity, and without the controlling centre of a dominating narrative authority, in order to convey a sense of the rich variousness of his characters' lives. This is exemplified in the plotline that revolves around the primary character in the novel, Philip Feeney's great-uncle, Joejoe, who claims that someone has shot a bullet through his living room window and the complex array of talk and innuendo that thereafter accompanies this claim allows each of the central characters to express themselves—the true story, of course, is more complicated than Joejoe's suggestion. Philip (or Mister Psyche, as he is generally known), who has just finished the leaving certificate, is the nearest we have to a formal narrator, but he tells us that his "head was tormented with words" (426), and his descriptions of the world frequently admit a multilayered consciousness of being that both enriches the world and simultaneously ensures that material reality is always just a surface phenomenon that masks endless depths:

> Sometimes I'd be building walls in my dreams.
> Some of the stones I used had come inland in storms. But today I started to haul from an old ruin up on the bank overlooking the sea. I got an awful bad feeling as I pulled the rocks out of the ruin. I had to tell myself over and over that they were going back into another wall. The ruin was supposed to have been a henhouse way back, but it was the strongest-built henhouse I ever came across. There were massive stones in her. I could have been demolishing a small church, and sometimes I thought I was.
> A beehive hut it might have been.
> A monk's chamber.
> I could even feel the sense of balance of the man who had built it.
> He drew the stone from the coral beach by ass and cart to the spot I was taking them from. As he built alongside me, I was pulling his work down. As he dropped a stone into place, I lifted it and carried it away. He built towards me, and I built away from him. I could feel the way he carried himself. He could have been a great-great-granduncle of mine. (128)

With relative ease, Philip's self slips into a more diffused sense being, imagining a former builder, long since vanished in time, building beside him, with the effect that material reality is imaginatively transfigured into a commingling of the landscape and the multiple modes of mind that so fascinate Healy. Many of the other characters appear to both participate in the action and simultaneously exist as separate creatures, aloof in their own consciousnesses, like Philip's mother who at one point pauses on the stairs lost in a moment only to, a second later, look "to where she had been standing on the stairs and g[i]ve this quaint satisfied nod to herself" (28). For a brief moment, she steps out of herself and becomes a kind of ghost to her own conscious mind. Characters exist in a curious relationship to any material sense of reality throughout the novel which, nevertheless, is nominally based in Sligo during the Celtic Tiger years. The contemporary social context is purring in the background but its felt significance is apparent primarily in terms of how it impinges on the extraordinary mythic small-town lives of these characters. Furthermore, without a persistent anchoring narrative voice, the fictional landscape doesn't have an obvious, overt, fixed shape, a feature that accommodates a more fluid sense of how one might aesthetically reflect reality in fiction.

All of Healy's fiction reflects a fascination with the process of naming material reality and the communication of states of being that are not so readily expressed in linear narrative forms that are firmly anchored to a concrete sense of the real. As with *Sudden Times* and *Long Time, No See*, *A Goat's Song* bears the imprint of Healy's fascination with the complex relationship between literary forms and the mutable nature of not-so-material reality. As mentioned earlier, *A Goat's Song* has been frequently read through the cultural lens of Northern Irish-border fiction, for obvious reasons, with all the attendant socio-political implications that its content embraces. But the novel is also one of those rare creatures, a writer's novel, a technically sophisticated narrative admired by many of his peers and yet somewhat ignored in the harsh world of popular fiction and the contemporary obsession with prizes. Echoing the work of his early mentor, Aidan Higgins, work that Derek Mahon provocatively claims is too "difficult" for a contemporary readership (75), Healy's *A Goat's Song* is framed by an extremely sophisticated variation of the use of analepsis or, more crudely, the flashback technique, and many critics have overlooked the key temporal variation in the formal structure of the novel. The enduring and haunting fascination that this novel holds for its admirers can be primarily explained by the effect generated by the aesthetically-daring variation, and this also, consequentially, explains its relative marginality in the popular marketplace.

Brian Richardson names six kinds of temporal reconstruction which are distinct from the "realistic temporality" that one finds in realist sequential novels, one of which is the "circular": "this kind of fiction instead of ending returns to its own beginning, and thus continues infinitely. Its circular temporality partially mimes but ultimately transforms the linear chronology of everyday existence; it always returns to and departs from its point of origin—which is also its (temporary) conclusion" (48). Similarly, Ken Ireland explains the function of analepsis as that which "signals the retrospective evocation of an event" (591). The narrative impact of such a device on many major novels, from García Márquez's *Love in the Time of Cholera* and *One Hundred Years of Solitude* to Conrad's *Nostromo* is obvious, and, at first glance, *A Goat's Song* appears to employ a similar technique. But there is a key difference: it does not simply generate "a temporally second narrative," as Shlomith Rimmon-Kenan indicates more generally about analepsis (47). Healy's novel is a bogus analeptic text in the sense that we do not technically return to the actual beginning or experience a temporally second narrative. Rather, it is an imagined second narrative. Technically, the account that we experience from section II onwards is an imaginative invention rather than a tale told about events from a different temporal zone based in the actual past. While the illusion of re-telling is maintained because of the re-appearance of Jack and Catherine, and by the plot being played out in a similar landscape, everything that we experience from the end of section I onwards occurs, as Jack puts it as he sits down to write, "in a different world," a world in which we "enter a new story," in which Catherine must be "imagined" into existence (84). This fictional sleight of hand holds enormous implications for the relationship between the life lived and the imaginative reconstructions that emerge from that life.

Offering due acknowledgement to the implications of the layers of fictional reality in the novel is essential to the way we read *A Goat's Song*. For example, Stephanie Schwerter interprets the novel as a straight realist political text, without acknowledging that everything after section I is a frame narrative. Consequentially, the novel is simply read as an allegory of Northern Irish conflict, and she concludes that "Healy works against the narrative image of reconciliation . . ." (179). Observing the political implications of a novel that features emotionally-connected characters from both sides of the border is perfectly legitimate but the temptation to reduce the novel to allegory alone is reductive. Of course, the relationship between realism and allegory has always been contentious; for example, Auerbach felt that serious realism in France was "in danger of being choked to death by the vines of allegory" (261). While there are clearly allegorical elements in the novel, it is very difficult to argue for a sustained allegorical frame because, as David Lodge has it, "the development of an allegorical narrative is determined at every point by its one-to-one correspondence to the implied meaning" (143). The presence of such a one-to-one correspondence in a complex narrative like *A Goat's Song*, in which the very nature of sensual experience is perpetually under assault, seems unlikely. The novel, quite simply, is too much a meditation on the wildness of imagination—even the maddening Irish Atlantic coastal wind and rain is like a chorus in Jack Ferris's real and imaginary worlds— to be contained in a closed allegorical rhetorical system. Similarly, while the novel has clear framing correspondences with Greek myth, including that which names the novel, and the Dionysian dying god, and Orpheus's tortured journey to the otherworld to find his dead Eurydice, such devices appear to thicken the layers of significance rather than impose a fixed formal shape.[1]

From the beginning of section II the novel appears to plunge backwards in time to Catherine's childhood and into her father's turmoil, including his inner fears and obsessions, that could never have been known to Catherine, let alone Jack. What follows is Jack's sympathetic invention of a world he never knew, or as Hopper names it, his "act of creative contrition" (Hopper 19), while it simultaneously, and self-reflexively, speaks to the complex artistic endeavour that Healy's work has always been engaged with; the work of turning the world, or what one imagines of it, into literary shape. In fact the phrase, derived from several biblical sources,[2] "to give form to that which cannot be uttered" is like a commanding refrain through the novel, repeated three times (5, 99–100, 202). The phrase dominates Jack's imagined figure of Jonathan Adams, as it does the embedded story of Jack and Catherine, and comes to assume major significance as they all struggle to find ways to meet across their various cultural and communicative barriers. For Jonathan Adams the phrase is at the centre of his abandonment of the Presbyterian ministry that he had initially pursued. For his first sermon, he had "chosen as his homily the powerful line—*to give some form to that which cannot be uttered*" (99) but the moment he begins to preach he is ironically "possessed of such a feeling of disorientation that his chin and wrists shook uncontrollably [. . .]. Words refused to come to him. Meaning departed" (99). Adams had long dreamed of the sermon he would give, he knew what he wanted to say, but the words that might deliver his thoughts failed him: "If he could only enter their interior without words! If even words could be swept away" (100). The rupture between form and the desire to speak is laid bare to such a degree that he abandons his vocation and joins the Royal Irish Constabulary. His father's uncompromising advice—"Per-sev-ere" (101)—is underpinned by his insistence that the words will come "in time" (101) and echoes through the same sense of futility that Jack Ferris felt when he first thought of imaginatively assembling the life of Catherine, to "live on in a different world" (27) but he fails, not being yet ready; however, he perseveres and ultimately finds a form—the primary embedded narrative in the novel.

In the primary frame, Jack discovers the phrase used by Adams in his homily, apparently underlined in the Bible, imaginatively connecting Jack to Adams. The phrase, of course, couldn't have been underlined in the Bible because it is a very liberal approximation rather than a direct quotation. The phrase, in Jack's imagined construction of Adams's mind, becomes the centre from which the character of his lover's father fictionally emerges but it also effectively becomes a commanding injunction both in Jack's artistic motivation and in the embedded Jack's desire to name and thus, somehow, know: "The writing down of certain words would strangely enough bring her across the void, as if they contained some power of healing" (345). But it is a perpetual struggle that commands the trajectory of the story of Jack's consciousness through various stages of collapse, recovery and loss of a precise sense of self. In one pre-linguistic moment that prevents him from imposing an ordered narrative on his surroundings, he speaks of what it feels to be bereft of a system to inhabit: "He was thinking in another language. The eerie language of the half-formed and the unsayable" (380). In such moments, of which there are many in the novel, the consciousness of Jack forces the readers on an increasingly hallucinatory journey, a dark mirror of Orpheus's attempted recovery of Eurydice, during which material reality frequently gives way to a spectral world, uncovered, or invented, by Jack's unanchored groundings. He, variously, meets a man on a beach, magically reformulated into "a stooped creature with a broken wing" (381), becomes a tragelaph, "a deer with a beard, whining into the night," "for the return of his beloved" (371), and, of course, the goat, being milked by his imaginary Catherine, the goatsucker (394). One day, the land has no horizon, and the house is "reduced to a mere dot in time" (403), while mere objects refuse to remain still:

> Objects took on other presences. For a certain amount of time the objects remained what they were—chairs, stones, shadows, a holy picture, a bend in the bed, a bottle—then there would be a slight alien encroachment, a vague déjà-vu, but before they could entirely become something else, the hint of change receded. (405)

That some of Jack's difficulties with grasping a fixed sense of material reality are derived from his alcohol-fuelled, or -deprived, consciousness at different times is certain, but throughout the novel there is a profound sense of the world becoming far less securely fixed than the evidence of our minds suggests.

Healy himself has acknowledged this tendency in his work: "A lot of people are able to see better, see what's there, but I might see what I think is there" (qtd. in O'Hagan). This doesn't suggest a vague lyricism in any sense because the precise savagery of the images that Healy uses to speak of an ever-shifting world is extremely arresting and exact, as when he imagines he has transformed into a female body: "It was for a minute only. But he felt for a moment that he had become the woman beside him. As she moved around the room in her nightdress, he could feel that he himself was scuttling about in his womanness. He even felt the sensation of breasts" (321). *A Goat's Song* is an exploration of what it means to lose a sense of shape, to be bereft of a system with which to name a world framed by pain, self-deception, alcoholism and loss. And yet all are revealed to be wildly and dangerously pivotal to Jack's rebirthing consciousness. Even though Jack is the primary recipient of this traumatic gift of seeing, it is a common refrain that runs throughout the lives of the other characters. Jonathan Adams, for example, thinks that it must be "dreadful," "to step out into space" (202), and the youthful Adams daughters, Catherine and Sara, transfigure the death of Matti Bonner into a nightmarish, mythic tale in which the maddening fusion of dreams, gossip, imagination, terror and burgeoning sexuality, compose a gripping fantasy with the presence of the real that never leaves Catherine in the years ahead.

Healy's fixation with locating forms to speak of the world in some legitimate, if not, ultimately, authoritative, sense is directly linked to the sense that the material world is always on the verge of divulging some of its secrets, dark though they may be, and to the profusion of oddities and hallucinatory moments in his work. Beyond the veneer of civil organisational shapes there is a perpetual sense of another less-secure place, and this is usually where his central figures find themselves. It is a landscape which echoes that of Kavanagh, Heaney and McGahern, but is nevertheless far stranger than any of them; at times it is a world "rampant with hallucinations" (*GS* 79), at others we are offered sympathetic but harsh insights into the enclosed consciousnesses that live without ever breaking through the membranes that contain them.

When Healy takes us off the tramlines of sequential narrative he does so not to play intellectual, technical games but to seek some forms that might help him explain the oddness of living. The reason for his relative neglect likely lies in a combination of these factors. Small-town Ireland has always been unpleasantly exotic to the metropolitan imaginations that emerged from Dublin. The paradox of Healy's work, in particular *A Goat's Song*, is that while its daring accomplishment may be incomparable in contemporary Irish fiction, the subject matter is likely incompatible with the easily digestible agenda-driven fiction that drives the marketplace. Rural, small-town Ireland has always been "provincial," closed, and excruciatingly limited in the popular imagination but Healy shows us, over and over, that the depths of people's loves and sorrows are as profound in Sligo, Fermanagh and Ballintra as they are in Paris, London or Dublin—with the advantage that they can still shock our sensibilities with the strangeness that lies at the heart of Art.

Works Cited

Auerbach, Eric. *Mimesis: The Representation of Reality in Western Literature*. Trans. Willard R. Trask. Princeton: Princeton University Press, 1953. Print.

Gefter Wondrich, Roberta. "Islands of Ireland: A Tragedy of Separation in Dermot Healy's *A Goat's Song*." *Writing Ulster* 6 (1999): 68–87. Print.

Healy, Dermot. *A Goat's Song*. London: Harvill Press, 1995. Print.

———. *Fighting with Shadows*. London: Allison and Busby, 1986. Print.

———. *Long Time, No See*. London: Faber and Faber, 2011. Print.

———. *Sudden Times*. New York: Harvill Press, 2000. Print.

———. *The Bend for Home*. London: Harvill Press, 1996. Print.

Hoffmann, Catherine. "Dancing to Ollie's Tunes: The Rhetoric of Narrative Stutter." *Style* 43.3 (Fall 2009): 357–72. Print.

Hopper, Keith. "Everyday Things." Rev. of *Long Time, No See* and *A Fool's Errand*, by Dermot Healy. *Times Literary Supplement* 8 Apr. 2011: 19–20. Print.

Ireland, Ken. "Temporal Ordering." *Routledge Encyclopedia of Narrative Theory*. Ed. David Herman et al. London: Routledge, 2008. Print.

Lodge, David. *The Art of Fiction*. Harmondsworth: Penguin, 1992. Print.

MacNeice, Louis. "Snow." *Collected Poems 1925–1948*. London: Faber and Faber, 1951. 86. Print.

Mahon, Derek. "The Blithely Subversive Aidan Higgins." *Aidan Higgins: The Fragility of Form*. Ed. Neil Murphy. Champaign: Dalkey Archive Press, 2010. 72–8. Print.

McCabe, Patrick. *The Butcher Boy*. London: Picador, 1992. Print.

McCarthy, Dermot. "Recovering Dionysus: Dermot Healy's *A Goat's Song*." *New Hibernia Review* 4.4 (Winter 2000): 134–49. Print.

O'Grady, Timothy. "Dermot Healy: An Interview." *Wasafiri* 25.2 (June 2010): 26–31. Print.

O'Hagan, Sean. "Dermot Healy: 'I try to stay out of it and let the reader take over.'" Interview with Dermot Healy. *The Observer* 3 Apr. 2011. Web. 30 Dec. 2012.

Richardson, Brian, ed. *Narrative Dynamics: Essays on Time, Plot, Closure, and Frames*. Columbus: Ohio State University Press, 2002. Print.

Rimmon-Kenan, Shlomith. *Narrative Fiction: Contemporary Poetics*. London and New York: Methuen, 1984. Print.

Schwerter, Stephanie. "Transgressing Boundaries: Belfast and the 'Romance-Across-the-Divide.'" *Estudios Irlandeses* 2 (2007): 173–82. Web. 19 Apr. 2016.

Sloan, Barry. "'In My Father's House': Renegotiations of Boyhood in Life Writing by John McGahern, Ciaran O'Driscoll, Dermot Healy, and Ciaran Carson." *Éire-Ireland* 44.1/2 (Spring/Summer 2009): 218–41. Print.

Wallace, Kim. "'Here it begins': Figuring Identities in Dermot Healy's *A Goat's Song*." *Beyond Borders: IASIL Essays on Modern Irish Writing*. Ed. Neil Sammells. Bath: Sulis Press, 2004. 121–42. Print.

Notes

1. For an excellent exposition of the mythic parallels and echoes, see Dermot McCarthy, "Recovering Dionysus: Dermot Healy's *A Goat's Song*," *New Hibernia Review* 4.4 (Winter 2000): 134–49.

2. The recurring phrase echoes a line from Corinthians most emphatically but the following lines from Romans also resonate with Healy's phrase: "How that he was caught up into paradise, and heard unspeakable words, which it is not lawful for a man to utter" (*King James Bible*, 2 Cor. 12.4). And: "Likewise the Spirit also helps our weakness: for we know not what we should pray for as we ought but the Spirit himself makes inter- cession for us with groanings which cannot be uttered" (*King James Bible*, Rom. 8.26).

Guilt Trips: Dermot Healy's *Sudden Times* and the Meaning of Sin
Paul Fagan

Early in Dermot Healy's *Sudden Times*, the novel's traumatised protagonist Ollie Ewing records a fleeting conversation with a holidaying German psychiatrist on the subject of guilt:

> Well, I have no problems feeling guilty, I said.
> Ah the Irish [the German said].
> What do you mean—*Ah the Irish*?
> Because you have little to feel guilty about.
> I have, I said, a certain sufficiency. (*ST* 32–3)

The brief discussion gives voice both to the intuition that a certain relation to guilt is essential to the cultural category of Irishness and to a countering refusal of this identification. To this extent, the exchange mirrors a recurring trend in the criticism of Irish writing. At the outset of his *Tragedy and Irish Literature* (2002), Ronan McDonald offers the commonplace that "the Irish imagination teems with images and tropes of loss and guilt" (2). And yet, McDonald underlines, any critical attempt to pin down these concerns in unchanging forms across the Irish literary tradition proves untenable. One might reflect on the distance between the acts of contrition in Oscar Wilde's *De Profundis* and the attack on Catholic guilt that recurs throughout Austin Clarke's poetry; or between the policemen that govern Flann O'Brien's *The Third Policeman* through a sadistically arbitrary interpretation of guilt and Seamus Heaney's writing, in which the poet seems almost masochistically "guilty about being a poet at all [. . .], troubled by his art's apparent incapacity to make things happen" (Brown 190). Evidently, these figurations of loss, culpability, and (self-) reproach are shaped and reshaped by legal, religious, gendered, nationalistic, jurisdictive, or aesthetic discourses, each with its own history and power dynamics. As a consequence, the dramatisation of the interpersonal stakes of guilt, as well as the identities to which it gives rise, shifts and adapts constantly. Thus considered, writing itself emerges not so much as an act of documenting or narrativising individually embodied forms of national guilt, but rather as a space within which such images of guilt might be drawn together, set into dramatic tension, and explored for their ethical ramifications.

These tropes of loss and guilt are transformed also by the ways in which we, as readers, conceive of the genre of the tragic. Here, too, we find a term shot through with varied and even contradicting meanings and values, although we can broadly distinguish between stances that conceptualise the tragic as either destructive or productive. In the destructive definition, "tragedy evokes a profound sense of waste, an awareness of destruction without corresponding progress or redemption" (McDonald 14). The tragic is here appreciated as an articulation of pessimistic realism, which fatalistically traces how the traumatic forces of loss, suffering, and death all mark time's passing by engendering an irreversible disjuncture between an innocent, yet naïve, past, and a guilty, and thus fallen, present. Clearly, such a definition of loss, guilt, and tragedy is inextricably bound up with how we understand the nature of time's passing. It follows that to reconceptualise the nature of time away from the idea of "the present as a succession of now-moments" (Cahill 9) is to test our understanding of the tragic.

In his *Time and Free Will* (1889), Henri Bergson rigorously refutes the definition of time as a chronological sequence of equally self-contained and measurable present moments, and contests the notion that the human experience of time can be measured by the clock. For Bergson, the real nature and experience of "lived time" cannot be captured until we acknowledge that the past and future constantly alter the *actual* present through the *virtual* pulls of memory and desire (Bergson 107–8). Concurring with Bergson, Gilles Deleuze and Félix Guattari argue that a destructive and teleological framing of the tragic must, therefore, be a "low" and "neurotic" way of understanding the unique power of literature (Kafka 95), in which the present moment never "actually occurs," but is rather "always forthcoming and already past" (Deleuze, *Logic of Sense* 80). Against a narcissistic posture that lingers obsessively on personal guilt as an insurmountable sorrow, they insist on the tragic's productive, affirmative, even joyous power to overcome such passions (Borg, "Deleuze on Genre" 106).

In this essay, I wish to explore Dermot Healy's critically overlooked *Sudden Times* as a particularly significant and innovative re-examination of these interwoven themes of guilt, self, and time in the contemporary Irish novel. My intention is to show that a direct correlation exists between the novel's engagement with the problem of guilt, its innovative performance of narrative time, and its insistence upon the regenerative power of the tragic. In building this case, I demonstrate how Healy's novel invokes literary models of guilt's relation to time, being, and the tragic from John Milton, James Joyce, and Samuel Beckett, and contemplates each model in turn for its applicability to capturing this insight in the contemporary moment. And it will be my contention that in the care it takes to render more rigorously time's shaping influence upon liminal identities, spaces, and experiences, Healy's novel attests to the *productive* power of writing as a means of overcoming the navel-gazing circularity of tragic sentiment.

The Time Is Out of Joint

The plot of *Sudden Times* begins, unusually, in the fifth of its seven sections. There, the novel's first-person narrator Ollie Ewing informs us that he "flew over with Ryanair from Dublin to Luton on February 9th for £40" (*ST* 167). As a 'Ryanair generation' narrative of migration and displacement, *Sudden Times* is thematically "concern[ed] with borders and states of in-betweenness" (Nordin and Holmsten 7). This concern is manifested in Ollie's inhabitations of temporary structures on and around London building sites, and in his subsequent return to converted Sligo attics amid ever-expanding "Urban renewal" (*ST* 4). These profoundly decentring experiences with the border position Ollie in a liminal state between "exile and escape; leaving and arriving; staying and going; past and present; [...] memory and imagination" (Murray 3). To the extent, then, that Ollie's sense of self unravels through his attempts to give voice to his experience, his testimony necessitates a form of narrative that breaks free from the constraints of autobiographical rhetoric and universal clock-time.

Tony Murray notes how this emphasis on liminality informs the contemporary Irish migration novel's unusual relation to narrative time: "Migration is sometimes perceived as a form of traditional narrative itself. It appears to have a beginning, a middle and an end. When migrants recount their experiences, however, they rarely opt for linear forms of storytelling" (2). *Sudden Times* expands upon this topos of the non-linear unfolding of the autobiographical through its innovative narrative structure. In the opening chapters the reader is dropped *in media res* amid Ollie's mental and emotional experiences upon his return to Sligo following his vagrant stint as a carpenter-turned-builder in London (the details of which we will not learn until the novel's close, and then only ambiguously). It is through and between these textual and contextual tensions that the novel's central narrative arc slowly comes into view. We learn how the death of his friend Marty Kilgallon and Ollie's subsequent involvement with protection racketeer Silver John initiated a series of events that lead to the tragic death of his own brother Redmond in London. Ollie's thoughts are shaped by sensations of culpability and guilt for each of these deaths, and by his consequent estrangement from his father Eamon. The 'plot' ends at the novel's halfway point, with Ollie's troubled reunion with his father in Coventry, before returning to the events in London which had given shape to his state of mind as depicted in its opening chapters.

Yet, as John Kenny notes, "while Ollie's story holds together as a fictionally 'true' plot," Healy's emphasis on the virtual plane of Ollie's memories, desires, and fantasies "appears to aim mainly to capture the processes of a consciousness trying to sift the *real* from the *imagined*" (B9). Appropriately to this aim, Ollie's agitated and darkly comic monologue is "characterized by repetition, fragmentation, fuzzy temporality" (Hoffmann 357). His sparse sentences are light on exposition and context, as his refracted internal monologue pieces together an impressionistic scrapbook of overlapping experiences, recollections, and reveries in and of Sligo pubs, supermarkets, and attics, and London pubs, building sites, and courtrooms. Consequently, unlike more linear realist modes which anchor context through exposition and guide the reader towards a dominant reading, these highly subjective and idiosyncratic shifting scenes engender a number of (potentially contradicting) effects, impressions, and readings. As Gordon Burn underlines, "Healy's great achievement here is the way he allows his characters to find their coherence in confessed incoherence" (n. pag.).

The long trial section concerning the circumstances of Redmond's death in book IV is the only sequence that leaves Ollie's refracted perspective for an omniscient view. In stark contrast to Ollie's narrative, the court case is presented as a distinctly 'realist' narrative mode *via* the genre of the transcript—a project to re-order the events of London into an authoritative, chronologically linear account populated by accountable agents who are the sole authors of their destructive thoughts and deeds. In other words, this episode—suggestively titled "The Case History of Ollie"—captures attempts to encode the world of Ollie's experiences within a system of laws and narratives that traduce the tragic "into moralistic sentiment" (Borg, "Deleuze on Genre" 107). As the lawyer for the prosecution announces: "what we are doing is trying to separate fact from fiction" (*ST* 279). I suggest that this brief, but jarring, shift in perspective is carefully chosen in order to stage the novel's central conflicts. Through its temporal anomalies, *Sudden Times* confounds these realist, legalistic, and moralistic discourses for encoding and shaping Ollie's guilt, and demonstrates the impossibility of cleanly separating 'fact' from the transformative 'fictions' of memory, fantasy, and desire. And ultimately, the novel moves beyond such moralistic concern with the proper and proportional attribution of guilt through its sustained challenge to the humanist concept of the self as an agent with libertarian free will upon which such an understanding of sin rests.

"The Meaning of Sin"

The novel's contemplation of the correlation between sin, guilt, and the nature of 'being in time' is established in a significant scene early in the book (yet close to the plot's *denouement*). Back in Sligo, the conversation between Ollie and the German psychiatrist turns to the relation of sinning and being:

> Do you know, he asked, the meaning of the word sin?
> I have an idea.
> You are thinking of religion.
> I suppose I am.
> I mean the meaning of the word.
> OK, I said, fire ahead.
> It means, in most languages, he said, to be. To exist.
> Go 'long.
> It is true [. . .]. I found it in a dictionary in Berlin and thought of you.
> That threw me.
> To be, I said. (*ST* 33)

Echoed at a number of crucial points throughout the narrative (*ST* 37, 41, 89), this etymological debate with the German psychiatrist (whom Ollie later improbably, and comically, refers to as "Sean McGuilty"; *ST* 37), announces that the novel's concern with "the meaning of sin" (*ST* 32), while not indistinguishable, is closely related to its concern with the meaning or nature of 'being.'

Healy's interest in the creative potential of etymology is well-established (see Healy, "Small Talk"), and most famously turned to good account in the title of his 1994 novel *A Goat's Song*, a literal rendering of the etymology of the word 'tragedy' (Greek *tragōidia*, from *tragos* 'goat' + *ōidē* 'song'). In that novel, which also employs a cyclical structure, Jack Ferris accounts for this derivation with a fable of lovelorn bucks and nannies separated by ancient Greek agricultural practices (227). The concept foregrounded in *Sudden Times* that 'sin' is etymologically related to 'being' extends in the modern imagination back, at least, to the nineteenth-century philologist Walter William Skeat's *Etymological Dictionary* (555). Indeed, the relevance of the *German* psychologist in Healy's text—beyond the comparative force of that nation's own twentieth-century wrangling with national guilt—might well be the fact that the connection between 'sinning' and 'being' is "the most obvious in the case of the modern German *sein*" (Forsyth 207). Yet, even as he evokes this etymological dimension to language, Healy does not duplicate the purely chronological "practice of grammarians who refer to the history of a particular idea only as a means of illustrating and ultimately justifying its current sense"—a linear view of meaning as a diachronic succession of prioritised 'present meanings' (Borg, *Measureless* 10). Rather, as in the case of Jack's tale in *A Goat's Song*, his focus lies primarily with the literary compulsion "to *create* fables that account for (and negotiate between) all the accumulated semantic"—emotional, and impressionistic—"variations" of a particular word's history in a single narrative image (Borg, *Measureless* 11).

The most prominent example of such a project implicitly evoked in *Sudden Times* is John Milton's *Paradise Lost*, with its germane themes of guilt, fate, and free will. The novel's engagement with Milton's epic is signalled in Ollie's dialogue with the figure of Ray: "The town of Sligo should be a paradise [Ray] said [. . .], but it's not. / It's not, I said" (*ST* 110). The significance of this textual echo is to be found in Milton's staging of Satan's conspiracy against God in Heaven, in which the birth of 'Sin' is indistinguishable from the birth of the 'sign':

> amazement seiz'd
> All th' Host of Heav'n; back they recoil'd, afraid
> At first, and call'd me *Sin*, and for a Sign
> Portentous held me. (II, 758–61)

Milton's considered punning of "*Sin*" and "sign" engenders a narrative image that attempts to account for their homophony by tracing their genealogies to a common origin in rebellion against a divine order. Thus Milton's fable of sin's etymology "goes in a different direction [to Skeat's], not towards being [*sein*] but towards meaning [*sign*]" (Forsyth 207). In Healy's text, the German psychiatrist sets these contrasting accounts of the significance of sin (as *meaning* or *being*) into direct creative tension: "You are thinking of religion [. . .]. I mean the meaning of the word" (*ST* 33). Milton's narrative etymology offers an enlightening coordinate by which to consider the implication that *Sudden Times* is an act of writing engendered, in its broader project, by an attempt to narrativise the homophony of 'sin,' 'sign,' and 'sein' in a world in which the fleeting concerns of the self can no longer be subordinated to a divine plan and will.

In both Milton's poem and Healy's novel, this relationship between 'sin,' 'sign,' and 'sein' is carefully related to models of time. If the etymological view of the sign is linear and teleological, Stanley Fish notes that Milton's alignment of 'sin' and 'sign' unfolds the poem's deeper concern with literary representation and narrative as threats—in and of themselves—to God's 'eternal' word. For Milton:

> Narrative and plot are vehicles of idolatry because they locate significance in some insight to be generated by time, rather than in the timeless, always present obligation to be aligned with the will of deity; plot and narrative tell us that there is somewhere to go, whereas the true question (posed by every indifferent moment) is: What way shall one *be*? (Fish 492)

As in *Paradise Lost*, Ollie's descent after the rupture of the tragic events in London is figured as a fall into a world of alienating signs and inauthentic representations which seem to trap him in a cycle of guilt-laden obsession with the self: "*I don't like these signs*," he tells us, "*I've seen them before.* They were everywhere, on the boat across [on his return to England], the train, in slight changes of consciousness [. . .], the broken cup that spilled pills, the quirks of light on the street, sudden shifts in perspective. [. . .] I was in a world of signs" (*ST* 138–9). Throughout his account, Ollie obsessively notes every sign in his environment: "PLEASE DO NOT FLUSH AFTER MIDNIGHT!"; "9 DURE STREET, COVENTRY"; "a cup that says DADDY"; "THE PALISADES WELCOMES YOU TO BIRMINGHAM"; "BRITISH TRANSPORT POLICE"; "START A NEW DAY WITH JESUS"; "FANNY ELEANOR WYNNE— JUST AS I AM, WITHOUT ONE PLEA"; "I AM THE TRUE VINE"; "TRESPASSERS WILL BE PROSECUTED"; "KEEP OUT"; "WARNING. THESE PREMISES ARE PROTECTED

BY EXECUTIVE SECURITY PATROLS"; "NO HAT NO BOOTS NO JOB!"; "FIRE ACTION! FIRE ACTION!" (*ST* 7, 25, 100, 148, 150, 153, 171).

Thus fallen, Ollie seems to long for an external force that will define and fix his guilt, and thus relieve him of burden:

> The worst thing is I turned sort of religious. That can happen. It can happen the best of us. I walked to the window in the hostel and looked out at the monastery that had not been inhabited in over two centuries. In my head I heard beautiful psalms. This need of mine for God is a travesty. (*ST* 46)

The "travesty" of Ollie's "need" is for a divine order which foregoes a significance rooted in isolated events in time (the traumatic events of Marty's and Redmond's deaths) and their representation (in Ollie's guilt as rendered through thought in the form of his first person narrative) for a "timeless, always present obligation to be aligned with the will of deity" (Fish 492). And yet, as I shall argue presently, the way out of this predicament is ultimately to be found in embracing Ollie's radical experience of the coexistence of past in present *via* his reverie of the "beautiful psalms" of the suddenly inhabited monastery.

Advising Ollie in spiritual matters, Ray evokes the parable of Job:

> [Your] mind is contaminated [Ray said]. Think of Job. You know your Job?
> I do.
> Well, everything was against him and look what he done. Right? Job was the boy.
> He was. (*ST* 109)

In the parable, Job's insight was that one should not quarrel with God's will by recourse to human concepts of right and wrong, as it is for God to handle all guilt in his own time, whether on Earth or in Judgement. The tragic aspect of Ollie's predicament that initiates his need to give voice to his experience, is that neither the linear model of time and subjectivity put forward by the law nor the eternal model encoded in a divine universe can fix his 'guilt' and free him from self-reproachment. He is on his own.

"If I Start to Think I Get the Tenses Mixed"

In his *Irish Times* review of *Sudden Times*, John Kenny emphasises "Healy's Viconian conception of narrative time" (B9). Kenny's reference is to eighteenth-century Italian philosopher Giambattista Vico, who propounded a cyclical theory of human history (as well as a project to explore etymology as a philosophical tool) that most famously informs the structuring principle of Joyce's *Finnegans Wake*. The *Wake*'s opening lower-case sentence fragment—"riverrun, past Eve and Adam's, from swerve of shore to bend of bay, brings us by a commodius vicus of recirculation back to Howth Castle and Environs" (3)—constitutes a continuation from its unpunctuated, unfinished closing sentence fragment, "A way a lone a last a loved a long the" (628) to forge an ostensibly never-ending cycle. *Sudden Times* invites direct comparison by virtue of the omitted full stop in Ollie's final sentence:

> I don't forgive you, I heard [my father] saying again.
> *I don't forgive you.*
> I pulled the hood of my sweater over my head and sat on the bed waiting till the listening stopped (*ST* 341)

As in *Finnegans Wake*, Healy's text opens with a suggestively uncapitalised phrase: "*after London*" (*ST* 3).

It would be simple to argue that this structure mirrors the destructive cyclical nature of guilt and remorse. However, I contend that by taking its cue from Joyce's text, the structure of Healy's novel works in more significantly productive ways to overcome the circularity of traumatic rehearsals of guilt. As it ends at the plot's halfway point, Ollie's narrative is non-linear in the sense that it is both cyclical and non-chronological; yet its temporality is even more radical than a mere dis-ordering of events, to be re-ordered and 'set right' by a reflecting, omniscient reader. Indeed, the cyclical structure of *Sudden Times* radically alters the reading experiences and the processes of signification in ways that cannot be returned to a standard linear realist retelling.

As I have argued elsewhere, in *Finnegans Wake* signification and significance are constantly deferred, revealed, and transposed by the novel's cyclical recontextualisation of its signs against the reader's shifting familiarity with the book's points of reference (Fagan 2010). By employing a cyclical *in media res* structure, rather than a linear *ab ovo* structure, Healy's novel likewise rewires the mechanisms of context so that an ineluctable distinction between the reader and re-reader is woven into the fabric of the text. In a localised sense, this dynamic works through the various headings that adorn each chapter's brief fragments: "Sometimes the paragraph titles function as signposts pointing directly to the content or theme of the individual section, other times, one must read right to the end of the paragraph in order to understand why the headline was placed their in the first place" (McCourt, n. pag.). In a global sense, early uncontextualised references to "Redmond" and "Marty," Ollie's statement that "the bride" in the Sligo launderette window was "like one of the Luton ladies I used to follow" (referring to *ST* 323–4), snatches of courtroom transcripts, and oblique references to "those things that happened in London" (*ST* 3, 5, 7, 12, 16) create a distinction between an uninitiated first-time reading of a passage (of the 'present' scene) and a recontextualised future reading of the same scene (the 'present' refigured as 'past' in the 'future'). The extent to which the reader is reading a passage rich with unobtainable information yet to be unveiled in the book's narrative cycle, or re-reading a passage with retroactive insight, appreciably alters both the possible signification and emotional content of a given word or line. In other words, owing to its cyclical structure, there are signifieds present at all times in the text which are, for all practical purposes, simultaneously present and impossible to infer until a 'future' acquaintance with 'past' contexts opens up these channels of signification.

Consider, for instance, how on a first reading the early passage in which Ollie arrives home from the pub and wakens his sleeping mother seems to bear purely procedural and referential content:

> Ma, I said.
> What?
> She grabbed the armrests. She was on the verge of a scream.
> What? she said again as her eyes focused.
> It's Ollie.
> Her face lit up when she saw it was only me.
> Ollie?
> Yes.
> Dear God, I didn't know who it was. I was dreaming. I was dreaming of your brother.
> I'm sorry. (*ST* 24)

It is only on rereading the scene that we can realise the emotional weight of Ollie's "I'm sorry" not only as an apology for disturbing his mother (as we might first assume), but also, and simultaneously, as an apology for his perceived accountability in his brother's death. This "understanding of time as a multiplicity of coexisting temporalities rather than a continuous, even stream" (Hannken-Illjes, n. pag.) is manifested in the narrative's "constant shifts from past tense to present tense" (Hoffmann 359). As Ollie attests: "If I start to think I get the tenses mixed. It's neither here nor there" (*ST* 71). Through the novel's narrative structure, the reader of *Sudden Times* is compelled to share in Ollie's experience.

Thus initiated, the reader slowly learns that the virtual "world of signs" in which Ollie is trapped is not only referential and spatial. Walking the streets after his tragic association with Silver John, Ollie relates: "I found myself in the centre of Luton at the junction between Silver Street and John Street. I was terrified" (*ST* 326). By thus lingering upon the ways in which signs can bear the weight, at once, of both objective present and subjective 'future-past' meanings, *Sudden Times* emphasises that 'signs' external to the mind can function as embodied extensions of that mind, storing its episodic, semantic, and emotional memories. Early in the book, Ollie describes his Sligo lodgings: "I had all of Marty's things round me. His atlases, *dawk-cue-ments*, travel books, his bearded heads of fishermen. I had my brother Redmond's box of cassettes" (*ST* 5). Again, it is only on rereading this scene that we can realise the emotional weight of this image of Ollie holed up in this attic surrounded by the relics of his departed friend and brother, and their significance to him as repositories of memories and emotions that he does not want to forget even as he suppresses them. The inverse implication—that the absence of certain items reveals an intention to keep at length memories and emotions at present too painful to bear—is seen in the noted absences in Ollie's father's apartment: "My mother's picture was on a chest of drawers. Redmond's picture was on the wall. I was nowhere to be seen" (*ST* 135). Relatedly, we find 'things' figured in the present as holders of past identities unable to be done away with given an unforeseeable futurity: "Being a chippie was a thing of the past, though in case I ever changed my mind I still kept my spirit level, saw, the two hammers, a fine chisel and one Stanley tape measure in a duffel bag under the sill" (*ST* 6).

The idea, so prevalent throughout the novel, that signs (words, things) do not refer to the discrete reality of a present moment but are shot through with the memories and potential of future/past significance, organises the very nature of Ollie's narrative rhetoric and logic:

> I went back to London. [. . .]
> I catch a glimpse of a vague place I once was daily. The vagueness hurts. It has no name. [. . .] It goes.
> I search for a familiar place [. . .]. No one's there but ghosts, fast-receding ghosts. [. . .] And then I realize that where I am now, in this chemist's doorway, will in the distant future be forgotten. [. . .]
> The ground is disappearing under my feet. And I get a longing, a sickening nostalgia.
> I try to put myself there as I once was. (*ST* 86)

While readers may at first conjecture that they are reading an actual return to London, such assumptions have to be retroactively modified as it is disclosed that we are reading a virtual return, as Ollie's Sligo self is trying to place himself back in his past, while simultaneously imagining his present moment from a future vantage. Significantly, we discover Ollie trying to access and narrativise his story as a clear chronological sequence of distinct 'past,' 'present,' and 'future' moments and finding such a project undone by the reality of a multitemporal experience of time in which all three planes are folded into each other simultaneously as coexistent and mutually informing forces.

This idea that the true nature of time as experienced is radically different from the commonplace literary and scientific models for its measurement is most economically captured in the novel's title. Marty's father, having come to London for the tragic task of claiming his son's body and possessions, gives voice to the novel's driving image: "These are sudden times" (*ST* 204). Of course, on one level he means a time in which tragedy arises without notice, and shakes one out of complacency to realise time's irreversibility. But when carefully considered against the novel's cyclically regenerative representation of the openness and polysemantic potential of the present moment, this image also offers a space within which to overcome the destructive understanding of time's linearity.

Challenged by the prosecution as to his motives leading up to his brother's death, Ollie repeats "It fell out like that" and "It just happened that way" (*ST* 284, 288). In a particularly telling exchange, Ollie aligns the suddenness of the time he experiences to chance:

> Mr Ewing, are you telling the court that all that happened to you is based on chance?
> > Most things in life happen like that.
> > Like what?
> > Like suddenly. (*ST* 295)

The trajectory of Ollie's redemption in the novel's first four books takes this realisation as its point of departure. The encounter with the German psychiatrist that initiates Ollie's apprenticeship in the relation of 'sin,' 'sign,' and 'sein' happens by chance: "I followed [a stranger] for no good reason. And that's how I found the German psychiatrist sitting by the stove" (*ST* 32). This suddenness opens him up to his burgeoning relationship with Liz and moves him towards a difficult reunion with his father in Coventry. Here, too, the ambiguity between will and chance is emphasised, as this encounter with his father is (purportedly) forced by Ollie and Liz's inability to reach their planned holiday destination of Morocco due to financial constraints. It is this encounter with time's suddenness that opens Ollie's experience to the reality, and ethical imperative, of an encounter with the unexpected.

"There I Was, from Inside Out"

Ollie's continual encounter with time's unexpected suddenness seems to suggest that he cannot fully be found guilty. And yet, this steady untangling of the *fact* of his guilt does not save him from the *feeling* of guilt. Indeed, we soon realise that Healy's novel is less concerned with traumatic events themselves, than with the mental state of guilt to which they give rise. As Ollie testifies: "The first time you do wrong is bad enough. The actual event will bring its own shame. But it's when you run it through your brain, again and again, down the years, that it grows enormous. The afterlife of sin is more horrendous than the sin itself" (*ST* 89).

The novel's opening paragraph aligns this state of constant self-interrogation with the involuntary force of thought located within the narrator's skull:

> After London [. . .] I found it hard to talk to anyone with that constant argument in my head. [. . .] Then would start the lament: *If I had done this, none of that would have happened. If I hadn't. If I had.* It went on till I was sick of my own consciousness.
>
> This guilt was stalking me. (*ST* 3)

Suggestively, Kenny characterises this central dynamic as Ollie's darkly comic "Beckettian converse with himself" (B9), an appropriate resonance given that "the theme of guilt is one of Beckett's most obsessive concerns" (McDonald 34). Beckett's legacy for Tiger-era migration narratives is the insight that the project of "bear[ing] witness" to a clear, transparent memory of a pivotal moment, prior to trauma, "ultimately proves unsustainable" given "the inescapability of the body" (Cahill 1). This thought is figured explicitly in Liz's response to Ollie's casual mention of an "old" girlfriend: "There is no such thing [. . .]. They're always hanging about in there somewhere, and she tapped her skull" (*ST* 126). Ollie's sense of being a 'self' that is simultaneously 'Other' is compounded by the inescapability of his own mind, as when we find him simultaneously attempting and failing to summon up and shut out images of his brother: "I've got to stop this. I'm away. I'd be obliged if you'd lay off, will you? Thank you. Thanks awfully" (*ST* 88).

Given this self-division, a number of commentators pathologise Ollie as not only traumatized but also "mentally deranged" (Hoffmann 357)—an unreliable because paranoid, even schizophrenic narrator. However, to my reading Ollie has not fallen outside of a normative understanding of mental health through trauma and guilt. Rather, his disjoined narration and decentred picture of mind offer a thoroughgoing contemplation of the authentic nature of being in time. Indeed, we read rhetoric out of any number of characters' mouths that distinctly echoes Ollie's. Ollie makes casual reference to a television set playing in the background on which "transvestites talk on Channel 4 of out-of-body experiences" (*ST* 67), and to a "low-slung man" muttering to himself: "I'm glad you asked me that, he said to himself, yes" (*ST* 32). In a particularly pertinent example, May discusses her inability to go through with a parachute drop: "I saw myself doing it [. . .] but I couldn't [. . .]. I'm saying to myself the next time, the next time I will but [. . .] I didn't and it was terrible" (*ST* 57). In a sudden moment, May unexpectedly encounters her self as an "Other," so that her access to her own motivations and anxieties becomes opaque. Yet if she is thus not accountable for her inability to go through with the jump, why is she so wracked with guilt by the fact that she did not?

The stakes of this process—by which the telling or writing of the self does not lead to an expression of pure subjectivity (a directly communicable and accessible subjective experience) but rather to an expression of alterity (the discovery that the self is opaquely "Other" even, or especially, to itself)—are carefully staged in two revealing tableaux. In the first, we learn of Ollie's experience of "*mirror images*" (*ST* 53) with his boss Gilmartin:

> [I]t strikes me, not for the first time, that we're eating in unison. If I lift a spud to my mouth he does the same. I cut my chop, he does his. So I slow down and try to vary my moves but darn it if he doesn't do the same.
> Are you copying me? I ask and leave my utensils down.
> What are you talking about, professor? he says and leaves down his.
> You're eating the same as me.
> What do you expect? he asks astounded. Weren't we given the same shagging dinner? (*ST* 54)

Ollie's eroded sense of the unity of the self in this comic scene is acknowledged directly: "I don't know whether it's me imitating him, or he me. Whenever Gilmartin is around I feel like I'm the victim of mirror images" (*ST* 55). This peculiar logic, by which the terms 'self' and 'other' are no longer seen as clear and mutually-exclusive binaries, informs Ollie's sense that his mind is neither confined to within his own head, nor is he the exclusive author of its own thoughts: "This happens a few times, so that I'm thinking other people's thoughts and making them my own" (*ST* 71).

In the second, and crucial, tableau, Liz takes a cast of Ollie's face:

> She lifted the cast off and took the linen from my eyes. [. . .]
> Look, she said.
> She showed me the cast.
> That's you in there.
> There I was, from inside out. Smiling. (*ST* 70)

The power of this narrative image is Ollie's surprised discovery that his mirror image, his other self, is smiling. The force of this shock moves Ollie beyond self-obsession and opens him to a more radical, and outward-reaching, experience of alterity:

> Stop laughing at me [Liz said].
> *I can't help it.*
> Well it's not funny.
> I'm sorry.
> You're not sorry. If I was you and you were me I'd be laughing too.
> You are laughing.
> That's because *I can't help it.* [. . .] I'm having an identity crisis." (*ST* 124–5)

For Deleuze, "One cannot help but laugh when the codes are confounded"; thus it is humour and irony that have the power to destroy "the whole tragedy of interiority" through a form of "schizophrenic laughter" that reaches outward rather than inward ("Nomad Thought" 147). As such, it is these comedic moments of confusion between self and 'Other' in Healy's novel that introduce the possibility of reconciliation to the narrative. Thus we find that, in the end, the routine that helps Ollie to survive—that restores his black sense of humour and returns him to Coventry to force a reconciliation of sorts with his estranged father—is not that which he professes: tidying, working in supermarket aisles, keeping on the move. Rather, it is the repetitive, even involuntary, routine of giving voice to his experience that allows Ollie to encounter difference and open himself up to the unforseeability of the future. In other words, the act of writing.

Thus Ollie's first-person testimony, for all its repetitive self-recriminations and dis-ease, ultimately adheres to Deleuze's insistence that "writing cannot be [. . .] the *product* of one's neuroses or psychoses," a form of record which simply "regress[es] into a state of inaction, having accepted a catastrophic diagnosis" (Hainge 234)—in this case, Ollie's paralysing rehearsal of his guilt. In *Sudden Times*, the act of writing is a "health-giving exercise" (Hoffmann 358) that actively takes the tragic diagnosis of guilt as a starting, rather than an ending point. It is this routine of rehearsing, telling, and writing that drives the plot to its culmination. Ollie, haunted by his last conversation with his father in which forgiveness for his responsibility in his brother's death was withheld, is finally confronted by Eamon in a heated, drunkenly sleepy exchange:

> I'm out of order, he said.
> It did my head in once, I said, and I don't want it to happen again.
> I know.
> I thought he wouldn't like that phrase—*it did my head in*. [. . .] A few minutes before I thought he would hit me. I knew he wanted to. He stirred at my feet.
> It did my head in too, he said. (*ST* 163)

If this is the moment that allows the plot to come to a close, even as so much of the characters' futurity remains unforeseeable, it is because it offers an unexpected, sudden insight. What Ollie finds in his reunion with his father is not forgiveness but rather something more profound: an affirmation of shared experience.

"Sorrow Can Be Like Joy"

It would be simple to read the novel's insistence that "to sin is to be" in the destructive tragic mode: a demonstration that sin and guilt are inevitable, that we are all trapped in a cycle of sin by the virtue of merely existing. It is my argument that Healy's novel makes a much more compelling claim. At the outset of Ollie's repetitive rehearsal of his experience of 'being in time,' signs are figured as a form of 'sin' that ensnare him in guilt: orienting him towards repetitive narcissistic concern with the self, trapping him in a time that does not seem to pass, stunting his self-development, alienating him from others. Yet through their temporal, semantic, and emotional malleability, such signs also have the power to alleviate and transform Ollie's undesirable way of 'being': enlightening him to the unexpected forces of time and subjectivity; testifying to the continued possibility of life and creation; allowing for a refocusing from narcissistic sentiments to an intersubjective encounter with an other, with difference; and enabling a reorientation from lost time (and the time of loss) to the openness of the future. It is by its refiguration of guilt on these terms that *Sudden Times* displays its alliance with Deleuze's definition of great literature:

> What springs from great books is schizo-laughter or revolutionary joy, not the anguish of our pathetic narcissism, not the terror of our guilt. [. . .] There is always an indescribable joy that springs from great books, even when they speak of ugly, desperate, or terrifying things. (*Desert Islands* 258)

Or, as Ollie puts it, "I lay staring at the ceiling and was full of regret but for what I could not say. It was enough to know I was sorry. But sorrow helped me sleep. Sorrow can be like joy" (*ST* 216).

Works Cited

Bergson, Henri. *Time and Free Will: An Essay on the Immediate Data of Consciousness*. Trans. Frank Lubecki Pogson. London: George Allen and Unwin, 1911. Print.

Borg, Ruben. "Deleuze on Genre: Modernity between the Tragic and the Novel." *Deleuze and the Schizoanalysis of Literature*. Ed. Ian Buchanan, Tim Matts, and Aidan Tynan. London: Bloomsbury, 2015. 99–115. Print.

———. *The Measureless Time of Joyce, Deleuze and Derrida*. London: Continuum, 2007. Print.

Brown, Terence. "Seamus Heaney: The Witnessing Eye and the Speaking Tongue." *The Literature of Ireland: Culture and Criticism*. Cambridge: Cambridge University Press, 2010. 190–8. Print.

Burn, Gordon. "The Art of Overhearing." Rev. of *Sudden Times*, by Dermot Healy. *Times Literary Supplement* 17 Sept. 1999. Web. 15 Feb. 2015.

Cahill, Susan. *Irish Literature in the Celtic Tiger Years 1990 to 2008: Gender, Bodies, Memory*. London: Continuum, 2011. Print.

Deleuze, Gilles. *Desert Islands and Other Texts 1953–1974*. Ed. David Lapoujade. New York: Semiotexte, 2004. Print.

———. *Difference and Repetition*. Trans. Paul Patton. New York: Colombia University Press, 1994. Print.

———. *The Logic of Sense*. Trans. Mark Lester and Charles Stivale. Ed. Constantin V. Boundas. New York: Columbia University Press, 1990. Print.

———. "Nomad Thought." *The New Nietzsche: Contemporary Styles of Interpretation*. Ed. D. B. Allison. Cambridge: MIT Press, 1988. 142–9. Print.

Deleuze, Gilles, and Félix Guattari. *Kafka: Toward a Minor Literature*. Minneapolis: University of Minnesota Press, 1986. Print.

——— *A Thousand Plateaus*. London: Continuum, 2004. Print.

Fagan, Paul. "'Forget, Remember! Forget!': Memory, Amnesia and the Cyclical Metamorphosis of Meaning in *Finnegans Wake*." *Joyce Studies in Italy 11: James Joyce, Metamorphosis and Re-Writing*. Ed. Franca Ruggieri. Rome: Bulzoni, 2010. 53–66. Print.

Fish, Stanley. *How Milton Works*. Cambridge: Belknap Press of Harvard University Press, 2001. Print.

Forsyth, Neil. *The Satanic Epic*. Princeton: Princeton University Press, 2003. Print.

Hainge, Greg. "'*L'Invention du Troisième Peuple*: The Utopian Vision of Philippe Grandrieux's Dystopias." *Nowhere is Perfect: French and Francophone Utopias/Dystopias*. Ed. John West-Sooby. Newark: University of Delaware Press, 2008. 228–39. Print.

Hannken-Illjes, Kati. "Temporalities and Materialities: Introduction to the Thematic Issue on Time and Discourse." *Forum: Qualitative Social Research* 8.1 (2007). Web. 15 Feb. 2015.

Healy, Dermot. *A Goat's Song*. London: Flamingo, 1995. Print.

———. "Small Talk: Dermot Healy." Interview with Anna Metcalfe. *Financial Times* 30 Apr. 2011. Web. 15 Feb. 2015.

———. *Sudden Times*. London: Harvill Press, 1999. Print.

Hoffmann, Catherine. "Dancing to Ollie's Tunes: The Rhetoric of Narrative Stutter." *Style* 43.3 (Fall 2009): 357–72. Print.

Joyce, James. *Finnegans Wake*. 1939. New York: Penguin, 1999. Print.

Kenny, John. "Past Master of Re-invention." Rev. of *Sudden Times*, by Dermot Healy. *The Irish Times* 2 Oct. 1999: B9. Print.

McCourt, John. "Dermot Healy." *Post-War Literatures in English*. Ed. Geert Lernout. Groningen: Martinus Nijhoff uitgevers, 2000: loose-leaf. Print.

McDonald, Ronan. *Tragedy and Irish Literature: Synge, O'Casey, Beckett*. London: Palgrave, 2002. Print.

Milton, John. *John Milton: Complete Poems and Major Prose*. Ed. Merritt Y. Hughes. New York: The Odyssey Press, 1957. Print.

Murray, Tony. *London Irish Fictions: Narrative, Diaspora and Identity*. Liverpool: Liverpool University Press, 2012. Print.

Nordin, Irene Gilsenan, and Elin Holmsten, eds. "Introduction: Borders and States of In-Betweenness in Irish Literature and Culture." *Liminal Borderlands in Irish Literature and Culture*. Bern: Peter Lang, 2009. 7–13. Print.

Skeat, Walter William. *An Etymological Dictionary of the English Language*. Oxford: Clarendon Press, 1888. Print.

Psyche's Garden: The Labour of Mourning and the Growth of the Self in *Long Time, No See*
Dermot McCarthy

> "In the stories it invents or finds to tell you can see the mind heal itself[,] close its gaping differences . . ." (Frost 235)

In the late summer of 2006, in a small Sligo community at the edge of the sea, an adolescent boy hovers on the brink of adulthood. Philip Feeney is waiting to hear the results of his Leaving exams, but he is also haunted by loss. A year before he was with his friend, Mickey Brady, celebrating his exam results, when Mickey crashed the car they were in and died from his injuries. Family, friends, and community tiptoe around Philip's pain, respectful of his grief and guilt. Philip, who also goes by the name of Psyche,[1] passes his days odd-jobbing for others—cutting lawns, trimming hedges, helping take in hay, and building a walled garden for his mother. His primary pastime, however, is attending to the needs of his granduncle Joejoe, in particular, keeping him and his old friend, the Blackbird, supplied with rum and cigarettes. He also hangs out with his childhood friend, Anna. The days pass, summer turns to autumn, storms arrive, the garden walls grow, and Psyche is drawn deeper into the lives and pasts of Joejoe and the Bird. For some reviewers such proceedings do not proceed enough: "nothing much happens" (Eagleton 23) in *Long Time, No See* (2011), although the claim of deficit is always qualified with praise for the novel's dialogue, characters, sense of place, and humour.[2] The story Philip Feeney tells, however, is as momentous as a change of season, the reverse of a tide, the cycle of a storm, the arrival and departure of migratory birds, or the passing of a generation. Most important, it is a story of working through mourning.

Dermot Healy wrote strange books of great integrity and the Orphic quest to recoup loss through the power of art is at the centre of his narrative, lyric and dramatic writing. At one point in his story Psyche describes feeling "in two worlds at once" (260) and ontological versatility is the essence of the "sense of balance" that he learns from the ghostly "stone man" (128) when building the walls of his "special garden" (315). It is also a feature of Healy's poetic. In *Long Time, No See*, the hyper-real dialogue sings of character rooted in place and time, but the action often slides suddenly, like a collapsing beach cliff, into the surreal. Commonplace actions recur until they take on the vestments of ritual, and banality begins to glow with intimations of myth. Commonplace objects on a shelf are talismans re-arranged daily as if their order composed a psychic seawall. To read Healy is to be led into a double-take because his essentially revelatory poetic is so quietly, humbly apocalyptic.

Long Time, No See is an old man's coming of age novel, a harvest story full of death, told through a first-person voice with such tongue-in-cheek wit that the self that slips through the intricate knot of character, place and time is a transparent self-haunting. Like Jack Ferris of *A Goat's Song*, who experienced a therapeutic effect from listening to the stories of his fellow inmates in the Castlebar hospital, Psyche benefits from his attendance upon Joejoe and the Bird. His bewilderment by the nature and origins of their mysterious suffering seems ultimately, and ironically, to have a penitential effect in the alleviation of his own. While he eventually settles for the most sensible explanation of the bullet hole in Joejoe's window, Psyche remains at a loss to understand the precise cause of the grief and regret that haunted and joined both men. But epistemological certainty is less important than ontological aplomb in Healy's last novel. The sexual, geographic, religious and moral "tensions" (Crowe 25) that dominate *Fighting with Shadows* and *A Goat's Song* persist but no longer dominate; they have subsided into the greater bio-rhythms of sea and land, history and landscape, life and death. For all its formal similarities with the post-traumatic narrator-character of *Sudden Times*, *Long Time, No See* evinces a sharper focus on the interplay of conscious and unconscious, accident and coincidence, the mysterious consolations of the quotidian and the redemptive banality of the universal. Tension builds over Joejoe and the bullet hole, drama builds between Joejoe and the Bird, the General, Miss Jilly, and the memory of the mysterious Bridie, and it all seems connected. But the past never comes out of the shadows in which it is present.

Long Time, No See is one half of a diptych, the other half being *A Fool's Errand* (2010), the long poem written during the same period. Novel and poem share the same setting in the West of Ireland that MacNeice described as "always more than matter," a place inhabited by "brute and ghost at once" (267). In the novel characters lament the absence of fairies and affirm the presence of ghosts. Psyche admits that he lives in a haunted land. As with Ollie's self-narrative in *Sudden Times*, the "spatial emphasis" (Hoffmann 363) in Psyche's also functions to express the dynamic relationship between the interior processes of thought, memory and feeling, and the places and spaces he moves through, labours and socialises in. Healy's use of the religious ritual of the Stations of the Cross as a metaphor for Psyche's movement through his world accentuates this synchrony of past and present in place in his narrative, most obviously in his repeated return to the crossroads where his friend died. Healy's careful construction of the village of Ballintra, Dromod House, Joejoe's, the Bird's and Psyche's houses, the pub, the pier and beach, the roads and fields, always with people moving, conversing, working, socialising, going about their living and dying, results in a storyworld that is a felt habitus and *shows* how the sense of belonging Psyche feels for the place and community is integral to his recovery. Healy's characterisation of the richly idiosyncratic, hospitable and neighborly men and women (as well as dogs, horses, donkeys, hares and herons) of Ballintra is the generous dividend of his own living and writing for twenty-five years within "a sustained marginality" (Clark 12).[3]

Philip Feeney's multiple names do not signify a multiple or unstable so much as a fluid, performative self. Joejoe even calls him a "trickster" on one occasion (127). As such this narrator-character is a figure for Healy's own creative voice and the ventriloquism that is its greatest strength. The names are interpersonal and contextual. But Healy's transgendered Psyche seems more Hermes Psychopompos than the foolish lover of Apuleius's tale. His frequent visits to pray at the crossroads where Mickey died suggest he is still shepherding his friend's soul to its resting place, and after attending to both the Bird and Joejoe as they approach their deaths, he is instrumental in ensuring that both receive successful wakes. Psyche moves through the novel as if he is living above and below ground simultaneously, in the social world of family and community and the underworld of grief and guilt, with his dreams the littoral where these worlds conduct the business of mourning. The *Bildung* in this novel of growth takes the form of successful grieving, but the mythopoeia seems driven by the same need to come to terms with Healy's own dying that dominates *A Fool's Errand*. The long poem is a 'key' to the metafictive symbolism that anchors the narrative and the mythopoeia of the novel. Like the mausoleum overlooking the sea that Psyche and his father build for Miss Jilly and the "special garden" that Philip builds for his mother, novel and poem depend on their maker's "sense of balance" between light and dark, living and dying, humour and pathos, sense and absurdity.

Grave and garden figure prominently in Healy's encryption of Psyche's inner life in his therapeutic journey through the labyrinth of beach, stone, wall and wave. After the storm that begins the novel, Psyche discovers an "ancient stone wall" (51) at the bottom of the cliff below his house. The sea's uncovering of the wall begins the pattern of revelation that is the 'missing plot' of *Long Time, No See*, revelation that is in effect recovery.[4] In a rare instance of explicit interior reporting, Psyche admits "I was a happy man to have found something that no one else had seen in years" (52). The first of many marvels in a story that fluctuates between the naturalistic and preternatural, the wall is a sudden "wonder" and a metonym for the central mystery in the novel, the affective presence of the past in the present. Psyche builds the four walls around the garden with stones he takes from the beach and from a nearby ruin. Handling the latter, however, awakens his historical sense and Healy turns the experience into the first turning-point in Psyche's story. At first he feels guilty undoing another man's work and rationalises it with the thought that he was recycling the stones in "another wall." Then, like Yeats with his Fisherman, Psyche 'sees' the man working in the past *as* he works in the present, building and rebuilding occurring simultaneously, now and then suddenly synchronic. Psyche feels the "sense of balance" (128) of the long dead builder in the stones as he handles them, and it seems to inform his own intuitive sense of how to set the stones so that they will 'settle' properly into their new place in *his* wall. Then Healy achieves a moment of numinous simplicity when the ghostly tutor suddenly morphs into Psyche's father.

The building of the walled garden is cognate with the telling of the story. The search for, selection, and laying of the right stones in the right order and leaving them to 'settle,' is a precise metaphor for Healy's art and enterprise, the work of words grounded in the labour of being-in-the-world. In the important chapter titled "The Curve," following the earlier hint that the shape of the wall emanates from his dream world, Psyche describes his sense not only of labouring in continuity with the past, but of solving the 'problem' of the wall—"trying to get the curve right"—by listening to the voice in the stone: "Every time I lifted a rock I heard the command from somewhere in the past—let the rock find its own balance, let it sit on its own weight, and when it does, only then push in the slanted stones to right the position" (242). In *A Fool's Errand* Healy describes the same problem of the curve in the wall as "something [that] is missing . . . // That leads back upward / Toward that first unspoken word" (35). For Healy, the natural object is the given symbol. In the poem the "curve" in the wall is a pre-lingual intention, the *fiat* of original impulse or yearning, the nagging remnant of dream that the poet has laboured to settle in the developing shape, the arc of emotion that is the poem. In *Long Time, No See* the word that Psyche cannot speak when challenged by the octopus in his nightmare is his name (152). Psyche's story is Philip Feeney's account of working his way "back upward" from the place of grief and guilt to recover his sense of being who he really is. Healy told Sean O'Hagan that *Long Time, No See* was "a bit of a curved mystery" and Eleanor Wachtel that "I wanted [Psyche] to remain a mystery . . . because he's a mystery to me." Psyche confesses, "I have rules for everything" (242). Earlier, his father had remarked, "What you imagine soon becomes a law" (140) and the 'law' Psyche *feels* to apply, the 'rules' he sets for the laying of stones and the building of the wall, is an *imagined* truth, an intuited *ancestral* wisdom, a discovery or learning of a *right way of building*. Rock and hand converse. There is a genius in the way Healy 'fits' the metafictive and the moral by encoding his own poetic in the development of his narrator's character. Laying stones, ordering words, building walls, constructing sentences, planning a garden, shaping a paragraph: the layering of sense and sound, the attention to balance, is aesthetic and psychoanalytic. Psyche articulates the patience and humility of Healy's creative process and *ethos* (243), which the reader experiences as his *hommage* to the beloved habitus of the world of Ballyconnell.

Building the garden focuses Psyche's negotiation with the demons of his unconscious. After the fireworks on the beach trigger his memory of the accident, he dreams of a Jehovah-like octopus demanding his identity. His inability to say his name could be the result of his having too many, just as his struggle "to get the curve right" may be the issue of finding the right path out of the labyrinth. The nightmare at the bottom of the sea ends with a waking vision of the way "back upward": "It was Saturday morning. I saw the curve. I could not get out of the bed. By the time I woke the next time I had finished the wall. Then when I really woke I knew I hadn't. Everything was there for me to do in the long future. I felt this terrible sense of loss. I was thinking of Mickey" (243). The connection between building the wall, the search for the curve, and the unconscious labour of grief and guilt is made clear. The curve of the wall is a symbol of the natural arc of grief, the shape of Psyche's suffering and his emergence from it; the latter leads back to the crossroads where Mickey died and forward to his finishing the wall and taking up the future that will come with his successful 'leaving.' But first he must finish his mourning, which he achieves, symbolically, when he finishes the garden.

The garden is mandalic, an archetype of transformation.[5] It is a version of the sacred place, the *temenos*, the 'squared circle': a place where the unconscious is released and the individual can engage with archetypes. The four-walled garden Psyche builds for his mother symbolises his emergent orientation towards life and individuation. The symbol combines the mandala's "conservative purpose" of restoring "a previously existing order" and the "creative purpose of giving expression and form to something that does not yet exist, something new and unique" (von Franz 247). Building the garden for his mother connects Psyche to the collective past that "the stone man" represents, the history of constructive-creative labour but also the universal experience of suffering, loss and change. The experience of connection transcends Psyche's grief and guilt but also 'settles' it, helping him to accept its proper place in the structure of his selfhood. What it restores is the maternal world that Mickey's death symbolically announced to Psyche would be irrevocably lost with his own successful Leaving; the garden restores the loss as gift, an act of giving to rather than giving up, and a gift that is accompanied by the special lore of the anima-figure who guides Psyche from the world of mother and son to that of adult sexual relations. When Anna tells Psyche he is a closed door but she is the 'open window' she is telling him she is the way to his seeing "something that does not yet exist, something new and unique." Psyche's patience and humility, his rejection of any stone too "proud" (242) to submit itself to the good of the whole, his willingness to "wait" for the run of stone to settle based on his trust in the nature of the process and belief in the truth of the 'laws' of his imagination, go a long way to explain his reticence and laconic conversation, his guarded interiority and reluctant socialising. The way he builds the wall reflects the way he is waiting on his unconscious to 'gather' and 'settle': the building of the wall and the making of the garden are *how* Psyche works out the final stages of his mourning for Mickey. The symmetry between the descriptions of building the wall and later of Psyche and his father building the mausoleum for Miss Jilly suggests that the garden is "special" not just because it is his gift to the mother who has nursed him through this year of grief, but because it will displace the deadly crossroads through its *containment* of death within the natural cycle of renewed life. In Peter Homans's term, the walled garden is a "transitional space" (4–5) between Psyche's private, introspective individuality and the public-communal world where his creativity can create 'new ground' out of 'old': the latter is represented by the historically and geologically 'rich' soil of Dromod House that is used for the garden as well as by the stones taken from the ancient church (or henhouse); the former is the new life, the 'journey' that Philip intends to take with Anna.[6]

The climax of the novel begins when Psyche completes the garden; this is his 'squaring the circle.' When Joejoe tells Gary to leave his house and "square the circle" he upsets him; Gary intuits the authoritative voice of the Wise Old Man but is mystified by the command. Psyche tells him it means "go the full jaunt"; Anna adds "do the impossible . . . And make sense of it all" (332). The scene occurs immediately after Psyche has finished building the garden for his mother. The "squared circle" is a metaphor of psychic wholeness.[7] But what is the bullet hole in Joejoe's front window that turns Psyche's father into a Doubting Thomas and then a charismatic believer, and 'bewilders' (302) Psyche to the point of obsession? The bullet hole is a window in a window, a hole in a hole, and the doubled liminality it figures is a metonym for the double or split nature of all the structures of experience and meaning in the novel—time, place, subject and world. Joejoe makes the hole when he shoots at his own reflection, or as Psyche's mother suggests, at "[s]omeone . . . he once was" (333), his reaction to the self-haunting of regret and remorse. Joejoe himself offers a clue to the mystery when he tells Psyche that "memory is a stranger who comes to call less and less" and "sometimes he's not welcome" (4). The bullet hole is a tear in the fabric of the self that inner and outer, past and present, wash through like waves on the beach. Joejoe is deeply troubled from the outset of the story: he asks Psyche, "is it possible to see the world through new eyes" (7), but Psyche has no answer to this until he himself learns that it is possible only if the 'I' changes.[8]

Philip/Psyche embodies the fusion of self-telling/self-making that this kind of first-person narrative presents to the reader. The novel's formal concern with its own poiesis accentuates the preoccupation with the labour of mourning that the narrative process performs. Healy said that "the authentic is a trick" (qtd. in Kenny) but the artful dodge of dialogue in *Long Time, No See* captures cognitive, expressive, and communicative processes as they evolve and intersect. Dialect and dialogue, humour, rhetoric, wit, negotiation, coded sociolect and proffered translation emphasise the centrality of language in sustaining the 'social contract' of life in Psyche's community, from the serio-comic vernacular accommodation of contradiction—"I headed up the road head-down"; "We have a wee problem, and it's a big one" (8, 9)—to the *performing* of Psyche's opening outward to the social world. The oral dimension of the story *is* the medium of the narrator's interiority. The dominance of dialogue over narration-description diminishes explicit attribution of mind by the narrator and draws attention to Healy's refusal to 'colonise' his creations by speaking for them; instead he *shows* interiority implicitly in a nuanced, oblique way through dialogue and behaviour. It is up to the reader to 'see' what is going on within and between Psyche, Joejoe, the Bird, Anna, and Miss Jilly. The paradox of Healy's style is that it cherishes the real so lovingly that it conceals in serious play what it teases out of the apparently random and inconsequential. But everything the narrator-character recounts, every conversation, sentence, phrase and image moves wave-like towards the last page and the final wave that breaks with the awakening of the last word.

When Philip begins his story he is in danger of slipping from mourning into melancholy. His story is how he finds a way through the "hinterland between grieving and moving on" (O'Hagan). Healy constructs a complex simplicity in his narrator-character by concealing in Philip/Psyche's guilt and grief the 'call' of the Self to change.[9] Mickey died after celebrating his own successful Leaving results. Philip has injected his own anxieties about leaving childhood, parents, and home into his guilt at being 'party' to Mickey's death. Joejoe's remark, "The *Leaving* is a sad word for an exam" (8), suggests Healy consciously uses this plot element symbolically. For Philip, Mickey's death summons an archetype of initiation. The account of (his) Psyche coming to terms with Mickey's death while waiting for his Leaving results, 'attending' to Joejoe and the Bird, building the garden for his mother, and spending his days helping out others in minor and profound ways describes a regimen of good deeds which effects his successful initiation into adulthood, symbolised by his completion of the garden for his mother, his building of the mausoleum with his father, his dancing with Anna (prompted by Joejoe's example), his rejoining his circle of friends, and in the final phrase of the novel, returning to the "Wake" (438)—the last word a less than sly allusion to Joyce's punning euphemism for Life.

Paradoxically, the wakes that close the novel are rites of initiation that mark Psyche's liberation from grief. While he tells his story out of loss, he tells it against the loss of the future that his extended grief threatens. Healy's world-making gift of vernacular orality may seem to result for some readers in a limited and infrequent disclosure of his characters' interiority but that is an illusion brought on by the narrator's extraordinary focus on the external-material world through which he moves. It is important to see how this continuous movement in the narrative marks the characters' changing emotional dispositions. The weather is constantly changing. Storms off the Atlantic frame the story. Joejoe is plagued by pustular psoriasis but also by regrets and guilt: "Memory . . . is a scourge, a scourge," he tells Psyche (399).[10] But unclogging a chimney leads to a dinner of thanksgiving and the opening of lines of communication long closed by regret and insecurity. For Healy, mind and body, weather and landscape, moods and relationships are interwoven in a liminal ecology. It is not that there is no inner life represented in the novel but rather that Healy's characters' inner lives are so close to the surface, informing word and deed. "I'm seeing things," Psyche tells his father (304), subtly answering both the title of the novel as well as Joejoe's leading question in the opening chapter. To engage in the process of individuation, the ego must quiet itself to attend to the inner urge to growth (von Franz 164). Psyche's quiet demeanour, reticence, and in particular, solitary activity of building the garden suggest that at some level he knows what he has to do and why. Joejoe recognises this. "Do you think a lot?" he asks him, and when Psyche confesses, "I do . . . I think a lot," Joejoe remarks, "But you don't tell us what you're thinking, do you . . ." (132). Joejoe understands that "[t]he mind is a terror," and like everyone who knows what Psyche is going through—the Tingles, the Judge, the Bradys, Miss Jilly, Anna, Psyche's parents and friends, even John Sweet the publican, he sees that interior activity manifest in his behaviour and demeanour. In hospital visiting the Bird, Psyche hears a baby crying "like an old man giving a lecture on the inner self" and then a voice say, "Sorry pet . . . you've got to stop" (276). This is perhaps Healy's most explicit explanation of his decision to *show* rather than report his narrator-character's inner labours.

When Psyche's mother arranges to host the Stations at Joejoe's house as a way of cheering up the old man, the Stations are explained as communal confessions or a Mass celebrated in a home followed by food, drink and conviviality. Religion in Ballintra is a catalyst for a party, but by the same token, the social can be numinous. As he travels through his community each interaction is a kind of 'station' in Psyche's progress. The synchronicity of grief, guilt and growth in garden and grave, the meeting of sea and land, the conjunction of storms and strangers, waves and hippies on the beach, trimming a donkey's hooves and cleaning a chimney, staring at the stars beside a room full of ferrets, or a bullet hole in a window but no bullet found are all occasions of numinous possibility. The first and paramount station is Joejoe's cottage. Every morning Psyche arrives to light the fire, make tea, read aloud the newspaper and then a 'psalm'; the scene takes on the ritual aura of a private morning mass, with Psyche playing attendant to Joejoe's celebrant. One morning the Bird is present and puts the question that is really the challenge facing Psyche: "So what are you going to be?" (7). Psyche cannot answer because he "cannot see the world through new eyes" yet; he cannot see himself *after* his leaving the state he has been trapped in since Mickey's death. The meaning of Psyche's frequent return to the crossroads is clear and his reply to the Bird is ironically precise: whatever he will become depends on his leaving his grief and guilt behind and moving on. Soon after this his discovery of the "mystery wall" (323) on the beach is coincident with a change in his receptivity to change. This leads to his encounter with "the stone man" and the beginning of progress towards self-understanding, seeing a future for himself, perhaps even as a writer, if that is what Joejoe is suggesting when he contrasts himself with Psyche in terms of his ability to write down what Joejoe has had to remember (399). It is interesting, too, that Psyche senses from "the way he carried himself" that this ghostly predecessor "could have been a great-great-granduncle of mine" (128), which makes him a *type* of Joejoe and further confirms the latter's role as mentor.[11] What he learns from "the stone man" is important because it occurs as Psyche descends to a threshold zone which is part Dantescan purgatory with "souls in coats" (124) and part nightmare (the dream of the octopus). This is ground he must cross, not avoid. When he admits to Joejoe that he feels "fierce low," Joejoe tells him to pray; however, his prayer of thanksgiving to the sea, the Bird, and the dog, cannot keep him from calling 'Good night' to Mickey in his head as he leaves and looks toward the crossroads. It is on this night that the octopus of identity appears.

Psyche's dreams are signposts in a book full of signs and Healy constructs a dream logic to suggest the unconscious process of Psyche's quest. Following his first glimpse of the curve that he knows he must get right if his walls are to stand, Psyche is overwhelmed by guilt that he is going to have a future and Mickey will not. This guilt keeps him in bed for two days; he declines to accompany his parents on the weekly outing to town, and he dreams that he "threw his mobile in the ocean after I received a text from Mickey" (244). In this dream when the setting shifts to an exam room and an exam paper in which "I recognised nothing," the weight of his guilt pulls him down to the world of the octopus and induces his panic that he will not find the way to the 'curve' that will lift him free. He is trapped at the intersection of past and future, childhood and adulthood, who he was and who he must become. Then the classroom becomes the garden, and

> Then myself and Mickey took the corner at Templeboy.
> Are you coming or what?
> In a minute, Ma.
> . . .
> I'll stay.
> Why?
> I don't know. (244)

"Are you coming or what?" is spoken by Psyche's mother outside the dream but it could just as well be Mickey's voice within it, one calling him 'back' to life, the other to join him at the bottom of the sea. The ambiguity of Psyche's reply, "I'll stay," effectively answers both: he *must* stay to finish his labour of mourning, but he will *not* remain with Mickey in the land of the dead. Psyche reaches the lowpoint of his traumatic distress in this chapter.

It is his "dear friend" (5), "the beautiful Anna" (12), who helps Psyche out of this impasse. An anima figure, she is his most important guide. All her exchanges with him are subtle directives and gentle pushes in the right direction, toward nature, the social world, and most importantly, mature love. She repeatedly asks him to go dancing. He 'finds' her most often close to the sea where she shares with him her sense of the world's "[i]ncorrigibly plural" wonders (MacNeice 24). Psyche's name for her, Lala, links her to song, the pre- or supra-linguistic, the Kristevan semiotic, and suggests her role is to help him negotiate his 'leaving' of the world of the mother on terms that will enable his successful individuation. It is Anna who helps him complete the "special garden" by supplying the seeds (of his future) and the acumen for planting them appropriately. At one moment, she seems to reveal herself to him as "a goddess" (103) and the effect of her ministrations when he is bedridden during his crisis has the aura of a divine intervention. Feeding him tidbits of knowledge picked up from her literary 'globetrotting,' she cuts away from the subject of "what's between your brain and whatever" to tell him something that helps him complete what he is trying to build in his mind.

> All space is crooked, nodded Anna. Did you know that?
> I do now.
> Good.
> I saw a curve among the shadows.
> Get better soon, she said, we need you. (246)

Psyche's four-walled garden is the individuated self. The 'problem' of the wall is the curve of space, the shape of the universe, and the nature of the mind. The curve goes on forever, it contains everything, and the arc of an individual's life and death fits, belongs, is joined with it. Expressing this visionary intuition is a central preoccupation of *A Fool's Errand*, where Healy expresses it with the same symbolic language.[12] In *Long Time, No See* the novelist configures the perspective and preoccupations of a poet in his sixties increasingly aware of the coming end of his life and labours, in a fictive adolescent's preoccupation with the death of his 'double,' and further, through his metafictive symbols, shows the boy's struggle through the dark dream-night of his psyche to lead to his discovery of the consolatory discipline of the poet's "plain dear labour" (*Errand* 28). The "curve among the shadows" Psyche glimpses following Anna's therapeutically coded non-sequiturs is the gift of his creator, who himself "would love / to have [. . .] the shadow / chased away by prayer" (*Errand* 28) but who could only imagine it for his creation.

Psyche's liberation begins at the Stations at Joejoe's. Psyche is "the last penitent" and the priest asks him how the evening has gone. Psyche's reply is his second glaringly Freudian slip: "Fine. Possession is ended" (163).[13] Psyche comes out with this "mistake," ironically, after he has already received the only absolution he really needs from Mickey's father (159). It is partial, but it's enough to end his 'possession' by guilt and grief.[14] His absolution is completed at Joejoe's wake when "Mrs Brady leaned over and kissed my cheek" (433). A lot happens between these scenes. Psyche publically acknowledges Anna as his girlfriend, 'crashes' after receiving his Leaving results, endures the last assaults of guilt and grief, solves the mystery of the bullet hole, 'wakes' the Bird, and suffers the loss of Joejoe. When he tells Miss Jilly at Joejoe's wake that he is "really" Philip, not Psyche, we conclude that he knows that a stage in his life and identity has come to an end and a new phase is about to begin. The final 'leaving' in the novel is when Philip lets Psyche leave *with* Joejoe and the Bird.

And yet *Long Time, No See* ends with a return. Psyche's last station is quite appropriately Mr Sweet's pub, the secular church where he abandons his search for a passage of scripture to read at Joejoe's funeral, deciding instead "to just let the book fall open at random" (437). He is ready to trust himself to the serendipitous nature of meaning. After all, it is his reading of scripture and *Moby Dick* with Joejoe that has taught him the way of bibliomancy, and now he shows his coming of age by deciding to continue alone. The significance of his decision and its connection to self-trust are signalled by Psyche's language—"then I thought *leave* it . . ." (437, emphasis added)—

and its echo of the motif that has borne so much of the archetypal meaning in the novel. Psyche finalises his decision by drinking "a glass of Malibu," Joejoe and the Bird's 'sacramental wine' of choice.

While Healy told Wachtel that he "wanted [Psyche] to remain a mystery . . . because he's a mystery to me," there is a strong sense at the end of the novel that Healy was fully at home with his own mystery. Symbols of the Self abound in his writing and a common symbol of transcendence is the figure of a bird in flight. As an animal that can live in two environments, the bird is a universal symbol of transcendence—bearing a message from the unconscious to consciousness. *A Fool's Errand* is a sustained meditation on the meaning of the flight of the barnacle geese for *him*, for *his* psyche. Like Yeats's swans at Coole, Healy's barnacle geese at Ballyconnell are harbingers of something he was obsessed with understanding—his own meaning. But where Yeats's imagining of a future from which he was absent was an occasion for self-mourning, Healy's meditation on the cycle of the geese's annual coming and going produces the mantric effect of 'settling' him into a cycle of eternal return, like one of his beloved stones, lifted and placed over and over again into the wall of being. The labour of being for Healy "fine tunes the instrument" for the psalm of praise that he strove to make of his work (*Errand* 93). In *Long Time, No See* Healy writes in such an uncelebratory celebratory way of simple communal-social acts and manners—meals, drinks, music, singing, working and playing together, walking, shopping, feeding animals, helping another, courtesy, kindness to strangers and familiars alike, respect, curiosity, sincerity, humour, imagination, compassion and love—and the aggregate effect is his most finely balanced song of life.

Works Cited

Clark, T. J. "False Moderacy." Rev. of *Picasso and Modern British Art*, by Tate Britain, and *Mondrian Nicholson: In Parallel*, by Courtauld Gallery. *London Review of Books* 34.6 (22 Mar. 2012): 11–3. Print.

Crowe, Catriona. "Dark Shoes on a Doorstep." Rev. of *The Bend for Home*, by Dermot Healy. *London Review of Books* 19.15 (31 July 1997): 25–6. Print.

Eagleton, Terry. "An Octopus at my Window." Rev. of *Long Time, No*

See, by Dermot Healy. *London Review of Books* 33.10 (19 May 2011): 23–4. Print.

Frost, Robert. *The Notebooks of Robert Frost*. Ed. Robert Faggen. Cambridge: Belknap, 2006. Print.

Healy, Dermot. *A Fool's Errand*. Oldcastle: The Gallery Press, 2010. Print.

———. *Long Time, No See*. 2011. New York: Penguin Books, 2012. Print.

Hoffmann, Catherine. "Dancing to Ollie's Tunes: The Rhetoric of Narrative Stutter." *Style* 43.3 (Fall 2009): 357–72. Print.

Homans, Peter. *The Ability to Mourn: Disillusionment and the Social Origins of Psychoanalysis*. Chicago and London: University of Chicago Press, 1989. Print.

Jarman, Mark Anthony. "A brilliant return for Dermot Healy." Rev. of *Long Time, No See*, by Dermot Healy. *The Globe and Mail* 8 July 2011. Web. 7 Nov. 2014.

Jung, Carl G. *The Archetypes and the Collective Unconscious*. 1959. Trans. R. F. C. Hull. 2nd ed. New York: Princeton University Press, 1980. Print.

Kenny, John. "*Sudden Times* by Dermot Healy." *ARAN—Access to Research and NUI Galway*. n.d. Web. 14 Nov. 2014.

MacNeice, Louis. *Collected Poems*. Ed. Peter McDonald. Winston-Salem: Wake Forest University Press, 2013. Print.

Nolan, Val. "Long Time No See, Indeed: Healy's First Novel in a Decade is Mesmerizing." *The Irish Examiner* 19 May 2012: 16. Web. 14 Nov. 2014.

O'Hagan, Sean. "Dermot Healy: 'I try to stay out of it and let the reader take over.'" *The Observer* 3 Apr. 2011. Web. 7 Nov. 2014.

O'Hanlon, Eilis. Rev. of *Long Time, No See* by Dermot Healy. *Independent*. 4 Oct. 2011. Web. 7 Nov. 2014.

Von Franz, Marie-Louise. "The Process of Individuation." *Man and His Symbols*. Ed. C. G. Jung. New York: Dell, 1964. 157–254. Print.

Wachtel, Eleanor. "*Long Time, No See* with Dermot Healy." Interview. *Writers and Company*. 15 Jan. 2012. CBC. Web. 7 Nov. 2014.

Notes

1. The Philip/Psyche split is Healy's figure for the self-narrator (Psyche) constructed by the narrating self (Philip). I hear Philip using his self-construction as Psyche to recover himself as Philip. The climax of this

process comes at the end of the story when he tells Miss Jilly that he is "really" Philip and not Psyche (434).

2. See also the reviews by O'Hanlon and Jarman.

3. For Clark, modernist art rests on the "balance of distance and literalness," which is modernism's way of keeping the half-truths of the parent culture at bay [and] . . . cannot possibly be an individual creation. It comes out of a habitus—a sustained marginality, keeping alive a fragile way of life" (12).

4. Healy presumably parodies this critical complaint in Psyche's anecdote of his 'missing mickey' (267).

5. See von Franz (195, 218, 224, 234).

6. For Homans, the process of individuation mediates between self and society and is "the creative outcome of mourning, a building up of new structures of appreciation born of loss" (263).

7. See Jung 388. Joejoe seems to be telling Gary to begin the path to individuation by escaping the terror of the mother who has rejected him.

8. The completion of the wall and the solution to the mystery of the bullet hole are linked by Psyche (302).

9. See von Franz (169).

10. See Healy, *Errand* (57).

11. This connection is strengthened at the end of the novel when Psyche, after giving up his search for the passage of scripture, "heard a command, and tried one more time" (437), which recalls his hearing "the stone man" when he was selecting stones for the garden wall.

12. See Healy, *Errand* (28).

13. For the first see note 4 above.

14. For a discussion of post-traumatic pathology as 'possession,' see Cathy Caruth, *Unclaimed Experience: Trauma, Narrative, and History* (Baltimore: Johns Hopkins, 1996).

Mister Psyche's Microcosmos
Catherine Hoffmann

In its minute recording of everyday life in a small area of North West Ireland, Dermot Healy's fourth and last novel, *Long Time, No See*, brings to mind some of the techniques and effects of *Microcosmos*,[1] a documentary in which the lives of various insects in the same field are observed and filmed as feats of resilience and tragicomedies. While the close-up photography of *Microcosmos* generates the illusion that the insect-actors are filmed from the perspective of other insects, there is no such conceit in the novel, since its narrator, Philip Feeney, a.k.a. Mister Psyche, is himself a participant in the local life he records and magnifies. Dermot Healy had already experimented with autodiegetic narration in his previous novel, *Sudden Times*. Abandoning the distancing authority of a heterodiegetic narrator allows him to leave "out all motives" (Healy *Guardian*), so that the text registers without mediation the protagonist's embodied experience. In turn this affects the reader's emotional involvement and active participation in the performance of the text—the word "performance" being used here by analogy with music, rather than "interpretation," which fails to capture the intensity of the experience of reading *Long Time, No See*.

The novel also shares with its predecessor the retrospective nature of the narrative. From the beginning the preterit is used to relate story events, that are set, it emerges, in August and September 2006, a transitory period for Psyche who was then awaiting the results of his Leaving Certificate. While it is impossible to determine how long after this period he undertakes his narration, the rupture between his narrating present and the past events he records is made clear by the early sentence "[Joejoe] was my granduncle but sometimes I called him just Uncle and sometimes Grandda" (*Long Time* 3), which suggests, besides, that Joejoe is dead. Indeed, the ritual preparations for his funeral bring to a close—with the noun "wake"—Psyche's narrative which had opened with a typical morning visit to the old man. In the short time span of the story, two more deaths occur: the death of Joejoe's friend, known as the Blackbird, and the death of the Feeneys' sick cow. The period narrated is also the anniversary of the death of Mickey, Psyche's best friend, killed in a car crash the year before. On one level Psyche's narrative may be read as a means of taming the words that tormented his head during those weeks and assuaging his pain (426). It is also an attempt to keep a tangible trace of the dead, yet the text is not a shrine or mausoleum, for Psyche, like Healy himself in the last part of his memoir, is "putting together the banal events of these days" which he "would otherwise not recall" (*Bend for Home* 288). In its chronological recording of details, eschewing the structural complexities of Healy's previous novels, the narrative interweaves the usual and the unexpected, the humorous and the elegiac into "a celebration of the whole gift of existence" (Hopper 20), and resembles Philip's building of a curved wall for his mother's new garden, a process which runs through most of the story time. Completion is achieved when, as in Healy's poem which the novel echoes, "the stones / are finding their place, and are sitting on their own weight at last" (*Fool's Errand* 35). The curved wall is both a concrete object in the making and a metaphor of the narrative with its egalitarian treatment of the story material: "every rock," says Psyche, "will find its place in the wall. No stone should be proud; and stand out from the rest. It is the small stone that no one sees gives all the balance" (242). This democratic conception of wall building and of narration is, this essay will argue, at the heart of the novel. Psyche's world may be tiny but it is also one which knows no hierarchies or distinctions.

A Hospitable Miniature World

Mister Psyche's microcosm, which lies on the very edge of the country, defies precise location on the Ordnance Survey map. Some toponyms refer to actual places, mostly in South Donegal: Bundoran, Killibegs, and Ballintra itself, the townland where the story is set. Yet referentiality here is largely illusory, since other place names—Templeboy and the Nephin range for instance—are imported from Sligo and Mayo into Ballintra or within sight of it, so that Psyche's world is experienced upon reading as a condensed fictional version of North West Ireland. In this, the novel echoes, without the satirical purpose, the compression of all western Gaeltachtaí in Flann O'Brien's *The Poor Mouth (An Béal Bocht)*.[2] In its amphibiousness, the violence of its storms and lashing rain, Psyche's world suggests a literary filiation with the West of *The Poor Mouth*, although in *Long Time, No See* elemental turmoil does not give cause for lament. Mostly it accentuates the porosity between sea and land: "The spray was scattering over the meadows. Salt was raining and the bent grass was burnt black at the tips as if there had been frost overnight" (8).

The centre of Psyche's world consists of a group of cottages by the shore and boats moored alongside the pier. The Feeneys' house is within walking distance from Joejoe's cottage and the cottage in Cooley Lane where the Blackbird lives. This diminutive territory allows close proximity between characters and short frequent journeys to the old men's cottages and the boats. Beyond these, Psyche's microcosm includes the local pub, the garage, the T-junction of Templeboy where Mickey died, Dromod House—Miss Jilly's estate, a remnant of Anglo-Irish landownership—and the nameless town, perhaps loosely based on Donegal, where Geraldine, Philip's mother, works as a hospital nurse and which is also the destination of the Feeneys for the performance of their ritual Saturday night tour.

The characters are constantly on the move within their own familiar world which, far from excluding outsiders, has become home, permanently or transiently, to "strangers," many from Eastern Europe. The patterns of migration had been reversed in the North West, reflecting the general situation in the Ireland of the economic boom years. With Poland playing Lithuania and Latvia in the Night Field (268), the tiny territory becomes the locus of a linguistic medley and a condensed version of the wider globalised world. Of Psyche's father, Gary the lorry driver observes: "Your man Tom Feeney speaks a myriad. [. . .] It's like being on a site with men from all over the world. I thought he was from round here, but the truth is he is a global local" (330). "Global local" cooking, mixing domestic and exotic traditions, offers another instance of this openness to outside influences: Psyche's wok ingredients, for example, involve garden marjoram, oregano, chives, parsley and sage added to mince, red pepper, basil, pine nuts, tomato and pesto (411).

Like his cooking, Mister Psyche's microcosm may be said to contain the world at large: "the men in the North Pole" and the Indian of Dromod House,[3] the stars which can be seen through the telescope in the Watch Room (228, 352), news from Russia which Joejoe watches on the *Russia Today* channel (369), all co-exist within sensory reach of the local characters untroubled by these eclectic presences. Psyche's world proves equally hospitable to supernatural beings and is home to an assortment of fairies and ghosts, including the ghost hens of the Blackbird's imagination at its most unhinged:

> Just before you came in, he said, the room was full.
> Full of what, I asked.
> Why, he says, the ghosts of hens. Did you ever get that? (25)

The Blackbird's ghost hens may be a personal Malibu induced hallucination but nobody in the area will touch a fairy fort, not for all the money in the world (57–8). The fairy fort found by Philip's father is one of the vestiges of a distant past concealed under the surface of the microcosm, which is not only an all-embracing world in miniature but also a layered one. Occasionally sediments of the past come into view. Such is the case of the curved wall in the cliff:

> The storm had [. . .] uncovered this ancient stone wall, about twenty foot long, cemented with sandy clay.
> It was the same rock that built our house and built the walls in the fields. It was everywhere around me [. . .]. (51)

The wall materialises the connectedness between past and present, making it visible and tangible. Elsewhere in *Long Time, No See*, this connectedness takes the form of a transfer of material or objects to new surroundings. Thus, the stones that Philip uses to build the wall of his mother, Geraldine's, new garden come from an old ruin, while the Protestant earth of the Anglo-Irish estate is shifted to this Catholic garden to provide fertile top soil for her *hortus conclusus*.

In a parallel move many years before, the Dromod Bible came to the Catholic home of Joejoe to whom it is still a daily source of delight and wonder, on an equal footing with *Moby Dick*. Since the old man is illiterate, his knowledge of those works is mediated by Psyche's almost daily reading to him of passages from this Bible, which provides an opportunity for quoting texts within the narrative text. The inclusiveness of the microcosm is thus mirrored in the text's inclusiveness.

In spite of the biblical quotations, there is a pre-lapsarian feel about Psyche's world where humans and animals generally live in reciprocal affection, and from which evil is conspicuously absent. Psyche's feeling of guilt about Mickey's death does not alter this impression of innocence and all falls in the novel are accidental. Strife, when present, is reduced to a few old grudges, and the bullet hole in Joejoe's window, which initially shatters the routine of his relatives' lives, turns out to be a sign of the old man's senility, not of anyone's hostility. All that is left of Ireland's colonial past in the area is Dromod House, yet Miss Jilly, its owner and the only local survivor of the ascendancy, now shares fond memories with Joejoe, her family's former servant. Thus, whereas Healy's first two novels vividly conveyed Ireland's territorial, political and sectarian divisions, Psyche's microcosm is, in 2006, a small island of peace, sporadically reached by news of distant wars and conflicts. The Ballintra of *Long Time, No See*, however, is no Arcadia but a place of physical work, required by seasonal cycles, animal health, or weather conditions. It is not that, in Terry Eagleton's words "nothing much happens" (23) in the novel, but, rather, that humble or banal actions performed by ordinary characters are deemed worthy of detailed narrative development which centuries of literary convention had generally reserved for dramatic or heroic action.

Narrative Democracy and the Stuff of Everyday Life

In his essay on modern fiction, "Le Fil perdu du roman," Jacques Rancière analyses the radical departure, in some novels of the later nineteenth century, from the teleological plot dynamics prevailing in earlier fiction centred on great actions and their ends. Breaking with the rules of causal consequences and narrative etiquette founded on the old social order, modern fiction, he argues, gives pride of place to the all-embracing democracy of the humble world of work and days (25–6). Though Rancière here is analysing Flaubert's fiction, many of his observations fit the case of *Long Time, No See*, which, if it relates to any older literary tradition at all, may be regarded as a twenty-first-century variation on the georgic tradition.

In the transitory period of late summer/early autumn, Psyche's jobs include cutting grass, baling hay, planting bulbs, feeding horses and donkeys, looking after a sick cow, digging and excavating, driving tractors, and collecting lobsters from Joejoe's pots. The chapter titles chart some of his activities—Fixing the window (chapter seven), Hoof-cutting (chapter ten), Working the Beach (chapter sixteen)—although the complete list of titles seems at first an enigmatic collage of various items (people, places, animals, objects, quotations . . .) and syntactical forms (nouns, verbs, onomatopoeia, sentences . . .), an impression dispelled upon reading the novel, when the cohesion between the narrative and the headings becomes clear. In particular, the juxtaposition among the titles of the mundane and supernatural or biblical (Fixing the Window / The Fairy; Passing the Time / The Dark Saying)[4] reveals the absence of hierarchy characteristic of the narrative. The democratic nature of the text originates first in Psyche's position in relation to his environment, which he experiences at close quarters by physically engaging with it. A direct consequence of his being level with the world is that the narrator cannot offer panoramic views of his surroundings or transform them into landscape. When Philip/Psyche is not working, he affectionately observes the other living beings who share his territory: humans, animals and plants alike.

> I saw the robin on the toe of his boot. I stood and watched. The bird looked my way, then turned to him. It lifted one claw and looked at it, scattered its wings, closed them and brushed its breast with its beak. Then it looked off to the left

as if remembering something, bowed quickly, hopped onto his knee, fidgeted, then back again to the toe of his boot. Good man, said Joejoe smiling. (54)

As it does for humans, the narrative pays minute attention to the attitudes and movements of the bird, some of them described in terms that would equally apply to those of human beings. The scene leaves Psyche and his great uncle sitting "there considering the wonders" (55), in a quiet elation at the small marvels of the world which the narrative invites the reader to share. Elsewhere, the resemblance of animals to humans is conveyed by vivid and often humorous similes, drawing on scenes of everyday life: "A starling like a gent on a street corner was whistling at the ladies" (307–8), or: "the hare drummed forward and stopped, bounced left right, left right, then strolled into the ditch like a person entering a shop" (211). Although the preposition "like" prevents complete merging of animal and human attitudes, the similes reduce the ontological distance between them, while simultaneously demonstrating Psyche's acute attention to all living beings.

Blurring of ontological distinctions also appears to extend to inanimate objects. The impression derives in particular from the frequent gendering of pronouns referring to such things as a window, a barrel, or, in the following example where the choice of verbs accentuates the effect, a drain pipe: "In the big winds she'd roar, in the breezes she'd whistle. And in the storm she'd become stuck" (68). This grammatical feature possibly reflects the transposition to English of a characteristic of the Irish language, though in almost all examples, the pronoun used is feminine, even when the corresponding Irish noun is masculine (the barrel— Ir. *Bairille*, for instance). How far grammatical gender as used in Healy's novel may be distinctive of local speech is difficult to assess without recent first hand experience.[5] What is certain is that, by defamiliarising contemporary English, it brings things to life in a way impossible to achieve by the same means in languages like French, Irish or German.

Human beings, animals and objects are all treated as worthy of narrative and linguistic respect: nothing seems too small, humble or banal to be narrated. The magnifying of ordinary tasks and everyday things, the detailing of gestures, draw attention to what constitutes the fabric of life for most people, far from heroic action, and the thrills of a dangerous life.

The levelling of categories and abolition of boundaries in Healy's novel concern all the components of the text: typography, grammar, story world material, and narrative discourse. Thus, in general, there is no typographical distinction between narrative of actions or events and direct speech, which allows the text to flow freely from one to the other. On the page, dialogue is usually identifiable, in spite of the absence of demarcation, by the brevity of its lines, sometimes scrolling down the left hand margin. Yet, very short descriptive or narrative sentences are often inserted in the dialogue with no differentiation from it, whether typographically, syntactically or by punctuation as in the following elliptical conversation between Psyche's father, Joejoe, and Psyche:

> The weather is mighty.
> It is.
> More silence.
> And the lad found a wall beneath the cliff.
> You did not?
> I did, I said.
> Now.
> Centuries old.
> More silence. (57)

The narrator's own economical notations fit the reticence of the speakers and ensure continuity, both visually and "musically" so to speak, in that his words do not disturb the tonality and rhythm of the halting conversation. In *Long Time, No See*, literary democracy goes together with narratorial unobtrusiveness.

Patterns, Echoes and Variations in Narrative Texture

The absence of narrative hierarchies and the abolition of ontological and textual boundaries in *Long Time, No See* do not result in formlessness. Various types of patterning, rather than the more traditional causal relationships of plot, shape the story world and the text which embodies it. A first obvious type concerns the repetition of similar actions or ritual scenes, which gradually acquire significance beyond the routine of everyday life. Among the recurring actions, grave-digging, performed first for an anonymous neighbour, then for the Blackbird, and finally for Joejoe, figures almost as prominently as wall-building. The latter, however, is an ongoing process which the narrative traces from its beginning in chapter nine to its completion at the end of chapter thirty-three. Building the curved wall for his mother's garden seems, somehow, to hold Mister Psyche and his narrative together. Grave-digging, an episodic activity, works differently. It connects metonymically the living who dig the graves and the dead who will rest in them, and emphasises proximity, physical or emotional, between generations and between friends or relatives. Thus, when digging the Blackbird's grave, Psyche and Frosty "hit a few bones of the ancestors" (383); later "the same crew" digs Joejoe's "alongside Grandma's and Grandda's" (428). Not only do the two actions echo each other, but, being performed by the same men, they underline the connection between their deaths, which Philip eventually recognises: "I suddenly realised that when we buried the Bird we were putting Joejoe in the grave" (431).

Other types of repetitions include recurring images which require active memorisation on the reader's part. For instance, the "wren [. . .] chiselling the question mark" (307) makes no sense, unless one recalls "the wren, with a tipped-up tail [. . .] keeping time to a questioning song she sang alone" (242). Even more demanding is the following image which appears first as a simile on page 92, then on page 298: "The clouds overhead passed by like more of the apostles on the dance floor," "Up overhead the clouds stepped out like three of the apostles out onto the dance floor," and finally in the metaphor "a new storm was throwing her skirts in the air. The Apostles were gathering" (389). In this case, memory is helpless in making sense of the incongruous simile, and this reader is left wondering.[6]

If the recurring images may be regarded as visual rhymes, the repetition of phrases within the text and from the headings to the narrative forms a series of refrains contributing to the novel's texture, a device already used in *Sudden Times* as I have outlined elsewhere.[7] The title of the novel itself is the Blackbird's traditional greeting, used at least three times in the body of the text (39, 62, 273). The onomatopoeic headings "Bang!" and "When Whack!," borrowed from the Blackbird and Joejoe's vivid rendering of the respective noise of the ghost hens (27) and of the bullet (34, 36) visibly amplify the imitative soundscape of the old men's speech. Strategically placed, "First Call" (chapter one), "The First Fall" (Book Four and chapter twenty-two) and "The Second Fall" (forty-fifth and penultimate chapter) rhyme with each other at regular intervals, as if the novel was a long prose poem. The three titles do not just chart the narrative's chronological movement: they signpost the relationship between Mister Psyche, Joejoe and the Blackbird, and suggest a shift from routine to personal disaster. In the body of the text verbatim repetition is sometimes used to convey heightened emotional intensity. Thus, the Blackbird's delirious litany in chapter twenty figures again, in italics, when, after the old man's burial, Philip and Joejoe walk to the various places on the familiar territory mapped by the Bird: "then it was off walking again, up to Cooley and back as if he was following the Bird's litany . . . *Up Cooley and across Poll an Baid. [. . .]. Through the Bent. The Night Field. [. . .]. Dromod. Through the willows. Take a left. Onto the New Road*" (387). In this elegiac walk—one of the private rituals which punctuate the narrative—Joejoe's own geography and existence merge with his dead friend's.

The use of italics in the above example immediately attracts attention and constitutes one of the visual variations in the narrative's texture. Such alterations of the smooth surface of the text heighten the audience's sensory perception of some undercurrent at work, without necessarily prompting unequivocal interpretation. A case in point concerns passages where direct speech is signalled by dashes framing each utterance, in a striking departure from the prevailing typographical indistinction. Sometimes, the dashes signal a moment of intense emotion which makes utterance physically difficult, as in the exchange between Psyche and Gary about Mickey's death:

> He was driving. I was beside him. It was a year ago. He had done his final paper in the Leaving, and a crowd of us were on the raz in the town and he said to me—Let's go out to Sweet John's, the local pub, for a breath of fresh air and that's when it happened. He hit the wall above in Templeboy—
> —I see—
> —That's it—
> —It's tough—
> —I could have driven, I was sober—(326)

The staccato effect of the dashes is preceded by the repetitive, minimal syntax of the three opening sentences, hammering the bare facts in halting rhythm. In this example, syntax and typography reinforce the emotional impact of understated grief. In other cases—for instance the three direction-giving scenes of chapter thirty-four—where the precise purpose of the dashes is harder to pinpoint, their immediate effect is still to isolate the dialogue visually and introduce a rhythmic alteration, a kind of breathlessness, in the smooth flow of the text. In those places, the reader is encouraged to *listen* to the text, to perform silently the sounds, rests and rhythms of its music. Apart from typography and punctuation, the visual means used to prompt this activity include passages where the text is exceptionally compact and runs on in long uninterrupted sentences, which sharply contrasts with the usual economy of dialogue and brief notations. There are two striking occurrences of that kind, the first recording the Feeneys' Saturday night tour of town, the second recording Philip's stroll through the hospital:

> I went from Medical North to Medical South, then down the stairs and by the Eye, How is things? A nurse in a blue top and black trousers going one way asked a nurse going the other. The same as usual, she replied; I went on past

> the Heart, all the blue-handled doors, and down the stairs into Emergency where a gypsy cornered me and asked was I O'Neill? You have the wrong man, I said; *Going up, Doors closing*, and I took the lift to fifth where a baby was crying like an old man giving a lecture on the inner self, Sorry pet, said a voice, you've got to stop [. . .]. (276)

The passage, which extends over two pages, reads like an experience in the phenomenology of perception, Philip's body being "not only an object among all other objects [. . .] but an object which is sensitive to all the rest, which reverberates to all sounds, vibrates to all colours" (Merleau-Ponty 236). Indeed, this passage interweaves in a dense fabric Psyche's journey through the hospital with the kaleidoscope of his perceptions of sights and sounds. The impression of indiscriminate recording is belied by the narrator's similes and by the inclusion of fragments of conversation which bring out the involuntary comic effects of everyday speech: "another woman was saying, *Brilliant, absolutely* into a mobile, then she added: The problem is that the undertaker is on his holidays in Lithuania, Yes, I know, but there was a fair gathering, nevertheless" (278).

If nothing spectacular happens at story level in *Long Time, No See*, the reading experience is one of intense activity, of sensuous delight in Mister Psyche's world and language, of puzzlement too, for his narrative and familiar microcosm remain "a bit of a curved mystery" (Healy *Guardian*).

The Strangeness of Mister Psyche's Familiar World

This quality of the text arises from a combination of linguistic, stylistic and narrative features, including the defamiliarisation of English mentioned earlier. Partly, this is due to the presence in the speech of the characters and the narrator of "the tones and rhythms of Irish, so that from the viewpoint of Standard English [the novel's idiom] is [. . .] persistently off-key" (Eagleton 24). Occasionally nouns of Irish origin are used: the alt, a dudeen [dúidín], the gra, or the buachalawn [buachalán],[8] as in the sentence "the dying buachalawns were bunched up in dry stacks of brown" (307) where the plant name allows a fleeting moment of alliterative poetry impossible to achieve with the unexotic English "ragwort." Also exhibited in the novel's language are grammatical and syntactical features characteristic of Hiberno-English, such as the use of the definite article where none would be used in Standard English—"[i]nstead of going on to the Donegal, we turned in at Dromod" (226)—of the present tense instead of the present perfect, and the prepositions "in" or "on" to express "various physical and mental sensations, states or processes" (Filppula 220), as in "[h]e is very tired in himself these last few days" (375). Sometimes, however, it is difficult to determine whether linguistic strangeness originates in the spectral Irish haunting of the characters' English or in idiolectal turns of phrase, recycled and transformed by Dermot Healy.

His ear for linguistic idiosyncrasies, surrealistic conversation, and phrases short-circuiting logic or conventional semantics, is even more evident in *Long Time, No See* than in *Sudden Times*. When the Judge, feeling depressed, says "it [is] getting late very early these days" (188), the oxymoron produces a humorous effect, yet, for all its seeming illogicality, the sentence, by destabilising semantics, makes sense more profoundly than the conventional "it's getting dark very early."

The humorous strangeness of the text often results from ellipsis and condensation, as in the following exchange between Philip's father and the Blackbird, when the latter refuses to open his door:

> Blackbird, he yelled again
> Yes, came a quiet voice.
> Where the hell are you?
> I'm in the letter box. (42)

The incongruous image conjured up by the literal meaning of the Bird's answer is superimposed on the actual and obvious meaning.

Defamiliarisation is further generated by the narrative technique of slow motion in those parts of the text which describe gestures and movements, usually unregistered in such detail in novels, and often performed mechanically and hardly noticed in real life:

he closed the door with a polite tap of his fingertips, and shook his head in dismay; lit up a cigarette made of yellow paper rolls and stepped aside like a gentleman and sat to the side of the shed [. . .]; kicked out, and shook himself viciously, then went perfectly still, [. . .] with his two fists sitting one on top of the other on his left knee. (21)

Such passages bear witness to Psyche's power of observation while highlighting the fact that so much human communication is of a nonverbal kind. They contribute to the "corporeality" of the narrative (Bolens 25), and displace narrative interest from the motives of plot to the motifs and motions of the physical world. Slow-motion recording and magnifying of the "dispositions of the body" (Eagleton 23) provide a narrative equivalent to miming and achieve comparable comic and surreal effects. As observed by Eagleton: "The more scrupulously you detail human action in this relentlessly externalising way, the more you estrange it" (23).

In part the strangeness of Psyche's world and of his narrative originates in the absence of a boundary between reality on the one hand and the world of the imagination, dreams, hallucinations and legends on the other. The levelling technique analysed earlier also enables the seamless shift from one world to another. Thus, the dream in which sea and land merge so that "[a]n octopus clung to the window and [. . .] looked at me" (152)[9] starts midway in the sentence "I got into bed and sailed off in the boat-house" (151) where grammatical conjoining erases the difference between fact and dream. If Psyche's hold on reality tends to dissolve into hallucinations and haunting reminiscences, this is largely because reality itself is fundamentally eerie. The local beach, for instance, assumes a sinister otherworldly appearance after the storm, and looks "like it was inhabited by aliens" while the roots of seaweed "clenched the stones with a drowning man's grip" (139). A liminal site of transaction and transition between the land and the sea, it bears the signs of disasters and potential tragedies, as in chapter forty-three, "A Jacket and Shoes" when, after yet another storm, Psyche comes upon a jacket hanging from a stake, "looking fierce human on the edge of the pier" (405), then finds the debris of a wreck and a pair of "sad shoes" which he imagines having been carefully placed there "by [a] man about to take a leap" (407). Jacket and shoes disappear as mysteriously as they first appeared, yet their ghostly presence hovers over the last chapters leading to Joejoe's fatal fall. Halfway between the Bird's death and his friend's death, the jacket and shoes are not only enigmatic diegetic objects but also visual *memento mori* and textual signs of impending tragedy and loss.

Conclusion: Reading the Signs

Signs, whether referring to the past or to the near future, abound in Psyche's world and accumulate in his narrative, especially in the last book entitled "The Signs." Some are written on Joejoe's body in the form of the marks left by his increasingly uncontrollable scratching; others are detected in simple acts such as the Blackbird's surrender of the key to his cottage because "he could not give a fuck if [he] died" (281); others, still, lie in the biblical passages which Psyche reads to Joejoe whose reactions suggest that the enigmatic texts bear a relation to his own life. For instance, listening, shortly after the Blackbird's funeral, to the sentence from Psalm 49, "*I will open my dark saying upon the harp*," the old man reacts with the cryptic remark that he "might meet someone on the other side" (396). The reader too comes to assign a prophetic significance to the biblical texts in relation to story events, for despite being presented as randomly chosen, the extracts, ranging from the Psalms to Revelations, seem to prefigure Joejoe's journey towards death. They anticipate the old man's decline and dejection in "*My days are like a shadow that declineth*" (*King James Bible* Ps. 102) (149), and the brief scene at the end of chapter forty-four where Joejoe, after uttering a terrible roar, "all of a sudden without a stitch on him [. . .] stood at the gate waving his arms" (417) which echoes Revelations 16, read to the old man a few pages earlier and interpreted by him as signs (392).

In the narrative, all extracts from the Bible appear in italics so that they form chains of linguistic signs immediately distinguishable from the rest of the text, and materialising the link between Psyche and Joejoe. What the Bible provides, beyond the affection involved in the young man's reading to the illiterate old one, is a shared world of powerful literary images and signs. In Joejoe's words, Psyche and himself are "in this together" (5) and when the old man dies, the link is snapped and the sense of loss acutely experienced as a sudden alienation from the biblical text:

> As I read the lines I did not rightly understand them. It felt false reading them alone. I knew what the words meant, but I needed his reply. I had never read the book alone. It was him who shared with me the sound that made sense of the words. Joejoe's absence suddenly emptied my head. (436–7)

Ultimately, the biblical fragments, far from destabilising Psyche's narrative, combine with it in a contrapuntal writing which, distantly echoing the tradition of allegorical interpretation, invites parallels between the narrator's microcosm and the now timeless world of the Bible. Joejoe's favourite book becomes the textual means by which his simple existence and banal death are transformed into a universal story of human life, death and loss.

Works Cited

Beal, Joan C. *Language and Region*. London: Routledge, 2006. Print.
Bolens, Guillemette. *The Style of Gestures: Embodiment and Cognition in Literary Narrative*. Baltimore: Johns Hopkins University Press, 2012. Print.
Eagleton, Terry. "An Octopus at my Window." Rev. of *Long Time, No See*, by Dermot Healy. *London Review of Books* 33.10 (19 May 2011): 23–4. Print.
Filppula, Markku. *The Grammar of Irish English: Language in Hibernian Style*. London: Routledge, 1999. Print.
Healy, Dermot. *A Fool's Errand*. 2010. Oldcastle: The Gallery Press, 2014. Print.
———. *A Goat's Song*. London: Flamingo, 1994. Print.
———. *Fighting with Shadows*. London: Allison and Busby, 1984. Print.
———. Interview with Sean O'Hagan. *The Observer*. 3 Apr. 2011. Web. 18 Jun. 2014.

———. *Long Time, No See*. London: Faber and Faber, 2011. Print.

———. *Sudden Times*. London: Harvill Press, 1999. Print.

———. *The Bend for Home*. London: Harvill Press, 1996. Print.

Hoffmann, Catherine. "Dancing to Ollie's Tunes: The Rhetoric of Narrative Stutter." *Style* 43.3 (Fall 2009): 357–72. Print.

Hopper, Keith. "Everyday Things." Rev. of *Long Time, No See* and *A Fool's Errand*, by Dermot Healy. *Times Literary Supplement* 8 Apr. 2011: 19–20. Print.

Merleau-Ponty, Maurice. *Phenomenology of Perception*. 1945. Trans. Colin Smith. London: Routledge and Kegan Paul, 1962. Web. 19 Nov. 2014.

Microcosmos, le peuple de l'herbe. Dir. Claude Nuridsany and Marie Pérennou. Bac Films, 1996. Film.

O'Brien, Flann. *The Poor Mouth (An Béal Bocht)*. 1941. Trans. Patrick Power. 1973. London: Paladin, 1988. Print.

Ó'Muirithe, Diarmaid. *A Dictionary of Anglo-Irish. Words and Phrases from Gaelic in the English of Ireland*. Dublin: Four Courts Press, 2000. Print.

Rancière, Jacques. "Le fil perdu du roman." *Le fil perdu. Essais sur la fiction moderne*. Paris: La Fabrique, 2014. Print.

Trudgill, Peter. *The Dialects of England*. 1990. Oxford: Blackwell, 1994. Print.

Notes

1. *Microcomos, le peuple de l'herbe*, directed by Claude Nuridsany and Marie Pérennou, released in 1996.

2. From the different apertures of the narrator's childhood cottage could be seen the Rosses and Gweedore, Bloody Foreland and Tory Island, the rocks of Connemara, Aranmore, the Great Blasket and Dingle! (O'Brien 21)

3. The Indian is in fact "a picture of a Red Indian" in the hallway of Dromod House (82) while on the third floor of the house stands "a full-length Arctic explorer" (83).

4. The Dark Saying, the title of chapter forty-two, is a quotation from Psalm 49.

5. Grammatical gendering survives in some English dialects as traces of

Old English, especially in the South West where the masculine pronoun is used for "things which can be picked up, moved around and counted" (Trudgill 88; see also Beal 72).

6. Investigation into the origin of the image of the dancing Apostles has yielded little that was not far-fetched. Given the biblical references in the text, one possibility might be the ring dance of the Apostles around Jesus prior to his arrest, described in the Apocryphal Acts of John. The Apocryphal New Testament would not, however, have been part of the King James Bible read by Psyche.

7. See Hoffmann 362.

8. Respectively: a cliff, glen-side or gully; a short smoking pipe; love; ragwort. See Ó Muirithe 26, 88, 114, 48.

9. This passage inspired the title of Eagleton's review.

The Bend for Home: Truth, Beauty, Such Things
Derek Hand

There has been a turn in some recent Irish literary scholarship toward 'memory' as an object of study.[1] It is a manoeuvre that widens a traditional historical approach to the past to include the ephemerae of everyday culture as focal points for significance and meaning. This reorientation is a means of overcoming, or trying to, the divisions of Irish life in the past and the present. Memory becomes its own justification because in memory objective truth no longer matters, nothing and no one is more important than anything or anyone else as everything and everyone's remembrance is equally valid. For Irish writing it has been argued that an accompanying factor along with this reorientation is the increasing emphasis placed on trauma as central to Irish experience: the result being that Irish history is always already tragic, experience always already categorised as miserable. R. F. Foster argues that much recent autobiographical writing exploits the sense of exceptionality in the Irish experience, using a quote from Frank McCourt's *Angela's Ashes* to illustrate:

> Worse than the ordinary miserable childhood is the miserable Irish childhood and worse yet is the miserable Irish Catholic childhood . . . [N]othing can compare with the Irish version: the poverty; the shiftless loquacious alcoholic father; the pious defeated mother moaning by the fire; pompous priests; bullying schoolmasters; the English and the terrible things they did to us for eight hundred long years. (11)

Joe Cleary is also suspicious of this seemingly easy retreat into a traumatic past, away from the sheering immediacy and attendant traumas of the present moment, suggesting that contemporary Irish writers encode a fear and rejection of modernity within their stories at the level of plot and form (203). The literary past in this argument is thus fetishized, a reservoir of images and ideas that forestalls any real engagement with the present. While there is much to laud in these considerations, opening up as they do, the gap between the much vaunted modernity and originality of the Celtic Tiger moment with the seemingly traditional cultural fixation with de Valera's Ireland, they miss a most obvious point that such a fixation actually, in a way, signals how different the contemporary moment really is from anything which has gone before it. In other words, what is being articulated in this writing is the utter heterogeneity of the present globalised world where everything and everywhere is the same as everywhere and everything else. The past, even the relatively recent past, is a moment of local Irish difference to be celebrated in the face of an all too bland present. A previous generation in the 1960s had looked at their own recent past, not as trauma per se, but as a version of the 'rare ould times,' a sentimentalised Ireland fit for consumption by the newly minted bourgeoisie at home, and abroad, in search of harsh, gritty realism so different to the sleek modernity of their present. Still, the risk of nostalgia is an ever-present one in modern Ireland, as elsewhere, a form of entertainment that offers easy access to emotion.

One imagines that it is the phenomenal reach of Frank McCourt's book that generates much of these critical responses to Irish writing in the contemporary moment as it seemed to set the agenda for Irish writing generally as it became a defining text on the international and national publishing scene. The danger is that admission into this international market simplifies the nature of the Ireland on display, steering clear of the subtleties and complexities a local reader might appreciate and expect. Ireland is rendered as conveniently one-dimensional so that the rough edges of literary expression are pared down for readers who know what to expect and get what they want.

Of course, there is more to this engagement with the past than simply setting up an opposition between then and now. What both Foster and Cleary miss is that an important element of this turn to memory and the past is how, as Robert F. Garratt suggests, the operations of memory come into view, with the act of remembering itself being brought to the fore. While this can be observed in much contemporary fiction writing generally[2] the most obvious manifestation of self-aware acts of memory come in memoir and autobiographical writing. Central to any autobiographical project is the self: the creation and the projection of a self into the historical realm. Indeed, it might be argued that in the Irish context this is centrally important, in that it is a recognition that history is always personalised, or ought to be. Eamonn Hughes argues that for the revivalist generation of the late nineteenth and early twentieth centuries autobiography was one means by which Revivalists could come to know themselves, precisely as themselves. And, as W. B. Yeats wrote:

> The friends that have it I do wrong
> When ever I remake a song,
> Should know what issue is at stake:
> It is myself that I remake. (778)

Yeats's acknowledgement here gives lyrical expression to the centralisation of the story of the self as being the only important story to be told in Irish writing through the twentieth century and perhaps, indeed, the only story that it is possible to tell. One major consequence of this was the proliferation of personalised fiction: from James Joyce to John McGahern, the autobiographical impulse underpins much Irish writing of the twentieth century. The story of becoming is paramount, as illustrated by the narrator in Frank O'Connor's "The Guests of the Nation," who famously declares at the close of the short story: "And anything that ever happened me afterwards, I never felt the same about again" (353). What is being signalled is how profound moments of change, transformation and development of the individual self are the central story to be reiterated.

Highlighting the productive gap between the past and the present coupled with the focus on the self gives a critical context to better understand the proliferation in the 1990s of autobiographical writing in Ireland and how to best place Dermot Healy's memoir *The Bend for Home* within that moment. Certainly it was a time of huge success for an autobiographical work such as McCourt's

1996 *Angela's Ashes*. Healy's memoir was also published in that year and was met with an undoubtedly positive response. Fellow author Patrick McCabe labelled it as "probably the finest memoir . . . written in Ireland in the last 50 years" (qtd. in O'Hagan) and George O'Brien, in the *Irish Times*, called it "remarkable" (O'Brien B8). It did not, perhaps it could not, garner the kind of fame enjoyed by Frank McCourt's tome. However, if McCourt's popularity had everything to do with assumptions and stereotypes of Ireland and Irishness that promoted an image that was already known: both traumatic *and* sentimental, Healy's memoir explored an alternative history, challenging and deconstructing some of the easier expectations of what Ireland was, and is. He also managed to make his memoir not so much a mediation on his youthful self but on the nature of the artistic enterprise itself, teasing out what it is a writer does or tries to do.

George O'Brien's review went on to correctly register the nature of this work of memory precisely as "work," that is as a form of creation or fiction (B8). From the very first page Healy warns his readership that fact might have very little to do with what is going to unfold on the following pages. After detailing the night of his birth he says:

> As for the child, it did not grow up to be me, although till recently I believed this was how I was born. Family stories were told so often that I always thought I was there. In fact, all this took place in a neighbour's house up the road . . . It's in a neighbour's house fiction begins. (*The Bend for Home* 3)

Healy's 'story,' then, it is clear, will be as much about the nature of stories as it will be about the growth and development and forging of a unique and worthy self. To suggest that autobiographical writing is concerned with construction or fiction-making is nothing new of course. The lesson for the reader is that stories are made up, and for a variety of reasons. Healy's early life was spent in the village of Finea in County Westmeath, located right on the border with County Cavan. It is a place made famous in a song by Percy French, "Come Back Paddy Reilly to Ballyjamesduff":

> The Garden of Eden has vanished, they say
> But I know the lie of it still;
> Just turn to the left at the bridge of Finea
> And stop when halfway to Cootehill.

We are told, though, in Healy's memoir, that it is impossible to turn left at that bridge:

> It can't be done. No matter how you try you can't turn left at the bridge of Finea, unless you go up Bullasheer Lane which leads eventually to the banks of floating reeds on Kinale . . . It's all a cod . . . For the sake of a song Percy French got his geography amiss. Even road-engineers are capable of giving wrong directions in order to get a couplet true. And that's how I found out writers not only make up things, but get things wrong as well. Language, to be memorable, dispenses with accuracy. (10)

It might be argued here that what Healy is championing is the Irish tendency for loquacious exaggeration, an updating of the Arnoldian warning that the Irish chaffed under the "despotism of fact." That, of course, would be to fall into the comforts of stereotype and that is what Healy is attempting to avoid. As he says a little later he must buttress himself against "nostalgia" because it "steals material from the same source as fiction, and then leaves the reality wanting" (25). What Healy highlights is how the artist in the act of creation, of making things up, can deliberately mislead, deflect and obscure in order to be memorable or to be true, not just to reality, but to the demands of form. In Ireland writers continue to operate within the Dinnseanchas tradition of Gaelic culture which powerfully combined poetry and place lore and where the stories of place excite the imagination as much as the material reality of the landscape itself. The point being made, though, is how completely enveloping is this realm of story and how we live in the realm of story, and how it is not separate from our everyday existence, something practised by a privileged few, but something everyone, everywhere does and understands at a fundamental level. So Percy French's lie productively leads to more tales and stories, more reimaginings of the actuality of place and landscape. Healy is no postmodernist in that the world outside language *is* there, but is there to be actively retold, to be made a part of the ongoing story which in turn brings itself back into the realm of the everyday. Mapping landscapes is thus a process between the real world and the imagination and, in the end, it is impossible to disentangle where each begins and ends.

These moments suggest that the distinctions between words, and concepts, such as truth and falsehood melt away in the emerging pre-eminence of fiction, as the mediator between the world out there and the human realm, within this narrative. Fiction, in this sense, is liberating: it allows things to happen, to be made and, ultimately, to be shared. Healy tells a tale of how on a trip home from London to Cavan he had told a journalist from the Anglo-Celt newspaper of how a play of his was to be aired on British TV. It was, of course, a lie, made up on the spur of the moment to impress. However this anecdote is central to his story as he goes on to say:

> Everything I write now is an attempt to make up for that terrible lie. Had I not lied I might never have tried my hand at fiction. The truth is the lie you once told returning to haunt you. (60)

Again and again throughout the memoir Healy acknowledges this interaction between imagination and the real world and how interchangeable they are for him:

> I've stolen so many of Maisie's phrases over the years and inserted them into the mouths and minds of fictional characters that she herself has become a work of the imagination. (241)

Fiction might begin in a neighbour's house but it is also a two-way street, enmeshed in the human experience of being-in-the-world.

Healy's mediation on the constructed nature of memory and memoir does not overtly intrude upon his tale; he is still concerned with telling the story of growing up in Westmeath and Cavan and detailing the rituals of family and community life. The usual scenes are recalled: the exuberance and excitement of the cinema, the classroom interaction between teachers and pupils, and the religious world of the Catholic church. A central element of *The Bend for Home* is the overly familiar preoccupation for Irish writers in the twentieth century, the sexual awakening of the young author. So much so that as one commentator put it, Healy "saddles the town of Cavan with a merry sexual ferment" (Craig 146). What is missed in these responses to the work is how Healy's 1950s and 60s Ireland is not such a blighted place after all: there is money and music and lovemaking aplenty. In other words, there is a life to be lived; there are opportunities to be taken, and things to do. John McGahern declared that "one room or town or locality can be made into an everywhere. The universal is the local, but with the walls taken away," and Healy's market town of Cavan is such a location (McGahern 11). Transcending the embrace and comfort of stereotype he begins to bridge the gap between the Irish past and the Irish present. In his rendering, therefore, the concerns of its inhabitants are not made exotic or strange either by time or place; rather, their lives are made contemporaneous and relevant.

What is remarkable is how Healy manages to be true to all these aspects of his life and his environment: no one thing or element dominates all others as he strives to render the multifariousness of his experience. In a way, like all narratives, Healy's is self-consciously struggling toward coherence and completeness and thus being true to the multiplicity of lived experience undermines such a unifying vision. In consequence at times what the reader is dealing with are 'scenes,' or single moments, captured amidst the flow of the story of growth and development. Some are more isolated than others, though all are luminous in their power. One very good example of this is chapter fourteen (77–80) which describes Cavan on a Thursday which was a half-day for businesses in the market town. Employing a condensed version of the Joycean technique made use of in the 'Wandering Rocks' episode of *Ulysses*, the eye of the narrator moves and flits through the town detailing how various people bring the shutters down on their shop or business, and what other characters are doing and not doing. People are named, places and shops are named, the high and the low and in-between are given mention and are made a part of this diorama of a moment. As with Joyce the notion of simultaneity is paramount: each character and vignette is at once apart from the others but in Healy's account made a part of the overall depiction, his vision at once panoptic and focused.

This technique is made use of again, later in the narrative, to offer a snapshot of life in his school (230ff.). This shift in register and perception, in formal approach, is of interest because it does suggest an author at work, an author experimenting with various literary methods, acknowledging the need for different styles at different moments for differing effects. Still later the narrator tells us that:

> We are trapped in what apparently is. We cannot take off elsewhere. But though this is not a fiction where everything happens in the so-called world of make-believe, sometimes the mundane everyday feels like an illusion—anything might happen, the authentic is a trick, and the story is not really known till it's told. (259)

Again, what Healy as a writer is stressing is how the everyday is the location of potential magic and wonder and how his writing, his act of fiction, is an effort to enter into that space and express the world as it is. The declaration that knowledge does not come except in the act of telling is important because it signals that art, certainly his art, is an on-going project of discovery: it is the process which is of importance and not the end itself.

Such moments as these, as has been argued, when the narrator, self-consciously and self-reflexively, begins to ponder his own art are central to the unfolding narrative. But, it becomes even clearer how central these moments are with the introduction of the found object of his diary that Healy's mother had kept and returns to him in the present moment of his 'writing' of the memoir. It is easily incorporated into the narrative structure, offering yet another perspective—the immediate felt moment of the action—to this encounter with the past. Obviously access to diaries and letters are legitimate in any act of autobiography, adding another layer of the real and the authentic, enacting the movement from the private to the public realms, thereby exposing the interiority of the narrator/subject to revelation. Healy's diary doubles this act of revelation by having been written in code in order to hide its true meaning and its message from the prying eyes of his mother and aunt in his youth.

While obviously this appeal to the authenticity of the immediate moment is an element of Healy's deployment of the diary it also forces the reader to consider the act of writing itself, as opposed to the act of telling. It is introduced as "A Version of a Diary 1963" (129) suggesting that, once more, facts and truth might not necessarily be paramount. The inclusion of the diary is also disruptive of the narrative flow. While ostensibly it takes up the narrative from where it has been left off, continuing to tell the story of Healy's youth, it surreptitiously blurs the two time frames that underpin any act of memory: then and now. The youthful object and the present day subject come together with the introduction of this text into the narrative. Of more significance, though, is how Healy manages with this one gesture to open up a consideration of genre. Certainly it is worth acknowledging that there is genre slippage at work in much 'life' writing which can access and use diaries, journals and letters as well as employ the myriad techniques of fiction. Here the diary acts as something of a series of notes toward a novel that might never be written. Or, it can be argued, it is a series of notes toward what will eventually become the memoir that is now being written. The panoptic technique discussed earlier, from his school days, appears in the diary and so, in terms of strict chronology, the more expanded use comes *after* that. Thus, the 'writer' Healy uses the diary as a means of testing, in nascent form, many styles and perspectives, as if he is working towards a particular style that will allow him to tell his own story to himself and to others.

This blurring of distinct lines between genres was very much a part of the critical context of the moment of *The Bend for Home* with Seamus Deane's disguised memoir *Reading in the Dark* also appearing in 1996—a family story presented in a novelistic fashion. Crucially, too, Deane's work also plunders the possibilities of considering the nature and power of stories in an Irish context, offering a magisterial critique not only of how stories are made but also how they are read and interpreted. An interesting anxiousness central to Deane's novel which revolves round various acts of betrayal, that of being an informer, of losing something essential in one's relationship to others in the act of writing their story, can also be observed in Healy's work.

The dominant in autobiographical writing is the self, the 'I,' or it is usually thought to be in the traditional sense. The processes of memory and memoir, of writing the story of the self are, as stated, an act of discovery and revelation. No matter that many such texts position the self in relation to something other: be it the nation or the family, it is the triumph of the individual that provides focus, momentum and energy. To be sure, the younger Healy is central to the narrative: it is his curious perceptive that brings coherence to the memoir. And yet, it might be argued that it is in fact not himself that Healy is in pursuit of, rather it is others that he really wants to come to know.

Throughout the memoir Healy comes back to moments of what can be labelled deflection. To return to the opening page and the reflection that "[i]t's in a neighbour's house fiction begins" (3): this can be read as the first instance of the author diverting attention from the self. He flags a shift away from himself as an author, as a creator of fictions, as a creator of a self, into the public and communal realm. Stories do not come from within but come from the world around, come from others and come from other places. It is one of the more curious aspects of *The Bend for Home* how, in many ways, the 'I' of the story told, of Healy, is constantly being erased though never annihilated. Simply put, while undoubtedly a story of the self, this is more a story of others, of rendering the public shared space as opposed to the inner intimacies of the individual. One powerful image has the youthful Healy awake and looking out on a storm:

> Last night stood by the window looking out at a storm. Everyone else was asleep in the dorm . . . Then came this distant thunder that was really wind. Rain lashed against the windows and the trees were waving and waving. Then the

wind, slapping like sheets, thumped against the black college
. . . The world outside howled. Branches swept across the
lawn . . . I stood there in my pyjamas for maybe half an hour,
then got into bed, but every few minutes I was out again to
look, and there was the storm still going on, making faces in
the trees, and the wind barking. The rain curved against the
window panes. The boys asleep. (219–20)

There is something of the romantic sublime in this moment with the world of nature raging on without care for the human observer who is nonetheless drawn to this spectacle. More important, though, is the way in which this vignette of a watcher emphasises how apart from the raging scene outside his dorm window the viewer actually is. In terms of a developing sense of the artist it is a central picture of the writer as silent observer, cut off from that which is being observed.

Another moment that reverberates with possible aesthetic concern is Healy's description of the large mirror to be found in the 'Milseanacht Breifne' restaurant in Cavan town where his mother and aunts worked and above which the family lived:

Facing us was the huge mirror which was nearly the width of an entire wall. That mirror had given my family and me a second identity.

We ate looking at ourselves in it. We were never fully ourselves, but always possessed by others. When someone entered the room we spoke to them through the mirror. The family, when they conversed, never had to look directly at each other. We all spoke through the mirror. We learned faithfulness and duplicity from an early age. Always there were two of you there: the one in whom consciousness rested with the other, the body, which somehow didn't belong and was always at a certain remove.

This mirror and our use of it threw visitors off balance. They looked at you directly but you looked at them in the mirror. Even if the person was standing in front of you you looked over their shoulder. That warped perspective stayed with me for years. (73–4)

Walter Benjamin notes that the mirror in café society of Paris brings the movement of the city streets into the café so that there is "no telling outside from in" (*The Arcades Project* 536). But here the mirror functions as a means of framing everyday interaction, of framing it and containing it. Again Benjamin suggests that, "The feeling of strangeness that overcomes the actor before the camera, as Pirandello describes it, is basically of the same kind as the estrangement felt before one's own image in the mirror" (*Illuminations* 230). As a metaphor for literary art and enterprise we can understand how writing both bridges this gap, or attempts to, and necessarily makes the gap real in the very act of naming it. Healy ends his pen-picture of the mirror and the family by stating: "This distance between my mind and my body has always remained and is insurmountable" (74). The kind of healing and reconciliation that memoir might offer seems thoroughly absent here.

The lingering possibility is that the 'self,' the supposed object of memoir, becomes lost in this endlessly reflecting hall of mirrors. As he says the mirror allows him a double or second identity. Again, at the very beginning we are offered this modern and postmodern image of the double, in the guise of a younger cousin of his also named Dermot:

> By the time he was three Dermot had come to despise the sound of his own name because it called to mind his alter ego in Finea. He was tormented. It was Dermot Healy this and Dermot Healy that till he was sick of me. (5)

An alternative 'self' obviously means an alternative life story, if only it could be told. Consequently this constant displacement of the narrative leads away from the self and means a move outward toward the world and others in the world. Such self-effacement is discovered in the author's often monosyllabic replies in the rendered dialogue: yes, no, maybe. The desired absence of a dominating self points to a concomitant presence of an openness to an engagement with that world of others. There are glimpses of other narratives, other possible stories, scattered throughout the text. For instance, we are told of Healy's wife, and a son, and a sunlit walk by the banks of the Thames in London (72) and, save for another occasion when his wife is mentioned once again, they exit the memoir. Obviously on display is how purposefully selective the memoirist can be: characters and events can be weighted according to the requirements of the story being told. Literary critic Barry Sloan suggests that the prominent focal point of this memoir is the father-son relationship thus linking Healy's work with that of John McGahern and others (218). To be sure, the figure of the father in Irish writing generally is prominent and having a father who is a Garda would signal that authority—state and familial—is something palpable and yet, in truth, Healy's narrative is actually more concerned with the strong female characters of his mother and aunt. More to the point, though, is how the perspective of the memoir is turned outward rather than inward: the public and shared realm of family and society rather than the intimacies of the interior are what is recorded.

Without that cohering presence of the self, what the reader is left with are numerous moments, pen pictures, vignettes of Healy, his family and the hustle and bustle of small town Irish life in the 1950s and 60s. The author understands, though, that that lack of wholeness can be translated into all areas of his experience:

> Before sleep that night I remember a moment in time—myself, nineteen, maybe twenty, walking along in a blue trench coat, under trees, in the rain. I'm going somewhere. I try to imagine where I was going to but can't. No matter. I have great expectations. In the dark the leaves are glistening. I'm happy it seems. (247)

When this is accepted by the reader it is possible to begin to appreciate how narrative disruptions and breaks operate within the text. The disturbing jump from schooldays to dropping LSD in London is just one such example (92), emphasising as it does dislocation and displacement on numerous levels. Formally it is chronology which is being undermined in these moments and the kind of teleological knowledge of cause and effect that chronology necessarily imposes on narrative. One consequence of this is that *The Bend for Home* does not possess that element of fault finding that underpins a lot of Irish autobiographical writing of the recent past which is an expression of the cultural relationship between the past and the present as one of blame. In Healy's world things just are: he is not looking to explain or to blame. Again, it is a comment on an aesthetic that refuses to be compromised by the need to be socially engaged, to adhere to a condemnatory or revelatory social realism.

One very curious anecdote comes, appropriately enough, near the close of the narrative. The scene is once again London and a séance that Healy and his friends go to in order to please an acquaintance interested in astrology. The medium sees a vision of a boy astride a big horse with a policeman holding the reins. Healy's insistence that he was never on a horse in his life brings the séance to an unhappy and abrupt close. However, he goes on to say:

> Years later I told the story to Anne-Marie after we got married. One night she came racing into our bedroom in the Breifne with an old Healy family photograph album she'd been looking at. She placed it in front of me and pointed. There was a photograph of my father standing, with just the side of his head in view, by a horse in great wonderful winkers, Tom Keogh's horse in Finea, while I, about four years of age, sat astride it happily. (284–85)

As Yeats knew the figure of the medium is a way to begin to think about creativity and the art of literature. In one of his great late plays, *The Words Upon the Window-Pane*, he hovers between the poles of the natural and the supernatural, between the realms of enlightenment reason and all that cannot be, or will not be, known. Healy too, in this moment, embraces the limits of his knowledge and, indeed, his autobiographical venture. The question remains as to how well can he know himself, how well can he know his father or his mother or, indeed, anyone? The workings of fiction and art, of writing and the truth and the beauty that it tries to give expression to, cannot be broken down to observable pieces, cannot be known in any easy way.

The memoir comes to an end with the funeral of his mother. The story began with a birth: his own, though deflected and diverted, and finishes with a death. The shape of the story, then, follows that natural pattern of all beginnings and all endings. What has been explored—certainly in a roundabout way and not-so-obvious fashion—is the very idea of modern authorship. The famous catch cry of the 'death of the author' that heralds the advent of textual studies is here refashioned in a manner that signals the end of the story of the singular self as being the only story worth telling. Healy recognises that in Ireland anyway that story has been told enough and a new story ought to be told. His reorientation of his writerly perspective outwards and away from himself is an integral element in that process, acknowledging that the communal story can be articulated. As with writers such as James Joyce and John McGahern, Healy too desires for the ordinary and everyday world to speak for itself, for characters to speak for themselves. His last novel, *Long Time, No See* (2011) is perhaps the best expression of that desire in his own oeuvre. This memoir contains within it notes towards a novel that might not have been written but it certainly begins the processes of making that shift into the realm of other voices.

Works Cited

Benjamin, Walter. *The Arcades Project*. Trans. Howard Eiland and Kevin McLaughlin. Cambridge: The Belknap Press of Harvard University Press, 2002. Print.

———. *Illuminations, Essays and Reflections* Ed. with Introduction by Hannah Arendt. New York: Schocken Books, 1969/1985. Print.

Cleary, Joe. *Outrageous Fortune, Capital and Culture in modern Ireland*. Dublin: Field Day Publications, 2006. Print.

Craig, Patricia, "From the Rannafast Summer." *Irish Pages*. 3.1 (Spring/Summer 2005): 100–52. Print.

Garratt, Robert F. *Trauma and History in the Irish Novel: The Return of the Dead*. London: Palgrave Macmillan, 2011. Print.

Healy, Dermot. "I try to stay out of it and let the reader take over." Interview by Sean O'Hagan. *The Observer* 3 Apr. 2011. Web. 9 Jun. 2015.

———. *The Bend for Home: A Memoir*. Florida: Harcourt Brace & Company, 1996. Print.

Hughes, Eamonn. "'The Fact of Me-ness': Autobiographical Writing in the Revival Period." *New Perspectives on the Irish Literary Revival.* Spec. issue of *Irish University Review* 33.1 (2003): 28–45. Print.

McCourt, Frank. *Angela's Ashes: A Memoir.* New York: Scribner, 1996. Print.

McGahern, John. "The Local and the Universal." *Love of the World: Essays.* Ed. Stanley van der Ziel. London: Faber and Faber, 2009. Print.

O'Brien, George. "Home is Where the Art is." *The Irish Times* 28 Sept. 1996: B8. Print.

O'Connor, Frank. "Guests of the Nation." *The Oxford Book of Short Stories.* Ed. William Trevor. Oxford: Oxford University Press, 1989. Print.

Sloan, Barry. "'In My Father's House': Renegotiations of Boyhood in Life Writing by John McGahern, Ciaran O'Driscoll, Dermot Healy, and Ciaran Carson." *Éire-Ireland* 44:1 & 2 (Spring/Summer 2009): 218–241. Print.

Yeats, W. B. "The friends that have it I do wrong." *The Variorum Edition of the Poems of W. B. Yeats.* Ed. Peter Allt and Russell K. Alspach. London: Macmillan, 1989. Print.

Notes

1. See for instance the series edited by Oona Frawley, *Memory Ireland*, (Syracuse: Syracuse University Press).

2. See for instance John Banville's *The Sea* and *Ancient Light* or Anne Enright's *The Gathering*.

Dermot Healy: Local, National and International Drama
Michelle C. Paull

Dermot Healy's career as a playwright has, to date, not been well known. Despite his quietly lauded reputation as the author of such novels as *A Goat's Song* (1994) and *Long Time, No See* (2011), Healy's work as a dramatist is largely unheard of. Yet before his untimely death in 2014 he had written twelve original plays, as well as an adaptation of Lorca's *Blood Wedding*.[1] A few of these plays garnered national attention: *The Music Box* was staged at the Peacock Theatre Dublin in 1998, *Mr Staines* was produced by the internationally renowned Pan Pan Theatre Company and staged at the Samuel Beckett Theatre in Dublin in 1998, while *Men to the Right, Women to the Left* premiered at Dublin's Abbey Theatre in 2001 and was later broadcast on RTÉ Radio 1 in 2002. Most of Healy's theatre, however, has been built on a quieter, less public process of collaborative work with local groups and smaller, more enclosed communities, and especially with people not used to having their lives the subject of representation on stage. Healy's drama thus explores in a theatrical context the real problems of particular demographics or under-represented social groups—for example, prisoners in *Serious* (2005) or teenagers in *A Night at the Disco* (2006). Even the Abbey production of *Men to the Right, Women to the Left* was itself devised as part of the "Season of Creativity in Older Age" project.[2] In all these plays there is a sense of Healy acting as a guiding voice: an enabler of disenfranchised communities and the conduit speaker for unheard voices whose life experiences are rarely presented on stage. Two of his plays considered here—*Here, and There, and Going to America* (1985) and *Metagama* (2004)—are typical of Healy's theatrical style, and demonstrate how his drama can be seen as part of his re-working of theatrical traditions, just as his novels work to challenge literary expectations and conventions.

Alongside the marginalised voices, Healy regularly returns to those figures who are silenced through absence, namely the exile and the migrant. *Here, and There, and Going to America*, his very first play, focuses on the lives of two young brothers ultimately determined to get to the United States. The men leave Sligo for London in the 1980s on the pretext of having jobs waiting for them in the building trade. In fact, they have no work lined up in London, but use the promise of jobs as a way of getting the Sligo Dole Office to pay their fares to the UK. On arrival they find no support from the British version of the same office, and have to sleep rough in Victoria Station until they are eventually placed in a hostel. Unemployed and without money, they drift into a life of squatting and petty crime, a depressingly familiar outcome of the quest for the American Dream.

But Healy's work is not a simple naturalistic recreation of the miserable life endured by some Irish immigrants in London. For Healy a story is never just a story. Every community depicted speaks not only of the people themselves but also suggests a wider national and international context. The fractured love affair of Catherine and Jack in *A Goat's Song*, for example, frames the political tension between Dublin, Belfast and London within a more personal world. Similarly, though Healy's plays often represent a particular local or social group, the issues they raise resonate well beyond the focus audience or the group that co-developed the work.

Metagama (2004), for example, which is set in the Scottish Hebrides, takes as its main theme the story of local crofters forced out of their environment by landowners and by changing economic requirements, when the mass production of kelp undermined the local industry. Although the story does explore the history of the area, and outlines the specific problems of local issues, it also resonates beyond the specific nature of the Hebrides. The particular problems of the area are carefully documented: the forced evacuations; the starvation due to famine and unemployment; the stoic decision to try and stay on the islands (despite the betrayal of promises made at national political level by the then Prime Minister, David Lloyd George). The play also details the specific pressures that the crofters and their families were subject to, in targeted attempts to force them to leave—including refusing to repair their houses, leaving the land unfertilized and unable to grow crops, and breaking up the crofts to become "sheep walks." But although the local experience is fully addressed, *Metagama* also holds this up as being typical of a national and international experience of displacement and emigration—a resonant topic for the Irish in particular.

Metagama is theatrically styled in a classically modernist way, rather akin to the minimalism and abstraction of a Beckett piece. The set is simply described as "*Open space.*" A mound of kelp and peat is present, but aside from a boat and some timber there is nothing to give a detailed local or national context. The locale will, however, be evoked mostly by its sounds, not by its images. The stage directions specify "*an intermittent sound of the sea*" during the scenes on Lewis. This eerie aural signifier is used in the play as a kind of chorus in sound, to add moments of ironic commentary. When the blatant contradictions of the Hebridean landowners are most plain—and their offers to help the crofters most deceptive—the sound of the wind appears like a warning banshee wail for the audience, suggesting a distorted logic or a glaring falsehood.

The heavy and physically challenging nature of the work being represented is also carefully physicalized. The stage directions insist that incessant stage movement be maintained throughout the scene: the men and women on stage are required to fork piles of seaweed to the front of the stage "*to form a ridge*," and "*they do not stop moving over and back.*" The relentless back-breaking work of the crofters is thus established, and a sense of the relentless rhythm and pulse of the island is characterised through their working practices; it is clear to see how the work of the people is their life, and vice versa. This physicalizing of thematic narrative links Healy's work closely with contemporary physical theatre practices, such as Philippe Gaulier and Jacques Lecoq.

On stage the physical bodies of the actors playing Healy's characters form a united entity as they work together, but their minds are rather more divided. The combined history of the island—part Gaelic, part English, part Scottish—is demonstrated through sound and often through speech. The songs sung by the workers are recited in a combination of Gaelic and English. However, as might be expected for a writer whose primary medium has been narrative prose, the conflict between the people of Lewis and the landowners really takes place at the level of language. This variation between languages and the loaded inflections between the two is reminiscent of Brian Friel's complex negotiation between the status and hierarchy of each language in *Translations* (1980).

Healy shows elements of Friel's exploration of the hierarchies of language through his theatrical movement between Gaelic and English in *Metagama*. A clannish expression of a shared community is expressed in Gaelic, whereas English is reserved to describe the kind of work the islanders are forced to carry out to survive economically. When the workers sing shared songs, the repeated refrain, sung in Gaelic, is "Lifting the kelp, turning the kelp," emphasising the repetition and routine of their working lives. However, the description of the crofters' identity, perceived through their work, is expressed in English: "My hair is made of kelp / My legs are kelp / My head is kelp." The bodily identification of the kelp and its resonance—"My arms are kelp / my blood is kelp / my heart is kelp"—figures the heart and soul of the crofter in Gaelic as more greatly connected to their role on the land.

This separation between the work of the crofters in Lewis, those connected to the land through their jobs, and those landlords who oversee the supply of goods made by the crofters to the metropolitan centre, is clearly posited again through physical means. The play draws a parallel between the women covered in the black grime of the seaweed of their geographical area and the women who use the soap produced from the seaweed outside their space: "In London the ladies are cleaning their faces on the weed that we collect." Connections between those wealthy enough to buy the soap and those strong enough to farm it are clearly emphasised; the remote Highland islands may seem far away but their link to the metropolitan economy is direct and defined. The workers are at once central to, and detached from, the results of their day's work:

> AENGUS: So the rest of the country can wash themselves and preen themselves, we must be covered in dirt.
> MISS MacDONALD: And the thing is I never once saw the soap that comes from the kelp.
> MISS TULLO: Nor did I.

The crofters and the workers serve only to provide the goods, not to benefit from them personally. But there is a curious complication in that the workforce see the use or ownership of the material goods they produce as being outside of remit of their culture. The soap they produce is only for outsiders or for those natives who want to leave the community. For the workers, then, soap is a marker of otherness and exile:

> MISS MacDONALD: You think I will see that soap someday?
> MacKENZIE: I do, if you were meant to see the soap then you can take the boat.
> MacTAVISH: To Canada.
> MISS MacDONALD: And I can give myself a good rinse there.
> MISS TULLO: A good rinse.
> MacKENZIE: You can if you want, with the rest of them who left—the incessant complainers.

The stoicism and pride in the workers' ability to do without the fripperies of the landowning classes, associating the use of the goods they make with a kind of weakness akin to leaving the country, is the dominant rhetorical overtone here. MacKenzie sees those who complain about the lack of access to the goods they create as being similar to those who bemoan the state of the land and environment they live in. For MacKenzie, these are the islanders who will betray their land by moving abroad to Canada:

> MISS MacDONALD: Do you not think it strange that soap rhymes with kelp?
> AENGUS: You're wrong there Blondie, kelp rhymes with help.
> MISS TULLO: And soap rhymes with boat.
> AENGUS: And that's the story.

Aengus's comments imply his recognition of the economic situation of the islanders. The kelp workers need financial assistance and investment in the land in order to survive, but the only real alternative to their current way of life is to emigrate. Even the stage directions point to the doomed nature of their current lifestyle: in an eerie, Beckettian-style stage direction Healy notes: "*This is tight concentrated work. Done neatly, like making a grave.*"

However, it is the combination of Gaelic and English in the dialogue that demonstrates the full complexity of the divided national identity of each figure (and again the link to Brian Friel's use of language in *Translations* is clear). English, when spoken exclusively, is associated with the landowner and not the worker. The interloper and the outsider do not understand the language of the people in either a literal or metaphorical sense. Throughout the play, the landowning class is depicted as being curiously uninterested in the future of the land they own. For instance, Murdo, one of the crofters, is caught attempting to take home a bag of kelp; when challenged, he explains that he is taking it to use as fertilizer on his potatoes, which will help to feed his children. Murdo speaks in Gaelic, showing his affinity with the local environment and the land that he works. The landowner replies exclusively in English, and is unaffected by the crofter's concern for the future of the land:

> SIR: The kelp is for incineration. It shall not manure the land. Every scrap of seaweed shall find its way into the kiln. You hear?
> MURDO: How am I to maintain the earth?
> SIR: The earth is not my concern.
> MURDO: But it is mine.

The landowner, concerned only with immediate profit and return, does not think of maintaining the croft for future generations. His overriding consideration is that the land should yield maximum profit for him now, not for Murdo's children or for farming to continue in the future. While Murdo's holistic understanding of the land is expressed in Gaelic, his uncompromising insight into the consequences of the landowner's behaviour is conveyed in English, the language of his oppressor:

> MURDO: That kelp along with the machair has gone to

manure the earth for centuries. You are trying to kill off the earth and kill off my family.

Healy's characters are not three-dimensional or psychologically-realized figures, as they are in his novels. But that is not their purpose on stage. Instead, they function to demonstrate an attitude, a point of view and a feeling—not as stereotypes, but as an expression of a human and emotional response to an issue. We do not have insight into Murdo's family, nor do we meet the children that he needs to feed by taking the kelp. It is as if the playwright feels that approaching the issue of exploitation and land clearance through a family tale would be too straightforward, even bathetic. What Healy does instead is allow the audience to see the consequences of each action in an emotional—but unsentimental—manner. There is a reserve in Healy's representation of character, a theatrical detachment which has more in common with Brecht's attempts to maintain his audience as engaged observers and critics, rather than to present the audience with an emotional encounter. Like Brecht, Healy does not seek to encourage *faux* emotion in his audience; they are not asked to feel sorry for individuals but instead to direct their distress towards questions about the social, political and national choices which create these problems.

"The Figure in Robes," for example, declaims that "the kelp worker is a burden on the state" and explains that while to date their rents have been paid in a combination of cash and produce, in future all rent is to be "paid in hard cash. [*Pause.*] This will spur on emigration." Rather than tell the story of one family's experience of this kind of policy, Healy's play presents the statement of policy, and allows the audience to imagine the consequence of such a ruthless approach themselves. How will a family who have no money—and who have been used to paying their rent in kind—be able to transform themselves overnight into tenants who pay in cash alone? Thus the stage "*Pause*" allows a grim Pinteresque reflection on exactly what that will mean for the people involved. The pause contains all the misery, starvation and trauma that the audience knows the family will experience before the next clause in the sentence will be enacted—the "spur" to emigration will be certain death if they do not go.

Similarly, the depiction of life in the croft—unsupported economically and rife with disease—is alluded to rather than fully demonstrated. Although the harsh living conditions are ardently denied by The Figure in Robes, they are in the process made manifest: "These black houses reared healthy men. Talk of illness is mere lies . . . The Hebrideans are lying on their backs waiting for you to feed them. I think the people should be left to work out their own salvation."

The history of the Hebridean croft—the long exploitation of the workers, the clearance of the crofts to make way for sheep walks that would provide a cheap source of raising meat for the capital, the potato blight, the enforced displacement and pressure to emigrate— is carefully depicted in such a way that the story of the Hebrides as a lived environment remains paramount. The play is not simply a family story or a personal history; instead, it is an account of a landscape, where the place itself is embodied and becomes the focus of the drama.

This kind of detached storytelling is underpinned by Healy's use of stage form in a self-conscious and often cinematic manner. *Metagama* intercuts different styles of communication to present the story of what happened to the islands in ironic terms, which requires the audience to critique unreflective assumptions about place and people. The sense of loss and damage to the community as a result of the emigration policy promoted in The Figure in Robes' speech, for example, is also dramatised on stage without language, via a series of poetic stage images. After The Figure's callous pronouncement—"I suggest that a third of the population should be moved abroad . . . Immediately . . . To the new lands of Canada"—the spotlight goes out on him and the sound of nearby sheep is transformed into a "*nightmarish sound*"—a ship's horn which then segues into an "*almighty*" sound of wind and rain. In a scene where "*no human is on stage*," the cinematic stage direction states that the lighting should "*pan*" across the stage, thereby revealing a series of connections between an Island life that has been lost and other displaced communities. This shared heritage is evoked by the use of emblematic clothes hanging on a washing line, which are described as "*blowing*" in the wind. The clothes depicted include:

> *a complete soldier's army outfit, with rifle; a fisherman's outfit from the eighteenth century; a kelp worker's clothes; a large wet cloth of tweed . . . a landlord's silks;* MISS MacDONALD's *dark religious church-going clothes; a child's nineteenth-century long trousers outfit, complete with cap; a Viking outfit, with headgear; a Red Indian's headdress; and, lastly, a vicar's outfit with collar.*

These visual signifiers link together the contemporary narratives of emigration of the current Hebrideans with the historical migration and colonisation of other oppressors and the oppressed, from the Vikings to the Red Indians. The play thus connects historical emigration over multiple continents and extended time periods. This is not an attempt to flatten the experience of emigration into a deeply conservative narrative of colonisation as a never-ending and unavoidable part of an international condition of change and development. Instead, the play casts a regretful eye over such a lamentable tradition of repetition and cultural exchange—Red Indians for Caucasians; kelp workers for the sheep and fishing industry—and asks the audience a pointed question: how much longer can this continue? The inclusion of clerical clothing suggests the religious complicity in the justification of land domination, and questions the contradiction between spiritual faith and the exploitation of indigenous peoples. There is no commentary or dialogue as these clothes simply blow in the wind on stage; instead, the clothes are almost inhabited by the wind and become ghost-people, creations of the air. That the time of these people and their heritage is over is also suggested through the gradually dying wind. This mystical moment of connection between the colonised past and an uncertain present is brought back to reality as the "*wind eases, the clothes go still, the wind turns into a version of mouth-music.*" For a brief moment the play has linked national and international, present and historical colonisation, and is now transformed back into a more naturalistic setting.

While the wind symbolises the independence of the Hebridean people, the *Metagama*—the name of the ocean liner on which hundreds of islanders migrated to North America in 1923—

becomes a symbol of their betrayal. The journey on the liner marks the end of the islanders' long struggle to gain their own land after years of rescinded promises. In the play, Lord Leverhulme arrives in Lewis after World War I offering the islanders a new industry in fishing. But the islanders are more anxious to take ownership of their land, which is the one consistent request they have made throughout their history:

> JOHN CAMPBELL: What of the promises made to us that every man upon his return from war would be given a new croft with a number of acres?
> LORD LEVERHULME: I am promising you something greater than that. Forget the cursed croft. It is an obsession that will keep you impoverished [. . .].
> JOHN CAMPBELL: [. . .] But when will we be given the croft and the land that we were promised?
> LORD LEVERHULME: [*To himself*] Dear God. This constant refrain would drive one senseless.

The desire of the people to own the land they work had been a regular refrain as Leverhulme's character suggests. The play makes it clear that the one desire that the locals have is the one desire that will never be granted, since it is not understood as being reasonable or relevant to those who live outside the area. In the years immediately after the war it is clear that those islanders who became soldiers in World War I, on the understanding that their wish for independence would be granted at the end of the conflict, realise that they have been betrayed by a landowner's vacuous promise:

> AENGUS: We came back, that's what's wrong with us. We should be "Presumed Dead." Or "Missing." Or "Lost in Action." Not in the Great War but in the Great Lie. On all of the other islands the soldiers are getting the land they were promised. But here we are getting nothing . . .

The experience of the crofters clearly mirrors that of the Irish soldiers who fought in World War I who believed that their desire for independence would be granted as a result of supporting the British in the conflict. Like the Irish, the people of the islands of Lewis and Harris were betrayed by those in charge. Whereas in Ireland, however, the consequence of this betrayal was the growth of an even stronger sense of national identity and determination to be an independent nation, for the crofters there is simply a complete destruction of who they are. As Aengus says, "We are ghosts now. Ghosts only. We are not clan. Nor family." The empty clothes on the washing line are even more significant now, suggesting the sense of an entire legacy being lost.

Once again it is the surreal quality in Healy's drama that evokes the pain and loss of the decision to make the voyage to Canada. The islanders are gradually starved out of their homes, partly because of the famine of 1921–22, and partly because there is no work and no prospect of owning their land, despite the promises of Lloyd George. The children of the islanders are shown films in schools, featuring attractive scenes of the fertile Canadian landscape:

> AENGUS: The lush fields. Apples and oranges. Apples and oranges.
> MacKENZIE: Your mouth would water at the thought of Canada.
> AENGUS: We learned more of that country than we did of our own history.

The returning soldiers faced prosecution for trying to re-inhabit or "raiding" their own farms after the war, and even the most loyal islanders are finally driven to book their passage to Canada. One short scene, again expressed through sound rather than language or plot, characterises the reaction to this final decision to leave their native land. When the islanders are examined to be passed as fit for the journey, Murdo, a doctor, asks Aengus to "Say Ahh." Aengus replies with a sound that *"rises into a great long echo of pain that is amplified throughout the theatre."* This howl of pain expresses the anguish of those leaving their homeland far more eloquently than any scene of fond farewells. The evocation of loss is underpinned by the gradual loss of the sound that has accompanied the play's aural landscape so far. As the boat moves further away from the Hebrides and closer to Canada, "*the last sound to fade is the sound of the sea.*" As the next scene opens with the islanders having arrived in Canada, the first stage direction is simply "*Silence. No sound of sea.*" This sense of an alien environment is evoked by silence, not as in Pinter or Beckett but through the disjuncture between rhythm and lyricism, and the breakdown of comforting harmony; it is when the music of the sea stops that the sense of loss is most acute.

What the migrants do not yet realise is that their new life in Canada will be much the same poverty as their old life in the croft. "When they were showing us the slides they didn't mention the snow," says Murdo. The cattle that they buy are caught up in storms and killed by lightning, and they still have to repay their passage into the country. The migrants have thus been sold into a kind of indentured servitude. They do not belong in this new country, nor can they let go of the old. As the Doctor remarks, when he translates Miss Tullo's views of her new life to the interviewer from The Emigration Board:

> MURDO: When she was in Lewis her thoughts were always abroad, away from the Great War, and now that she's abroad she is home in Lewis. She brought Lewis here, so she is home.

The Irish diaspora of the mind maintains a sense of place wherever the migrant individual is geographically located. But here the sound of the sea dramatises the islanders' complete dislocation. As Aengus says to his fellow workers, "What is it you can't hear? [. . .] The sea. That is what we can't hear. And we lived with it all our lives." The sea, the wind and the land are all integral to our understanding of what has been lost; not only people but a whole place.

In *Men to the Right, Women to the Left* (2001), it is once again clear that Healy's work has a much wider reach than the particular context of its own creation. Written in collaboration with The Clones Drama Group as part of an outreach and education programme, the play might seem to address a very specific local area and circumstance. However, a distinct change in tone and style from the previous play is immediately evident. In contrast to the large ensemble cast of *Metagama*, *Men to the Right, Women to the Left* features only three characters, a man and two women (one younger, one older). Unnamed, the three figures converse with one another about people and incidents they know, in a manner which will later become familiar to audiences of Enda Walsh's plays—in Walsh's *Ballyturk*, for example, when two unnamed men are shut in a room together, and manically theatricalise the stories of people they appear to know (but whom the audience are never sure actually exist).[3] Healy introduces a similarly inexplicable context in his play. The location is unnamed, the audience looks at a geographically-sparse environment, as minimalist as any Beckettian set. Three chairs are fixed onstage beside one another. Next to the chair stage right is *"an old pram."* The stage directions indicate the potential significance of the pram, since "cries mimed by W1" [Woman 1] will emanate from within. Otherwise, only a *"small table and small bed"* feature onstage, alongside a more curious prop—*"A pulley rope dangling from above."* The Pinteresque sense of menace and inexplicable anxiety about the presence of such an unusual object is palpable. But the only sense of connection with Ireland is suggested by the presence of "*The Irish Press newspaper*" in the pocket of the middle-aged man, and his working-class background is suggested by a *"cap"* in his other pocket.

This unidentified place contains only one bed shared between three people. The play gives no local, national or international location. Instead, only the sound of a train offers a hint of the approximate time or place, but even that is subject to question. Instead of the comforting regularity of a train running to a known timetable, the sound of it only provokes doubt. The play opens in darkness, with only the sound of the train and two voices:

> *In the far distance the roar of the train.*
> *Darkness on stage.*
> MAN: Ah Christ. Is that the . . . [*Searching*] . . . the Ballyhaise?
> W2: No.
> MAN: Well blast it. Hold it—Clones, hah?

> W2: No.
> MAN: Well, pray tell?
> W2: That'd be the 6.15 ta Dundalk I'd warrant.
> MAN: Is that her? Be god!
>   [*Lights up.*]

Although this does give a national location, and situates the play very clearly in an Irish context, an eerie resonance is also evoked by the darkness and the sound of the train. There is a kind of otherworldly-quality about it all, a mystery to be solved. The appeal to Christ suggests not only a figure of speech, but also a strong need for spiritual support. This atmosphere of disturbance and distortion is maintained throughout by the recurring sound of the train. The older woman, W2, explains to the audience that "for my sins, I was born in a railway house." Again, the colloquial phrase sounds inoffensive enough, but the connection established between the railway and "sins" becomes increasingly resonant when we discover that the trains are memories associated with World War II. W2, it transpires, operated the gates on a level crossing for the trains to pass through, and the dialogue conjures up a network of national journeys connecting towns all over Ireland:

> W1: When you heard the code of rings you knew the train was due from Clones.
> MAN: [*Finger up, knowing a thing or two.*] Or Newbliss.
> W2: Maybe Cavan.
> W1: Or Drogheda.
> MAN: Or – [*losing the knowledge*] – where was it . . .
> W1: Belcoo?
> MAN: The very place, you're right.

The train continues to be a troubling symbol throughout the play, uniting various disjointed narratives as the play shifts back and forth in time (all three characters play themselves as younger and older versions, alongside the many other characters that they tell stories of). W2 recounts her past life as a nurse, travelling to Belfast and all over Ireland as part of her job. The train also functions as a link between North and South as well as between Ireland and England, as W1 travels to Birmingham to work in hospitals there. Again, there is a resonant quality about her accounts of what she witnessed, which seem to echo beyond the specifics of the role itself:

> W2: I heard things as a nurse in Belfast and later in Birmingham that would turn your head. What the doctors told you would sicken you. The things that happen to a body are beyond belief.

The suffering of the human body thus becomes integrated into the narrative, and the connections between the story of a rural Irish family and the wider context of international conflict is increasingly suggestive. The play introduces various allusions to World War II as a background context for W2's memories of her childhood. W2 gives an account of herself as the eldest of seven children, who became the substitute mother to her siblings during the war. She struggles to feed them all in a time of rationing, and describes them as voracious eaters incessantly demanding more. Her only means of control was to threaten them with the prospect of war: "Hitler'll blow you all to hell in your beds." Thus the link between domestic abuse and international conflict is firmly established:

> W2: And all the time I couldn't think with thinking we would be bombed. Every time ya turned on the radio it was going on. I used to terrify myself. I'd lie down in the bed at night and listen. And hear her crying. And downstairs my father telling my mother what would happen. Oh God!!

Domestic events in the household and in the local community form a perverse allegory of what was happening in the wider world. W2 tells a story about being unable to make her pot fit inside her new oven. So she takes the pot to the blacksmith "and had the legs took clean off." This is followed by the story of W2's abuse and beatings both at school and at home. However, the structure of Healy's play is such that these memories are interspersed with the sound of the train, which is already associated with feelings of "sin":

> W1: She [W2] was mocked, laughed at, kept in at break and lunchtime, made to pull briars and nettles with her bare hands for getting something wrong. [. . .]
> W2: Then back to the house and drop potatoes into drills that seemed to go on forever and ever.
> W1: And we reported nothing.
> W2: No.
>> W2 *sits.*
>> *Distant train.*
>> MAN *leans his elbow onto the pram.*
>> *The women kneel sideways to their chairs.*
> W1: Bless me, Father…
> W2: For I have sinned.
> W1: [*Quietly.*] It has been a week since my last confession.
> MAN: Speak up!
> W1: I nearly died of shame.

The significance of trains, ovens and sin in the context of World War II is not difficult to imagine, but Healy draws attention to these dark events without ever directly addressing the subject of the Holocaust. Moreover, the worlds of the living and the dead are also connected through the dramaturgical metaphor of dance. This dance of life and death operates in tandem as W2 and the Man offer a prayer together:

> W2: Hail Holy Queen . . .
> MAN: Mother of Mercy . . .
> W2: Hail our light, our sweetness, and our hope . . .
>> [MAN *rises, pulls the pulley.*
>> *Mother throws open the gates. Light drops, train bells in the far distance. The train goes by, light rises, hummed music begins.*]
> W1: And it was . . .
> MAN: Men to the right . . .

> W2: Women to the left . . .
> W1: And off you'd go.
> [*Pause.*
> *Humming continues from all three as they rise to dance.*]

This moment of the play provides both the play's title and its central theme: the rural idyll of Ireland, the friendly local dances and the relatively harmless segregation of the males and females on the dance floor, set against a more insidious kind of separation in the wider world.

Dermot Healy's drama is evocative, lyrical and disturbing. Working with specialist groups on local subjects does not limit his theatrical reach but instead widens the dramatic resonance. By allowing the local to speak for the national, his work points to the underlying connections between personal stories and international events. While his narrative fiction celebrates the evocative nature of language, his drama explores the visceral impact of that which cannot be captured on paper, using sound, visual imagery and music to offer the audience the feeling of an experience rather than simply present a rational or intellectual explanation of things. Healy's theatre is above all a theatre of the physical and, as such, his work deserves to remain at the centre of contemporary stage practice and design.

Notes

1. All thirteen of Healy's plays are due to be published as *Dermot Healy: The Collected Plays*, ed. Keith Hopper & Neil Murphy (Victoria/Dublin/London: Dalkey Archive Press, 2016). All references to the plays in this present essay are taken from the unpublished and unedited typescript versions provided by the editors.

2. *Men to the Right, Women to the Left* was first published in *Stories of the Drumlins: Men to the Right, Women to the Left—a Collaborative Theatre Project Developed by the Abbey Theatre, Positive Age and the Health Service Executive*, ed. Sharon Murphy (Dublin: Outreach/Education Department of The Abbey Theatre, 2005).

3. Enda Walsh, *Ballyturk* (Nick Hern: London, 2014).

Banished Misfortunes?:
Dermot Healy and the Rise of the Posthuman
Michael Cronin

For the fiftieth birthday of *The New York Review of Books* the well-known British historian Timothy Garton Ash was invited to comment on what he felt had fundamentally changed in the world since the *NYRB* first appeared on the magazine racks in 1963. Seeing the magazine as a "light-house at the centre of the Western world" he wanted to show "how the world has changed under its steady illumination" (Garton Ash 51). "Human rights" and a concern with same are first picked out under the sweeping beam of retrospection. He then sheds light on the rise and staggered fall of the US as "hyperpower," the increased prominence of the Arab world, the inexorable ascension of China and the explosion of "digital opportunity," the binary revolution that leaves expression gloriously unbound. Not a word, however, about the Stern Review on the Economics of Climate Change. Not a line about the Intergovernmental Panel on Climate Change. No melting ice. No rising sea levels. No acidic oceans. No species loss. For Garton Ash, all is gloriously quiet on the weather front. Our duty in this changing world, if we have one, is to "remain true to the core values of a modernized Enlightenment liberalism, Western in origin but universal in aspiration" (53).

In thinking about Dermot Healy and the importance of his work for the coming times, my argument will be that the "modernized Enlightenment liberalism" Garton Ash has in mind is no longer effective or persuasive as a means of liberation because it is based on a set of assumptions around what it is to be human which can no longer remain uncontested. In the first half of this essay, I will sketch out the background to new thinking around the notion of the human. In the second half, I will explore Dermot Healy's penultimate poetry collection, *A Fool's Errand* (2010), in terms of a move towards what has been dubbed, by Rosi Braidotti, as the "posthuman."

Central to my argument is an idea that has been borrowed from the Nobel Prize-winning chemist Paul Crutzen and his collaborator, a marine scientist specialist, Eugene F. Stoermer, namely, the idea of the "Anthropocene." Crutzen's contention is that in the last three centuries, the effects of humans on the global environment have escalated dramatically. As a result, anthropogenic emissions of carbon dioxide are very likely to significantly affect the climate for millennia to come, so "[i]t seems appropriate to assign the term 'Anthropocene' to the present, [. . .] human-dominated, geological epoch, supplementing the Holocene—the warm period of the past 10-12 millennia" (Crutzen 23).

The Anthropocene and the Posthuman

The Anthropocene is traced back to the latter half of the eighteenth century when analyses of air trapped in polar ice showed the beginning of growing global concentrations of carbon dioxide and methane. The principal consequence of anthropogenic climate change is that humans have now become capable of affecting all life on the planet. As Dipesh Chakrabarty pointed out in 2009, when the collective actions of humans fundamentally alter the conditions of life on the planet they move from being biological agents to becoming a geological force in their own right, "For it is no longer a question of man having an interactive relationship with nature. This humans have always had, or at least that is how man has been imagined in a large part of what is generally called the Western tradition. Now it is being claimed that humans are a force of nature in a geological sense" (Chakrabarty 207). With this shift in status comes a shift in perspective. It is no longer tenable to conceive of humans as a species apart. We must think again about what it is to be human and if we think again about what it is to be human then we must inevitably think again about one of the activities that humans engage in, namely, poetry.

Joseph Stalin, no friend it is fair to say of humanists or poets, in his *Dialectical and Historical Materialism* (1938) claimed that "changes in geographical environment of any importance require millions of years, whereas a few hundred or a couple of thousand years are enough for even very important changes in the system of human society." Stalin's distinction between natural history and human history had a certain credibility as long as the human remained in Fernand Braudel's words, a "prisoner of climate" rather than a maker of it (qtd. in Crosby 1185). In the era of the Anthropocene, however, the distinction no longer holds. Once humans move from being biological agents to geological agents, dominating and determining the survival of many other species on the planet, they then become not so much subject to nature as a condition of nature itself. This dominance comes, of course, at the cost of the very survival of humanity. For this reason, trying to conceive of a sustainable future for humans means the convergence of human history with the history of life on the planet to produce a form of "deep history." Implicit in the notion of deep history is that thinking about a variety of historical phenomena does not involve an excessive privileging of the printed word. Historical evidence can take other forms. Daniel Lord Smail in *On Deep History and the Brain* (2008) points out that the ancient world is unimaginable without archaeological evidence and this also holds for what we now know about the Middle Ages. He adds:

> So what does it matter that the evidence for the deep past comes not from written documents but from the other things that teach—from artefacts, fossils, vegetable remains, phonemes, and various forms of modern DNA? Like written documents, all these traces encode information about the past. Like written documents, they resist an easy reading and must be interpreted with care. (Smail 6)

The biologist Edward O. Wilson in *The Future of Life* (2002) sees such long-range historical thinking as crucial to curbing humanity, as "planetary killer, concerned only with its short-term survival" (202). Wilson argues it is only when humans begin to think of themselves as species that they can begin to take the longer view not only as an important exercise in critical self-understanding but as a means of securing the future. For Rosi Braidotti this move towards species awareness is a necessary step towards post-anthropocentric identity. Critical at the present moment is the de-centring of *anthropos*, "the representative of a hierarchical, hegemonic and generally violent species whose centrality is now challenged by a combination of scientific advances and global economic concerns" (Braidotti 65). Out of this vision comes a notion of relationality and ontological equality that does not privilege one life form over another.

The theorist Louis Borges once grouped animals into three classes: those we watch television with, those we eat, and those we are scared of (Braidotti 68). Another more psychoanalytically inflected way of classifying these relationships might be the Oedipal (you and me on the same sofa), the instrumental (you will end up being eaten) and the fantasmatic (how exotic, sleek, dangerous you are). In Braidotti's view a posthuman ethics implies an end to forms of "anthropolatry" which not only obscure emergent forms of species thinking but consign all other species to dangerous, destructive and ecologically untenable forms of subordination. "Becoming animal" in Hiberno-English for Braidotti is a way of realising the irretrievably embodied, material nature of our existence on a planet that we share with innumerable other species that we continue to destroy in vast numbers. The current rate in the loss of species diversity alone is similar in intensity to the event that sixty-five million years ago wiped out the dinosaurs.

The backdrop to the end of anthropolatry is the rise of geocentrism, the notion that the planetary must now be figured into all our thinking. This includes everything from the Great Coral Reef and the Gulf Stream to the future of the honey bee. In Braidotti's interpretation of Spinoza's monism, she emphasises not so much the tyranny of oneness or the narcissism of separateness that is often associated with monism as the freedom of relationality, "[monism] implies the open-ended, inter-relational, multi-sexed and trans-species flows of becoming through interactions with multiple others" (89). Being "matter-realist" to use her term is to take seriously our multiple connections to natural and material worlds. If we conceive of the notion of subjectivity to include the non-human then the task for critical thinking is, as Braidotti herself admits, "momentous." This would involve visualising the subject as "a transversal entity encompassing the human, our genetic neighbours the animals and the earth as a whole, and to do so within an understandable language" (Braidotti 82).

Deep Time

Visualising what such a subject might look like is part of the creative labour of a poet that was continually attuned to the music of what might be. In section six entitled "The Wild Goose Chase" in *A Fool's Errand*, Dermot Healy speaks of the old friendship between the "beginning" and the "end." He sees a faultline in that friendship, however, in the imperiousness of the present, and the dead lines of the short-term:

> There is a rule—the time you live, in the long run,
> is the best. Forget the rest, the debt is paid. Anything else
>
> is sentiment. We invent anew an old arrogance.
> So the man in the 7th century took the man in the 3rd for
>   a fool.
> The woman in the 12th had little time for the handmaid in
>   the back
>
> row at school. The 21st
> sees the rest as cursed.
>
> And the scientist in the 30th
> will see us as the worst. (Healy 61)

Healy takes the "old arrogance" of presentism and exposes it to the long view of the centuries. The irony is that the rule which may provide subjective comfort—the time you live in is the best—has no particular validity in "in the long run." However, there is a deeper logic at work in these lines which goes beyond a kind of chronological relativism—a notion that each age has its own form of internal coherence and is no better or worse than any other—to suggest a different relationship to time itself as opposed to a different relationship to different times. Healy's scientist a thousand years hence looks back at our century in despair. What the scientist finds particularly distressing, we may never know, but we find a hint in the dismissive certainty of "Forget the rest, the debt is paid." The problem in the age of the anthropocene is that forgetfulness is not an option. The accession to the status of geological agent means a recognition that the ecological debts have not been paid and that remembering rather than forgetting the "rest"—what was previously marginalised or left over—is essential to any notion of recovery, restitution or sustainability. The "old arrogance" of amnesia, of viewing the world as an endlessly repeated tabula rasa ready for the inscriptions of the exploitative, leads to the fraught terminus of the "worst" of centuries. Healy's move, however, to pull away from the fragmented intransigence of the present to the long now of millennia is embedded in a broader vision of time that informs the collection throughout.

In section three, "The Beaten Sound," the poet looks at other journeys etched out in the landscape. Nothing is immovable in what he sees:

> Far from home
> the freed fossils
>
> of coral
> tumbled
>
> in the rising tides, then later travelled with the ice
> up the mountains and on through the valleys
> till they reached the heights
>
> where they sat forgotten in old forts
> to look back through to the gap
> at the distant equator
>
> where their ancient parents
> are laid out

> in spiralling tropics
> around the Serpent's Rock. (Healy 30)

This is a world that is not frozen but fluid. The verbs are active, verbs of movement and becoming, "tumbled," "travelled," "reached." This movement too is part of the purview of the "scientist" of "The Wild Goose Chase" section but with a dramatic expansion in the range of time surveyed. The time of Healy's fossils is part of the "deep history" of Chakrabarty or Smail. It is a time that becomes possible or conceivable from the end of the eighteenth century with advances in palaeontology, geology and biology. The age of the earth formerly bounded by the speculations of biblical scholars and situated within the comfortable timeframe of a few millennia suddenly balloons into the runaway digits of "deep time" (Gould 2). The philosopher Michel Serres describes this advent of time in the science of the nineteenth century:

> Au début de leurs recherches respectives, Lamarck et Darwin se trouvèrent face à une discipline que dominait la question de la classification des vivants. Leur geste commun consista, dès lors, à faire ruisseler le long de ses classes, genres ou règnes une cataracte temporelle telle qu'elle permit, par exemple, à l'espèce de passer de passer d'un concept abstrait ou arbitraire à une existence concrète et vivante. (Serres, Legros, Ortoli 304) *[In their early research, both Lamarck and Darwin had to deal with a discipline that was dominated by the question of the classification of living beings. What they both did, in effect, was to make time flow like a cataract through these classes, genera and kingdoms, so that the concept of species from being abstract and arbitrary became something concrete and alive.]*

From the static typologies of a Linnaeus and the mania for collection and classification that will hold the eighteenth century in its thrall, Lamarck, Lyell and Darwin are going to infuse the universe with a sense of history, a kind of narrative friendship between the "beginning" and the probable "end" that seeks to deepen and problematise conventional understandings of time and duration. In Healy's vision, it is not only the barnacle geese that are on the move but the whole of the natural world. The cataract of time unleashed by Lamarck and Darwin is captured by these freed fossils of coral "tumbled" in the rising tides. The sense of time itself falls away from the historical time of the older biblical narratives of the age of the earth to embrace the challenges of deep time and deep history. Central to the notion of time and memory as articulated in the poet's final collection is a sense of expansiveness, a movement beyond anthropocentric notions of what temporally matters to a more inclusive notion of time that sees the surrounding world of the Sligo coastline as containing the history of more than one species. When the "orchestra of memory / takes to the air" (16), the accounts of human losses and the burial of friends are enfolded into forms of memory that take seriously Daniel Lord Smail's contention mentioned earlier that it does not matter that the evidence for the deep past comes not from written documents but from other things that teach—such as artefacts, fossils and vegetable remains.

Healy's vision, like the flight of the barnacle geese he celebrates, constantly moves between earth and sky. If he tracks what happens on the ground, he is also mindful of what happens in the heavens. In section seven, "The Late November List," the poet sees the stars in the night sky morph into the migrating geese:

> While the birds bed down
> the stars gently
>
> beat their wings
> searching the earth below
>
> for a place
> to land sometime
> after this long
>
> night flight
> over everything
> is finished.

> The movement of the stars
> is infinitesimal
>
> as they climb the stairs
> to the opening. (Healy 76)

What is striking in the evocation of the night flight of these stars is Healy's deliberate shunning of any sense of the easy sublime. In other words, the stars are not choreographed through a desire to overwhelm or belittle, or to pander to the facile cosmological pieties of the insignificance of the human in the vastness of the galaxies. Rather the stars like the fossils are in movement. They too are swept along by the cataract of history, as they move through time. Serres notes how to see the stars in this way points to a profound change in our apprehension of the natural world and our cosmology:

> Les astres, qui apparaissaient autrefois comme des éléments stables de l'espace, sont aujourd'hui emportés dans le flot du temps. En les observant, nous pensons temporalité et non plus stabilité. Quand vous regardez une étoile, vous savez qu'elle est peut-être "morte," même si vous continuez d'en percevoir le rayonnement: Grâce à ce savoir, vous percevez un objet temporel autant qu'un objet spatial. (Serres, Legros & Ortoli 309) [*The stars which previously appeared to be stable elements in space, are now carried along in the flow of time. When we look at them we no longer think of stability but of temporality. When you look at a star, you know perhaps that it is "dead," even if you still see it shining. Because of this knowledge, what you are seeing is as much a temporal as a spatial object.*]

For Healy, there is no escape from history in the mythified infinities of the heavens above. The movement of the stars may be "infinitesimal" but they are not ahistorical in his expanded and inclusive sense of time and history.

The sense in which time troubles more spatialised visions of the environment in *A Fool's Errand* is crucial to a release of the poet from the clutches of the picturesque. In the documentary that drew heavily on the poems in the volume, *The Writing in the Sky*, first broadcast on RTÉ 1 television on 4 January 2011, the poet is shown in various locations around his home in Sligo and the camerawork is heavily invested in capturing the visual beauty of the surrounding landscape. There is a repeated sense of the poet dissolving into the dramatic land and seascapes of his adopted county. Such seamless fusion, of course, is not without its problems. The primary difficulty is that the static space of the picturesque evacuates the developmental time of the poetic. Writing on the centrality of the West of Ireland landscape to the construction of Irish identity and the emerging tourism industry, Catherine Nash notes the particular nature of its metaphorical appropriation:

> The West came to stand for Ireland in general, to be representative of true Irishness. It could be seen as a way into the Irish past through its language, folklore, antiquities, and way of life, yet also be conceived of as outside time, separated from normal temporal development, as evoked later by Seán Ó Faoláin as "lost islands, lost consciousness, lost time." (Nash 86–7)

For a site to attract tourism, it is important to trade on difference. Finding sameness is not generally what impels people to go elsewhere. The construction of this difference in the case of Ireland will come to focus heavily on the West of Ireland both as a bastion of difference against the encroachment of colonial power and as the fountainhead of separatist authenticity. The political project folds into the touristic enterprise with the West as the sublime cypher of otherness, good for the soul and good for the bottom line. When Healy brings the stars down to the earth and turns these spatial objects into temporal objects, he stages his own form of resistance to this essentialisation of the West of Ireland as a place "outside time," lost in the soft-focus dreaminess of the establishment shot. Healy's poem sequence is no nostalgic pastoral but a deeply felt evocation of what it means to be a geological agent in the anthropocene age. That is to say, it is about "lost consciousness" and "lost time" but not in the sense of a never-never land assuaging the consciences of anguished day trippers but in the sense of a loss of consciousness that comes with the loss of a deeper sense of time. If in the course of the sequence, he moves heaven (stars) and earth (fossils), it is to make the reader aware of the multiple timelines of the lived world and how alterations in the timescale of exploration and sensibility allow us to make sense of our post anthropocentric present as opposed to dwelling on idealized pasts trapped in heavily iconicized landscapes. Healy's poems are alive with a strikingly contemporary sense of what it is to live in an age of dramatically altered ecological sensibility and what a lived geocentrism might translate into on the printed page or in the mouth of the poet.

Becoming Animal

When Rosi Braidotti speaks above of conceptualising the post-human subject as "a transversal entity encompassing the human, our genetic neighbours the animals and the earth as a whole," she argues that this must be done using an "understandable language" (Braidotti 82). Formulating a new vision or version of subjectivity puts ordinary language under pressure and demands a translation practice that is adequate to the needs of this new "transversal entity." In section eight, "The Arrowhead," Healy traces the contours of an emerging subject that seeks to encompass rather than exclude:

> The beyond can belong
> to the past:
>
> this I see
> as now is nearly over.
>
> But later in my bed
> a swan goes over the house
> I grew up in.
>
> A silence comes down.
> The dog nods at something
> in her sleep. The sea wind

> is gathering
> at the gable
>
> When the engine stops
> that's when you wake. (Healy 86)

At one level, of course, "as now is nearly over," the planet definitively entering the age of the anthropogenic climate change, the "beyond" (what lies ahead) is irretrievably bound up with the "past" (what has gone before). At another, the waking subject in Healy's lines knows that inhabiting the "earth as a whole" means accommodating the "swan," the "dog," the "sea wind," "the engine." The beyond can indeed belong to the past but as the poet reminds us in section three, "The Beaten Sound," "The past is the present tense / of the verb to be" (26). What the animals and the elements and the engines bring into focus is the continuity of the connectedness of the subject from the past into the present with a range of species, objects and phenomena which lead to that subtle de-centring of *anthropos* running right through the collection. The waking subject here is not a master of all he surveys but a consciousness enmeshed in a world that no longer tolerates the condescension of anthropocentric largesse.

In a sense, what Healy articulates throughout the work is a specific kind of post-Stoic sensibility. Typically, the Stoic posture was predicated on the notion that some things depended on the operations of our will but most things did not. There was no point, therefore, in being troubled or anxious over so many things over which we had no control. The very fact that the world around us, in particular, the natural world, was indifferent to our actions meant that in the words of Marcus Aurelius in Book Seven of his *Meditations*, one could aim "To live each day as though one's last, never flustered, never apathetic, never attitudinizing—here is the perfection of character" (Aurelius 118). The advent of modernity and the age of the anthropocene fundamentally alters, however, this Stoic wager. Now most things depend for the survival on humans but in a paradoxical flip in the circle of ecological vulnerability, humans now depend on the world which depends on them. If humans through their activities make the earth uninhabitable, they too will disappear along with the other inhabitants. Marcus Aurelius's injunction to "live each day as though one's last" takes on a radically more unsettling resonance in an age of anthropogenic climate change where formerly discounted environmental externalities come back to undermine anthropocentric fictions of a subject nature and a compliant universe (see Bonneuil and Fressoz 20–28). The subject in *A Fool's Errand* is acutely sensitive to networks of dependency that spread through the natural and material worlds described in the volume. The litany of observation in section four, "The Thrashing Shadows" which begins, "You are the spit on the footpath / under the May bush" (38) intimates that subject/object discriminations break down under the exacerbated awareness of inter-species and ecological interdependency. The Stoic *ataraxia* (a state of serene calmness) of the biological agent gives way in the expanding universe of the volume to the matter-realism of geological force and responsibility.

Actual Places

Cheryll Glotfelty in her definition of ecocritcism presents it as a theoretical approach that "takes as its subject the interconnections between nature and culture, specifically the cultural artefacts of language and literature. As a critical stance, it has one foot in literature and the other on the land; as a theoretical discourse, it negotiates between the human and the nonhuman" (Glotfelty xix). A critical juncture for this meeting between "nature and culture," the "human and the nonhuman" is place itself. It is the interrogation and the situation of place that brings forth buried contexts and elided futures that lie beyond conventional horizons of reference.

In section three, "The Beaten Sound," the poet intimates that "You have to be there / in the actual place / listening to what never can be heard till the next time" (Healy 25). The actual places get mentioned, "Carney," "Maugherow," "Easkey," "Cloonagh," "Aughris" and the barnacle geese on their odyssey from Newfoundland sweep into known territories. However, it is the relationship to place and the possibilities of place that mark out Healy's writing as an invitation to exploration rather than as a summons to reverence. In his introduction to a series of ecocritical readings of Irish texts (2010), the teacher and essayist John Elder notes "that many Irish writers from the late nineteenth century to the present have sought to escape from the elegiac mode in their depiction of Ireland's deeply rooted culture and history" (Elder 1). Healy is no exception. Though the collection may lament the death of friends and the passing of acquaintances, there is no sense in which the poet sees the world of the Sligo coast as an elaborate metaphor of loss. The places, people and species within this landscape "knit joy / to terror" (Healy 14). If there is no easy sublime, neither is there decorous pastoral elegy. There is a resistance throughout to any facile sentimentalisation of the barnacle geese or their chosen sanctuaries, a refusal to orchestrate threnodies on endlessly fragile ecosystems. Healy's concern with "the actual place" is not to pinpoint historical loss in the plaintive Come-all-ye of the elegiac mode but to show how the particularity of place, what Tim Robinson has called its "echosphere" (Robinson 208) sustains solidarities of feeling and understanding without on the one hand, falling for the blandishments of messianic universalism or on the other, surrendering to the exclusivist pieties of blood and soil.

In the kinetic euphoria that accompanies contemporary eulogies to the global, the dizzying rate of global exchange is often equated to the relentless onward march of liberal democracy and the advent of a world marketplace of ceaseless cultural exchange (see Friedman). The defensive local allegiance of the particular has no place in the fraternal embrace of the universal. Enlightened supra-national governance or the inclusive joys of global citizenship are the termini of the accelerated voyage away from the retrograde claims of the specific. Universal love for all peoples and all species represents a kind of radical externalisation of sentiment which envelops the planet in an outward burst of fellow feeling. However, are internal repudiation and external celebration the only grounds for intelligent sympathy or due care?

The philosopher and critic Val Plumwood has expressed a useful scepticism with respect to the viability of sympathies which are too indiscriminate in their focus: "this 'transpersonal' identification is so indiscriminate and intent on denying particular meanings, it cannot allow for the deep and highly particularistic attachment to place that has motivated both the passion of many modern conservationists and the love of many indigenous peoples for their land" (Plumwood 152). Plumwood argues that, in fact, it is internalisation not externalisation which becomes the effective basis for a meaningful engagement with struggles and issues elsewhere: "Care and responsibility for particular animals, trees, and rivers that are known well, loved and appropriately connected to the self are an important basis for acquiring a wider, more generalized concern" (145–6).

It is in fact the local connection, the ready identification of a particular animal, tree, river, predatory oil company or abusive state practice in a local setting which makes possible the ethical imagining of the importance of species preservation or social justice in other proximate, micro-sites. The movement inwards is an opening up, not a shutting down. As Alastair McIntosh observed in 2002, "I must start where I stand. As children, we used to be told that if you dug a really deep hole, you'd come out in Australia. I think in some ways this is very true. If any of us dig deep enough where we stand, we will find ourselves connected to all parts of the world" (McIntosh 7). Healy's barnacle geese in a very obvious way connect the islands and town lands of Sligo to "other parts of the world." The poet, however, goes beyond the migratory possibilities of the birds to set the known, particular worlds of the lands around his home in motion. At one stage in "The Beaten Sound" we move from "the stairs / to the Chinese Pagoda" to a red bead of "Ecuadorean sunlight" to the fog "off Cloonagh" to "Duark" and the smell of burning kelp (Healy 33). Healy, in other words, is not consumed by the indiscriminate universalism of the Friend of the Earth but locates his openness to the world in a deep and lasting engagement with the particularities of place. It is this openness that makes Healy's legacy transformative. His importance for our collective future is how through his writing he has sought to develop a transformative ecology of place and new, emergent forms of subjectivity that would bring humanity back from the fool's errands of species supremacism and Garton Ash's triumphalist amnesia.

Works Cited

Aurelius, Marcus. *Meditations*. Trans. Maxwell Staniforth. Harmondsworth: Penguin, 1964. Print.

Bonneuil, Christophe, and Jean-Baptiste Fressoz. *L'événement anthropocène: la terre, l'histoire et nous*. Paris: Seuil, 2013. Print.

Braidotti, Rosi. *The Posthuman*. Cambridge: Polity, 2013. Print.

Chakrabarty, Dipesh. "The Climate of History: Four Theses." *Critical Inquiry* 35 (2009): 197–222. Print.

Crosby, Alfred W. "The Past and Present of Environmental History." *American Historical Review* 100 (Oct. 1995): 1185. Print.

Crutzen, Paul. "Geology of Mankind." *Nature* 415 (3 Jan. 2002): 23. Print.

Cusick, Christine, ed. "Mindful Paths: An Interview with Tim Robinson." *Out of the Earth: Ecocritical Readings of Irish Texts*. Cork: Cork University Press, 2010. 205–11. Print.

Elder, John. "Introduction." *Out of the Earth: Ecocritical Readings of Irish Texts*. Ed. Christine Cusick. Cork: Cork University Press, 2010. Print.

Friedman, Thomas. *The World is Flat: The Globalized World in the Twenty-First Century*. London: Penguin, 2006. Print.

Garton Ash, Timothy. "From the Lighthouse: The World and the *NYRB* After Fifty Years." *The New York Review of Books* 60.17 (7–20 Nov. 2013): 51. Print.

Glotfelty, Cheryll. "Introduction: Literary Studies in an Age of Environmental Crisis." *The Ecocriticism Reader: Landmarks in Literary Ecology*. Ed. Cheryll Glotfelty and Harold Fromm. Athens: University of Georgia Press, 1996. Print.

Gould, Stephen Jay. *Time's Arrow, Time's Cycle: Myth and Metaphor in the Discovery of Geological Time*. London: Penguin, 1990. Print.

Healy, Dermot. *A Fool's Errand*. Oldcastle: The Gallery Press, 2010. Print.

McIntosh, Alastair. *Soil and Soul: People versus Corporate Power*. London: Aurum, 2002. *Millennium Ecosystem Assessment Report*. Washington: Island Press, 2005. Print.

Nash, Catherine. "'Embodying the Nation'—The West of Ireland Landscape and Irish Identity." *Tourism in Ireland: A Critical Analysis*. Ed. Barbara O'Connor and Michael Cronin. Cork: Cork University Press, 1993. 86–112. Print.

Plumwood, Val. "Nature, Self and Gender: Feminism, Environmental

Philosophy, and the Critique of Rationalism." *Reflecting on Nature: Readings in Environmental Philosophy*. Ed. Lori Gruen and Dale Jamieson. Oxford: Oxford University Press, 1994. 142–59. Print.

Serres, Michel, Martin Legros, and Sven Ortoli. *Pantopie: de Hermès à Petite Poucette*. Paris: Le Pommier, 2014. Print.

Shubin, Neil. "The Disappearance of Species." *Bulletin of the American Academy of Arts and Sciences* 61 (2008): 17–9. Print.

Smail, Daniel Lord. *On Deep History and the Brain*. Berkeley: University of California Press, 2008. Print.

Stalin, Joseph. *Dialectical and Historical Materialism*. 1938. Web. 22 Apr. 2015.

Wilson, Edward Osborne. *The Future of Life*. New York: Vintage, 2002. Print.

SELECT BIBLIOGRAPHY

PRIMARY WORKS BY DERMOT HEALY

Novels
A Goat's Song. London: Harvill Press, 1994; New York: Harvest, 1994; Harmondsworth: Viking, 1995; London: Flamingo, 1995; London: Faber & Faber, 2015.
Fighting with Shadows, or Sciamachy. Dingle: Brandon Books, 1984; London: Allison & Busby, 1984; London: Allison & Busby, 1986; Victoria/Dublin/London: Dalkey Archive Press, 2015.
Long Time, No See. London: Faber & Faber, 2011; repr. 2012.
Sudden Times. London: Harvill Press, 1999; New York: Harcourt, 1999; London: Faber & Faber, 2015.

Short Stories
After the Off: Photographs by Bruce Gilden / Story by Dermot Healy. Stockport: Dewi Lewis Publishing, 1999.
Banished Misfortune and Other Stories. Dingle: Brandon Books, 1982; London: Allison & Busby, 1982.
Dermot Healy: The Collected Short Stories. Ed. Keith Hopper and Neil Murphy. Illinois/Dublin/London: Dalkey Archive Press, 2015.

Poetry
A Fool's Errand. Oldcastle: The Gallery Press, 2010.
Neighbours' Lights. London: Turret Books, 1992.
The Ballyconnell Colours. Oldcastle: The Gallery Press, 1992.
The Reed Bed. Oldcastle: The Gallery Press, 2001.
The Travels of Sorrow. Oldcastle: The Gallery Press, 2015.
What the Hammer. Oldcastle: The Gallery Press, 1998.

Memoir
The Bend for Home: A Memoir. London: Harvill Press, 1996; Florida: Harcourt Brace & Company, 1996; London: Faber & Faber, 2014.

Drama

Dermot Healy: The Collected Plays. Ed. Keith Hopper and Neil Murphy. Victoria: Dalkey Archive Press, 2016.

———. *A Night at the Disco* (2006)
———. *Blood Wedding* (1989)
———. *Here and There and Going to America* (1985)
———. *Last Night's Fun* (1996)
———. *Men to the Right, Women to the Left* (2001)
———. *Metagama* (2004)
———. *Mr Staines* (1999)
———. *On Broken Wings* (1992)
———. *On the Ramparts* (1994)
———. *Serious* (2005)
———. *The Long Swim* (1987)
———. *The Music Box* (1998)
———. *Where Are You?* (2010)
———. *Stories of the Drumlins: Men to the Right, Women to the Left—a Collaborative Theatre Project Developed by the Abbey Theatre, Positive Age and the Health Service Executive*. Ed. Sharon Murphy. Dublin: Outreach/Education Department of The Abbey Theatre, 2005.

Film and Television-Related Work

Our Boys [drama documentary]. Dir. Cathal Black. Script by Cathal Black and Dermot Healy. Ireland: RTÉ, 1981. 42 mins.

I Could Read the Sky [feature film]. Dir. Nichola Bruce. Starring Dermot Healy. UK and Ireland: Hot Property Films, 1999. 86 mins.

Prison Door [short drama]. Dir. Kevin McCann. Script by Kevin McCann and Dermot Healy. Ireland and UK: Maccana Teoranta, 2015. 10 mins.

The Writing in the Sky [documentary on Dermot Healy]. Dir. Garry Keane. Ireland: RTÉ, 2011. 54 mins.

Interviews

"An Interview with Dermot Healy." Interview by Tim O'Grady. *Wasafiri* 62 (Summer 2010): 26–31.

"Dermot Healy Interview." Interview by Luke Henderson. *Sligo Weekender* (4 July 2014).

"Finding beauty and inspiration on his doorstep." Interview by Carty Ciaran. *Irish Independent* (20 Apr. 2013).

"Headland: An Interview with Dermot Healy." Interview by Brian Leyden. *The Buzz* 10 (July 1994): 5.

"Interview with Dermot Healy." Interview by Damian McCarney. *Anglo-Celt* (4 Oct. 2012).

Interview by Mike McCormack. Centre for Irish Studies Archive. Galway: National University of Ireland. (5 July 2004). 90 mins.

"'I try to stay out of it and let the reader take over.'" Interview by Sean O'Hagan. *The Observer.* (3 Apr. 2011). Web. 30 Jan. 2015.

"*Long Time, No See* with Dermot Healy." Interview by Eleanor Wachtel. *Writers and Company* Canada: CBC/Radio-Canada. 54 mins.

"Novelist puzzled at row sparked by *Irish Times* review of latest book." Interview by Ronan McGreevy. *Irish Times* (1 Apr 2011).

"Small Talk: Dermot Healy." Interview by Anna Metcalfe. *Financial Times* (30 Apr. 2011).

"'Some think I'm wasting my time.'" Interview by John McEntee. *Irish Press* (15 July 1982): 9.

"Taking the edge to the centre." Interview by Helen Meany. *Irish Times* (10 Aug. 1995).

"When best left alone." Interview by Ciara Dwyer. *Sunday Independent* (15 May 2011).

"Writer with a bright future." Interview by Joe Donlan. *Longford Leader* (18 Feb. 1983): 14.

Journals

Ed. *Force 10.* Issues 1–13 (1989–2008).
Ed. *The Drumlin.* (1978–1980).

Work in Progress Extracts

"An Interview in the City." *Cyphers* 16 (Winter 1981). Ed. Leland Bardwell, Eiléan Ní Chuilleanáin, Pearse Hutchinson, and Macdara Woods: 26–32. Repr. *The Anthology.* Ed. Leland Bardwell and Joseph Ambrose. Dublin: Co-Op Books, 1982. 131–40. [Variant of Chapter 40, *Fighting with Shadows.*]

"Extract from a novel by Dermot Healy." *Connacht Tribune* (20 July 1984).

"From *Fighting with Shadows*." *A Christmas Feast: Incorporating Winter's Tales*. Ed. James Hale. London and Basingstoke: Macmillan, 1983. 283–5. [Variant of Chapter 24, *Fighting with Shadows*.]

"Helen Allen." *Aquarius* 15/16 (1983). Ed. Eddie S. Linden. 65–8. [An endnote calls it "Extract from *Fighting with Shadows*, a novel by Dermot Healey [sic] to be published in 1984 by Allison & Busby." Variant of Chapter 2, *Fighting with Shadows*.]

"Legal Times." *Icarus* 75 (1980). Ed. Gerry McDonnell. 35–41. [Subtitled "(An Excerpt from 'Sciamachy'—A Novel in Progress)."] Repr. *Dermot Healy: Collected Short Stories*. Ed. Keith Hopper and Neil Murphy. Victoria/Dublin/London: Dalkey Archive Press, 2015. 222–29.

"The Midgets on the Pass." [Sub-titled "Work in Progress: Dermot Healey [sic]."] *The Fiction Magazine* 1.3 (Autumn 1982): 4–66. [Variant of Chapter 25, *Fighting with Shadows*.]

"Voting for Dead Men." *Books Ireland* 86 (Sept. 1984): 151–2. [A headnote calls this "An extract from *Fighting with Shadows* by Dermot Healy, to be published this month by Brandon/Allison & Busby." Variant section of Chapter 38, *Fighting with Shadows*.]

"Work in Progress." *Icarus* 73 (Winter 1977-78). Ed. Ed McGuire. 61–6. [Subtitled "(Excerpt from Dermot Healy's 'Sciamachy,' now being forged in the smithy of his soul 3 miles outside Cootehill, Co. Cavan.)."]

Reviews by Dermot Healy

"A Flawed and Rootless Psyche." Review of *As Towns with Fire* by Anthony C. West. *Fortnight* 216 (18–31 Mar. 1985): 18.

"Art and Extinction." Review of Diarmuid Delargy's paintings at Taylor Galleries, Dublin. *Irish Arts Review* 26.1 (Spring 2009): 65.

"Let The Hare Sit." Review of *Rise Up Lovely Sweeney* by Tom MacIntyre. *Theatre Ireland* 11 (Autumn 1985): 9–10.

"Other worlds." Review of *Fairy and Folk-tales of Ireland*, ed. W. B. Yeats. *Irish Press* (9 June 1973): 10.

Review of *Behind the Scenes at the Museum* by Kate Atkinson and *Captain Corelli's Mandolin* by Louis de Bernieres. *Irish Times* (25 Feb. 2013).

Review of *Jumping Off Shadows*, ed. by Greg Delanty and Nuala Ní Dhomhnaill, and *Ruined Pages, Selected Poems* by Padraic Fiacc. *Poetry Ireland Review* 48 (Winter 1996): 92–5.

"When is an Irish Writer an Anglo-Irish Writer? Review of *Language and Society in Anglo-Irish Literature* by A. C. Partridge. *Fortnight* 222 (24 June 1985): 13.

SECONDARY CRITICISM

Selected Essays/Commentaries

Barry, Kevin. "Sligo Occult: On Dermot Healy's Radical Style." *The Stinging Fly* (Winter 2014–15). Web. 10 Feb. 2015. Repr. *Writing the Sky: Observations and Essays on Dermot Healy.* Ed. Neil Murphy and Keith Hopper. Victoria: Dalkey Archive Press, 2016: 100–3.

Browne, Vincent. "Profile: Dermot Healy." *Film West* 37 (July 1999): 16–8. Repr. *Writing the Sky: Observations and Essays on Dermot Healy.* Ed. Neil Murphy and Keith Hopper. Victoria: Dalkey Archive Press, 2016: 143–7.

Bruce, Nichola. "Remembering Dermot Healy and *I Could Read the Sky.*" *Writing the Sky: Observations and Essays on Dermot Healy.* Ed. Neil Murphy and Keith Hopper. Victoria: Dalkey Archive Press, 2016: 137–42.

Coulouma, Flore. "Reveries of the Solitary Self in *Banished Misfortune.*" *Writing the Sky: Observations and Essays on Dermot Healy.* Ed. Neil Murphy and Keith Hopper. Victoria: Dalkey Archive Press, 2016. 231–45.

Craig, Patricia. "From the Rannafast Summer." *The Literary World* 3.1 (Spring/Summer 2005): 100–52.

Cronin, Michael. "Banished Misfortunes?: Dermot Healy and the Rise of the Posthuman." *Writing the Sky: Observations and Essays on Dermot Healy.* Ed. Neil Murphy and Keith Hopper. Victoria: Dalkey Archive Press, 2016. 381–98.

Fagan, Paul. "Guilt Trips: Dermot Healy's *Sudden Times* and the Meaning of Sin." *Writing the Sky: Observations and Essays on Dermot Healy.* Ed. Neil Murphy and Keith Hopper. Victoria: Dalkey Archive Press, 2016. 292–313.

Fennell, Jack. "Dermot Healy's Heterotopias: Fanacross and Northern Ireland in *Fighting with Shadows.*" *Writing the Sky: Observations and Essays on Dermot Healy.* Ed. Neil Murphy and Keith Hopper. Victoria: Dalkey Archive Press, 2016. 246–58.

Foster, John Wilson. "Dermot Healy." *The Field Day Anthology of Irish Writing*. Vol. 3. Ed. Seamus Deane. Derry: Field Day, 1992: 1093.

Gallagher, Tess. "Sea-strangeness: Memories of Dermot Healy." *Writing the Sky: Observations and Essays on Dermot Healy*. Ed. Neil Murphy and Keith Hopper. Victoria: Dalkey Archive Press, 2016. 49–55.

Gefter Wondrich, Roberta. "Islands of Ireland: A Tragedy of Separation in Dermot Healy's *A Goat's Song*." *Writing Ulster* 6 (1999): 68–87.

Golden, Seán. "Oriental Sense of the Border." *Fortnight* 210 (3–16 Dec. 1984): 18.

———. "'The small stone that no one sees gives all the balance': Unique Perspective and Personal Idiom in the Works of Dermot Healy." *Writing the Sky: Observations and Essays on Dermot Healy*. Ed. Neil Murphy and Keith Hopper. Victoria: Dalkey Archive Press, 2016. 159–81.

———. "Traditional Irish Music in Contemporary Irish Literature." *MOSAIC* 12 (1979): 1–24.

Hand, Derek. "*The Bend for Home*: Truth, Beauty, Such Things." *Writing the Sky: Observations and Essays on Dermot Healy*. Ed. Neil Murphy and Keith Hopper. Victoria: Dalkey Archive Press, 2016. 349–64.

Harding, Michael. "The Rogue Wave." *Writing the Sky: Observations and Essays on Dermot Healy*. Ed. Neil Murphy and Keith Hopper. Victoria: Dalkey Archive Press, 2016. 84–6. [First published as "Dermot Healy was afflicted with an unruly mind." *Irish Times* (1 July 2014).]

Hoffmann, Catherine. "Dancing to Ollie's Tunes: The Rhetoric of Narrative Stutter." *Style* 43.3 (2009): 357–72.

———. "Mister Psyche's Microcosmos." *Writing the Sky: Observations and Essays on Dermot Healy*. Ed. Neil Murphy and Keith Hopper. Victoria: Dalkey Archive Press, 2016. 331–48.

Hogan, Robert. "Old Boys, Young Bucks and New Women: The Contemporary Irish Short Story." *The Irish Short Story: A Critical History*. Ed. James Kilroy. Boston: Twayne, 1984. 169–215.

Hopkin, Alannah, and Aidan Higgins. "Dermot Healy: Newcomer, Mentor, Old Hand." *Writing the Sky: Observations and Essays on Dermot Healy*. Ed. Neil Murphy and Keith Hopper. Victoria: Dalkey Archive Press, 2016. 78–83.

Hopper, Keith. "Everyday Things." Review of *Long Time, No See* and *A*

Fool's Errand by Dermot Healy. *Times Literary Supplement* (8 Apr. 2011): 19–20.

———. "'The Passionate Transitory': Dermot Healy and the Sense of Place." *Writing the Sky: Observations and Essays on Dermot Healy.* Ed. Neil Murphy and Keith Hopper. Victoria: Dalkey Archive Press, 2016. 210–30.

Hopper, Keith, and Neil Murphy. "Editors' Introduction: Making it New." *Dermot Healy: The Collected Short Stories.* Victoria/Dublin/London: Dalkey Archive Press, 2015. xi–xxvii.

Jordan, Neil. "Foreword." *Writing the Sky: Observations and Essays on Dermot Healy.* Ed. Neil Murphy and Keith Hopper. Victoria: Dalkey Archive Press, 2016. ix–xi.

Keane, Garry. "At the End of the Day." *Writing the Sky: Observations and Essays on Dermot Healy.* Ed. Neil Murphy and Keith Hopper. Victoria: Dalkey Archive Press, 2016. 148–54.

Lazenbatt, Bill. "Editorial." *Writing Ulster* 6. (1999): ix–x.

Leyden, Brian. "A Short History of *Force 10* (A Journal of the North-West)." *Writing the Sky: Observations and Essays on Dermot Healy.* Ed. Neil Murphy and Keith Hopper. Victoria: Dalkey Archive Press, 2016. 87–92.

———. "The Place of Writing." *The Leitrim Guardian* 47 (2015): 20.

McCabe, Patrick. "Wings 2/6: Memories of Dermot Healy." *Writing the Sky: Observations and Essays on Dermot Healy.* Ed. Neil Murphy and Keith Hopper. Victoria: Dalkey Archive Press, 2016. 29–39.

McCarthy, Dermot. "Psyche's Garden: The Labour of Mourning and the Growth of the Self in *Long Time, No See.*" *Writing the Sky: Observations and Essays on Dermot Healy.* Ed. Neil Murphy and Keith Hopper. Victoria: Dalkey Archive Press, 2016. 314–30.

———. "Recovering Dionysus: Dermot Healy's *A Goat's Song.*" *New Hibernia Review* 4.4 (Winter 2000): 134–49.

McCloskey, Molly. "On *The Bend for Home.*" *Writing the Sky: Observations and Essays on Dermot Healy.* Ed. Neil Murphy and Keith Hopper. Victoria: Dalkey Archive Press, 2016. 128–35.

McCormack, Mike. "Testing, said a voice. Testing, one two three . . ." *Writing the Sky: Observations and Essays on Dermot Healy.* Ed. Neil Murphy and Keith Hopper. Victoria: Dalkey Archive Press, 2016. 104–9.

McCourt, John. "Dermot Healy." *Post-War Literatures in English*. Ed. Geert Lernout. Groningen: Martinus Nijhoff uitgevers, 2000.

Morrison, Danny. "A Song for Ireland." *Writing the Sky: Observations and Essays on Dermot Healy*. Ed. Neil Murphy and Keith Hopper. Victoria: Dalkey Archive Press, 2016. 66–71

Murphy, Neil. "Dermot Healy's *A Goat's Song*: 'To give some form to that which cannot be uttered.'" *Litteraria Pragensia* 22.44 (Dec. 2012): 108–20. Repr. *Writing the Sky: Observations and Essays on Dermot Healy*. Ed. Neil Murphy and Keith Hopper. Victoria: Dalkey Archive Press, 2016. 277–91.

Murphy, Neil, and Keith Hopper. "Editors' Introduction: 'Anything Strange?'" *Fighting with Shadows*. By Dermot Healy. Victoria/Dublin/London: Dalkey Archive Press, 2015. vii–xx.

———. "Dermot Healy: A Modern Master." *Irish Times* (21 Oct. 2015).

Murray, Tony. *London Irish Fictions: Narrative, Diaspora and Identity*. Liverpool: Liverpool University Press, 2012.

Ó Ceallaigh, Philip. "Anonymous is best . . ." *The Stinging Fly* (10 Sept. 2015). Repr. *Writing the Sky: Observations and Essays on Dermot Healy*. Ed. Neil Murphy and Keith Hopper. Victoria: Dalkey Archive Press, 2016. 72–5.

O'Brien, George. "Reading *Force 10*." *Writing the Sky: Observations and Essays on Dermot Healy*. Ed. Neil Murphy and Keith Hopper. Victoria: Dalkey Archive Press, 2016. 93–8.

O'Grady, Timothy. "Only myself, said Cúnla." *Irish Times* (22 May 2015). Repr. *Writing the Sky: Observations and Essays on Dermot Healy*. Ed. Neil Murphy and Keith Hopper. Victoria: Dalkey Archive Press, 2016. 16–28.

Paull, Michelle C. "Dermot Healy: Local, National, and International Drama." *Writing the Sky: Observations and Essays on Dermot Healy*. Ed. Neil Murphy and Keith Hopper. Victoria: Dalkey Archive Press, 2016. 365–81.

Patterson, Glenn. "After the Event." *Writing the Sky: Observations and Essays on Dermot Healy*. Ed. Neil Murphy and Keith Hopper. Victoria: Dalkey Archive Press, 2016. 76–7.

Proulx, Annie. "Dermot Healy's *A Goat's Song*: A Writer's Appreciation." *Litteraria Pragensia* 22.44 (Dec. 2012): 121–30. Repr. *Writing the Sky: Observations and Essays on Dermot Healy*. Ed. Neil Murphy and

Keith Hopper. Victoria: Dalkey Archive Press, 2016. 112–23.

———. "Review Essay: Dermot Healy's *Sudden Times*." *Writing the Sky: Observations and Essays on Dermot Healy*. Ed. Neil Murphy and Keith Hopper. Victoria: Dalkey Archive Press, 2016. 124–7.

Robin, Thierry. "The Importance of Being Dermot: Healy's Idiosyncrasies." *Writing the Sky: Observations and Essays on Dermot Healy*. Ed. Neil Murphy and Keith Hopper. Victoria: Dalkey Archive Press, 2016. 197–209.

Rocks, Seán. Presenter. Interview with Keith Hopper about Dermot Healy. *Arena*. Ireland: RTÉ Radio 1 (18 May 2015).

Schwerter, Stephanie. "Transgressing Boundaries: Belfast and the 'Romance-Across-the-Divide.'" *Estudios Irlandeses* 2 (2007): 173–82.

Sheehan, Ronan. "Dermot Healy: A Cavan Antaeus." *Writing the Sky: Observations and Essays on Dermot Healy*. Ed. Neil Murphy and Keith Hopper. Victoria: Dalkey Archive Press, 2016. 56–63.

Sloan, Barry. "'In My Father's House': Renegotiations of Boyhood in Life Writing by John McGahern, Ciaran O'Driscoll, Dermot Healy, and Ciaran Carson." *Éire-Ireland* 44.1/2 (Spring/Summer 2009): 218–41.

Smyth, Gerry. "'The orchestra of memory': Music, Sound and Silence in *A Goat's Song*." *Writing the Sky: Observations and Essays on Dermot Healy*. Ed. Neil Murphy and Keith Hopper. Victoria: Dalkey Archive Press, 2016. 259–76.

Swainson, Bill. "Dermot Healy—Art into Life: Life into Art." *Writing the Sky: Observations and Essays on Dermot Healy*. Ed. Neil Murphy and Keith Hopper. Victoria: Dalkey Archive Press, 2016. 182–96.

Tóibín, Colm. "Alone in a Landscape: The Poetry of Dermot Healy." *Writing the Sky: Observations and Essays on Dermot Healy*. Ed. Neil Murphy and Keith Hopper. Victoria: Dalkey Archive Press, 2016. 5–14.

Wallace, Kim. "'Here it begins': Figuring Identities in Dermot Healy's *A Goat's Song*." *Beyond Borders: IASIL Essays on Modern Irish Writing*. Ed. Neil Sammells. Bath: Sulis Press, 2004. 121–42.

Woods, Vincent. Presenter. "Dermot Healy: A Consideration of his Writing and Literary Work." *Arts Tonight*. Ireland: RTÉ Radio 1 (18 May 2015). [Featuring Neil Jordan, Bill Swainson, Peter Fallon, Keith Hopper, Timothy O'Grady, and Mary O'Malley.]

Reviews of Healy's Work

Adair, Tom. "Tale of an Irish boy hits heights by not going over the top." Review of *Long Time, No See* by Dermot Healy. *The Scotsman* (30 Apr. 2011): 4.

Anon. "A lot to take on board." Review of *I Could Read the Sky* by Nichola Bruce. *Irish Times* (16 July 1999).

———. "Audio fun!" Review of *Last Night's Fun* by Dermot Healy. *Southern Star* (9 Sept. 1995): 9.

———. Review of *Banished Misfortune* by Dermot Healy. *Kirkus Review* (21 Nov. 1982). Web. 20 Nov. 2014.

———. "Bizarre, touching, comic and romantic." Review of *Mr Staines* by Dermot Healy. *Kilkenny People* (10 Sept. 1999): 4.

———. "Buried memories, secret histories." Review of *I Could Read the Sky* by Dermot Healy. *Irish Times* (3 July 2000). Irishtimes.com. Web. 4 Feb. 2015.

———. "Comic and absurd." Review of *Mr Staines* by Dermot Healy. *Kilkenny People* (1 Oct. 1999): 4.

———. "Extraordinary celebration of the ordinary." Review of *Long Time, No See* by Dermot Healy. *Irish Independent* (9 Apr. 2011).

———. "Issue 9 of *Force 10* is another tour-de-force." *Leitrim Observer* (11 Dec. 1998): 19.

———. "*Last Night's Fun*: Healy's latest offering." Review of *Last Night's Fun* by Dermot Healy. *Anglo-Celt* (17 Aug. 1995): 28.

———. "Launch of Dermot Healy's Autobiography in Cootehill." *Anglo-Celt* (3 Oct. 1996): 6.

———. "Long Time, No See . . . But he's back! Dermot Healy's latest book is on the shelves now." *Anglo-Celt* (31 Mar. 2011).

———. "Mister Staines—comic and absurd." Review of *Mr Staines* by Dermot Healy. *Kilkenny People* (17 Sept. 1999): 4.

———. "New play for Sligo." Review of *The Long Swim* by Dermot Healy. *Irish Times* (26 Sept. 1987).

———. "*On Broken Wings*— one man's struggle with life." Review of *On Broken Wings* by Dermot Healy. *City Tribune* (11 Nov. 1994): 10.

———. "*Banished Misfortune* by Dermot Healy." *Longford Leader* (3 Sept. 1982): 14.

———. "*Fighting with Shadows* by Dermot Healy." *Irish Independent* (17 Nov. 1984): 9.

———. "*Sudden Times* by Dermot Healy." *Irish Independent* (16 Oct. 1999): 45.

———. "*The Bend for Home* by Dermot Healy." *Meath Chronicle* (11 Jan. 1997): 30.

———. "Scenes from the Border country." Review of *Men to the Right, Women to the Left* by Dermot Healy. *Irish Times* (24 Apr. 2002). Irishtimes.com. Web. 4 Feb. 2015.

———. "World premiere of Cavan author's play [*The Long Swim*]." *Anglo-Celt* (8 Oct. 1987): 1.

Banville, John. Review of *Sudden Times* by Dermot Healy. *Irish Times* (26 Mar. 2011).

Battersby, Eileen. "From chatty comments to chilling observations." Review of *Long Time, No See* by Dermot Healy. *Irish Times* (26 Mar. 2011).

Boland, Rosita. "A bit of a two-horse race." Review of *After the Off* by Dermot Healy and Bruce Gilden. *Irish Times* (18 Dec. 1999).

———. "Scenes from the Border country." Review of *Men to the Right, Women to the Left: Stories of the Drumlins* by Dermot Healy. *Irish Times* (25 Apr. 2002).

———. Review of *Sudden Times* by Dermot Healy. *Irish Times* (3 July 2000).

Bredin, Hugh. Review of *The Ballyconnell Colours* by Dermot Healy. *Fortnight* 318 (June 1993): 50.

Brooke, Peter. Review of *Fighting with Shadows* by Dermot Healy. *Linenhall Review* 1.4 (Winter 1984/85): 19.

Browne, Harry. "Child's play magic." Review of *The Three Boxes* by Dermot Healy. *Irish Times* (24 June 1998).

Burn, Gordon. "The Art of Overhearing." Review of *Sudden Times* by Dermot Healy. *Times Literary Supplement* (17 Sept. 1999).

Coleman, Philip. "Decommissioning the Blurb." Review of *The Reed Bed* by Dermot Healy. *The Irish Review* 30 (Spring–Summer 2003): 158–62.

Colgan, Gerry. "Comedy with a quirky character." Review of *Last Night's Fun* by Dermot Healy. *Irish Times* (14 Aug. 1995).

———. Review of *Last Night's Fun* by Dermot Healy. *Irish Times* (11 Oct. 1996).

———. "Topsy-turvy laughs in theatre of the absurd." *Irish Times* (23 Sept. 1999).

———. "When style clouds the story lines." Review of *Banished Misfortune* by Dermot Healy. *Irish Independent* (28 Aug. 1982): 8.

Courtney, Kevin. "Unhurried in a harried world." Review of *Art Lives: The Writing in the Sky*. *Irish Times* (8 Jan. 2011).

———. "Word on the Street: Manbagging." *Irish Times* (9 Apr. 2011).

Craig, Patricia. "Forms of Fecklessness." Review of *Banished Misfortune* by Dermot Healy. *Times Literary Supplement* (11 June 1982): 642.

Crowe, Catriona. "Dark Shoes on a Doorstep." Review of *The Bend for Home* by Dermot Healy. *London Review of Books* (31 July 1997): 25–6.

Dawe, Gerald. Review of *A Goat's Song* by Dermot Healy. *Fortnight* 330. (July–Aug. 1994): 27.

Dillon-Malone, Aubrey. "Vim and Vinegar." Review of *Fighting with Shadows* by Dermot Healy. *Books Ireland* 89 (Dec. 1984): 232–3.

Donovan, Katie. "Who Read What—Philip Casey on Dermot Healy's *Sudden Times*." *Irish Times* (4 Dec. 1999).

Downes, Daragh. "Paperbacks: *Long Time, No See*." *Irish Times* (5 May 2012).

Dunne, John. "First Person Singular." Review of *The Bend for Home* by Dermot Healy. *Books Ireland* 199 (Nov. 1996): 320–1.

———. "Terrible things happen." Review of *A Goat's Song* by Dermot Healy. *Books Ireland* 178 (Summer 1994): 159–60.

Eagleton, Terry. "An Octopus at the Window." Review of *Long Time, No See*. *London Review of Books* (19 May 2011): 23–4.

East, Louise. "What is the stars?" Review of *Footfalls* by Samuel Beckett, directed by Dermot Healy. *Irish Times* (7 Oct. 1999).

Gaffney, Eamonn. Review of *Long Time, No See* by Dermot Healy. *Anglo-Celt* (21 Apr. 2011).

Golden, Seán. "Oriental Sense of the Border." Review of *Fighting with Shadows* by Dermot Healy. *Fortnight* 210 (3–16 Dec. 1984): 18.

Grace, Edwina. Review of *Mr Staines* by Dermot Healy. *Kilkenny People* (8 Oct. 1999): 2.

Graham, Colin. "Words on the wing." Review of *A Fool's Errand* by Dermot Healy. *Irish Times* (20 Nov. 2010).

Groarke, Vona. "Conjuring the landscape." Review of *What the Hammer* by Dermot Healy. *Irish Times* (25 Feb. 2013).

Harte, Liam. "How the Irish autobiography went from 'we' to 'I.'"

Review of *The Bend for Home* by Dermot Healy. *Irish Times* (5 May 2007).

Haze, Richard. "A Place Called Fruitfulness, a Space Called Silence." Review of *The Ballyconnell Colours* by Dermot Healy. *The Poetry Ireland Review* 37 (Winter 1992/3): 115–21.

Hazeldine, Peter. "Barricades." Review of Dermot Healy's *Banished Misfortune* and *Fighting with Shadows*. *PN Review* 13.3 (1986): 87–8.

Higgins, Aidan, ed. "Cantraps of Fermented Words." Review of of *Fighting with Shadows* by Dermot Healy. *Windy Arbours: Collected Criticism*. Illinois/London: Dalkey Archive Press, 2006. 192–3.

Hogan, Sinead. Review of *A Fool's Errand* by Dermot Healy. *Anglo-Celt* (21 Oct. 2010).

Hughes, Eamonn. Review of *A Goat's Song*. *The Irish Review* 19 (Spring–Summer 1996): 146–51.

Imhof, Rüdiger. Review of *A Goat's Song*. *Linen Hall Review* 11.2 (Autumn 1994): 26–9.

Jarman, Anthony Mark. "A Brilliant Return for Dermot Healy." Review of *Long Time, No See* by Dermot Healy. *The Globe and Mail* (8 July 2011).

Johnston, Fred. "Innocence and Angst." Review of *The Ballyconnell Colours*. *Books Ireland* 169 (Summer 1993): 136–8.

———. "Two Irish Novelists." Review of *Fighting with Shadows* by Dermot Healy and *Ringmaster* by Lee Dunne. *Irish Times* (3 July 2000).

Kearney, John. "Borders of misunderstanding." Review of *Fighting with Shadows* by Dermot Healy. *Sunday Independent* (25 Nov. 1984): 16. *The Irish News Archive*.

Kenny, John. "Past Master of Re-invention." Review of *Sudden Times* by Dermot Healy. *Irish Times* (2 Oct. 1999).

Kiely, Kevin. "Meaning?" Review of *A Fool's Errand* by Dermot Healy. *Books Ireland* 334 (Nov. 2011): 212–3.

Koenig, Marianne. Review of *Fighting with Shadows* by Dermot Healy. *Irish University Review* 15.1 (Spring 1985): 112–5.

Linehan, Hugh. "Back to the future." Review of *I Could Read the Sky*. *Irish Times* (18 Aug. 2000).

Logue, Antonia. "Last Night's experiment works out." Review of *Last*

Night's Fun by Dermot Healy. *Irish Independent* (11 Oct. 1996): 26.

McCabe, Eugene. "Another take on *Long Time, No See*." *Irish Times* (29 Mar 2011).

Morrison, Danny. Review of *The Bend for Home* by Dermot Healy. *Fortnight* 355 (Nov. 1996): 36–7.

Morton, Brian. "In the Border State." Review of *Fighting with Shadows* by Dermot Healy. *Times Literary Supplement* (11 Jan. 1985): 41.

Nolan, Val. "Long Time No See, Indeed: Healy's First Novel in a Decade is Mesmerizing." Review of *Long Time, No See* by Dermot Healy. *The Irish Examiner* (19 May 2012): 16.

O'Brien, George. "Home is where the art is." Review of *The Bend for Home* by Dermot Healy. *Irish Times* (25 Feb. 2013).

O'Byrne, Patrick. "Another take on *Long Time, No See*." Review of *Long Time, No See* by Dermot Healy. *Irish Times* (30 Mar. 2011).

O'Hanlon, Eilis. Review of *Long Time, No See* by Dermot Healy. *Independent* (4 Oct. 2011).

Parry, Gwyn. "Some More Versions of Pastoral." Review of *What the Hammer* by Dermot Healy. *The Poetry Ireland Review* 61 (Summer 1999): 106–11.

Proulx, Annie. Review of *Long Time, No See* by Dermot Healy. *Guardian* (2 Apr. 2011).

Rafroidi, Patrick. "Dermotitis." Review of *Banished Misfortune* by Dermot Healy. *Irish Press* (22 Jul. 1982): 11.

Reddin, Daragh. "Another take on *Long Time, No See*." *Irish Times* (31 Mar. 2011).

Redmond, Lucile. "Smokeless Fuel." Review of *Firebird I: Writing Today*, ed. T. J. Binding. *Irish Press* (20 May 1982): 6.

Sealy, Douglas. "Concorde, Healy." Review of "Music from the Reed Bed" [reading by Dermot Healy]. *Irish Times* (3 July 2000).

Sommerville-Large, Gillian. "Novels of the Week: Borderland." Review of *Fighting with Shadows* by Dermot Healy. *Irish Times* (24 Nov. 1984).

Tongue, Alan. "Percy French." Response to George O'Brien's review of *The Bend for Home* by Dermot Healy. *Irish Times* (17 Oct. 1996).

Traynor, Desmond. "Culture I Loved." Review of *What the Hammer* by Dermot Healy. *Books Ireland* 217 (Nov. 1998): 308–9.

———. "Intellect and Feeling." Review of *Sudden Times* by Dermot Healy. *Books Ireland* 236 (Dec. 2000): 356–7.

Walsh, Caroline. "Loose Leaves: End of an epic wait." Review of *Long Time, No See* by Dermot Healy. *Irish Times* (3 Apr. 2010).

General News Articles

Anon. "Busy residency." *Irish Times* (24 Jan. 1992).
———. "Deeply rooted in a local world." *Irish Times* (18 Sept. 1999).
———. "Film and Literary World Acclaim Cavan Writer's Latest Novel." *Anglo-Celt* (9 June 1994): 6.
———. "Healy in the wind." *Irish Times* (22 Feb. 1997).
———. "Mammy, I'm poignant." *Irish Times* (20 Feb. 1999).
———. "New Irish Writing—Hennessy Literary Awards: Winners through the Decades." *Irish Times* (24 Jan. 2015).
———. "New Irish Writing Awards: Four Authors Honoured." *Irish Press* (28 Sept. 1974).
———. "Hennessy Story Awards." *Irish Press* (16 Oct. 1976): 3.
———. "Novelist and poet who captured ordinary truths." *Irish Times* (12 July 2014).
———. "President among hundreds at funeral of Dermot Healy." *Irish Independent* (4 July 2014).
———. "The Humours of Ballyconnell." *City Tribune* (11 Nov. 1994): 10.
———. "Trad with a twist." *Irish Times* (30 Jun. 2000).
———. "€25,000 literary award for Healy." *Irish Times* (25 June 2002).
Battersby, Eileen. "Poet and novelist Dermot Healy dies aged 66." *Irish Times* (1 July 2014).
Boland, John. "It's flash, it's trash, but is it art?" *Irish Times* (16 Mar. 1996).
———. "Judging a book by its cover." *Irish Times* (21 Sept. 1996).
Burke, Dermot. "Dermot Healy's latest double success." *Anglo-Celt* (29 Aug. 1999): 9.
Dunne, Aidan. "Punter photos are a racing certainty." *Irish Times* (5 Feb. 2000).
Harding, Michael. "The War Is Over. Feral Boys Are Everywhere." *Irish Times* (20 Aug. 2013): 11.
———. "'There's quite a difference between 'dismount' and 'go down.'" *Irish Times* (8 Apr. 2011).

McCarney, Damian. "'He wrote like an angel.'" Tribute to Dermot Healy. *Anglo-Celt* (3 July 2014): 2.

McCormack, W. J. "Diverse voices of the regions." *Irish Times* (14 Aug. 1993).

McDonagh, Marese. "Dermot Healy laid to rest in Sligo amid music, dance and poetry." *Irish Times* (1 July 2014).

McGarry, Patsy. "Sudden death of writer Dermot Healy inspires many tributes." *Irish Times* (1 July 2014).

Moynihan, Ciara. "Dermot Healy to share literary insights." *The Mayo News* (2 Oct. 2012).

Murray, Catherine. "Poetry in the making." *Longford Leader* (30 July 1993): 21.

O'Faolain, Nuala. "An epic of love, drink, fear and politics." *Irish Times* (14 Nov. 1994).

O'Hagan, Sean. "Dermot Healy Obituary." *Guardian* (30 June 2014).

O'Hanlon, Eilis. "An extraordinary insight into an ordinary life." *Sunday Independent* (10 Apr. 2011).

O'Mahony, John. "Let the West of the World go by." *Guardian* (3 June 2000).

Ryan, Áine. "Literary event to survive in Mayo." *Irish Times* (3 July 2000).

Sheridan, Kathy. "100 Key Names in Irish Literature." *Irish Times* (25 July 1985): 10.

CONTRIBUTORS

KEVIN BARRY is the author of the Rooney prize-winning short story collection, *There Are Little Kingdoms*, the Edge Hill winning short story collection, *Dark Lies the Island*, and the IMPAC Dublin Literary Award-winning novel, *City of Bohane*. His most recent novel, *Beatlebone*, was published by Canongate in 2015. He lives in Sligo.

CAROLINE BRACKEN has had poems published in *Skylight 47*, *The Scaldy Detail*, *The Clare Champion*, *Headspace*, *The Gathering Poem*, *The Ogham Stone* (University of Limerick), *Poets Meet Painters*, and *Words on the Waves*. Her poems were shortlisted in the Bridport Prize (2014), the Swift Satire Festival (2014) and the WOW Awards (2015), and she was the winner of the Writing.ie/Anam Cara International Poetry Competition (2013). She works in RTÉ Radio and lives in Bray, Co. Wicklow.

VINCENT BROWNE is a freelance writer, bookseller and broadcaster living in Galway, Ireland. He contributes to a number of publications and presents a weekly Arts programme on Galway Bay FM. He has been working as a manager of Charlie Byrne's Independent Bookshop since 1990. He currently sits on the board of The Galway Arts Centre and has been involved with the Cúirt International Festival of Literature since 2003.

NICHOLA BRUCE works with the moving image, and directed Dermot Healy in *I Could Read the Sky* (1999). Her work is primarily about expressing the way the mind composites vision through memory. She films elements of her life almost every day and has an extensive archive, which informs her larger projects. These projects include experimental work, dramas and documentaries. She was awarded a National Endowment Science Technology and the Arts Fellowship for her study of perception. Her work is exhibited through cinema, broadcasts, installations, single and multiple screenings at galleries and other venues, and is available online: <www.nicholabruce.com>.

HARRY CLIFTON was Ireland Professor of Poetry from 2010 to 2013. *The Holding Centre: Selected Poems 1974-2004* was published in 2014 by Bloodaxe Books.

FLORE COULOUMA is an Associate Professor in the English Department at the Université Paris Ouest Nanterre, where she teaches English linguistics and Irish literature. She is the author of *Diglossia and The Linguistic Turn: Flann O'Brien's Philosophy of Language* (2015), and has written on contemporary Irish and American literature and on American and Irish TV series, applying pragmatics and discourse analysis to literary and fictional texts. Her research interests include ecocriticism, social justice, and law and linguistics. She is currently working on the representation of linguistic, social and legal norms in both fictional and real-life corpuses.

MICHAEL CRONIN holds a Personal Chair in the Faculty of Humanities and Social Sciences at Dublin City University, Ireland. He is the author and editor of many books including *Tourism in Ireland: A Critical Analysis* (1993), *Translating Ireland: Translation, Languages and Identity* (1996), *Reinventing Ireland: Culture, Society and the Global Economy* (2002), *Translation and Globalization* (2003), *Time Tracks: Scenes from the Irish Everyday* (2003), *Irish Tourism: Image, Culture and Identity* (2003), *The Languages of Ireland* (2003), *Irish in the New Century/An Ghaeilge san Aois Nua* (2005), *The Barrytown Trilogy* (Ireland into Film series, 2007), *Transforming Ireland* (2009), and *The Expanding World: Towards a Politics of Microspection* (2012). He is a Member of the Royal Irish Academy.

GERALD DAWE's most recent publications include *Selected Poems* (2012), *Mickey Finn's Air* (2014) and *Of War and War's Alarms: Reflections on Modern Irish Writing* (2015). He teaches at Trinity College Dublin.

RODDY DOYLE was born in Dublin in 1958. He is the author of ten novels, including *The Commitments* (1987), *Paddy Clarke Ha Ha Ha*, for which he won the Booker Prize in 1993, and *The Guts* (2013). He has written two collections of short stories, including *Bullfighting* (2011); *Rory & Ita* (2002), a memoir about his parents; and a series of dialogues, called *Two Pints* (2012) and *Two More Pints* (2014). He has written seven books for children, and has also written for stage and the small and big screens. He lives and works in Dublin.

KATE FAGAN is a poet, musician, and academic who lectures in Literary Studies within the School of Humanities and Communication Arts at Western Sydney University. She is a prominent Australian innovative poet, and her most recent volume of poems *First Light* (2012) was shortlisted for both the Age Book of the Year Award and the NSW Premier's Literary Awards. She is a former editor-in-chief of *How2*, the American-based journal of contemporary and modernist innovative poetry and poetics scholarship. Kate Fagan is well known across Australia and the U.K. as a folk-roots songwriter, and her album *Diamond Wheel* won the National Film and Sound Archive Award for Folk Recording.

PAUL FAGAN is a lecturer and researcher at the University of Vienna and a Senior Scientist at the University of Salzburg. He is the co-founder and president of the International Flann O'Brien Society, as well as co-founder and series editor of the peer-reviewed society journal *The Parish Review*. He is the co-editor, with Ruben Borg and Werner Huber, of *Flann O'Brien: Contesting Legacies*, and has published articles and reviews in *James Joyce Quarterly*, *European Joyce Studies*, *Joyce Studies in Italy*, *The Parish Review*, and *Partial Answers: Journal of Literature and the History of Ideas*, with chapters in edited collections from Syracuse University Press, Manchester University Press, Cork University Press, and Brill/Rodopi. He is currently completing a monograph under the title *Positions of Distrust: The Literary Hoax from Swift to Beckett*.

JACK FENNELL teaches and researches at the University of Limerick, where he teaches American Literature, Postcolonial Literature and Utopian Studies; his primary research interests are Irish literature, science fiction and Gothic literature, and he has published on topics such as Catholic ideology, the depiction of justice in comic books, monstrous communities, and the science fiction of Flann O'Brien. He is the author of *Irish Science Fiction* (2014), a former Irish Research Council scholar, and a visiting fellow at the Moore Institute, NUI Galway. He has also contributed a number of translated short stories to *The Short Fiction of Flann O'Brien* (2013).

TESS GALLAGHER's *Midnight Lantern: New and Selected Poems*, from Bloodaxe Press in England is her ninth volume of poetry. Other poetry volumes include *Dear Ghosts, Moon Crossing Bridge*, and *Amplitude*. Blackstaff Press in Belfast published *Barnacle Soup—Stories from the West of Ireland*, a collaboration with the Sligo storyteller Josie Gray. She also spearheaded the publication of Raymond Carver's *Beginners* with Jonathan Cape as a single volume. Most recently she has been involved in the film *Birdman* with director Alejandro Iñárritu, which presents both a poem and a story from her late husband, Raymond Carver. She spends time in a cottage on Lough Arrow in Co. Sligo in the West of Ireland where many of her new poems are set, and also lives and writes in her hometown of Port Angeles, Washington.

SEÁN GOLDEN was born of Irish parents in London. Early childhood in Ballina and Ballaghaderreen (Ireland). Schooled in Connecticut and Massachusetts (USA). Returned to the home place in Ireland to live. Worked some years in Tianjin (China), later in Barcelona (Spain), while keeping a home in Ireland. Before China, a specialist in Irish Studies and James Joyce; after, a specialist in Chinese thought, politics, and international relations. Published in *The Crane Bag* and *The Field Day Anthology of Irish Writing*, as well as *Cyphers, Force 10, The SHOp* and *The Stinging Fly*. Co-editor with Peter Fallon of *Soft Day: A Miscellany of Contemporary Irish Writing*. Numerous translations of Chinese poetry, classical and contemporary. Divides his time now among Barcelona (Spain), Ballyconnell (Sligo, Ireland) and Beijing (China).

DEREK HAND is a Senior Lecturer and Head of the English Department in the English Department at St Patrick's College, Dublin City University. He is interested in Irish writing in general and has published articles on W. B. Yeats, Elizabeth Bowen, Colum McCann, Molly Keane, Benedict Kiely, Mary Lavin, and William Trevor, and on contemporary Irish fiction. He has lectured on Irish writing in the USA,

Portugal, Sweden, Singapore, Brazil, Italy, Sweden and France. The Liffey Press published his book *John Banville: Exploring Fictions* in 2002. He edited a special edition of the *Irish University Review* on John Banville in 2006 and co-edited a special edition of the *Irish University Review* on Benedict Kiely in 2008. He was awarded an IRCHSS Government of Ireland Research Fellowship for 2008-2009. His book *A History of the Irish Novel: 1665 to the present* was published by Cambridge University Press in 2011 and has recently come out in paperback. He is now working on a critical study of recent Irish fiction for Syracuse University Press tentatively entitled *The Celtic Tiger Irish Novel 1994-2010: Modernity and Mediocrity*.

MICHAEL HARDING is the author of three novels, two volumes of memoir and his weekly column in the *Irish Times* has been described as a "creative chronicle of rural Ireland." He is also a playwright and performer, and was a recipient of the Stewart Parker Theatre Bursary in 1990 and the Bank of Ireland/RTÉ award for excellence in the Arts in the same year. He won the Hennessy Literary Award for short stories in 1980, and became a member of Aosdána in 2000.

AIDAN HIGGINS (1927-2015) was considered by many as the natural heir to master stylists James Joyce and Samuel Beckett. His books include *Langrishe, Go Down* (1966) which won the James Tait Black Memorial Prize, and which was filmed for television with a screenplay by Harold Pinter. He travelled widely in Europe and Africa, and lived in Johannesburg, Berlin, Andalucía and London before settling in Kinsale. His much-lauded novel *Balcony of Europe* (1972) was published in a revised version edited by Neil Murphy in 2010. *Donkey's Years* and *Dog Days* were the first two volumes of his memoirs. The third volume, *The Whole Hog* was short-listed for the Irish Times Fiction Prize. These memoirs are also published in one volume entitled *A Bestiary* (2004). He was a member of Aosdána, and received an honorary Doctorate of Letters from the National University of Ireland in 2001. He passed away on December 27, 2015.

CATHERINE HOFFMANN is Senior Lecturer in English at the University of Le Havre (France), and a member of the research group

FoReLL at the University of Poitiers. Her main fields of research include narratological and intermedial approaches to the work of some twentieth-century English novelists, especially Anthony Powell, space and literature, geopoetics, and, since very recently, ecopoetics. Her interest in Dermot Healy's work began with the chance discovery of *A Goat's Song* and she is the author of an essay on *Sudden Times*, "Dancing to Ollie's Tunes: The Rhetoric of Narrative Stutter," published in *Style* 43.3 (2009).

ALANNAH HOPKIN lives in Kinsale, Co. Cork. She grew up in London and studied at Queen Mary University of London and the University of Essex. She has published two novels, *A Joke Goes a Long Way in the Country* and *The Out-Haul*; her non-fiction books include *Eating Scenery: West Cork, the People & the Place*. Her stories have appeared in the *London Magazine* and *The Cork Literary Review*, amongst others, and have been broadcast on Irish radio. She has written guides to Ireland for Fodor's, Insight and Berlitz. She is a regular contributor to the *Irish Arts Review*, and a member of AICA, the International Association of Art Critics. She currently reviews books for the *Irish Examiner*, and has led writing workshops to MA level. Her first story collection will appear shortly.

NEIL JORDAN was born in Sligo in 1950. His debut collection of stories, *Night in Tunisia*, won the 1979 Guardian Fiction Prize. His critically-acclaimed novels include *The Past*, *The Dream of a Beast*, *Sunrise with Sea Monster*, *Shade* and *Mistaken*. Of the many films he has written and directed, several have won multiple international awards, including an Oscar (for *The Crying Game*), a Golden Bear at Venice (for *Michael Collins*), a Silver Bear at Berlin (for *The Butcher Boy*) and several BAFTAs (for *Mona Lisa* and *The End of the Affair*). He lives in Dublin.

GARRY KEANE has been directing documentaries across all genres for over twenty years. A graduate of the London College of Printing and The National Film School IADT, he has filmed in over twenty countries worldwide and has worked for the BBC, Channel 4, PBS, the Biography Channel, MTV, Setanta Sports and RTÉ. In 2012 he won an IFTA for "Best Director in Television" for his Arts Lives documentary on Dermot Healy, *The Writing in the Sky*. He lives in Donegal with his wife Alison and their three children.

BRIAN LEYDEN is the author of the bestselling memoir *The Home Place*, the short story collection *Departures*, and the novel *Death and Plenty*. He won the RTÉ Radio 1 Francis MacManus Short Story Award in 1988. He has written extensively for RTÉ's *Sunday Miscellany*. His radio documentary work includes *No Meadows in Manhattan*, *Even the Walls Were Sweatin'*, *The Closing of the Gaiety Cinema in Carrick-on-Shannon* and most recently, *An Irish Station Mass*. He co-wrote the original screenplay for the feature film *Black Ice*, which premiered at the Jameson Dublin International Film Festival. He received an Arts Council of Ireland Literary Bursary in 2014. His most recent work is *Sweet Old World—New & Selected Stories* (2015).

MICHAEL LONGLEY has published nine collections of poetry. He is the winner of the Whitbread Poetry Award, the Hawthornden Prize, the T. S. Eliot Prize and the *Irish Times* Poetry Prize. His most recent collection is *A Hundred Doors* (2011), and his *Collected Poems* appeared in 2006. He has received honorary degrees from Queen's University Belfast, Trinity College Dublin, the Open University and University College Dublin. He is a Fellow of the Royal Society of Literature, a Fellow of the American Academy of Arts and Sciences, and a member of Aosdána. He was the winner of the American Ireland Fund Literary Award in 1996. In 2001 he received the Queen's Gold Medal for Poetry, and in 2003 the Wilfred Owen Award. He was awarded a CBE in 2010, and was the Ireland Professor of Poetry from 2007 to 2010. He and his wife, the literary critic Edna Longley, live and work in Belfast.

PATRICK McCABE was born in Clones, Co. Monaghan, where he still lives. He is the author of several novels: *The Butcher Boy* (1992), *The Dead School* (1995), *Breakfast on Pluto* (1998), *Emerald Germs of Ireland* (2001), *Winterwood* (2006), *The Holy City* (2008), and *The Stray Sod Country* (2010). He is also the author of a children's book, *The Adventures of Shay Mouse* (1985), and a collection of linked short stories, *Mondo Desperado* (1999). His play *Frank Pig Says Hello*, which he adapted from *The Butcher Boy*, was first performed at the Dublin Theatre Festival in 1992. He became a member of Aosdána in 2012.

DERMOT McCARTHY is Professor Emeritus of English Literature at Huron University College, London, Ontario, where he taught modern Irish, British, and Canadian literatures. He is the author of *Roddy Doyle: Raining on the Parade* (2003), *John McGahern and the Art of Memory* (2010) and *The Comfort of Love: The Fiction of Jennifer Johnston* (which has yet to find a publisher).

MOLLY McCLOSKEY was born in Philadelphia and grew up in Oregon. In 1989, she moved to Sligo, Ireland, where she published her first fiction in Dermot Healy's *Force 10* journal. She is the author of a collection of short stories, *Solomon's Seal*; a novella, *The Beautiful Changes*; a novel, *Protection*; and a memoir, *Circles Around the Sun*, concerning her brother Mike, who suffers from schizophrenia. She is a regular contributor to the *Irish Times* and the *Dublin Review*, and has taught writing at universities in Ireland and the US. She has also worked for the United Nations in their Kenya-based Office for the Coordination of Humanitarian Affairs for Somalia. After spending twenty-three years in Ireland, she now lives between Washington, D.C. and Dublin.

MIKE McCORMACK is the author of two collections of short stories, *Getting It in the Head* and *Forensic Songs*, and three novels, *Crowe's Requiem, Notes from a Coma*, and *Solar Bones*. In 1996, he was awarded the Rooney Prize for Literature and *Getting It in the Head* was chosen as a *New York Times* Notable Book of the Year. A short film, which he scripted from one of the stories in that collection, was long-listed for an Academy Award in 2003. In 2006, *Notes from a Coma* was shortlisted for the Irish Book of the Year Award; it was recently published by SOHO Press in New York. He was awarded a Civitella Ranieri Fellowship in 2007, and he has been the recipient of several Arts Council Bursaries.

EOIN McNAMEE was born in Kilkeel, Co. Down, in 1961. He has written seventeen novels including *Resurrection Man*, which was turned into a film in 1997, and *The Ultras*. His latest novel is *Blue is the Night*, the third book of the *Blue* trilogy. He lives in Co. Sligo.

DANNY MORRISON (b.1953) is a Belfast-based writer and political commentator. He is the author of four novels: *West Belfast*, *On the Back of the Swallow*, *The Wrong Man* and *Rudi: In the Shadow of Knulp*. His non-fiction books include *Then the Walls Came Down: A Prison Journal*; a memoir, *All The Dead Voices*; and *Rebel Columns*, a collection of political writings. He also edited *Hunger Strike: Reflections on the 1981 Hunger Strike*. His critically-acclaimed play *The Wrong Man* was staged in Belfast, Dublin, London and the Edinburgh Fringe. His short stories have been broadcast on BBC, RTÉ and Lyric FM and have appeared in a number of publications. He is currently working on a fifth novel, provisionally entitled *Band on the Run*, and a play, *The Mental*. He is a former national director of publicity for Sinn Féin and a former republican political prisoner.

PHILIP Ó CEALLAIGH won the Rooney Prize for Irish Literature in 2006. He has published two collections of stories: *Notes from a Turkish Whorehouse* (2006), which won the Glen Dimplex New Writers Award for fiction, and *The Pleasant Light of Day* (2009). Both books were shortlisted for the Frank O'Connor International Short Story Award. He also edited the anthology *Sharp Sticks, Driven Nails* for The Stinging Fly Press in 2010. He lives in Bucharest.

GEORGE O'BRIEN was born in Ireland, educated at Ruskin College, Oxford, and the University of Warwick, and is Professor of English at Georgetown University, Washington D.C. Among his various publications are three volumes of memoirs, *The Village of Longing* (1987), *Dancehall Days* (1988) and *Out of Our Minds* (1994). More recently, he has published *The Irish Novel: 1960–2010* (2012).

TIMOTHY O'GRADY was born in Chicago and has lived in Ireland, London, Spain and Poland. He is the author of three works of non-fiction and three novels. His novel *Motherland* won the David Higham award for the best first novel in 1989. His novel *I Could Read the Sky*, a collaboration with photographer Steve Pyke, won the Encore Award for best second novel of 1997. *I Could Read the Sky* was filmed and also travelled as a stage show. His most recent novel is *Light*, published in 2004. His non-fiction books are *Curious Journey: An Oral History of Ireland's Unfinished Revolution*, *On Golf* and *Divine Magnetic Lands*, an account of a return journey to the United States after thirty years of living in Europe, published in 2008. His book *Children of Las Vegas* is due to appear in 2016.

MARY O'MALLEY was born in Connemara and educated at NUI Galway. She has served on the council of Poetry Ireland and on the committee of the Cúirt International Poetry Festival. She taught on the MA programmes for Writing and Education in the Arts at NUI Galway for ten years; held the Chair of Irish Studies at Villanova University in 2013; and has held Residencies in Paris, Tarragona, New York, NUI Galway, as well as in Derry, Belfast and Mayo. Her published works include seven books of poetry, the most recent being *Valparaiso*, which arose out of her Residency onboard the Irish national marine research ship. She is a member of Aosdána, and is currently working on a memoir of childhood.

GLENN PATTERSON is the author of ten novels, the most recent of which, *Gull*, is based on the story of the DeLorean Motor Company. *The Mill for Grinding Old People Young* (2012) was Belfast's first One City One Book choice. *Here's Me Here*, a collection featuring his articles and essays for print and broadcast was published in 2015 by New Island, which previously published the collection *Lapsed Protestant*. A memoir, *Once Upon a Hill: Love in Troubled Times* was published in 2008. His first feature film *Good Vibrations* (co-written with Colin Carberry) was released in 2013.

MICHELLE PAULL is Senior Lecturer in Theatre & Performance Studies at St Mary's University, Twickenham, where she also teaches on the MA in Irish Studies and the MA in International Ensemble Theatre. Her publications include book chapters on George Bernard Shaw, Enda Walsh, and Sean O'Casey. Research interests include contemporary theatre and fiction, adaptation studies, and Daphne Du Maurier. She is currently writing a monograph on the later plays of Sean O'Casey entitled *Sean O'Casey: Critical Controversies*.

ANNIE PROULX, independent scholar and recipient of several literary awards, currently reads and writes in the Pacific Northwest state of Washington.

Contributors

STEVE PYKE moved to London in 1977. He became a singer in a number of bands and was involved with establishing a record label and several fanzines. In 1979 he became a photographer and from 1981 to 1984 worked continuously for a diverse mixture of publications including *The Face* and *NME*. He was made staff photographer at *The New Yorker* in 2004 and has been a regular contributor since 1998. Throughout his career he has developed, funded and published a number of personal projects. Best known are those on the world's leading thinkers—*Philosophers*. More recently he completed his series *Astronauts*. For the past two decades, he has worked consistently on his series collecting the *Faces of our Times*. He has published ten books. His photographs have been exhibited widely in the UK, Europe, Japan and North America. His work is held in international permanent collections. In 2004 he received the MBE in the Queen's New Year's Honours list for his services to the Arts. In 2006 he was made a Friend of the Royal Photographic Society. He lives in New York City.

THIERRY ROBIN has been a senior lecturer at the European University of Brittany, Brest, since 2005. His research focuses on contemporary Irish literature and the connections between ideology, satire, stereotypes, epistemology and the concepts of reality and identity. He has written on Samuel Beckett, John Banville/Benjamin Black, Anne Enright, and Dermot Healy, and is the author of a book-length study of Flann O'Brien's novels entitled *Flann O'Brien, Un voyageur au bout du langage* (2008). He is the co-editor (with Patrick Galliou) of a collection of essays entitled *Political Ideology in Ireland from the Enlightenment to the Present* (2009).

RONAN SHEEHAN was born in Dublin in 1953. He was educated at Gonzaga College, University College Dublin, and The Incorporated Law Society. Published works include *Tennis Players* (1977), *Boy with an Injured Eye* (1983), *The Heart of the City* (1988), and *Foley's Asia* (1999). The National Library of Ireland created an archive of his manuscripts in 2003. He worked on the cultural and political journal *The Crane Bag*, where he edited a special edition on Latin America. A passionate advocate of the Latin poet Catullus, he edited *The Irish Catullus: One Gentleman from Verona* (2010). He lives in Dublin.

GERRY SMYTH is originally from Dublin. He is Reader in Cultural History at Liverpool John Moores University, and has published widely on many aspects of Irish cultural history, with particular interests in music, fiction and modernism. His books include *The Novel and the Nation* (1997), *Space and the Irish Cultural Imagination* (2001), *Noisy Island* (2005) and most recently *The Judas Kiss: Treason and Betrayal in Six Modern Irish Novels* (2015). He is currently completing a book entitled *Celtic Tiger Blues: Music and Modern Irish Identity*, due for publication in 2016. He is also a musician, actor and playwright, with work performed throughout Ireland, Britain and Europe.

BILL SWAINSON is a British literary consultant and freelance editor with forty years' experience in independent and mainstream publishing. He was until recently Senior Commissioning Editor at Bloomsbury (2000 to 2015), and previously worked at the Harvill Press, Fourth Estate, Allison & Busby, and John Calder (Publishers) Ltd. He has published fiction and non-fiction, including books by Mourid Barghouti, Javier Cercas, Rajiv Chandrasekaran, Paul Durcan, Carlos Fuentes, Nadine Gordimer, Al Gore, A. C. Grayling, Oscar Guardiola-Rivera, Dermot Healy, Aidan Higgins, Rachel Holmes, Elizabeth Kolbert, David Kynaston, John Lahr, Gerald Martin, Amin Maalouf, Magnus Mills, Laurie Penny, Jacqueline Rose, Boualem Sansal, Judith Schalansky, W. G. Sebald, Will Self, Hasan Ali Toptaş, Juan Gabriel Vásquez, and Delphine de Vigan. He has been a board member of the Poetry Society, the Poetry Book Society and The Poetry Translation Centre, and a literary advisor to the British Centre for Literary Translation and, since 1999, to the Santa Maddalena Foundation in Italy. In 2015 he was awarded an OBE for services to literary translation.

COLM TÓIBÍN, the author of eight novels, is Mellon Professor of Humanities at Columbia University. His latest book is *On Elizabeth Bishop*.

ABOUT THE EDITORS

Neil Murphy teaches contemporary literature at NTU, Singapore. He is the author of *Irish Fiction and Postmodern Doubt* (2004) and editor of *Aidan Higgins: The Fragility of Form* (2010) and of the revised edition of Higgins's *Balcony of Europe* (2010). He co-edited (with Keith Hopper) a special Flann O'Brien centenary issue of the *Review of Contemporary Fiction* (2011) and *The Short Fiction of Flann O'Brien* (2013). He has published numerous articles and book chapters on contemporary fiction, Irish writing, and theories of reading, and is currently completing a book on John Banville.

Keith Hopper teaches Literature and Film Studies at Oxford University's Department for Continuing Education, and is a Research Fellow in the Centre for Irish Studies at St Mary's University, Twickenham. He is the author of *Flann O'Brien: A Portrait of the Artist as a Young Post-modernist* (revised edition 2009), general editor of the twelve-volume *Ireland into Film* series (2001-7), and co-editor (with Neil Murphy and Ondřej Pilný) of a special "Neglected Irish Fiction" issue of *Litteraria Pragensia* (2013). He is a regular contributor to the *Times Literary Supplement* and is currently completing a book on Neil Jordan.

Writing the Sky: Observations and Essays on Dermot Healy (2016) is part of a multi-volume sequence published by Dalkey Archive Press and edited by Neil Murphy and Keith Hopper. It also includes *Dermot Healy: The Collected Short Stories* (2015), *Fighting with Shadows* (2015), and *Dermot Healy: The Collected Plays* (2016).

Reviews of *The Collected Short Stories* and *Fighting with Shadows*

"Dalkey Archive Press has republished Dermot Healy's first novel, *Fighting with Shadows*, and issued his *Collected Short Stories*. These books provide an insight into the most extraordinary Irish literary consciousness of the last fifty years. [. . .] What lies before you in these books is both a gift to see the world with a clarity not often granted, and the immense will and virtuosity to render that vision as art." (Eoin McNamee, *Irish Times*, 2015)

"Before Murphy and Hopper's accomplished reissue of *Fighting with Shadows* the novel has been out of print since 1986. What was a reasonably chaotic text has become lucid and elegant under editorial guidance, and is now rigged with an introduction, a glossary of Irish terms and a list of published extracts from the novel that gives readers a view into Healy's methods of composition and revision. The clarity of the editorship supports an appreciation of Healy's style: his innovations with dialogue and reported speech have flowered, free of typographical weeds. Much the same can be said for the editors' work on *The Collected Short Stories*, which is a triumph of colourful and rational compilation." (Luke Maxted, *Times Literary Supplement*, 2016)

"If these stories haven't previously found favour with a popular audience, that's probably because the images contained within all of them are unsettling, violent and troublesome. But maybe that's the point: Healy doesn't want to make us feel warm or sentimental. Questioning everything – out past, our identity, our tribal allegiances, our quarrels, and our very existence – isn't supposed to be easy. But Healy's magisterial writing makes it a noble quest worth returning to." (John Paul O'Malley, *Sunday Independent* 2015)

"In a development that should help redress the neglect of a significant and highly distinctive Irish writer, Dalkey Archive Press has now published Healy's collected stories along with a reissue of his first novel, *Fighting with Shadows*. Encompassing more than four decades of work, *The Collected Short Stories* is a perfect introduction to Healy's voice, showcasing his intense engagement with language and his imagistic, often mesmeric writing style. Keith Hopper and Neil Murphy are conscientious, unpatronising editors. Their introduction locates their subject within the literary tradition from which he has been largely excluded. They point out that Healy is essentially a modernist, a descendant of Joyce, Beckett and other experimental writers such as Faulkner, Kafka and Borges. [. . .] But, as is so often the case with Healy, the brilliance lies beneath the surface of the work, which, like the majority of these stories, conjures up an entire world with all of its mind-sets, prejudices and shifting tensions." (Joanne Hayden, *Sunday Business Post*, 2015)

"The publication of this collection serves Healy scholars as well as readers fundamentally interested in the art of fiction. The pieces exemplify what's possible in fiction and likewise suggest how elusive those opportunities are but for the most capable creators." (John G. Matthews, *Library Journal*, 2015)

SELECTED DALKEY ARCHIVE TITLES

MICHAL AJVAZ, *The Golden Age.*
The Other City.
PIERRE ALBERT-BIROT, *Grabinoulor.*
YUZ ALESHKOVSKY, *Kangaroo.*
FELIPE ALFAU, *Chromos.*
Locos.
JOE AMATO, *Samuel Taylor's Last Night.*
IVAN ÂNGELO, *The Celebration.*
The Tower of Glass.
ANTÓNIO LOBO ANTUNES, *Knowledge of Hell.*
The Splendor of Portugal.
ALAIN ARIAS-MISSON, *Theatre of Incest.*
JOHN ASHBERY & JAMES SCHUYLER, *A Nest of Ninnies.*
ROBERT ASHLEY, *Perfect Lives.*
GABRIELA AVIGUR-ROTEM, *Heatwave and Crazy Birds.*
DJUNA BARNES, *Ladies Almanack.*
Ryder.
JOHN BARTH, *Letters.*
Sabbatical.
DONALD BARTHELME, *The King.*
Paradise.
SVETISLAV BASARA, *Chinese Letter.*
MIQUEL BAUÇÀ, *The Siege in the Room.*
RENÉ BELLETTO, *Dying.*
MAREK BIENCZYK, *Transparency.*
ANDREI BITOV, *Pushkin House.*
ANDREJ BLATNIK, *You Do Understand.*
Law of Desire.
LOUIS PAUL BOON, *Chapel Road.*
My Little War.
Summer in Termuren.
ROGER BOYLAN, *Killoyle.*
IGNÁCIO DE LOYOLA BRANDÃO, *Anonymous Celebrity.*
Zero.
BONNIE BREMSER, *Troia: Mexican Memoirs.*
CHRISTINE BROOKE-ROSE, *Amalgamemnon.*
BRIGID BROPHY, *In Transit.*
The Prancing Novelist.

GERALD L. BRUNS, *Modern Poetry and the Idea of Language.*
GABRIELLE BURTON, *Heartbreak Hotel.*
MICHEL BUTOR, *Degrees.*
Mobile.
G. CABRERA INFANTE, *Infante's Inferno.*
Three Trapped Tigers.
JULIETA CAMPOS, *The Fear of Losing Eurydice.*
ANNE CARSON, *Eros the Bittersweet.*
ORLY CASTEL-BLOOM, *Dolly City.*
LOUIS-FERDINAND CÉLINE, *North.*
Conversations with Professor Y.
London Bridge.
MARIE CHAIX, *The Laurels of Lake Constance.*
HUGO CHARTERIS, *The Tide Is Right.*
ERIC CHEVILLARD, *Demolishing Nisard.*
The Author and Me.
MARC CHOLODENKO, *Mordechai Schamz.*
JOSHUA COHEN, *Witz.*
EMILY HOLMES COLEMAN, *The Shutter of Snow.*
ERIC CHEVILLARD, *The Author and Me.*
ROBERT COOVER, *A Night at the Movies.*
STANLEY CRAWFORD, *Log of the S.S. The Mrs Unguentine.*
Some Instructions to My Wife.
RENÉ CREVEL, *Putting My Foot in It.*
RALPH CUSACK, *Cadenza.*
NICHOLAS DELBANCO, *Sherbrookes.*
The Count of Concord.
NIGEL DENNIS, *Cards of Identity.*
PETER DIMOCK, *A Short Rhetoric for Leaving the Family.*
ARIEL DORFMAN, *Konfidenz.*
COLEMAN DOWELL, *Island People.*
Too Much Flesh and Jabez.
ARKADII DRAGOMOSHCHENKO, *Dust.*
RIKKI DUCORNET, *Phosphor in Dreamland.*
The Complete Butcher's Tales.

FOR A FULL LIST OF PUBLICATIONS, VISIT: www.dalkeyarchive.com

SELECTED DALKEY ARCHIVE TITLES

RIKKI DUCORNET (cont.), *The Jade Cabinet.*
The Fountains of Neptune.
WILLIAM EASTLAKE, *The Bamboo Bed.*
Castle Keep.
Lyric of the Circle Heart.
JEAN ECHENOZ, *Chopin's Move.*
STANLEY ELKIN, *A Bad Man.*
Criers and Kibitzers, Kibitzers and Criers.
The Dick Gibson Show.
The Franchiser.
The Living End.
Mrs. Ted Bliss.
FRANÇOIS EMMANUEL, *Invitation to a Voyage.*
PAUL EMOND, *The Dance of a Sham.*
SALVADOR ESPRIU, *Ariadne in the Grotesque Labyrinth.*
LESLIE A. FIEDLER, *Love and Death in the American Novel.*
JUAN FILLOY, *Op Oloop.*
ANDY FITCH, *Pop Poetics.*
GUSTAVE FLAUBERT, *Bouvard and Pécuchet.*
KASS FLEISHER, *Talking out of School.*
JON FOSSE, *Aliss at the Fire.*
Melancholy.
FORD MADOX FORD, *The March of Literature.*
MAX FRISCH, *I'm Not Stiller.*
Man in the Holocene.
CARLOS FUENTES, *Christopher Unborn.*
Distant Relations.
Terra Nostra.
Where the Air Is Clear.
TAKEHIKO FUKUNAGA, *Flowers of Grass.*
WILLIAM GADDIS, JR., *The Recognitions.*
JANICE GALLOWAY, *Foreign Parts.*
The Trick Is to Keep Breathing.
WILLIAM H. GASS, *Life Sentences.*
The Tunnel.
The World Within the Word.
Willie Masters' Lonesome Wife.
GÉRARD GAVARRY, *Hoppla! 1 2 3.*

ETIENNE GILSON, *The Arts of the Beautiful.*
Forms and Substances in the Arts.
C. S. GISCOMBE, *Giscome Road.*
Here.
DOUGLAS GLOVER, *Bad News of the Heart.*
WITOLD GOMBROWICZ, *A Kind of Testament.*
PAULO EMÍLIO SALES GOMES, *P's Three Women.*
GEORGI GOSPODINOV, *Natural Novel.*
JUAN GOYTISOLO, *Count Julian.*
Juan the Landless.
Makbara.
Marks of Identity.
HENRY GREEN, *Blindness.*
Concluding.
Doting.
Nothing.
JACK GREEN, *Fire the Bastards!*
JIŘÍ GRUŠA, *The Questionnaire.*
MELA HARTWIG, *Am I a Redundant Human Being?*
JOHN HAWKES, *The Passion Artist.*
Whistlejacket.
ELIZABETH HEIGHWAY, ED., *Contemporary Georgian Fiction.*
AIDAN HIGGINS, *Balcony of Europe.*
Blind Man's Bluff.
Bornholm Night-Ferry.
Langrishe, Go Down.
Scenes from a Receding Past.
KEIZO HINO, *Isle of Dreams.*
KAZUSHI HOSAKA, *Plainsong.*
ALDOUS HUXLEY, *Antic Hay.*
Point Counter Point.
Those Barren Leaves.
Time Must Have a Stop.
NAOYUKI II, *The Shadow of a Blue Cat.*
DRAGO JANČAR, *The Tree with No Name.*
MIKHEIL JAVAKHISHVILI, *Kvachi.*
GERT JONKE, *The Distant Sound.*
Homage to Czerny.
The System of Vienna.

FOR A FULL LIST OF PUBLICATIONS, VISIT: www.dalkeyarchive.com

SELECTED DALKEY ARCHIVE TITLES

JACQUES JOUET, *Mountain R.*
Savage.
Upstaged.
MIEKO KANAI, *The Word Book.*
YORAM KANIUK, *Life on Sandpaper.*
ZURAB KARUMIDZE, *Dagny.*
JOHN KELLY, *From Out of the City.*
HUGH KENNER, *Flaubert, Joyce and Beckett: The Stoic Comedians.*
Joyce's Voices.
DANILO KIŠ, *The Attic.*
The Lute and the Scars.
Psalm 44.
A Tomb for Boris Davidovich.
ANITA KONKKA, *A Fool's Paradise.*
GEORGE KONRÁD, *The City Builder.*
TADEUSZ KONWICKI, *A Minor Apocalypse.*
The Polish Complex.
ANNA KORDZAIA-SAMADASHVILI, *Me, Margarita.*
MENIS KOUMANDAREAS, *Koula.*
ELAINE KRAF, *The Princess of 72nd Street.*
JIM KRUSOE, *Iceland.*
AYSE KULIN, *Farewell: A Mansion in Occupied Istanbul.*
EMILIO LASCANO TEGUI, *On Elegance While Sleeping.*
ERIC LAURRENT, *Do Not Touch.*
VIOLETTE LEDUC, *La Bâtarde.*
EDOUARD LEVÉ, *Autoportrait.*
Newspaper.
Suicide.
Works.
MARIO LEVI, *Istanbul Was a Fairy Tale.*
DEBORAH LEVY, *Billy and Girl.*
JOSÉ LEZAMA LIMA, *Paradiso.*
ROSA LIKSOM, *Dark Paradise.*
OSMAN LINS, *Avalovara.*
The Queen of the Prisons of Greece.
FLORIAN LIPUŠ, *The Errors of Young Tjaž.*
GORDON LISH, *Peru.*
ALF MACLOCHLAINN, *Out of Focus.*
Past Habitual.
The Corpus in the Library.
RON LOEWINSOHN, *Magnetic Field(s).*
YURI LOTMAN, *Non-Memoirs.*
D. KEITH MANO, *Take Five.*
MINA LOY, *Stories and Essays of Mina Loy.*
MICHELINE AHARONIAN MARCOM, *A Brief History of Yes.*
The Mirror in the Well.
BEN MARCUS, *The Age of Wire and String.*
WALLACE MARKFIELD, *Teitlebaum's Window.*
DAVID MARKSON, *Reader's Block.*
Wittgenstein's Mistress.
CAROLE MASO, *AVA.*
HISAKI MATSUURA, *Triangle.*
LADISLAV MATEJKA & KRYSTYNA POMORSKA, EDS., *Readings in Russian Poetics: Formalist & Structuralist Views.*
HARRY MATHEWS, *Cigarettes.*
The Conversions.
The Human Country.
The Journalist.
My Life in CIA.
Singular Pleasures.
The Sinking of the Odradek.
Stadium.
Tlooth.
HISAKI MATSUURA, *Triangle.*
DONAL MCLAUGHLIN, *beheading the virgin mary, and other stories.*
JOSEPH MCELROY, *Night Soul and Other Stories.*
ABDELWAHAB MEDDEB, *Talismano.*
GERHARD MEIER, *Isle of the Dead.*
HERMAN MELVILLE, *The Confidence-Man.*
AMANDA MICHALOPOULOU, *I'd Like.*
STEVEN MILLHAUSER, *The Barnum Museum.*
In the Penny Arcade.
RALPH J. MILLS, JR., *Essays on Poetry.*
MOMUS, *The Book of Jokes.*
CHRISTINE MONTALBETTI, *The Origin of Man.*
Western.

FOR A FULL LIST OF PUBLICATIONS, VISIT: www.dalkeyarchive.com

SELECTED DALKEY ARCHIVE TITLES

NICHOLAS MOSLEY, *Accident.*
Assassins.
Catastrophe Practice.
A Garden of Trees.
Hopeful Monsters.
Imago Bird.
Inventing God.
Look at the Dark.
Metamorphosis.
Natalie Natalia.
Serpent.
WARREN MOTTE, *Fables of the Novel: French Fiction since 1990.*
Fiction Now: The French Novel in the 21st Century.
Mirror Gazing.
Oulipo: A Primer of Potential Literature.
GERALD MURNANE, *Barley Patch.*
Inland.
YVES NAVARRE, *Our Share of Time.*
Sweet Tooth.
DOROTHY NELSON, *In Night's City.*
Tar and Feathers.
ESHKOL NEVO, *Homesick.*
WILFRIDO D. NOLLEDO, *But for the Lovers.*
BORIS A. NOVAK, *The Master of Insomnia.*
FLANN O'BRIEN, *At Swim-Two-Birds.*
The Best of Myles.
The Dalkey Archive.
The Hard Life.
The Poor Mouth.
The Third Policeman.
CLAUDE OLLIER, *The Mise-en-Scène.*
Wert and the Life Without End.
PATRIK OUŘEDNÍK, *Europeana.*
The Opportune Moment, 1855.
BORIS PAHOR, *Necropolis.*
FERNANDO DEL PASO, *News from the Empire.*
Palinuro of Mexico.
ROBERT PINGET, *The Inquisitory.*
Mahu or The Material.
Trio.
MANUEL PUIG, *Betrayed by Rita Hayworth.*
The Buenos Aires Affair.
Heartbreak Tango.
RAYMOND QUENEAU, *The Last Days.*
Odile.
Pierrot Mon Ami.
Saint Glinglin.
ANN QUIN, *Berg.*
Passages.
Three.
Tripticks.
ISHMAEL REED, *The Free-Lance Pallbearers.*
The Last Days of Louisiana Red.
Ishmael Reed: The Plays.
Juice!
The Terrible Threes.
The Terrible Twos.
Yellow Back Radio Broke-Down.
JASIA REICHARDT, *15 Journeys Warsaw to London.*
JOÃO UBALDO RIBEIRO, *House of the Fortunate Buddhas.*
JEAN RICARDOU, *Place Names.*
RAINER MARIA RILKE,
The Notebooks of Malte Laurids Brigge.
JULIÁN RÍOS, *The House of Ulysses.*
Larva: A Midsummer Night's Babel.
Poundemonium.
ALAIN ROBBE-GRILLET, *Project for a Revolution in New York.*
A Sentimental Novel.
AUGUSTO ROA BASTOS, *I the Supreme.*
DANIËL ROBBERECHTS, *Arriving in Avignon.*
JEAN ROLIN, *The Explosion of the Radiator Hose.*
OLIVIER ROLIN, *Hotel Crystal.*
ALIX CLEO ROUBAUD, *Alix's Journal.*
JACQUES ROUBAUD, *The Form of a City Changes Faster, Alas, Than the Human Heart.*
The Great Fire of London.
Hortense in Exile.
Hortense Is Abducted.
Mathematics: The Plurality of Worlds of Lewis.
Some Thing Black.

FOR A FULL LIST OF PUBLICATIONS, VISIT: www.dalkeyarchive.com

SELECTED DALKEY ARCHIVE TITLES

RAYMOND ROUSSEL, *Impressions of Africa*.
VEDRANA RUDAN, *Night*.
PABLO M. RUIZ, *Four Cold Chapters on the Possibility of Literature*.
GERMAN SADULAEV, *The Maya Pill*.
TOMAŽ ŠALAMUN, *Soy Realidad*.
LYDIE SALVAYRE, *The Company of Ghosts*.
The Lecture.
The Power of Flies.
LUIS RAFAEL SÁNCHEZ, *Macho Camacho's Beat*.
SEVERO SARDUY, *Cobra & Maitreya*.
NATHALIE SARRAUTE, *Do You Hear Them?*
Martereau.
The Planetarium.
STIG SÆTERBAKKEN, *Siamese*.
Self-Control.
Through the Night.
ARNO SCHMIDT, *Collected Novellas*.
Collected Stories.
Nobodaddy's Children.
Two Novels.
ASAF SCHURR, *Motti*.
GAIL SCOTT, *My Paris*.
DAMION SEARLS, *What We Were Doing and Where We Were Going*.
JUNE AKERS SEESE, *Is This What Other Women Feel Too?*
BERNARD SHARE, *Inish*.
Transit.
VIKTOR SHKLOVSKY, *Bowstring*.
Literature and Cinematography.
Theory of Prose.
Third Factory.
Zoo, or Letters Not about Love.
PIERRE SINIAC, *The Collaborators*.
KJERSTI A. SKOMSVOLD, *The Faster I Walk, the Smaller I Am*.
JOSEF ŠKVORECKÝ, *The Engineer of Human Souls*.
GILBERT SORRENTINO, *Aberration of Starlight*.
Blue Pastoral.
Crystal Vision.
Imaginative Qualities of Actual Things.
Mulligan Stew. *Red the Fiend*.
Steelwork.
Under the Shadow.
MARKO SOSIČ, *Ballerina, Ballerina*.
ANDRZEJ STASIUK, *Dukla*.
Fado.
GERTRUDE STEIN, *The Making of Americans*.
A Novel of Thank You.
LARS SVENDSEN, *A Philosophy of Evil*.
PIOTR SZEWC, *Annihilation*.
GONÇALO M. TAVARES, *A Man: Klaus Klump*.
Jerusalem.
Learning to Pray in the Age of Technique.
LUCIAN DAN TEODOROVICI, *Our Circus Presents...*
NIKANOR TERATOLOGEN, *Assisted Living*.
STEFAN THEMERSON, *Hobson's Island*.
The Mystery of the Sardine.
Tom Harris.
TAEKO TOMIOKA, *Building Waves*.
JOHN TOOMEY, *Sleepwalker*.
DUMITRU TSEPENEAG, *Hotel Europa*.
The Necessary Marriage.
Pigeon Post.
Vain Art of the Fugue.
ESTHER TUSQUETS, *Stranded*.
DUBRAVKA UGRESIC, *Lend Me Your Character*.
Thank You for Not Reading.
TOR ULVEN, *Replacement*.
MATI UNT, *Brecht at Night*.
Diary of a Blood Donor.
Things in the Night.
ÁLVARO URIBE & OLIVIA SEARS, EDS., *Best of Contemporary Mexican Fiction*.
ELOY URROZ, *Friction*.
The Obstacles.
LUISA VALENZUELA, *Dark Desires and the Others*.
He Who Searches.
PAUL VERHAEGHEN, *Omega Minor*.
BORIS VIAN, *Heartsnatcher*.

FOR A FULL LIST OF PUBLICATIONS, VISIT: www.dalkeyarchive.com

SELECTED DALKEY ARCHIVE TITLES

LLORENÇ VILLALONGA, *The Dolls' Room.*
TOOMAS VINT, *An Unending Landscape.*
ORNELA VORPSI, *The Country Where No One Ever Dies.*
AUSTRYN WAINHOUSE, *Hedyphagetica.*
CURTIS WHITE, *America's Magic Mountain.*
The Idea of Home.
Memories of My Father Watching TV.
Requiem.
DIANE WILLIAMS,
Excitability: Selected Stories.
Romancer Erector.
DOUGLAS WOOLF, *Wall to Wall.*
Ya! & John-Juan.
JAY WRIGHT, *Polynomials and Pollen.*
The Presentable Art of Reading Absence.
PHILIP WYLIE, *Generation of Vipers.*
MARGUERITE YOUNG, *Angel in the Forest.*
Miss MacIntosh, My Darling.
REYOUNG, *Unbabbling.*
VLADO ŽABOT, *The Succubus.*
ZORAN ŽIVKOVIĆ, *Hidden Camera.*
LOUIS ZUKOFSKY, *Collected Fiction.*
VITOMIL ZUPAN, *Minuet for Guitar.*
SCOTT ZWIREN, *God Head.*

AND MORE...

FOR A FULL LIST OF PUBLICATIONS, VISIT: www.dalkeyarchive.com